Men of the Time

The Reprint Company
Spartanburg, South Carolina

This Volume Was Reproduced
From A 1902 Edition
In The
South Caroliniana Library
University of South Carolina
Columbia

The Reprint Company
Post Office Box 5401
Spartanburg, South Carolina 29301

Reprinted: 1972
ISBN 0-87152-094-X
Library of Congress Catalog Card Number: 74-187366

Manufactured in the United States of America on long-life paper.

MEN OF THE TIME.

SKETCHES OF LIVING NOTABLES.

A BIOGRAPHICAL ENCYCLOPEDIA OF CONTEMPORANEOUS
SOUTH CAROLINA LEADERS.

BY

J. C. GARLINGTON.

SPARTANBURG, S. C.
GARLINGTON PUBLISHING CO.
1902.

PRESS OF
FOOTE & DAVIES COMPANY,
ATLANTA, GA.

PREFACE

"Footprints on the sands of time."—LONGFELLOW.

This volume is designed to furnish concise biographical sketches of those who are at present active in intellectual, industrial and commercial life in South Carolina. It is not a collection of eulogies nor an aggregation of business advertisements. The compilation has been made without reference to the sale of the book, and in this important respect it claims to be more valuable than any other work of the kind ever attempted.

It is not easy to estimate the difficulties encountered in a work of this kind, where no single standard of selection can be adopted. The Editor has been greatly aided by suggestions from men of recognized discretion in different parts of the State, who furnished lists of names of those whose past achievements or present prominence warrant a place in this biographical encyclopedia of living South Carolinians. It is not claimed that every obstacle has been overcome, because the plan is comprehensive and embraces a variety of interests; but more than ordinary exertions have been made to secure accuracy and to make the work representative. The information has been obtained largely from original sources and is for the first time presented to the public.

The interest taken in the work by those whose relation to public affairs have put them in position to be of service has exceeded the expectations of the publisher, who takes this opportunity to thank the various persons throughout the State to whom he is indebted for important contributions.

Information has been frankly sought and freely given. In some cases, from the absence of parties or an occasional reluctance to publicity, names which have been selected as entitled to a place in the work have been omitted. These cases, however, are few.

In this day of rapid progress and development in South Carolina, it is important to know the men whose talents are promoting this growth, and it is the design of this work to furnish this information.

J. C. GARLINGTON.

MEN OF THE TIME.

ABLE, EUGENE W.—Lawyer. Born near Convent Church, Lexington County, South Carolina, October 2, 1872. Attended the common schools and the South Carolina College, from which he graduated with honors and the degree LL. B., in 1893. Has never sought political preferment. Married Miss Neil Gunter, December 18, 1895. Is now engaged in practicing law at Saluda and is secretary of the Saluda Oil Mill.

ACKER, WILLIAM B.—Baptist minister, Abbeville, South Carolina. Born July 20, 1839, in Greenville, South Carolina. Education acquired in Williamston Academy. Taught school at Donalds, South Carolina. In May, 1851, volunteered in Gist Rifles, a company gotten up at Williamston for the Confederate service. Joined the Hampton Legion. Lost an arm in the battle of Seven Pines. Is treasurer of the Abbeville Baptist Association. Taught school after the war. Later engaged in farming. Married Miss Barmore, a daughter of Larkin Barmore, October 8, 1862.

ADAMS, ROBERT.—Pastor of the First Presbyterian Church of Laurens, South Carolina. Was born in Eatonton, Georgia, March 24, 1852. Graduated from the University of Georgia. Decided to enter the ministry and went immediately to the Theological Seminary at Columbia, South Carolina. Married Miss Eudocia Hammond, on January 16, 1878.

ADAMS, THOMAS JOHN.—Editor "Edgefield Advertiser." Son of Hiram Adams and Lydia Giles. Born March 12, 1845, Edgefield County. Attended country schools, Erskine College, the University of Virginia and Union College, New York. Married Elizabeth Miller, May, 1869. Has never

1

sought or held military or civil office. Is a lawyer, but since 1874 has been editor and proprietor of the "Edgefield Advertiser," one of the oldest and best weekly newspapers in the State. He volunteered for service in the Confederate army at sixteen years of age, in April, 1861. Was wounded at Malvern Hill and discharged because he was under the conscript age. When he reached the age of eighteen, he re-enlisted in Second South Carolina Cavalry, Company B.

ADAMS, WILLIAM WRIGHT.—Merchant, Edgefield, South Carolina. Son of W. W. and A. E. Adams. Born at Edgefield, South Carolina, February 7, 1862. Educated at the common schools. For the past eight years mayor of Edgefield. Married Miss Hattie Wise, November 27, 1890. In early life he entered mercantile business and has been so engaged for twenty-five years, doing a general supply business. Captain of Edgefield Rifles for a number of years. President of the Edgefield Building and Loan Association, and vice-president of the Bank of Edgefield.

AIKEN, DAVID.—Eldest son of the late Honorable D. Wyatt Aiken, for many years a member of Congress from Abbeville County. David Aiken, the subject of this sketch, was born at Stony Point, in what is now Greenwood County, on November 4, 1857. Received his preliminary training under the instruction of Mr. W. C. Benet; spent one year under Rev. George Round, and two years at the Carolina Military Institute, at Charlotte, North Carolina. He married Miss Annie Mary Connor, of Cokesbury, November 12, 1878. After marriage he moved on the farm near the old homestead, where he remained until January, 1892, at which time he moved to Coronaco and engaged in merchandising. Moved, in 1899, to Greenwood, where he now resides and is engaged in the mercantile business.

ALDERMAN, OWEN.—Sheriff of Aiken County since 1893. Son of Owen Alderman. Born in eastern North Carolina. near Wilmington, October 31, 1849, of Scotch-Irish and English descent. Attended the common schools and high school

at Clinton, North Carolina. Married Mamie, daughter of
Colonel James L. Davis, of Barnwell County, South Carolina, December 17, 1879. Engaged in farming and turpentine
business several years. In 1890, elected to the Legislature
from Aiken County; served one term. In 1892, elected a
director of the penitentiary; served until 1893.

ALDRICH, JAMES.—Judge of the Second Circuit. He is
a son of James T. Aldrich and Isabel C. Pattison. Born
July 25, 1850. His father died in 1875, comparatively young,
though one of the leading lawyers of that section. Attended
the private schools in Barnwell, and graduated from Washington and Lee University, Lexington, Virginia, in 1872.
Member of the House of Representatives of South Carolina
from 1878 to 1881 and from 1883 to 1889. Member of the
Judiciary Committee, and chairman of the Committee on
Incorporation. Married Miss Fannie Lebby, on December
15, 1874. Was elected judge of the Second Circuit in 1889
and is now in his twelfth year of continued service. Was
admitted to the bar in 1873, at which time he moved to the
city of Aiken, the county-seat of the then new county of
Aiken. Judge Aldrich took an active part in politics, in 1874
and 1876, and was one of the Democratic speakers appointed
to "divide time" with the Republican speaker. He has
always taken considerable interest in educational matters,
and was the founder of the Aiken Institute and president
of same until his elevation to the bench. He is of English
and Scotch-Irish descent.

ALLEN, JOSEPH DUNCAN.—Elected probate judge of
Edgefield County to fill unexpired term of Honorable W. F.
Roath. Has been re-elected to said office, without opposi-
tion, at every election since 1887, and the present term will
expire in 1902. He is a son of O. W. and Mary Ellen Allen.
Was born August 6, 1858, at Fruit Hill Post-office, Edgefield
County, South Carolina. A common-school education. Mer-
chandised and appointed postmaster at Fruit Hill, South
Carolina from 1879 to 1882; then farmed until 1887. Never
married.

ALLISON, ROBERT ERASMUS.—Was born January, 1830, in York County, South Carolina. He received an academic education in York County, after which he went to Davidson College, North Carolina, from which he graduated, in 1852, with second honor. He was appointed by the faculty to deliver the salutatory. Taught school two years after leaving college. Then studied law at Lancaster under Major Clinton, the leading member at that bar. Settled in Lancaster and began practice there. Married Mary A. Chambers, of York County, in 1856. He represented Lancaster County four years in the Legislature. While a member of that body he served on the Ways and Means Committee, and also the Judiciary Committee. His ancestors were of English and Irish origin. His father, Robert Turner Allison, was a member of the Secession Convention from York County.

ANDERSON, ALBERT WILLIAMS.—Railroad superintendent. Born November 27, 1863, near Cartersville, Georgia. His father, Dr. William Anderson, a native of Abbeville County, South Carolina, of Scotch-Irish parentage, was for many years one of Laurens County's most prominent and honored citizens. His mother was, before her marriage Miss E. L. Watts, whose family on both sides were prominent in the State's history for years before, during, and since the Revolutionary War. The subject of this sketch attended the primary schools of Laurens up to his fourteenth year, when he entered Adger College, at Walhalla, South Carolina, and later the South Carolina College. Owing to the death of his parents, he left college in the latter part of his junior year. In the following spring, April 22, 1882, accepted a position as clerk and watchman for the Richmond and Danville Railroad at Clinton, South Carolina, devoting his spare time to the study of telegraphy. He was soon promoted. In

June, 1885, he accepted a position with the Port Royal and Western Carolina Railway, at Laurens, as agent, holding this and other advanced positions until appointed superintendent eight years later by Receiver John B. Cleveland. Three years afterwards, upon the consolidation of the Port Royal and Western Carolina and Port Royal and Augusta roads into the Charleston and Western Carolina Railway Company, he was at the age of thirty-one appointed general superintendent, which position he has since held.

ANDERSON, RICHARD WARNER, REV.—Son of M. L. and Elizabeth Anderson. Born in Albemarle County, Virginia, May 12, 1857. Of Scotch-Irish, English and Welsh ancestry. His education was obtained at home and at Hanover Academy under Colonel Hilary P. Jones. Later, he entered Randolph-Macon College, and Theological Seminary of Virginia. Taught school one year before entering Seminary. Has served as a missionary of the Protestant Episcopal Church in Virginia, Kentucky, Georgia, Arkansas, Texas and South Carolina. Taught school part of the time. Clergyman of Protestant Episcopal Church. Married Miss Mary A. Beatty, April 14, 1891.

ANSEL, MARTIN FREDERICK.—Actively engaged in the practice of law at Greenville, South Carolina. Was born in Charleston, South Carolina, December 12, 1850. His parents moved to Walhalla when he was four years of age. He went to Greenville in January, 1876. Attended the high schools in the town of Walhalla. He never had the advantage of a college education, but taught himself. Was elected to the Legislature from Greenville County, in 1882, serving until 1888, at which time he was elected to the position of solicitor of the Eighth Circuit, which office he held until January, 1901, when he voluntarily retired. Is now practicing law in Greenville and adjoining counties.

APPELT, LOUIS.—Born March 22, 1857, in the city of Troy, New York. When he was a small child his parents moved to South Carolina. He was educated in the public

schools of New York City and later at the Greenport High
School, Greenport, Long Island. He married Miss Eliza
Steinneyer Clark. Was for ten years probate judge of Clarendon County; city treasurer, postmaster and a member of
the staff of General Joseph L. Stopplebein, with the rank
of major. He is now Senator from Clarendon County, editor
and proprietor of "The Manning Times." He is a vigorous
writer and a forceful speaker.

ARCHER, HENRY P.—Superintendent of the public
schools of Charleston. Born in
Charleston, South Carolina, January
3, 1839. Son of Benjamin R. Archer
and Elizabeth M. (Hammett) Archer.
He received his elementary education
in the best private schools of the city,
and was graduated at the College of
Charleston in March, 1858, with second honor. He married Mrs. Emily
S. Miller, eldest daughter of Henry
S. Strohecker, a prominent merchant,
on April 2, 1872. He has devoted his
life to teaching, having held various
positions in Charleston. Member of the State Board of
Education from 1876 to 1890. Conductor of the State Normal Institute in 1885, and member of the advising board
of the State. Superintendent of Education. Served one
term as president of South Carolina State Teachers' Association. Is also a member of the National Educational
Association and the Southern Educational Association.
In 1900, he was elected vice-president of the former organization. Trustee of the Charleston College. He is a great
church-worker and was president of the Charleston Bible
Society two years, and member of the Society of Associated
Charities, and of the Vanderbilt Benevolent Association
Member of the Board of Managers of the Charleston Ly-
ceum and the Charleston Library.

ARDREY, JOHN WHITE.—Dealer in general merchandise, and one of the oldest and most successful merchants of Fort Mill, South Carolina. Commenced business at that place, in 1873, as a member of the firm of Cureton, Ardrey & Co. Since 1879, has been conducting his business alone. Mr. Ardrey was born in Mecklenburg County, North Carolina, November 30, 1845. He spent his early life on a farm, and at sixteen years of age entered the war with the first regiment of volunteers that was formed in North Carolina. The regiment was only enlisted for six months, however, and re- turned home in 1861. His father died about this time, and his brothers having already re-enlisted, he was prevented from returning immediately to the army. After arranging his father's estate, he returned in the spring of 1863, and served until the close of the war in the First South Carolina Cavalry. After the war, he attended school for a short time at Ebenezer, and in 1866, began trying to make something out of his farm. He borrowed $3,500, and at the end of six years, he was out of debt and $1,500 ahead. Married Miss Mary H. Massey, October 26, 1866. Has served five terms as intendant, and is now a director in the Manufac- turing Company and of the Savings Bank of Fort Mill.

ARNOLD, J. THOMAS.—Was born January 16, 1869, at Greenwood, South Carolina. Son of James B. Arnold. At- tended the Greenwood College under the management of Professor Geo. C. Hodges. He married Miss Ellen, daughter of D. H. Traxler, of Timmonsville, South Carolina, June 5, 1895. After leaving school accepted a clerkship in a general merchandise store at Greenwood, South Carolina. In spring of 1891, moved to Greenville and accepted a position as head salesman for Park & Jones. In the fall he changed houses and went with J. H. Morgan & Bro., the largest dry-goods and shoe house in the city at that time. The following spring he was made buyer, advertiser and general manager. This concern being burned out in 1898 he formed a partner- ship with G. H. Mahon, of Williamston, South Carolina, under the firm name of Mahon & Arnold, which business has in

two years grown to be the largest wholesale shoe and dry-
goods business in Greenville.

ASBILL, EDWARD LEE.—Practiced law at Lexington,
South Carolina. Was born April 3, 1871, near Ridge Spring,
South Carolina. His father, P. B. Asbill, and mother, Emeline Satcher, died when he was an infant. Prepared for college at Leesville, South Carolina. Entered Wofford College,
in 1888, and graduated in 1892. Studied law at Yale, in 1894-
95. Was principal of the Edgefield Graded School, in 1892
and 1893. Edited the "Edgefield Farmer" during part of
1893. Elected to the Legislature from Lexington, in 1896,
served during 1897 and 1898. Chairman of the Democratic
Convention for Lexington County, and also chairman of
Election Commissioners. He is now engaged in practicing
law and farming. Married Miss Julia Drafts, March 12, 1901.

AULL, ELBERT HERMAN.—Born in Newberry County,
August 18, 1857. Son of Jacob Luther
and Julia (Haltiwanger) Aull. He attended the country schools. Moved
with his parents to Edgefield County
in 1873. Was prepared for college by
George D. Haltiwanger. Entered the
sophomore class in Newberry College
in 1877. Graduated in June, 1880.
Taught in the Abbeville Graded
School, 1880-81. Professor in Newberry College, 1881-82. Studied law
in the office of Eugene B. Gary, at
Abbeville, and O. L. Schumpert, at
Newberry. Admitted to the bar in December, 1882. Practiced law at Newberry. In 1884, was editor of "The Newberry News" and afterwards of "The Newberry Herald and
News." In 1885, established the "Prosperity Reporter" which
he edited and published for five months, when he returned
to Newberry, and again edited the "Herald and News."
March 7, 1887, with Mr. W. P. Houseal, he purchased "The
Newberry Herald and News," and he has edited and pub-

lished it since, buying out Mr. Houseal's interest in 1894. Was elected president of the South Carolina State Press Association, in 1894, and has been continuously re-elected since. Established the "Saluda Sentinel," the first newspaper published in Saluda County. In May, 1898, the Lutheran Publication Board of the United Synod of the South was established, and he was made superintendent of this board. June 3, 1899, was appointed private secretary to Governor McSweeney. Was married to Miss Alice Kinard, February 14, 1881.

AUSTIN, J. THOMAS.—Was born in Greenville County. Is the son of the late Dr. Thomas C. Austin, a prominent physician of Greenville County. His ancestors are of English descent, and came from Virginia to South Carolina in 1761, and settled in Greenville County. His grandfather, Col. William Austin, was a soldier in the Revolutionary War, and commanded a regiment in the War of 1812. His father, Dr. Thomas C. Austin, was paymaster in said regiment. Educated at Wofford College. Elected to the Legislature in 1874, 1876 and 1878, and was a member of the Wallace House. In 1886, elected to the Senate of South Carolina, and, in 1892, elected Registrar of Mesne Conveyance; served two terms. Member of Constitutional Convention of 1895. At present a member of the Legislature, and chairman of the Democratic Committee of Greenville County.

AVERILL, JOHN H.—Director-general of the South Carolina Interstate and West Indian Exposition Company. Born in Plattsburg, New York, October 1843. Obtained education from Charleston High School. Superintendent of South Carolina Railroad twelve years. General manager of C. S. N. R. R. three years; receiver and general manager P. R. & W. C. Railroad three years. Married Miss Susan H. Marshall.

AYER, HARTWELL M.—Son of Gen. Lewis Malone Ayer, of Barnwell, South Carolina. Born in Barnwell County, South Carolina, January 7, 1869. Graduated in 1887 from

2

the South Carolina College. Admitted to the bar of the Supreme Court in 1897. Married Cornelia W. Smith of Charleston, South Carolina, June 25, 1890. He was employed as city editor of the "Charleston World." Telegraph editor of the "Enquirer Sun," of Columbus, Georgia, and "Savannah Morning News." Editor and founder of the "Charleston Evening Post," and is now editor of the "Florence Daily Times."

BABCOCK, JAMES WOODS, M. D.—Appointed superintendent of the State Hospital for Insane at Columbia, South Carolina, August 1891. He was born in Chester, South Carolina, August 11, 1856. Attended the schools in Chester; Philip Exeter Academy, Exeter, New Hampshire; Harvard College, class of 1882, and Harvard Medical School in 1886. Married Miss Katherine Guion, August 17, 1892. Assistant physician McLean Asylum, Somerville, Massachusetts, from 1885 to 1891. He has filled his present position with great honor and credit to himself. His services in the treatment of smallpox and special diseases place him high in the profession.

BACON, JAMES THOMAS.—Editor. Has been engaged in newspaper work since twenty-three years of age, and is now editor of the "Edgefield Chronicle." He is a son of E. L. and Mrs. Sara A. Bacon, at Edgefield Court-house, South Carolina. Finished a very fine course at Union College, Schenectady, New York, and studied afterwards in University of Leipzig, Germany. He is a well-known writer and lecturer. Not married.

BACOT, ROBERT DEWAR.—Son of Thomas Wright Bacot, Jr., of Charleston, South Carolina, who was assistant postmaster to his father, Thomas Wright Bacot, the first postmaster at Charleston under the United States Constitution of 1787, appointed by George Washington in 1791, and continued in office until his death in 1834. After his father's death T. W. Bacot, Jr., held the same position with W. Alfred Huger, who was postmaster until his death in 1851. The mother of Robert Dewar Bacot was Harriet S. Dewar. Mr. Bacot was born at Charleston, South Carolina, October 16, 1821. Attended the private schools in Charleston, and Flushing Institute, at Flushing, Long Island, with a view of going to West Point, but on account of political influence brought to bear he was unable to attend the last named institution. He embarked in business as a cotton merchant. In 1842 he entered the business house of William C. Murray, a cotton merchant of Charleston, as clerk. Finally he became the head of the house. He was for years a member of the Charleston volunteer fire department, being president of the Old Phoenix Fire Engine Company at the time of the great fire of December 1861. Served in the Confederate War. Married, April 18, 1843, Julia Amanda Huger, of Charleston, a daughter of Daniel Huger, at one time Secretary of State of South Carolina.

BACOT, THOMAS WRIGHT.—Son of Robert Dewar Bacot, of Charleston, a retired cotton merchant, and Julia Amanda, daughter of Daniel Huger, rice-planter and at one time Secretary of State of South Carolina. He was of French Huguenot origin maternally as well as paternally. Born April 14, 1849, at the old family homestead in the city of Charleston. Received the rudiments of education at home under his mother's eldest sister. Attended Bennett public school under Dr. William H. Carroll. During the Civil War he pursued his education in private schools at Society Hill, in Darlington County. In April, 1865, was appointed by Governor MaGrath to the battalion of Arsenal Cadets then in the field and ordered to report for duty to Capt. J. E. Thomas commanding the battalion at Greenville, South Carolina; but before he could join the battalion the end came in the surrender of Lee and his army at Appomattox. In 1867 entered the College of Charleston, where he graduated in 1870. Began the study of law in the office of McCrady & Son, of Charleston. Was admitted to the bar in 1871 and engaged actively in practice. Married at Charleston, April 18, 1877, to Miss Louisa De Berniere McCrady, daughter of Edward McCrady of Charleston. Formed a copartnership with George R. Walker for the practice of law, which continued to the death of Mr. Walker in 1882. In 1882 became associated with Edward McCrady and his two sons, General Edward McCrady and DeBass McCrady, until the death of the senior member of the firm. General Edward McCrady, Mr. Bacot and Colonel Lewis DeBass McCrady have been associated together in the practice of law since. First entered into politics in the Hampton campaign of 1876, though he had previously taken an active part in city, county and state campaigns, in efforts to overthrow the tyranny of "Reconstruction." In 1884 was appointed by Governor Hugh S. Thompson with W. R. Shands, of Columbia, and T. Q. Donaldson, of Greenville, a commission to consider and report a plan to simplify the mode of assessing and collecting taxes. Represented Charleston in the Legislature in 1892 and has been returned continuously ever since, being now chairman of the Judiciary Committee. In 1896 was elected a trustee in the South Carolina College. Was prominently mentioned in 1898 for the judgeship of the First Circuit, but declined to make the race.

BAILEY, CHARLES WILLIAMS, M. D.—Son of Dr. T. P. Bailey and Maria Laval Williams. Born at Georgetown, South Carolina, October 27, 1868. Of English and French descent. Attended the high schools of Georgetown. Graduated from South Carolina College. Afterwards licensed as Doctor of Pharmacy. Graduated from the Maryland Medical School with degree of M. D. in 1889, and began practice at Georgetown. In 1893 commissioned as sanitary inspector of Marine Hospital Service and sent for duty in London, Liverpool, Hull, and other places abroad. Returned to America in 1894. Married December 17, 1894, Miss Johnes Dalton Whitford, of New Berne, North Carolina. Has been county physician of Georgetown since 1895. Appointed acting assistant surgeon of the United States Marine Hospital. Placed in charge of the station at Georgetown, in 1898, and is still filling that position. He is surgeon of Camp Arthur Manigault's United Sons of Veterans.

BAILEY, JOHN CROOKS, SR.—Appointed probate judge to fill out an unexpired term, to which position he has been twice elected by the people. He was born in Edgefield Coun ty, July 1, 1840. His parents removed to Greenville when he was only two years of age. He attended the common and private schools of Greenville, and the Greenville Male Academy 1852 and 1854. His second marriage was in 1884 to Laura J. Gaulden, of Ninety-Six. He became editor of the "Greenville Enterprise" in 1861, which he conducted continuously until December 31, 1891. Was clerk and treasurer of the town council for six years. Being a delicate boy and having a widowed mother with six children dependent on him for support, did not enter the Confederate army. Besides aiding in the coming in and going out of the wounded and disabled soldiers, he published in his paper the laws of the Confederate Congress to the value of $5,000, for which he received no compensation. In 1873 he purchased the "Mountaineer" and united it with the "Enterprise." In 1876 he was secretary of a Democratic club, of which Dr. James C. Furman was president. In 1878 he was made chairman of the board of school trustees of Greenville, South Carolina. After visiting the Atlanta schools, returned and led in instituting the present system of graded schools in that city. In 1884 he was a member of the Farmers Alliance, and afterwards a strong supporter of the reform movement in State politics. Elected school commissioner in 1890. In 1891 he was compelled to sell his journal, the "Enterprise" and the "Mountaineer," owing to financial pressure, and retire from the vocation to which he had become very much attached. In 1893 he edited the "Greenville Democrat," and in the following year he was appointed to the position he now holds.

BAILEY, JOSEPH ABRAMS.—Merchant and treasurer of the Thornwell Orphanage. He is the eldest son of Rosanna Abrams, and Mercer S. Bailey. Born at Clinton, Laurens County, South Carolina, September 1, 1861. His primary education was received from the high schools of Clinton under N. J. Holmes, Stobo J. Simpson, and W. S. Lee. Graduated from Davidson College, North Carolina, June, 1883. His first wife was Jessie, daughter of Thomas L. Coleman of New Market, South Carolina, whom he married on September 9, 1886. His second wife was Nina Vance, of New

Orleans, Louisiana, to whom he was married on July 31, 1899. Elected warden in 1896 for town of Clinton. He is one of the firm of M. S. Bailey & Sons, merchants, who began business in 1883, succeeding M. S. Bailey, whose business was established in 1865.

BAILEY, MERCER SILAS.—A leading merchant and banker of Clinton, South Carolina. Was born on a farm seven miles south of Clinton, November 9, 1841. His youth was spent on a farm, where his educational advantages were limited and a college course out of the question. At the age of fourteen he went to Clinton, and secured a clerkship in a store. After clerking two years he returned to school for one year, then resumed his former occupation of clerking. At the age of nineteen he was married to Miss Rosanna Abrams, a daughter of Joseph Abrams, a farmer of Laurens County. In 1862 he entered the Confederate service in the James Battalion, with which he served as private for about three months, when ill health compelled him to return home. At the close of the war, Mr. Bailey engaged in business for himself, starting out with just four bales of cotton, but his business soon developed into a general merchandising trade. He followed this business for twenty years. He has since turned it over to his eldest three sons. In 1886 he established Bailey's Bank of Clinton, of which he is president and his son, W. J. Bailey, cashier. He organized and built the Clinton Cotton Mill, being made president with W. J. Bailey secretary and treasurer, and C. M. Bailey bookkeeper.

BAILEY, PUTSEY SILAS.—Member of the large mercantile firm of M. S. Bailey & Sons, of Clinton, South Carolina. He was born at Clinton, Laurens County, South Carolina, July 28, 1863. His education was acquired in the high schools of Clinton. He married Fannie, daughter of Mr. George P. Copeland, April 23, 1884. He is held in very high esteem by all with whom he comes in contact.

BAILEY, THOMAS PIERCE, M. D.—Son of Robert S. and Eliza Pierce Bailey, born near Charleston, May 21, 1832. Of English ancestry. Attended private schools and the Charleston High School. Graduated from the State Medical College in 1853. After leaving college practiced a few years in the Santee section of Georgtown County. Then entered Confederate army in 1862 as surgeon. Served in battles of Chickamauga, Murfreesboro and battles around Atlanta. After the war closed he returned to Georgetown and has since practiced his profession. At one time editor of the "Georgetown Times." Held a position on the Board of Health. He is also engaged in the drug business in connection with his practice. He is the author of a little book of poems, and has written several articles on his profession.

BAILEY, WILLIAM JAMES.—Cashier of the Bank of Clinton. Son of Mercer S. and Rosanna L. Bailey. Was born on December 12, 1865, at Clinton, South Carolina. Had the advantage of the common schools, and the Clinton Academy under Professor W. S. Lee. Married Miss Florence, only daughter of Dr. W. P. Jacobs, on September 12, 1888. He began clerking for his father when fourteen years of age, and later was made a partner of M. S. Bailey & Sons, merchants. In 1886 he helped to organize Bailey's Bank, the only bank at that time in Laurens County, and was made cashier. He and his father, M. S. Bailey, own Bailey's Bank and organized the Clinton Cotton Mill Company. The latter was elected president and the former secretary and treasurer.

BAIN, CHARLES WESLEY.—Professor of ancient languages at the South Carolina College. Son of George Martin Bain, and W. F. Cherry. Born in Portsmouth, Virginia, June 24, 1864. Acquired his education from the Portsmouth Male Academy, McCabes University School, Petersburg, Virginia, University of Virginia, and the University of the South at Sewanee. Married Isabel De Rippe Plummer. Instructor in

Savannah Academy, Savannah, Georgia, McCabes University School and head master of the Sewanee Grammar School. Editor of "Homer's Odyssey." Author of Bain's First Latin.

BAKER, SAMUEL CHANDLER.—Physician. Son of Dr. C. R. F. Baker, and Mary J. Burch, of Macon, Georgia. Born December 15, 1866 in Sumter County, South Carolina. Attended the neighborhood schools until twelve years of age. Then appointed a page to the secretary of the United States Senate where he served two years. Prepared for college at Mayesville High School and graduated from Davidson College with degree of A. B. in 1896. Married Jennie McClellan Moses, of Washington, D. C., April 30, 1890. Taught school one year. Since graduation in medicine has practiced continuously in Sumter, where he has established a private hospital. Member of the Sumter County Medical Association of the South Carolina Medical Association, and of the Tri-State Association of the Carolinas and Virginia. Member of the State Board of Examiners, and has served as secretary and treasurer since his appointment.

BANKS, JOHN FELDER.—Was born in Edgefield County, near Saluda, December 5, 1839. He had only the advantage of the common schools of that period. Joined the Confederate army in Company A, Thirteenth Regiment South Carolina Volunteers. Was first and second Lieutenant and then promoted to Captain. Served his county in the Legislature two terms. Married Miss T. R. Counts.

BANKS, WILLIAM.—On the editorial staff of "The State." Born at Fort Mill, York County, South Carolina. Son of A. R. Banks, a well-known educator. Attended Fort Mill Academy and Davidson College with a view of entering the ministry, but became infatuated with newspaper work and did not graduate. Married Laurens Louise Vance, of Laurens, South Carolina, April 25, 1900. Local editor of the "Rock Hill Herald." Reporter and local editor of the "Columbia Register" in 1897. War correspondent of "The State" with First South Carolina Volunteer Regiment.

BARKSDALE, COLLYAR DOUGLAS.—He is the second son of Dr. John A. Barksdale, the president of the National Bank of Laurens South Carolina, who for many years was one of the most prominent and skillful physicians of the State. Was born June 23, 1853, at Laurens, South Carolina. Had the advantage of Furman University, and took a course in the Eastman Business College, Atlanta, Georgia. Read law in the office of Col. James M. Baxter, at Newberry, South Carolina. He married Miss Lilly A. Fair, of Selma, Alabama, June 9, 1881. He was appointed Master of Laurens County in 1880, by Governor Simpson, and held the office until it was abolished by an act of the Legislature, in 1891. Has been a trustee of the Laurens graded schools for nine years. He was admitted to the bar in 1877, and has since 1891 practiced at Laurens, South Carolina. He bears the full name of his father's youngest brother, Captain C. D. Barksdale, who was a commission merchant in Charleston before the war, and served in the Confederate army as the captain of Company L (Carolina Light Infantry). His mother is a daughter of Mr. Drayton Nance, a lawyer of Newberry, and a sister of James D. Nance, who was the colonel of the Third South Carolina Regiment, Kershaw's Brigade, and was killed at the battle of the Wilderness.

BARKSDALE, JOHN A., M. D.—President of the National Bank of Laurens, South Carolina, since its organization in 1886. Was born in Laurens, South Carolina, on October 1, 1826. He received his literary education at the Laurens Male Academy, and his medical education at the Medical Department of the Pennsylvania University, and the South Carolina Medical College, graduating from the latter college in March, 1847. He practiced physics at Laurens, South Carolina, for nearly forty years. Was a director of the Georgia and Carolina and Laurens Railroad, and of Greenville and Laurens Railway. Was a member of the Legislature from 1880 to 1882. On October 7, 1852, he was married to Martha A., daughter of Drayton Nance, of Newberry, South Carolina. He was chairman of Committee on Agriculture, and carried through the general stock law.

BARNES, ALBERT.—Instructor in Mechanical Department at Clemson College since 1896. Was born at Lockport, New York, February 23, 1870. His early training was received from the Lockport High School, and he graduated with M. M. E. degree from Cornell University in 1895. Married Sara E. Donaldson, July 12, 1899.

BARNWELL, BENJAMIN SMITH.—Bank cashier. Son of William and Sara (Gibbs) Barnwell of Beaufort, South Carolina. Was born February 8, 1834. He attended the Beaufort College several years. He married Mary Anna McCaslan of Abbeville County, December 10, 1867. For several years before the Civil War, he was in the counting house in Charleston and since the war he has been engaged in the mercantile business for fifteen years. In 1885 he established the National Bank of Abbeville, and has been cashier since that time.

BARNWELL, JOSEPH WALKER.—Son of Rev. William H. Barnwell, and Catherine Osborn Barnwell. Born October 31, 1846, at Charleston, South Carolina. Attended private schools of Charleston, South Carolina, and Beaufort College in 1861, private schools of Columbia, the Citadel Academy, Charleston, in 1864, South Carolina University in 1866, and the University of Goettingen, Germany, in 1869. Married Harriott Kinloch, daughter of Dr. Charles M. Cheves. She died January 17, 1900. Admitted to the bar in 1869. Vice-president of Charleston Library Society. Vice-president South Carolina Historical Society. President of Charleston Club. Chief of Staff of Governor Hagood in 1880 and 1882. Member of House of Representatives from Charleston County from 1874 to 1876. Senator from Charleston County from 1894 to 1896, and from 1898 to 1902. Chairman of earthquake relief committee in 1886, and also of cyclone relief committee. Chairman of Democratic club of Charleston County in 1880. President of Auxiliary Board of South Carolina Interstate and West Indian Exposition. Wounded in leg at Tulafinni on line of Charleston and Savannah Railroad, December 7, 1864. Attorney-general on Haskell ticket in 1890.

BARNWELL, WILLIAM.—Cashier of The State Bank and Trust Company of Columbia South Carolina. Son of Charles Heyward Barnwell and Charlotte Thompson. Born at Fort Motte. South Carolina, March 7, 1862. Obtained education from the high schools of Columbia. Married Mary J. Uttey. Kept books in Columbia ten years. Was teller in Bank of Columbia six years.

BARR, CHARLES D.—Merchant and Mill owner. Was born March 17, 1863, near the town of Leesville, South Carolina, on his father's plantation. Education obtained from common schools of neighborhood, he being unable to avail himself of a college course. He was first engaged in farming and saw-milling, and in 1891 commenced the mercantile business. Began on small capital, and now owns and controls several large sawmills. Owns and manages the Leesville Roller Flour Mill, and also is proprietor of a large mercantile establishment at Leesville. Trustee of Leesville College and has aided materially in the support of this institution during the past eight years. Has been mayor of Leesville several years and has retired refusing re-election. Married Eula Mitchell, February 4, 1887.

BARRON, JACOB THOMAS.—Lawyer. Son of Bolin B. Barron, and Amanda Thomas, born in Edgecombe County, North Carolina, May 20, 1854. Of English and Scotch-Irish descent. Attended Bingham Military School, Mebane, North Carolina. Entered Virginia Military Institute, Lexington, Virginia, from which he graduated, July 1875. Married Floride Calhoun Rion, of Winnsboro, South Carolina, December 11, 1879. From September 1875, to December, 1875 tutor in private family in Kittrell, North Carolina. Read law in office of Col. James H. Rion, of Winnsboro, South Carolina. Admitted to the bar by the Supreme Court of North Carolina in 1879. Began the practice of his profession in Columbia in 1879. Made a specialty of corporation law. Connected with the Atlantic Coast Line Railroad since 1879. Chairman of board of trustees of the Columbia City Schools. Has held several offices in Knights of Pythias, Knights Templars, and R. A. M. Lodges.

BARTON, WILLIAM ALEXANDER.—Son of Alsbury and Susan Huldah (Woods). Born July 19, 1848, in Cass, now Bartow County, Georgia. His parents returned to South Carolina when he was three years old. He worked on the farm until October, 1864, when he entered the Confederate army at the age of sixteen. Served until the close of the war as corporal of his company, returning to the farm in Laurens County. December 26, 1871, he married Miss Josephine, daughter of Jonas M. Edwards. In 1873 he accepted a position as salesman and collector for a traveling stone company, resigning said position at Gainesville, Georgia, after a continuous service of five years. He went to Greenville, South Carolina, in the latter part of 1878, and entered the store of J. A. Goodwin & Company as clerk. He then went into the saddlery and harness business on his own account late in 1879, selling said business to McDaniel & McBee in 1888. Accepted a position as traveling salesman with R. Woolley & Sons, a wholesale saddlery and harness firm, of Cincinnati. In January, 1890, he embarked in the insurance business, and is now engaged in that business, at Greenville, South Carolina. Served the city of Greenville one term as alderman. Takes a great interest in educational and public affairs.

BATES, GEORGE HOLLAND.—Lawyer at Barnwell, South Carolina. Born July 27, 1853, in Barnwell, now Aiken County, South Carolina. Son of William Bates and Martha Kizana Holland. Obtained a good common-school education from Richland Academy, Barnwell, South Carolina. Read law under Major John W. Holmes, and was admitted to the bar in December, 1883. Married February 28, 1878, Elizabeth O.

Buckhalter of Aiken, South Carolina. Member of county Board of Education several years. Member of Constitutional Convention 1895. Chairman of board of trustees of the Barnwell Graded School, and also of the Columbia Female College. Soon after admission to the bar he became associated with Hon. Isaac M. Hutson in the practice of law, which continued until the latter's death in 1887. Now senior member of the law firm of Bates & Simms.

BAUER, JACOB W.—Section director on United States Weather Bureau. Born in Suffield, Portage County, Ohio, August 30, 1860. Of German parentage. Attended the country schools and three years at Mt. Union College, Alliance, Ohio, completing the junior year. One year in law at New York City. Married Esther Boyd Washburn, June 7, 1893. Entered the Weather Service, then the Signal Corps United States Army in 1883. Transferred to the Department of Agriculture in 1891. Stationed at Washington, Boston, Thatchers Island. Was two years at Mt. Washington, New Hampshire, for nine months each year with only one companion and a cook. Was seven years at New York City station. Has been in Columbia for the past eight years as section director, climate and crop service of the Weather Bureau.

BAUKNIGHT, JOSEPH H.—Banker. Has been engaged in farming and banking in Edgefield County all his life, and is now president of the bank of Johnston at Johnston, South Carolina. He is a son of William and Nancy (Huiet) Bauknight. Born near Mount Willing in Edgefield, now Saluda County, November 25, 1841. His ancestors came from Germany, and were among the early settlers of Edgefield County. Graduated from the State Military Academy at Charleston, South Carolina in 1864. In 1864 he entered the service of the Civil War as a member of the Battalion of Citadel Cadets, under the command of Captain J. B. White; served until the war closed. Appointed a member of Governor Hampton's staff with rank of lieutenant-colonel in 1878. Married Miss Emma, daughter of Benjamin Bettis, October 23, 1889.

BEATTY, J. H. MEANS.—Son of Captain James and Sarah T. Beatty. Born in Fairfield County, South Carolina, January 30, 1871. Grandparents came from Ireland. His father was for a number of years a prominent merchant of Winnsboro, South Carolina. Ancestors were Scotch-Irish. He attended Mt. Zion Institute, Winnsboro, South Carolina, till 1887 where he was prepared for college, then attended the South Carolina University until 1891. Afterward was with the Southern Railway at Columbia, South Carolina as machinist and draughtsman. After leaving their employ, in 1895, he was superintendent of several cotton mills. Was director of Clemson Textile School, the first director of the first school of this character in the South. He studied the business of cotton manufacturing, and textile school work to a great extent in the North, and is considered good authority on the subject by mill men both North and South. Offered position as director of Mississippi Textile School in August 1900, at quite an advance of salary, but preferred to remain in his native State. He has never married.

BEATTIE, WILLIAM EDGEWORTH.—President and treasurer of Reedy River Manufacturing Company, since 1898. He is a son of Hamlin Beattie, and Sallie Cleveland Beattie. Was born in Greenville, South Carolina, September 25, 1859. His earlier schooling was acquired from the high school of Greenville, and he was graduated from Princeton University in class of 1882. Three years later he was united in marriage with Miss Kitty, daughter of Samuel Marshall. He has been cashier of the National Bank at Greenville, since October, 1882; a director in Piedmont Manufacturing Company; Victor Manufacturing Company; and the Mountain City Land and Improvement Company.

BECKHAM, ROBERT S., M. D.—Physician. Born in Lancaster County, South Carolina, March 9, 1839. His father was clerk of the court of Lancaster twelve years. His ancestors were Scotch-Irish. Received literary education from the Cokesbury Conference School, and graduated in medicine from the Charleston Medical College. Practised his profession at Pleasant Hill, Lancaster County, until 1872. Moved to Lowndesville, Abbeville County, where he practised medicine and was trial justice four years. Has since practised medicine at Kershaw, and is also connected with the insurance business. Is Chancellor Commander of Knights of Pythias, Knight of Honor and Mason. Was delegate to the Haskell conferences in 1890. Married Miss H. Elizabeth Cauthen, May 3, 1860.

BECKWITH, JOHN GEORGE.—Minister. Born near Jamison, in Orangeburg County, South Carolina, September 25, 1873. His paternal ancestors were of old Cavalier stock, and came to this country in the seventeenth century with Lord Baltimore, and settled in Maryland, while his maternal ancestors, the Moorers, were among the earlier settlers of Orangeburg County. He is a son of Lawrence R. Beckwith and Ann Hesse Moorer. Prepared for college in Sheridan's Classical School, of Orangeburg, and graduated from the Citadel, the youngest man in his class, at the age of nineteen. He taught three years after leaving school, and then made his arrangements to enter the ministry. He was placed in charge of the church at Manning on account of the ill-health of the pastor. He then served the church at Rock Hill, South Carolina, four years. On February 3, 1897, he married Fannie A. Brailsford, of Richmond, Virginia. He is now pastor of the church at Barnwell. Delegate to the Grand Missionary Conference in New Orleans, in April, 1901.

BELCHER, R. EDMUND.—A native of Augusta, Georgia. Was born March 6, 1850. Had the advantage of the normal schools of Anderson. Founded the "Sun," a newspaper, at Anderson, in 1875. Changed the name to "The Journal," in January, 1876. Separated from it and established the "Sun" at Hartwell, Georgia, in 1876. He is now head of the firm of R. E. Belcher & Son, Job Printers, Anderson, South Carolina. He married Lucy, daughter of Colonel D. S. Taylor, on June 2, 1874.

BELL, JESSE RUTLEDGE, M. D.—A practicing physician of Due West, South Carolina. Son of J. H. Bell, M. D. His primary training was received in the common schools of the county. He graduated from Erskine College in 1893.

Principal of Preparatory Department of Erskine College, 1893-1896. He entered the Medical College of South Carolina in 1896, and graduated third in a class of ninety-nine, thereby winning a position on the staff of the City Hospital of Charleston, South Carolina.

BELL, JESSE W., M. D.—Son of the late Dr. Benjamin W. Bell, who was born in North Carolina, in 1826. Married Elizabeth A. Bleckley, of Anderson, South Carolina, a sister of the late Sylvester Bleckley and ex-Chief Justice Logan E. Bleckley, of Georgia. Jesse W. Bell was born in Walhalla, South Carolina, January 8, 1867. Attended the Anderson Military School and Adger College, in Walhalla. Studied medicine one year under the late Dr. L. B. Johnson, of Walhalla. In the fall of 1889 he attended Bellevue Hospital Medical College, New York City, graduating in the class of 1892. Attended lectures in same institute in winter of 1899. Married Caroline, eldest daughter of Captain W. A. Strother, of West Union, South Carolina. In 1892 located in Walhalla for the practice of medicine, which occupation he still follows in connection with a drug-store. County physician and alderman of the town several years. Member of the Board of Health since organization five years ago.

BELLINGER, GEORGE DUNCAN.—Attorney-general of

the State; elected in 1898 and again in 1900. Was born at Barnwell, South Carolina, November 4, 1856. His mother died in 1860, and three years later his father, Lieutenant John A. Bellinger, was killed by Lieutenant Rice, in the Confederate service, on James Island, South Carolina, in a duel. Left an orphan at the age of seven, he went to live with his guardian, where he resided until his admission to Furman University. Soon after entering college the estate left by his father and maternal grandfather was lost by unfortunate management, and it seemed that his education must be ended; but a relative came to the rescue, and gave him the necessary funds. He was graduated, June 16, 1879, with the degree of A. B. In October, 1879, he returned to Barnwell and entered the law office of ex-Judge John J. Maher, as a law student, being admitted to the bar in December, 1880. In 1882, he was elected to the Legislature from his county; and in 1883 was upon the unanimous recommendation of the bar appointed Master in Equity by Governor Thompson. For seven successive terms beginning in 1883 he held the office of mayor of his native town. He was president of the Enterprise Manufacturing Company and at one time vice-president of the Savings Bank of Barnwell. He was elected solicitor of the Second Circuit, in 1892, and re-elected in 1896. During his first term he became a member of the Constitutional Convention of 1895, in which he was the chairman of the Committee on Jurisprudence. He was the author of the three important sections relating respectively to change of venue on motion of the State in criminal cases, codification of the laws and prevention of lynching of persons in charge of officers of the law. The Broxton Bridge lynching, in his circuit, followed immediately after this, and to his vigorous prosecution in this celebrated case is probably due his election to the office which he now holds. He has been chairman of the Democratic party of Barnwell County since 1890. Married Miss Fannie J. O'Bannon, June 14, 1881. In all of the various public positions he has held, he has displayed unusual ability and fidelity, never wavering or bending because of popular clamor. As Attorney-general he has been called upon to decide many vexed questions growing out of the adoption of the new constitution, and in nearly every case his ruling was sustained by the Supreme Court.

BELUE, DANIEL HENDERSON.—Born at Walterboro, Colleton County, South Carolina, October 22, 1872. He was educated in the schools of his native town, and the University of Georgia. He was for six years engaged in newspaper work, from 1891 to 1897. Having completed his law studies, he was admitted to practice in the year 1897, at Saint

3

George, Dorchester County, South Carolina. He has been a member to every State Democratic convention since 1890. Served as colonel on the Governor's staff from 1894 to 1896. Was the youngest member of the Constitutional Convention of 1895, and a presidential elector on the Bryan and Stevenson ticket, in 1900.

BENTZ, RICHARD LAROCHE.—Son of John H. and Harriet B. Bentz. His ancestors were of English descent and settled in the lower portion of South Carolina on lands granted them by the King of England. He was born in Barnwell County, near Blackville, South Carolina, September 21, 1864. His education was received from the common schools of Charleston County. He married Miss Lydia E. LaRoche, of Charleston County, on August 24, 1885. In 1886 he moved to Greenville and engaged in the dry-goods business under the firm name of McAlister & Bentz, until 1894, at which time he sold out to McAlister, and began business alone.

BETHEA, PHILIP YANCEY.—Son of Colonel James R. Bethea, whose ancestors were English and settled in Marion just prior to the Revolution, and Mary McLeod, whose father came from Scotland and settled in Marlboro County. Philip Yancey Bethea was born near Latta, Marion County, South Carolina, October 5, 1849. Obtained education from the common schools and Wofford College. Taught school a few years. Married Florence A. Johnson, of Charleston, South Carolina, November 25, 1875. Was appointed county auditor in 1881; resigned in 1889 to accept the position as cashier of the Bank of Marion; held this position until 1899. In that year the Marion Bank was established, and he was made director and cashier, which position he still holds. President of the Marion Public Library.

BIGGER, ISAAC ALEXANDER.—A practicing physician of Kershaw County. He was born May 9, 1867, at Bethel, South Carolina. His education was obtained from the high schools of the neighborhood, and at Woodlawn Business

College. Graduated with second honor from the Medical
College of South Carolina, 1889. He then took a post-
graduate course in polyclinics at Philadelphia. He married
Miss Mary Neal Johnston, September 5, 1888.

BIGHAM, JOHN THOMAS.—Editor of the "Chester Lantern." He was born February 8, 1852, in Chester County,
five miles east of Blackstock. His earlier training was received from the country schools. Entered Erskine College,
in 1873, and graduated therefrom in 1876. Taught fifteen
years in North Carolina, South Carolina and Alabama. He
owned and edited the "Gastonia Gazette," (North Carolina),
the "Chester Enterprise" one year, and is now editing the
"Chester Lantern." Married Miss Mary Hamilton Miller,
daughter of Dr. J. L. Miller, of Due West, South Carolina, on
December 23, 1885.

BIRCHMORE, CHARLES WHITAKER.—Editor. Born in
Cheraw, South Carolina, November 10, 1860. Educational
advantages limited. Attended the common schools of Camden, South Carolina, where he lived after the death of his
father and mother, which occurred when he was only five
years of age. He is a son of William T. and Elizabeth E.
Birchmore. His father was a cabinet-maker. After working on a small farm a year or so, and doing such other work
as he might find, he was given a position as apprentice in
the office of the "Kershaw Gazette." Here he made the best
of his advantages, working through the day and spending
his evenings studying. Married, October 13, 1886, Eva B.
Sligh, daughter of Captain John Sligh, of Fairfield County.
In 1886, he was nominated at the primary election at the
head of the ticket for county commissioner. Was re-nomi-
nated in the election of 1888, and again stood at the head
of the whole ticket, serving two terms as chairman of
the board. Steward in the Methodist Church a number of
years. Is superintendent of the Sunday-school, and of the
Mission School at the Camden Cotton Mills, which school
he organized several years ago. He has been secretary
and president of the county Sunday-school convention, sec-

retary of the county Democratic Executive Committee, and
of the Camden Board of Trade, and member of the board of
directors of the Farmers and Merchants Bank. He established the "Wateree Messenger" in 1884, after having been
employed on the "Gazette" eight years.

BLACK, ALEXANDER MURRAY.—Was born in eastern
York County, February 24, 1837. Education was limited.
Married Miss N. Jane Roddey, daughter of John Roddey,
November 15, 1865. Was clerk two years, and has since
been engaged in farming. He assisted in raising Company
H, Twelfth Regiment, South Carolina Volunteers, in July,
1861. Cad Jones, Sr., was made captain of this company,
which became a part of the Twelfth Regiment, South Carolina Volunteers, Greggs Brigade, A. P. Hill's Division, Jackson's Corps, Army of Northern Virginia. Mr. Black entered the service as corporal, and at different times was
promoted, and was in command of the company at the surrender at Appomattox. The company was engaged in nearly
all the hottest battles of the war, and had three colonels
killed in action on the field. Mr. Black was twice wounded,
first at Cold Harbor, Virginia, then at Gettysburg, on July
1st. There were four Catawba Indians in this company, as
gallant soldiers as ever went into battle, and as true to
the cause as any of the other soldiers. Their names were
John Harris, Jim Harris, Bill Canty and Nelson George.
The first experience they had in fighting was at Hilton
Head Island, and at Port Royal Ferry, South Carolina.
They were engaged in the seven day's fight around Richmond, where they were attached to Jackson's Corps, following him through all his hard-fought battles until he was
killed. Mr. Black has always taken an active part in all
enterprises for the betterment of the community. He has
been a member of nearly every county convention since the
war. Was a member of the county executive committee in
1876, and was a supervisor at every election during Radical
times.

BLACK, D. SHULER.—He is a son of W. A. and Virginia A. (Shuler) Black. Born in Orangeburg County, South Carolina, sixteen miles from court-house, March 27, 1872. He was reared in Columbia, South Carolina. Took special course in chemistry at South Carolina College, and graduated in medicine at Memphis Hospital Medical College, in 1895. Was house physician Memphis City Hospital from 1893 to 1896. Acting surgeon in charge, May, 1896, to March, 1897. Assistant demonstrator of anatomy, Memphis Hospital Medical College, 1895 to 1896. Married Miss Mignonette B. Johnson, February 5, 1897. Vice-chairman of city board of health, 1899. County physician to the poor, 1897 to 1899, and again in 1900, at Georgetown, South Carolina.

BLACK, FINGAL C.—Was born at Euharlee, Bartow County, Georgia. Has been in South Carolina since 1874. He attended the South Carolina College in 1885 and 1886; entered the South Carolina Military Academy, October, 1886, and graduated in 1890. He taught in the public schools of the State two years, then commenced the practice of engineering. At the beginning of hostilities he was county engineer for Spartanburg County. Lieutenant Black was examined in Atlanta, Georgia, and, having a satisfactory examination, was commissioned first lieutenant of the Third Engineers, in 1898. He was appointed enrolling officer for the regiment, with headquarters at Spartanburg, where he was on duty until September, when he joined the regiment at Jefferson Barracks, Missouri. He was in command of Company H. Third Engineers, when this company with five others, marched from Young's High Bridge, Kentucky, to Camp Hamilton, Kentucky, a distance of twenty-eight miles. Lieutenant Black's foreign service was in and around Cienfuegos, Cuba, where, in addition to his duties as commanding officer of Company H, (Captain Thomas, of Company H, being on detached duty during the entire stay of the company in Cuba), he had charge of the topographical survey of the Spanish defences in and around Cienfuegos; made a map of the territory, and prepared the government wharf at Cienfuegos. He served with the regiment until it was mustered out of service, at Atlanta, in 1899. After which he resumed the practice of his profession.

BLACK, JAMES BENJAMIN.—Physician. Son of Robert and Elizabeth Caldwell Black. Born January 19, 1849, in Colleton County, South Carolina. Of Scotch-Irish descent. Attended the high schools of Colleton County. Attended lectures in the South Carolina Medical College, and graduated from the University of Maryland School of Medicine, in March, 1872. Married Sarah H., daughter of T. C. Ayer, of Barnwell County, August 1, 1873. After leaving college, located in Barnwell County for the practice of his profession. He is also engaged in the drug and general merchandise business. Member of the Legislature from Barnwell County from 1886 to 1890. Member of the same body from Bamberg County from 1899 to 1900. Member and ex-president of the Barnwell County Medical Society. Deacon in Baptist Church at Bamberg, and ex-president of the Barnwell Baptist Sunday-school Convention. He called the first meeting that resulted in creating the new county of Bamberg.

BLACK, JOHN G., M. D.—For many years a practicing physician of York County, now Cherokee. He was prepared for college, but the Civil War came on, and he volunteered, and remained until the close of the war. Graduated from the Charleston Medical College in 1868. Member of Legislature from 1880 to 1884. In 1888 was elected State Senator from York County. For past twenty years has been engaged in farming, and encourages every enterprise for the upbuilding and betterment of the community. Was influential in securing the C. C. & C. Railroad by Blacksburg.

BLACK, JOHN G., COLONEL.—Son of Captain James A. Black, who was a member of Congress for three terms, 1842. Was born near the site of Cherokee Falls Manufacturing Company, in 1830. Graduated from West Point Military Academy. After leaving college lived in Richland County until 1859, then removed to Fairfield County and engaged in farming. Was for several years connected with the fertilizer business at Charleston. Organized the Magnetic Iron and Steel Ore Mining Company, of which he was for several years managing director. Was among the first to volunteer when the Civil War broke out, and was soon promoted to Lieutenant-Colonel of First Battalion, South Carolina Cavalry. Later was placed in command of First Regiment, South Carolina Cavalry until close of war.

BLACKMON, ROBERT LEE.—Son of William J. and Polly (Catoe) Blackmon. Born at White Bluff, Lancaster County, South Carolina, May 24, 1862. Had only the advantage of the common schools. Farmed until 1891, when he moved to Kershaw and established a general merchandise business under the firm name of Blackmon, Estridge & Co. Trustee of graded schools of Kershaw. Married Miss Almetta J. Hinson, December 23, 1886.

BLAKE, JOHN RENNIE.—Treasurer of Abbeville County. Was born at Greenwood, South Carolina, October 4, 1852. Received academic training in the schools of Greenwood. and Cokesbury, South Carolina. Then entered the sophomore class of Erskine College, where he graduated with distinction, in 1871, at the age of nineteen. He married Miss Annie Johnson, of Lowndesville, South Carolina, on October 4, 1877. Taught school at Ninety-Six, Coronaco and other places. Was mayor of Greenwood, in 1876, and merchandised there for a few years. Was elected treasurer of Abbeville County in 1890. Has been treasurer and vice-president of the State Alliance for the past four years, declining the presidency of same. Is treasurer of State Alliance Exchange. a director of the Merchants and Farmers Bank at Abbeville, a commissioner of the South Carolina Interstate and West Indian Exposition, and president of the Abbeville County Fair Association.

BLAKENEY, EUGENE DUBOSE.—Son of General J. W. Blakeney and V. M. DuBose, of Darlington, South Carolina, whose ancestors were Huguenots and first settled in South Carolina. Father was a prominent lawyer. Mr. E. D. Blakeney's education was obtained at Cokesbury, South Carolina.

Read law under J. T. Hay, of Camden, South Carolina, and practiced there from May, 1886, to January, 1894; then moved to Kershaw, South Carolina. He was first married to Miss Kennedy, daughter of General J. D. Kennedy, of Camden, and second to Miss Piearce, of Kershaw, South Carolina. Attorney for Heath Banking and Mercantile Co., Kershaw Building & Loan Association and South Carolina & Georgia Railroad Company.

BLAKENEY, WHITEFORD SMITH.—Son of John Smith Blakeney and Rosa Vick. Born May 4, 1865, at Cross Roads, Old Store Township, Chesterfield County, South Carolina. Educated at Davidson, North Carolina, and at the South Carolina College, graduating with the degree of A. M. and LL. B., in 1887. Is now a Senator from Chesterfield County, and actively engaged in the practice of law. His ancestors were among the first settlers in Chesterfield County. He is unmarried.

BLANDING, JAMES DOUGLASS.—Son of Abram Blanding

and Mary C. (nee DeSaussure). Was born in Columbia, South Carolina, June 26, 1821. From the academy in Columbia he entered the South Carolina College, and graduated with distinction in the class of 1841. Read law under his uncle, William F. DeSaussure, in Columbia. Admitted to the bar in December, 1842. The following year, 1843, practiced at Camden. Removed to Sumter, December, 1843, where he continued the practice with his uncle, under the firm name of Blanding & DeSaussure. He married Lenora A. McFaddin, of Sumter County, February, 1849. Secretary of the board of trustees of the South Carolina College from 1843 to

1852, during which time he compiled the catalogue of all
trustees, officers and students of the college from its beginning to 1853, which was made by LaBorde part of the
appendix to his history of the college. Before the war he
was a trustee of the Sumter Academical Society, and after
the war a trustee of Davidson College, North Carolina; also
of the Agricultural and Mechanical College of South Carolina, from its re-organization in 1879 till 1892. Intendant
of Sumter from 1852 to 1856. Member of the Legislature
from Sumter County, from 1852 to 1858. Served as chairman
of Committee on Education and on the Judiciary Committee.
He proposed two amendments to the Constitution of the
State, both of which were carried through; one of local
interest being the change of the name of Claremont to
Sumter Legislative District; the other of general interest,
that all elections of the State should be held on Tuesday, and
for one day only, instead of Monday and Tuesday in October of election years. He was colonel of the Twenty-Second Regiment South Carolina Militia, in the forties. Was
mustered into United States service, in 1846, and served
from the seige of Vera Cruz to the capture of the City of
Mexico. Served as adjutant and promoted to captain after
Colonel Butler was killed. Mustered out of service in September, 1848. He raised the first company in Sumter District for State service, which became Company D, of the
second of the ten regiments raised by the State in anticipa-
tion of its Ordinance of Secession. It was the first regiment
to reach Morris Island before the fall of Fort Sumter. This
regiment was made the basis for the organization of the
second, the ninth, and the twelfth regiments mustered into
Confederate service from South Carolina, under command of
Colonel J. B. Kershaw, Lieutenant J. D. Blanding and Major
Dixon Barnes. Colonel Blanding carried the Ninth to Virginia, reaching First Manassas on the evening of the battle.
Being disabled, he again tendered his services to the Confederacy and was ordered to report to the inspector-general,
and was assigned to duty as inspector of sea-coast batteries, from Charleston to the North Carolina line, and of the
regiments of reserves on the coast. He also did duty in

the ordnance department, and so served until the end of the war. Democratic chairman of Sumter County from 1876 to 1884, and in the memorable campaign of 1876 his county, with five negroes and two whites, elected a full delegation to the House and all county offices. Served in all the Democratic State Conventions from 1876 to 1890. By that body, in 1884, he was nominated and elected presidential elector, and as such had charge of the campaign in the so-called Black District, and of course voted for Cleveland, whose nomination he had advocated in the State Convention. He retired, in 1890, at the head of Sumter County's delegation from the Democratic State Convention, and participated in organizing the Democratic Conservative Convention, and was a member of the State Executive Committee of that faction. Over forty years a deacon and elder in the Presbyterian Church. After fifty years of professional work he retired on account of hardness of hearing, the primary cause of which was the bursting of a shell near his ear during the Civil War. He organized the scheme, and was president of the Three C.'s Railroad, in operation from Camden, South Carolina, to Marion, North Carolina, now known as the South Carolina and Georgia Extension Company, the section from Camden to Sumter, thence to Lanes, and thence to Georgetown, having been constructed by separate companies and the connection from Marion, North Carolina, across the Alleghany and Cumberland Mountains, to the Ohio River, being now built by a combination of companies. When completed this will be the shortest railroad route from Cincinnati to the Atlantic coast. The Sumter and Wateree Railroad, now a part of the Southern, was also constructed under his organization and presidency.

BLASSINGAME, WILLIAM FIELD.—Born in Anderson County, November 4, 1868. Son of B. F. Blassingame, who was a son of Thomas Blassingame, who, with his brother, General John H. Blassingame, came to the upper part of the State from Marion County, in 1787. The subject of this sketch had the opportunity of attending a country school until 1886, when the family removed to Greenville, South

Carolina. He there entered Furman University, 1886, graduating, in 1890, with the degree of Master of Arts. Was principal, the following year, of the school at Cross Keys, Union County, South Carolina. Married Miss Eva Gregory, of Union County, October 25, 1893. She died September 12, 1894, in Greenville, South Carolina. He was admitted to the bar in December, 1895, and in April, 1896, began the practice of law at Pickens Court House, where he is now practicing as a member of the law firm of Morgan & Blassingame. Mr. Morgan resides in Greenville, South Carolina.

BLEASE, COLEMAN LIVINGSTON.—Lawyer. Son of Henry H. and Mary E. Blease. Was born in Newberry thirty-two years ago. He attended school in Newberry, and the Newberry College. Graduated in law from the Georgetown Law School, Washington, D. C., in 1881. Was admitted to practice before the Supreme Court of the District of Columbia the same year, before the Supreme Court of South Carolina a few days later, and before the United States Supreme Court in March, 1893. In politics is a Reformer. In 1890, was elected to the Legislature. Chairman on the Committee on Privileges and Elections. Twice elected speaker pro tempore of the House, and re-elected to the House in 1892 and 1898, leading the ticket each time. Member of the State Board of Canvassers four years. Member of the Board of Visitors of the South Carolina Military Academy. Presidential elector on the Democratic ticket in 1896 and 1900. Has been county chairman of Newberry County, delegate to several State conventions, and is now a member of the State Executive Committee from Newberry and attorney for the city of Newberry.

BOEHM, WILLIAM HENRY, B. S., M. M. E.—Professor of mechanical engineering, and director of mechanical department Clemson College, South Carolina. Born at Memphis, Tennessee, August 30, 1868. Graduated at the Rose Polytechnic, in 1891, and at Cornell University in 1893. Before entering College was drafting apprentice, office of J. B. Cook, architect, from 1881 to 1882. After completing undergraduate course was engineer on construction of Memphis Gas Works, from 1891 to 1892. On completing his course at Cornell, he was appointed mechanical engineer Chickasaw Iron Works, which position he resigned, in 1894, to become inspector of steam boilers Fidelity Loan and Casualty Company of New York. It was while here that he received and accepted the position of instructor in mechanical engineering, Washington University, St. Louis. Resigned to become inspector of machinery of St. Louis waterworks, from 1897 to 1898, after which he was appointed to the position he now holds.

BOGGS, AARON.—Was born December 21, 1822, in Pendleton District, now Pickens County. His education was limited, having only the advantage of the old field schools. He volunteered in Company C, when the Civil War came on; was elected lieutenant, and served in Major Stoke's Cavalry on the coast in this State. He is farming, and has made a success of same. He married Miss Elmira L. Stevens, January 17, 1850.

BOGGS, AARON JOHN.—Clerk of the court of Pickens County. Born December 7, 1864, in Pickens District, now Oconee County. Educated in the common schools until 1882, when he entered the Pickens High School, at Pickens, where he remained for three years. Mr. Boggs was appointed postmaster at Fort Hill, South Carolina, under Cleveland's administration, which position he held until November, 1900. He then resigned to accept the position as clerk of the court of Pickens County, having been elected over one of the best men in the county. He held the office twelve years. Mr. Boggs married Miss Sallie Looper, August 8, 1886.

BOGGS, JULIUS E.—Solicitor Eighth Circuit. Was born February 14, 1854, in Pickens County. Mr. Boggs was reared on a farm in Pickens County. His early education was acquired under the instruction of a Miss Clayton, one year under Rev. J. L. Kennedy, a noted educator, and one year at the Pickens Academy. For two years he taught an

academy at Liberty, South Carolina, and for one year a similar institution at Pickens, South Carolina. At the age of
twenty-two, he began the study of law under Captain C. I.
Hollingsworth, of Pickens. In January, 1880, was admitted
to the bar, and entered upon the practice of his profession at
Pickens. In December, 1881, he removed to Marshall, Texas,
and was admitted to practice in the courts of that State, but
two months later he returned to Pickens, where he has been
actively engaged in the practice of his profession. In 1882,
he was elected to the State Legislature, being next to the
youngest member in that body. He was re-elected in 1884,
and served another two years. Mr. Boggs is a member of
the Masonic lodge. At one time he represented his lodge
in the Grand Lodge of South Carolina. He is a member
of the State Bar Association. He married Miss Minnie Lee
Bruce, of Pickens, December 24, 1882. Is a stockholder in
the Easley Banking Company, of Easley, South Carolina, and
also a director. He is a stockholder in the Easley Oil Mill
and Fertilizer Company. He is president of the Pickens
Railroad Company, and solicitor of the Eighth Judicial Circuit.

BOGGS, WILLIAM LAWRENCE.—Pastor of the Third
Presbyterian Church of Greenville, South Carolina, son of T.
H. Boggs, Lieutenant-Colonel Second South Carolina Volunteers, Moore's Regiment. He was born at Liberty, Pickens
County, July 11, 1857 and died July 1862. His ancestors were
Scotch-Irish. Attended the common schools, and was for three
years a student under Dr. J. R. Riley. He entered the Theological Seminary at Columbia, South Carolina, remained two
years, and graduated from the Princeton Theological Seminary in 1887. In December of that year he was married to
Miss Nannie Cunningham, of Liberty Hill, South Caolina, was
pastor of Liberty Hill Church three years, and then supplied
several churches in Spartanburg County. Then went out as
an evangelist one year. He has been chairman of the Home
Mission Committee of Enoree Presbytery three years. He is
also a member of the Synodical Committee of Home Missions.

BOLEMAN, GEORGE NEWTON C.—Born July 26, 1849, near Providence Camp Ground, Anderson County, South Carolina. He attended school at Brown's Muster Ground, and at Townville. His education was, however, largely self-acquired. He was twice married; first, to Miss Molie Tribble, and second, to Miss Nannie, daughter of Capt. R. O. Tribble. He has never held any public office except that of Auditor of Anderson County. He was elected to this position in 1892; was re-elected two years later by a large majority, over two other competitors, and in 1896, was again elected County Auditor, this time without opposition, receiving the largest vote ever given a candidate for office in Anderson County. Has been elected Auditor for five consecutive terms. Previously taught school in South Carolina and Tennessee with marked success.

BOMAR, HORACE LELAND.—A rising young member of the Spartanburg bar. Youngest son of John Earle Bomar deceased. Was born July 15, 1874, at Spartanburg, South Carolina. His education was acquired from private schools, the city schools, and from Wofford College, where he graduated in 1894, taking Bachelor of Arts degree. Has since spent about six months in Europe and Africa. After finishing school he entered the law office of Bomar and Simpson, and studied law for one year. Was admitted to the bar in December 1895, and formed a partnership with Judge Thomason. Afterwards became member of the firm of Bomar and Simpson which, upon the death of John Earle Bomar, became Simpson and Bomar. The firm of Simpson and Bomar represent the city of Spartanburg as attorneys. Mr. Simpson, senior member of the firm, is general solicitor of the Charleston and Western Carolina Railroad; the junior member is secretary of the Bar Association of Spartanburg. In 1898 he was appointed by Judge Brawley the referee in bankruptcy for Spartanburg County, under the United States Bankruptcy Act. Is one of the trustees of Kennedy Library, a director in several corporations, a deacon in First Baptist Church, director and one of the organizers of the Choral Society and of Wofford College Lyceum.

BONHAM, MILLEDGE LIPSCOMB.—Son of Governor Milledge L. and Mrs. Annie Griffin Bonham. Was born at Edgefield Court-house, South Carolina, on October 16, 1854. He received his academic schooling at Edgefield and Columbia. Graduated from the Carolina Military Institute, under Colonel John P. Thomas, with the rank of adjutant. He began the study of law at Barnwell under his brother-in-law, Colonel Robert Aldrich. His studies were interrupted by calls to duty as a member of a Red Shirt company; but he took his full part in all the labors, hazards and victories of that epoch. He was admitted to the bar in February, 1877, and settled at Ninety-Six with a view to assist in the establishment of a county seat at that place—of a county to be formed of a part of Edgefield, Abbeville, and Laurens counties. Governor McSweeney at the same time, established the "Ninety-Six Guardian," of which young Bonham became editor. Two years later Mr. Bonham moved to Newberry and thence to Abbeville. Here he entered actively on the practice of his profession, and in 1881 was appointed by Governor Hagood, Master for the county. This office was held until 1885, when he voluntarily retired from it and took up the practice of law. He was captain of the Abbeville Rifles (in command of which he was at Yorktown, in 1881) in the regiment from this State in command of Hugh S. Thompson (afterwards governor). This regiment was sent by the State to take part in the ceremonies incident to the celebration of the centennial of the surrender of Lord Cornwallis in 1781. In August, 1886, on the death of General M. A. M. Manigault, adjutant and inspector-general of the State, he was appointed by Governor Sheppard to fill the unexpired term, and in November of that year, he was elected to a full term of two years. He held the office until 1890, when he was defeated. In 1894, he moved to Anderson, and formed a partnership with Captain H. H. Watkins for the practice of law. He married in 1878, Daisy, daughter of Judge A. P. Aldrich, of Barnwell.

BONNER, OLIVER YOUNG.—Son of Rev. J. I. Bonner D. D. Was born in Due West, South Carolina, on November 15, 1863. His father was the founder of Due West Female College, and its president for twenty years. He was also editor of the "Associated Reform Presbyterian." The subject of this sketch graduated at Erskine College, in 1883. Spent two years in Erskine Theological Seminary, and graduated at Union Theological Seminary, New York. He was pastor of churches for four years in Lineshe County, Tennessee, and since 1891 has supplied the Associate Reform Presbyterian Church of Due West, South Carolina. He is also one of the editors of the "Associate Reform Presbyterian." He married Miss Belle H. Neel, on November 15, 1892.

BOSTICK, ALEXANDER McIVER.—Member of the Legislature from Bamberg County. Born in Cheraw, South Carolina, January 4, 1863. Son of Rev. J. M. Bostick and Helen McIver. His ancestors were English, Scotch, and French-Huguenot. Was Bachelor of Arts of Richmond College, Richmond, Virginia, in 1885. Won writer's medal and philosophy medal. Married Cornelia Adams, of Arkadelphia, Arkansas, August 1, 1893. Was planter for several years after leaving college. Has practiced law for the past ten years in Hampton, Walterboro, and Bamberg.

BOWEN, ROBERT ESLI.—Son of John and Elvira (Hunt) Bowen. Born on George's Creek near Briggs Post-office, Pickens County, September 8, 1830. His ancestors were of Irish and Welsh descent. They came from Virginia, and settled in this section of the State about 1785. Colonel R. E. Bowen was reared to manhood on his father's farm, receiving a knowledge of the English branches at the common schools, and being instructed at the same time, by his father in surveying. In 1853 he went to Texas on horseback, remaining in that State about a year, and teaching school during five months of the time, the balance of the year being spent in traveling over the State. In the fall of 1854, he returned to South Carolina; and from that time until 1857 he superintended his father's farm. October 15, of that year, he married Miss Martha Oliver, daughter of Dr. James Oliver, of Anderson, South Carolina. In the early part of 1858, Colonel Bowen located upon the farm he now occupies, which

had been given him by his father. He remained there until
November, 1861. On the sixth of that month he entered the
Confederate army as first lieutenant of Company E, Second
South Carolina Regiment, commanded by Captain T. H.
Boggs. During the first two months, he was stationed on
Sullivan's Island, in Orr's Regiment of Rifles. In 1861 Com-
pany E, together with five other companies, organized the
First Battalion of Rifles, Captain Boggs being promoted to
major. In the early part of 1862 this battalion, and some other
companies which joined it, were organized into the Second
South Carolina Regiment of Rifles, and Lieutenant Bowen
was promoted to the captaincy of this regiment. In October,
1863, he was again promoted to lieutenant-colonel, and in
December of the same year was made colonel of the regiment. Continued in that capacity until the close of the war,
surrendering with Lee at Appomattox. He commanded Company E, in the seven days fight around Richmond, which included both the battles of Gaines' Mill, and Frazer's Farm. In
the battle of Fredericksburg, he was in command of the same
company. He was wounded in the battle of Willis Valley,
below Chattanooga, and compelled to spend two months in
the hospital and at home. He was at the head of his regiment in several other battles. In the Battle of the Wilderness, a cannon ball cut off the tail of his coat, but inflicted no
injury. At the close of the war he rode his army horse home,
and again took charge of his farm. In 1872 he was elected to
the Legislature. In 1874, elected State Senator from Pickens
County, and served four years. In 1877, he was chairman of
the special committee appointed to investigate the frauds
perpetrated by the Radicals during 1869 and 1876. In 1881,
he was elected president of the Atlantic and French Broad
Railroad Company, which position he held two years. He was
a director of the Carolina, Cumberland Gap, and Chicago Railroad from 1883 to 1886, and in June of the latter year was
made president. He is still a stockholder in the road and
also of the Easley Oil Mill. Trustee of Clemson College and
member of the Farmers' Alliance. Mr. Bowen was elected to
the Legislature, in 1864. While he was in the army, he served
out that term, and was re-elected in 1865.

4

BOWMAN, ILDERTON WESLEY.—Lawyer. Eldest son of the late Dr. O. N. Bowman, a leading physician of Orangeburg County. Born near Cattle Creek Camp Ground, in Orangeburg County, September 20, 1857. Attended Mount Zion Institute, and graduated from Wofford College, in 1879. Married Mary Ellen, daughter of Honorable John W. Crum, of Barnwell County, November 14, 1883. Member of the Legislature from 1894 to 1895, and also of the Constitutional Convention of 1895. Author of the bill forbidding divorces in this State. Has been practicing law at Orangeburg, since admission to the bar, in 1882. Now a member of the firm of Bowman & Wannamaker. Member of the fire department of the City, and charter member of the East End Reel Company. He is now assistant chief of the fire department. He is a Mason and Worshipful Master of Shibboleth Lodge, and member of the Grand Lodge of South Carolina. He is also a Woodman of the World.

BOYCE, JAMES.—Son of Rev. Ebenezer Erskine Boyce, D. D., and Rachel McElwee Boyce. Born January 25, 1860. He was prepared for college in Elk Shoals Academy, Iredell County, North Carolina, under Rev. W. B. Pressley; and Bethel Academy, York County, South Carolina, under Rev. James Douglas. He graduated from Erskine College, in 1878. Taught school one year at Woodward, South Carolina, and entered Erskine Theological Seminary, graduating in June, 1881. He married on October 17, 1883, Miss Jennie I. Thompson, at Millersburg, Kentucky, daughter of R. A. Thompson, a well-known farmer of Nicholas County. He was appointed by the Associate Reform Presbyterian Synod to take charge of the mission in Louisville, Kentucky, the most important mission to be filled at that time. Succeeded in the field, and raised the money for the erection of a handsome church. Received a call to the large and flourishing congregation in Huntersville, North Carolina, and moved to that place in December, 1896. In February, 1899, he was elected president of the Due West Female College, in Due West, South Carolina. In 1890, was elected stated clerk of the Associate Reform Synod of the South, the highest court of the church; and was re-elected to this office, in 1900.

BOOZER, DAVID LUTHER, DR.—Dentist. He is a son of David and Catherine (Rawl) Boozer. Born in Lexington, South Carolina, September 11, 1833. His father was a well-to-do farmer. Having determined to study dentistry, he entered the office of Drs. Roberts and Gregg of Columbia. In six months the senior partner died, and Dr. Boozer became a member of the firm. He joined the ranks of Hampton, and served until the close of the war. He returned home, to find his office had been destroyed by fire; but he went to work with renewed vigor. In 1866, he married Martha Caroline, eldest daughter of Jacob Barre, a wealthy planter of Lexington County. He withdrew from active practice, in 1898; purchased the Aull Mill, near Newberry; and erected the Newberry Roller Mills. He has, associated with him, his two younger sons. Dr. Boozer was one of the prime movers in organizing the State Dental Association, and was elected president, in 1884. He has invented several appliances for the extraction of teeth. He is a great church worker, and an ardent supporter of the Lutheran Church.

BOZEMAN, JAMES BRUNSON.—Pastor of Baptist Church at Yorkville, South Carolina. Was born in Darlington County, South Carolina, February 14, 1864. Prepared for college at the Dovesville High School, and graduated from Furman University, Greenville. Then took a two years' course at the Southern Baptist Theological Seminary, Louisville, Kentucky. Married Miss Nettie P. Blackwell, of Kershaw, South Carolina, March 2, 1897. He has supplied churches in Walterboro, Kershaw, and Yorkville.

BRABHAM, HENRY JASPER.—Banker. Was born September 3, 1843, at Buford's Bridge, Barnwell County, South Carolina. Attended school in Aiken two years, and one year at Cokesbury School. Married Mrs. Adelle Jennings, of Orangeburg County, December 17, 1868. After being in the mercantile business nineteen years, at Bamberg, retired. Later was elected cashier of the Bamberg Banking Company; and served as such twelve years, when elected president, which office he still holds. Served in the Confederate army, four years, in Hagood's First Regiment, Company C, as second sergeant; slightly wounded twice. Has been mayor of the town, and served several years as alderman. He was chairman of the committee to create the new county of Bamberg. Secretary of the Board of Control, of the Carlisle Fitting School. Commissioner of Bamberg County for the Charleston Exposition. Director in several cotton and oil mills.

BRADLEY, DAVID FRANKLIN.—Born in Pickens County, South Carolina, September 5, 1845. He passed his early life on a farm in his native county; but in 1859 he went to Florida from which State, in April, 1864, he entered the Confederate service, in Company A, Second Florida Regiment, known as the Pensacola Rifle Rangers. He served in this regiment until, in the Battle of the Wilderness, he lost his left arm. After this he spent one month in a hospital, where he was assigned to duty in the enrolling department of Florida. While en route he was intercepted by General Sherman, and obliged to return home. In 1865, he resumed his studies in a country school, and from that time until 1868. attended school and taught, alternately. In 1868, he was elected school commissioner of Pickens County, in which capacity he served for six years. In 1871, he helped to found the "Pickens Sentinel," of which he was sole editor until 1885. For a part of that time he was the sole owner. In 1874, he was elected to the Legislature, serving two terms; and in 1878, he was sent to the State Senate. Appointed, by President Cleveland, internal revenue collector for South Carolina, in 1885, and held the position four years. Was a member of the board of penitentiary directors of South Carolina, and during the last three years was chairman of board. He is a Democrat. President of Easley Oil Mill, Fertilizer and Ginning Company, in which he is one of the largest stockholders. He is also a stockholder in the Carolina, Cumberland Gap, and Chicago Railroad, only a portion of which is in operation. Trustee and chairman of the board of the Easley High School. In February, 1891, he assisted in the establishment of the "Easley Democrat," of which he has since been editor and joint owner. He is a member of the Masonic Fraternity. Major Bradley married Mary B. Breezeale, of Pickens, in 1865.

BRADLEY, WILLIAM RENWICK.—Son of Rev. R. F. and M. R. Bradley. Was born at Moffettville, Anderson County, South Carolina, March 5, 1873. After completing the course at the Troy High School, of Troy, South Carolina, he graduated from Erskine College, with the degree of Bachelor of Arts, in the year 1895. After teaching one year at Madison, North Carolina, he returned to his native State, and for four years has been engaged in educational work in Anderson County. He is now teaching in the Abbeville graded schools. While at college, he won considerable distinction as an orator.

BRANCH, WILLIAM TULLY.—Son of Dr. Isaac and Fannie Branch. His parents came from Vermont to Abbeville County, South Carolina, in 1825, and his father practiced medicine in Abbeville until 1872. W. T. Branch was born April 23, 1845. He attended the public school until sixteen years of age, and entered the South Carolina Military Academy, in 1862. In 1863, entered the Civil War with the South Carolina Military Cadets as a whole, and remained until the close of the war, Was under Brigadier-General Elliott, of Johnston's army. Surrendered at Hillsboro, North Carolina. In 1869, went into the insurance work, and has been at it ever since. He is Past Grand Master of Masons of South Carolina, Past Grand High Priest of the Grand Chapter Royal Arch Masons of South Carolina. In June, 1870, married Miss Annie C. Wilson, of Greenwood, South Carolina. Lives at Abbeville, South Carolina.

BRANTLEY, THOMAS F.—Lawyer. Son of E. W. Brantley. Born in Orangeburg County, January 28, 1867. Of French, Scotch and German descent. Prepared for college at the Bingham Military School, of Asheville, North Carolina. Graduated from the South Carolina College, in 1892; and the following year, 1893, completed the law course. Admitted to the bar in 1894. Taught school in the public schools of Orangeburg. Received an appointment in 1893, under Cleveland, as chief of Pension Division under Secretary Carlisle, but office was abolished. Returned to Orangeburg and engaged in the practice of law. Elected to Legislature, in 1899, to fill out unexpired term; served one term in the Senate; then resigned to enter the race for Congress, and was defeated by a small vote. He is unmarried.

BRAWLEY, WILLIAM H.—Prominent among the representative men of South Carolina, is Major William H. Brawley, a leading member of the Charleston bar. Major Brawley is a native of South Carolina, and was born May 13, 1841, at Chester. His early education was secured in the academy at Chester, from which he entered the South Carolina College at Columbia, where he was graduated, in 1860. In April, 1861, he entered the Confederate army as a private, joining the Sixth Regiment of South Carolina Volunteers. After the siege of Fort Sumter, his regiment was ordered to Virginia, and became a part of the Army of Northern Virginia. He lost an arm in the battle of Seven Pines, was confined to a hospital for three months, and then returned home. His father having died in the meantime, Major Brawley took charge of the plantation, and conducted the same until 1864, when, not having recovered his health, he determined to go abroad. In March of that year ran the Federal blockade at Wilmington and went to Europe, remaining abroad until 1865. Upon his return, he began reading law in the office of his uncle, Mr. James Hemphill, at Chester, and May, 1866, was admitted to the bar. Immediately after, he formed a partnership with Mr. Samuel McAliley, of Chester, the leading lawyer of that circuit. In 1868 Major Brawley was elected solicitor of the Chester Circuit, and was re-elected, in 1872.

In 1874, he resigned the solicitorship and moved to Charleston, where he formed a partnership in law, with Honorable W. D. Porter, and later, formed a partnership with Joseph W. Barnwell. He has several times been elected to the Legislature and has served in that body with distinction. Appointed district judge during Cleveland's second administration.

BREEDEN, JAMES FRANK.—Son of Rev. William K. and Martha J. Adams Breeden. Born in Marlboro County, South Carolina, October 3, 1848. Acquired education from the common schools of the neighborhood. Married Sallie J. Pearson, November 20, 1867. He was county commissioner eight years, and now is alderman of the town of Bennettsville. He joined the Confederate army, in 1864, at the age of sixteen, and remained in service until the close of the war. Member of the Finance Board of the South Carolina Conference twenty years. He is now engaged in planting.

BREMER, HERMAN FREDERICK.—Son of Herman F. and Carolina (Cook) Bremer. Born April 22, 1850. His father merchandised in Charleston several years. Ancestors came from Germany. Educated in the public schools of Charleston. Married Rebecca K. Keys, October 20, 1880. In early manhood clerked for F. W. Wagner & Company, Charleston, South Carolina. In 1889, became a member of the firm, with which he remained until 1896, when he withdrew and organized the Charleston Importing and Exporting Company, of which he is president and general manager. Secretary and treasurer of the Imperial Kaolin Mining Company, of South Carolina; director of the Charleston Freight Bureau, and director of the Philadelphia Museum, of Philadelphia.

BRIGGS, ELDRIDGE CUTTER.—A leading merchant of Clinton, South Carolina. Son of Robert P. and Frances Briggs, (nee Wilburn.) Born near Union, South Carolina, June 30, 1851. Attended only the country schools, and one year at J. B. Patrick's School, Greenville, South Carolina. His first wife was Laura Calmes. His second wife was Jennie Little, of Clinton, South Carolina. Was mayor of Clinton for one year. He is a cotton buyer, and buys for a great many of the cotton factories in the State. Engaged in farming and merchandising.

BRIGGS, HENRY.—Organized the American Bank in Greenville, in October, 1890; and was elected president. He was born in Pickens County, on October 12, 1851. Removed to Spartanburg when quite small, his father, Alexander Briggs, having been elected secretary and treasurer of the Spartanburg & Union Railroad. He attended the Gallard School of Greenville, and the common schools of Spartanburg. He married Emily Louisa McBee, April 18, 1883. He commenced business as a clerk in a store, in 1870, and engaged in the mercantile business on his own account, from 1876 until a short time before going into the banking business.

BRIGHT, WILLIAM WOOD FIELD.—Son of David Bright, of Blount County, Tennessee. Born December 19, 1840, near Louisville, Tennessee. His father was a farmer, of English Quaker descent, of Pennsylvania. His elementary training was received from the public schools. He attended Ewing Jefferson College, in Tennessee for a few months just before the war. He served in the Confederate War, joining Company K, Second Regiment of Tennessee Cavalry, as a private, from August 13, 1861, to May 3, 1865. Surrendered at Charlotte, North Carolina. Was a prisoner of war a few months. Has devoted most of his life to teaching. Taught in the Pickens public schools from 1868 to 1890. At that time he was elected county school commissioner, then taught for four years, and, in 1898 was elected county superintendent of education. Served out that term, and has been re-elected. Married Miss Margaret J., daughter of B. J. Williams, September 21, 1871.

BROCK, JOHN WILLIAM.—Son of J. L. and Barbara Brock, of Anderson County. Was born at Honea Path, August 29, 1860. Attended the Honea Path High School. Engaged in the telegraph business for one year. Clerked five years for G. W.

McGhee & Son, at Belton, South Carolina. Merchandised for three years under the firm name of McGhee & Brock. Then the latter bought out McGhee's interest, and is now the proprietor, doing business, since 1899, under the firm name of J. W. Brock, General Merchandise, at Honea Path, South Carolina. A director of the Citizens Bank at that place. Married Miss Mary Erwin, daughter of Malvern Erwin, December 27, 1900.

BROCK, LEWIS AUGUSTUS.—President of the Citizens Bank of Honea Path. A son of A. J. and Mrs. Ann Brock. Born at Honea Path, South Carolina, July 21, 1861. His education was received from the Honea Path High School. He married Lillian H. Mattison on May 29, 1900. Is a director of the Honea Path Oil Mill. A merchant, and a member of the firm of the Brock Fertilizer Company, of Honea Path.

BRODIE, PAUL THOMAS, B. S., A. B.—Professor of mathematics in Clemson College, South Carolina. Was born near Leesville, Lexington County, South Carolina, January 11, 1866. His father, T. F. Brodie, who died in 1871, was a successful cotton merchant of Charleston, South Carolina, whose paternal grandfather was a member of the Brodie Clan of Scotland and settled in Charleston. His mother is the daughter of General Paul Quattlebaum, who was an officer in the Florida War, a member of the Secession Convention, and for many years prominent in the political affairs of the State. He died in 1890. Mr. P. T. Brodie was prepared for college at the Stuart Classical School of Charleston. He graduated from Furman University, in June, 1897, and began at once the work of teaching. After a year of service in charge of the Lewiedale High School, he was for four years principal of the Lexington Graded School. In June, 1891, he was elected superintendent of the Spartanburg city schools, which position he held until June, 1895, when he accepted the superintendency of the Bennettsville Graded Schools. He has done post-graduate work in different universities during the summer. In August, 1899, he was elected head of the department of mathematics in Clemson College. He was married June 30, 1891, to Miss Isabel Bradford.

BRODIE, ROBERT LITTLE, M. D.—One of the oldest and most popular physicians of Charleston. Born in that city September 5, 1829. Graduated from Charleston College, and South Carolina Medical College. Took post-graduate course at Bellevue Hospital, New York. Assistant surgeon in United States army in 1854; assistant surgeon in Confederate army in 1861. Reported for duty to General Beauregard at Manassas. Medical director until surrender at Greensboro. Private practice since.

BROOKS, ULYSSES ROBERT.—Clerk of the Supreme Court of South Carolina, and a veteran of Company B. Sixth South Carolina Cavalry. Is a descendant of a noted and patriotic Southern family. His great-grandfather was Zachariah Smith Brooks, a lieutenant in the Revolutionary army under General William Butler, who married a sister of the General after the close of the war, and had one son, Whitfield Brooks. The latter married Mary Parsons Carroll; and one of their sons was Preston S. Brooks, Congressman previous to the Confederate era. James Carroll Brooks, father of Ulysses Robert, married Sarah Crawford Robert, a daughter of Colonel U. M. Robert of Mount Pleasant, Barnwell District, South Carolina, who was descended from Rev. Peter Robert, the first Huguenot minister in the Carolina Colony who landed at Port Royal, in April, 1670, under William Sayle, the first Governor of Carolina.

The subject of this sketch was born at Mount Pleasant, Barnwell District October 27, 1846. Was reared at the home of his parents in Edgefield District. He attended the Edgefield Male Academy about four years. On the third day of

December, 1862, he and his brother, Whitfield Butler Brooks, who was killed at the battle of Trevilian Station, Virginia, June 12, 1864, in the nineteenth year of his age, were mustered into the Confederate service by Captain Lewis Jones of Company B, Sixth South Carolina Cavalry. He served as a private with this regiment in South Carolina until the campaign of 1864, when he participated in the cavalry fighting in Virginia. In August, 1864, he was detailed as courier for General John Dunovant, with whom he served with credit until General Dunovant was killed. After this he was attached to the staff of General M. C. Butler as courier until the close of hostilities. In his speech at Edgefield, at the unveiling of the Confederate Monument, August 8, 1900, General Butler said that the subject of this sketch had always behaved gallantly in battle and had frequently acted as staff officer for him. Throughout this career he escaped without serious injury, being only slightly wounded twice. Receiving a Mexican Dollar as his share of the money available to pay the Confederate troops at Greensboro, he returned to his father's plantation. For five years from the fall of 1866, he was engaged in mercantile pursuits in Louisiana, then returned home. On December 5, 1871, was united in marriage, at Augusta, Georgia, to Mary E. adopted daughter of General James Jones, colonel of the Fourteenth South Carolina Infantry. After his marriage, he farmed, and studied law. Was admitted to the bar March 24, 1880. On the 8th of February, 1881, he made his home in Columbia, South Carolina, and began the practice of law; but on the 24th of January, 1883, he accepted a position under Honorable James N. Lipscomb, then Secretary of State. He has ever since held honorable and responsible positions in the State government, as chief clerk of the office of Secretary of State until December 6, 1894, and since then by election as clerk of the Supreme Court, his present term expiring in 1904.

Mr. Brooks is an author, and is now engaged upon a history of the Bench and Bar of the State. He is a member of Camp Hampton, United Confederate Veterans, and while aide-de-camp to General Walker, division commander with the rank of major, was elected colonel of the Richland Regiment, United Confederate Veterans, March 11, 1899, which is composed of the camps of Camp Hampton, Camp A. C. Haskell, Camp M. C. Butler, and Camp E. D. Bookter.

BRONSON, HARRY ALEXANDER.—Business manager of the "Florence Daily Times." Son of W. A. and Antoinette T. Bronson. Born November 4, 1869, at Florence, South Carolina. Of Scotch-Irish and Huguenot descent. Ancestors came to this State in 1670. Attended private schools and graduated from the South Carolina University, in 1889. Studied law; and was admitted to the bar in December, 1894. Taught in the graded schools at Georgetown, and was for three years principal of the Magnolia Street School in Spartanburg. Secretary and Treasurer of the Times Company at Florence, South Carolina.

BROWN, CLARENCE L.—Editor of the "New Sentinel," Barnwell, South Carolina. Son of Charles E Brown and Elizabeth Gilchrist. Born in Charleston, South Carolina, October 23, 1870. Of French and English descent. Acquired education from the high schools of Charleston, South Carolina. Married Louisa Bronson, in August, 1892. A reporter at Charleston several years.

BROWN, CLINTON CAPERS.—Pastor of the First Baptist Church in Sumter for the past twenty-seven years. Born in Barnwell, South Carolina, February 2, 1852. Educated at Furman University, Greenville, South Carolina; Washington and Lee University, Lexington, Virginia. Graduated at the Southern Baptist Theological Seminary at Greenville, South Carolina. Married Sallie Wright, November 26, 1878. Degree of Doctor of Divinity conferred by Furman University, Greenville, South Carolina, in 1858.

BROWN, JAMES ALFRED.—Pastor of Due West Baptist Church. A son of Daniel A. and Annie E. Brown. Was born August 24, 1856, in Montgomery County, Virginia. Graduated at Richmond College, Virginia, with the degree of Master of

Arts. Afterwards completed full course of Theological studies at the Southern Baptist Theological Seminary, and supplied churches in Chester County. Married Miss Carrie Scaife, October 31, 1888.

BROWN, JAMES COURTENEY.—Minister. Son of Elijah Brown, of Clarke County, Georgia. Born May 10, 1836. Graduated from Mercer University in class of 1859, with degree of Bachelor of Arts. Since then, received degree of Master of Arts from said college. Married first to Eva L. Culbertson, August 11, 1863; second to Mrs. M. A. Ray, October 4, 1881; and third to Miss Mollie A. Quattlebaum, of Lexington County, August 4, 1891. Began life as a teacher at Cave Springs, Georgia. Then entered the Confederate army in Cherokee Artillery, served four years, taken prisoner two days after the surrender of Lee in North Carolina. Returned to Cave Springs, Georgia, and taught school a short time. Then ordained to the ministry and supplied churches in Rome, and other parts of Georgia, for about ten years. In 1875, came to South Carolina and supplied a church at Beech Island. Then called to Aiken, and served the First Church seven years. He is now pastor of churches in Aiken and Edgefield counties.

BROWN, JAMES FLEMING.—Professor of mathematics in Converse College. Son of M. L. and M. W. Brown. Was born at Columbia, South Carolina, June 3, 1857. He was prepared for college at Mount Zion Institute, Winnsboro, South Carolina. Entered Wofford College, and graduated in June, 1876. Taught in what is now Cherokee County for five years after graduation, then Santuc; and Johnston where he had a very fine private school. Organized the Newberry Graded Schools and was first superintendent. He was called to fill the chair of mathematics in the Columbia Female College, and remained two years, when, in 1893, he was elected professor of mathematics in Converse College, which position he still holds. He is secretary and treasurer of Wofford College Alumni, and also treasurer of Converse College. Married Miss Bennie Scurry, November 10, 1885.

BROWN, JOSEPH JENNINGS.—Lawyer. Youngest son of Barnett H. Brown and Eliza Duncan. His grandfather, Bartlett Brown, came to South Carolina from Albermarle County, Virginia; in 1757. His grand-uncle, Tarleton Brown, came from Virginia and served in the Revolutionary War under Marion. Early training in the country school. In 1852, he went to the Citadel Academy. The class rebelled on account of unjust treatment, and marched out of Academy. He then read law, and was admitted to the bar in 1854. Married Virginia Harley, January 29, 1879. Captain of Company K, in Hagood's Regiment. Was present at the capture of Fort Sumter. At dissolution of regiment went to Virginia, and served as captain in command of General Curtis Lee. Served on the coast a short time, with Beaufort Artillery, and was badly wounded at Pocataligo. He was elected to the Legislature to succeed Judge Aldrich. Engaged in farming eight years after the war. In 1874, resumed the practice of law at Allendale, South Carolina, and, in 1882, moved to Barnwell, his old home.

BROWN, JOSEPH NEWTON.—Lawyer and banker of Anderson, South Carolina. He is a son of Samuel Brown and Helen T. (Vandiver) Brown, granddaughter of Edward Vandiver, a Revolutionary soldier. Was born near Anderson, South Carolina, December 16, 1832. His education was acquired under the instruction of O. H. P. Fant, Wesley Leverett, and Manning Belcher. He married Miss Lizzie L. Bruce, on February 28, 1866. He was a member of the Legislature from Anderson County for one year, from 1886 to 1887. Merchandised at Townville, South Carolina, for two years, and at Laurens, South Carolina, for two years. Read law under Colonel James H. Irby, in 1857, and the following year was admitted to the bar. Formed a partnership with Colonel James H. Irby, in 1858; and remained so until 1860, when he formed a partnership with R. P. Todd. In 1861, volunteered as a private in Gregg's Regiment, and was present at the fall of Fort Sumter. Appointed Captain, Company E, Fourteenth South Carolina Volunteers, February 20, 1863. Lieutenant-Colonel Fourteenth South Carolina Volunteers from February 20, 1863, to September 17, 1863. Colonel of same from September, 1863, until the surrender. Captured at fall of Petersburg, April 2, 1865. Imprisoned on Johnson's Island, Lake Erie, from April 16, to July 25, 1865. Commanded regiment at Chancellorsville, May 2 and 3, 1863. In command of McGowan's Brigade in the Bloody Angle, and Spottsylvania Court-house, Virginia, May 12, 1864, and in other smaller engagements. Served in numerous other battles. Severely wounded at Gaine's Mill, June 27, 1862, and at Gettysburg, July 3, 1863. In 1860, he went to Anderson, South Carolina, and formed a partnership with J. L. Tribble. At present he has no partner. He was president of the National Bank at Anderson, until 1891, when it closd up, paying stockholders $470.00 per share of $100.00 each.

BROWN, FREDERICK GARLINGTON.—Born at Anderson, South Carolina, October 28, 1860. The eldest son of Julia Reed and John Peter Brown. He was reared on the farm, and attended the country schools at intervals. When eighteen years of age, he entered Professor W. J. Ligon's High School at Anderson, but remained there only one year, being called home by the death of his father. For two years after, he taught a short-term country school. Mr. Brown lived in Florida one year, after which he returned to Anderson, South Carolina, and entered the store of Bleckley, Brown & Fretwell, in 1885, as salesman. Remained in that capacity until 1888, when he became a partner in the new firm of Sylvester, Bleckley & Co. In 1893 this firm sold out to the new firm of Brown, Osborne & Co., the senior member of which is the subject of this sketch. This firm did a large business until January 1, 1901, when Mr. Brown retired from the firm. He is now president and treasurer of the Anderson Fertilizer Co.; and vice-president of the Peoples Bank of Anderson, South Carolina. Is a director in the Orr Cotton

Mills; Riverside Manufacturing Company; Cox Manufacturing Company; and also in the Farmers' Warehouse Company, of Anderson, South Carolina. He is now serving his second term as Alderman from the First Ward. He is an enthusiastic Mason and has taken the Shriner's Degree. Married Miss Mamie McCrary, youngest daughter of Mr. Edmund McCrary, of Pendleton, South Carolina, in November, 1887.

BROWN, MICHAEL.—Born in New York City on the 27th of October, 1855. His father, Simon Brown, removed from New York to Blackville, South Carolina, when he was only three years old. Mr. Brown was given a good education in the schools of Blackville, and at the age of thirteen was sent to New York City to complete his scholastic training. Returning home after three years, he entered the mercantile establishment of his father, as bookkeeper and general manager. In 1884, he went to Barnwell and embarked in business for himself. The branch road running from that place and intersecting the South Carolina road at Blackville, is owned and operated by him. Vice-president of the Barnwell Bank. A stockholder in the Middle Georgia and Atlanta Railroad. He is president and principal owner of the Barnwell Oil and Fertilizer Company, and was largely instrumental in the erection of the Knights of Pythias Hall, and the Masonic Hall, in Barnwell. He is president of the Seaboard Construction Company, of Savannah. Married Miss Jennie Klein of Philadelphia, in 1877. He helped organize the Citizens Savings Bank of Barnwell, and the Southern Investment Co., of which he is general manager. Is now constructing the Carolina Midland, of which he is vice-president and treasurer.

BROWN, WILLIAM JAMES.—Son of M. H. and M. A. Brown. Born in Florence County, South Carolina, October 30, 1858. Moved to Florence, in 1869. Only such advantages as could be obtained from private schools at that time. Married Anna E. Mouzon, October 11, 1861. Clerked several years, then merchandised on own account, from 1887 to 1892. He then took the position as cashier of the Bank of Florence, which position he still holds. He is secretary and treasurer of several Building and Loan associations. Alderman of Florence, from 1889 to 1893. He is alderman and mayor pro tem., now serving second term of two years. Deacon in the Baptist Church, and treasurer of same.

BROWN, WILLIAM MONROE.—Was born in Oconee County, July 24, 1846. Father born in Anderson County and graduated in Laurens. Attended country schools. Married Miss N. Catherine Hunt, November 28, 1866. Served in Confederate army the last year of war. He is still farming and represents Oconee County in the Legislature.

BROWN, WILLIAM STEVENS, D. D. S.—Son of Dr. William S. Brown, one of the oldest and best physicians of Charleston during his life time. Was born February 25, 1869, in Charleston, where he has since resided. Attended the public schools of the City, B. R. Stuart's School, and the Charleston College. Left the College to take up study of dentistry with his father. Graduated from the University of Maryland, in 1890. Married Miss Marie Virginia Brown, January, 1896. He was once president of the South Carolina Dental Association. Practiced dentistry on his own account for ten years, but at the commencement of present year, joined forces with his father. Upon his father's death, which occurred soon after, succeeded to his practice.

BROWNE, HENRY BASCOM REV.—Presiding elder of the Orangeburg District. Son of J. M. and Lydia Coffin. Born in Anderson County, South Carolina, July 20, 1852. Of Scotch-Irish descent. Attended the private schools and academies of the county. Took literary and theological courses at Chautauqua in Boston. Married Mollie M. Moody. His second wife was Maria B. Chase. Entered the South Carolina Conference, in 1876, and served in Rock Hill, Florence, Charleston, and Greenville. Member and secretary of board of education. Connected with the "Southern Christian Advocate." Chairman of the Board of Control of the Carlisle Fitting School of Bamberg.

5

BROWNLEE, ROBERT CALVIN.—Son of Samuel R. and Louise Brownlee. He is merchandising at Due West, South Carolina. Was born in Due West, South Carolina, May 31, 1858. He graduated from Erskine College, in 1877. Married Miss Fannie F. Bonner, daughter of Rev. J. I. Bonner, in September, 1880. He was employed as salesman in Greenville for a few years after leaving college, and, in 1880, began business on his own account at Due West.

BRUCE, JOSEPH B.—Is engaged in the wholesale drug and retail business in Greenville, South Carolina. He was born in Iredell County, North Carolina, and remained on the farm until he was twenty-two years of age. Ancestors on mother's side came from England, and on father's from Scotland. Early training obtained from common country schools. Completed education at Rutherford College, North Carolina, in 1872. Came to South Carolina, the following year, and taught school four years. Afterward entered the mercantile business and has continued it since, with success. Married Miss Hammon, of Kershaw.

BRUCE, PHILIP THOMAS.—Auditor of Kershaw County since 1899. Son of James B. Bruce. He was born September 7, 1857, in Alexander County, North Carolina. Had only the advantage of a common school education, but made the best of his opportunities, and has acquired a very good English education. Was married to Miss Sarah A. Peach, March 28, 1886. He then taught in the public schools of the county, fourteen years.

BRUNSON, ALEXANDER NELSON, B. S.—Pastor of Trinity Methodist Episcopal Church, at Yorkville, South Carolina. Was born in Greenville, South Carolina, October 15, 1868. Son of George W. and Sophia Stephens Brunson. Graduated from the South Carolina Military Academy, in 1888, as captain of company, and valedictorian of class. Entered the Theological department of Vanderbilt University. Married April 3, 1894, Miss S. Philo Jones of Laurens, South Carolina.

BRUNSON, WILLIAM ALEXANDER.—Born in Darlington District, March 19, 1837. Son of Peter Alexander and Susannah P. Woods Brunson, both natives of Darlington District. Ancestors were, for generations, natives of South Carolina, and earlier English and French-Huguenots. He was prepared for college at the Darlington Academy, and entered Wofford College as a freshman, in October, 1858. Left at the close of his junior year to enter the army. He was mustered into service as a private at Richmond, in August, 1861, in Company D, Gregg's First Regiment, South Carolina Volunteers. The company was afterwards given a battery of Light-Artillery which was attached to Pegram's Battalion, Jackson's, afterwards Hill's, corps, American National Volunteers. Returned with battery to South Carolina, in June, 1864, to recruit for men and horses. He is now probate judge of Florence County. Married Antoinette Tyler Chandler of Winnsboro, South Carolina, December, 1865. In 1877, appointed trial justice by Governor Hampton; served four years. Served three terms as intendant of Town of Florence. Member of the Legislature from Darlington, from 1882 to 1883. Admitted to the bar in 1882, first with Boyd and Miller, and, later, with Boyd and Brown of Darlington. President of the Bank of Florence, from 1888 to 1896. Now probate judge of Florence County.

BRYAN, FRANCIS MARION.—Son of George D. Bryan. Was born in Charleston, South Carolina, June 22, 1875. Ancestors were Scotch-Irish. Attended the public schools of Charleston; the High School of Virginia, at Alexandria, completing his education at the South Carolina College, Columbia. He has never married. After leaving school, in 1896, he returned to Charleston, where he has since been engaged in the practice of law. Assistant to the Corporation Council of the City of Charleston, and chairman for Registration for that county.

BRYAN, GEORGE DWIGHT.—Son of Honorable George S. and Rebecca L. Bryan. Born September 26, 1845, at Charleston,

South Carolina. Was prepared to enter the sophomore class in the Charleston College, in 1860; but entered the United States Naval Academy. Resigned in March, 1861, and returned home. Was appointed midshipman in the South Carolina navy; and was present at the bombardment of Fort Sumter, in April, 1861. Upon the formation of the Confederate States navy, he was appointed midshipman. Captured in Brazil, in 1864, and confined in Fort Mann, Boston, until February, 1865. After the war, studied law; and was admitted to the bar, in 1867. Has continued the practice of law since, at Charleston, South Carolina, as member of the firm of Bryan & Bryan. Elected city attorney, in 1878, which office he held until 1887, when he was elected mayor of said city. He was appointed by President Cleveland, collector of customs, for the port of Charleston, on February 13, 1894; and served as such until 1898, when his successor was appointed by President McKinley. Married Miss May Middleton King, August 3, 1869.

BUCHANAN, JOHN HIDDIN.—Editor. Son of John R. Buchanan of Fairfield County, South Carolina. Born August 17, 1836, in Fairfield County, South Carolina. Graduated from South Carolina College in class of 1856. He spent eight years in teaching. On November 10, 1874, he was united in marriage to Miss Mary M. Mobley, of Rome, Georgia. Probate Judge of Chester County for six years. In 1890, became editor and proprietor of the "Chester Reporter," which position he still holds. Was in Confederate service one year, Bratton's Brigade, Army of Northern Virginia.

BUCHANAN, OSMUND WOODWARD.—Judge of Third Circuit. Born in Winnsboro, Fairfield County, South Carolina, on the 16th day of September, 1858. Son of R. A. Buchanan and Rebecca Woodward. On both sides, of Revolutionary stock. He is a nephew of John Buchanan, who signed the Ordinance of Secession, December 20, 1860. He was educated in the common schools of his county, and at Mount Zion College. He studied law in the office of James H.

Ryon, and after an examination by the Supreme Court, was admitted to practice, in 1880. He married Miss Sophia A. Tillman, a daughter of the Honorable George Tillman, of Clarks Hill, on January 2, 1889. Was twice elected a representative from Fairfield County to the General Assembly; was appointed assistant attorney-general by Attorney-General D. A. Townsend, and upon the election of General Townsend to the bench in 1893, was elected without opposition to fill the vacancy thus caused. December 4, 1894, was elected judge of the Third Circuit for four years, commencing on December 8, 1894; and re-elected, without opposition, for term commencing December 8, 1898; and is still serving as circuit judge.

BUFORD, M. M.—Is serving his second term as sheriff of Newberry County. Was born in Union County, South Carolina, February 13, 1846. Had only the advantage of a country school. Married Sara A. Bell, of Laurens County, March 15, 1870. In 1862, young Buford enlisted in Company K, Fifth Regiment South Carolina Cavalry, Hampton Command. He was one of the escorts of the officers bearing the flag of truce between the armies, at the surrender of General Joseph E. Johnston, but the day preceding the surrender he was off on picket duty; and the night before that memorable occasion, he, with others, came out without surrendering, and returned home to the farm. Thoroughly identifying himself with the farmers and their interests, was active in the organization of the Alliance. During the reign of the Red Shirts, Captain Buford commanded one of the crack companies of the Mollohon Section of the county. He enjoys the distinction of being the only member of the Ku Klux Klan that was ever brought to trial, from Newberry County in the United States Court. In 1896, he was elected sheriff by a majority of over four hundred votes, and re-elected, in 1900. Since his election, of the numerous murders committed in the county, with only one exception, every criminal has been arrested or surrendered.

BUIST, ARCHIBALD JOHNSTON, M. D.—Practicing physician of Charleston, South Carolina. Born February 7, 1872,

at Charleston, South Carolina. He attended the high schools
of Charleston; Pautops Academy, Virginia; and Lawrenceville
School, New Jersey. Graduated, with Bachelor of Arts degree, from Princeton University, in 1893, and from the Medical
College of South Carolina, in 1896. Instructor in histology,
pathology and bacteriology, and lecturer on surgery, in Medical College of South Carolina; also lecturer on physiology
and diseases of children in the Charleston Medical School.
Married Miss Alice S. Mitchell, daughter of Francis A.
Mitchell, of Charleston, South Carolina.

BUIST, GEORGE LAMB.—Third son of George Buist and
Mary Edwards Buist. Born September 4, 1838, at Charleston,
South Carolina. Of Scotch descent. Attended private schools
in Charleston, South Carolina, and Bridgeport, New Jersey.
Later went to the College of Charleston. Studied law in the
office of Honorable George Buist, and was admitted to the
bar, in 1860. In May, 1862, he was married to Martha Allston
White. Was lieutenant of Palmetto Guards in Iron Battery
on Morris Island, and major of artillery of South Carolina Artillery, at close of the war, in North Carolina. State Senator
from Charleston County for sixteen years. Has engaged in
practice of law under firm name of Buist & Buist, of Charleston, South Carolina, since 1865. As one of the school commissioners, has always taken a great interest in educational
matters.

BUIST, HENRY.—Eldest son of George Lamb Buist, and
Martha A. White. Born March 3, 1863, in Charleston County,
South Carolina. Of Scotch descent. Attended the private
schools of Charleston; the Episcopal Academy of Connecti-
cut, and graduated from Yale, in 1884. Read law in office of
Buist & Buist. Supplemented this reading by a course under
John B. Minor of the University of Virginia, and was admit-
ted to the bar in December, 1885. Married Miss Frances G.
Ravenel, October 20, 1887.

BUIST, JOHN SOMERS, M. D.—Practicing physician of
Charleston. Born in Charleston, South Carolina, November

26, 1839. Graduated from Charleston College, and Medical College of South Carolina. Attended lectures in University of Berlin, Paris, and London. Surgeon in Confederate States Army, and Army of Northern Virginia; also in Roper Hospital and City Hospitals, and in United States Marine Hospital. President of Medical Society of South Carolina. Member of Board of Health of City of Charleston. Professor of Principles and Science of Surgery in Medical College of South Carolina. Commissioner of Charleston Orphan House. Director in Consolidated Company of Charleston, and one of the promoters in opening up the Isle of Palms. Honorary member of the Supreme Council of the Medical College of South Carolina. Married Miss Margaret Sinclair Johnston, February, 1867. Is a Thirty-third Degree Mason.

BULL, JAMES ALBERT.—Son of Daniel H. and Martha J. (Fowler). His father was a farmer and merchant. Ancestors were among the early English settlers of upper South Carolina, settling there about 1835. Was born at Sandy Flat, Greenville County, March 28, 1872. Acquired education in the schools of the county. Married Miss Sunie S. Stroud, daughter of Henry T. Stroud, of Greenville County, November 14, 1896. Since eighteen years of age has conducted a staple and fancy grocery business in Greenville; and is at present a member of the firm of J. A. Bull & Co., grocers, of Greenville, South Carolina.

BURGISS, WILLIAM WESLEY.—President of Franklin Cotton Mills, Greers, South Carolina. Was born August 12, 1863, at Greenville, South Carolina. Had the advantage of the Greenville schools until he was eighteen years of age. He is a great advocate of the cotton-mill industry; and has built two, the Victor, and the Franklin Mills, both of Greers. Is president of the Franklin Mills. He married Miss Eatta Bailey, of Greers, September 14, 1887.

BURNETT, WILBUR EMORY.—Born September 29, 1854, at Alexander, North Carolina. Came to Spartanburg, in 1863. Graduated from Wofford College, June, 1876. Entered the

National Bank as bookkeeper in July, 1876; was elected cashier of National Bank in 1886, and treasurer of the Fidelity Loan & Trust Co., in 1887. Still holds these offices. Elected president of the Spartan Mills upon its organization, and was principal mover in its organization. Elected president of the Tucapau Mills, after the death of Dr. C. E. Fleming. Has had a number of opportunities to become head of manufacturing institutions, but declined. Elected trustee of Converse College when it was founded; and trustee of Wofford College, in 1900, by the South Carolina Methodist Episcopal Conference. Served on City Council and was mayor pro tempore during the term of office. Married Miss Gertrude DuPre. daughter of Dr. Warren DuPre, a former professor in Wofford College, and president of Martha Washington, at Abingdon, Virginia. Elected president of his class in 1876, and in 1898 was elected president of Wofford College Alumni Association, which position he still holds.

BURNS, C. R. D.—Clerk of the court of Oconee County, South Carolina. Was born in Laurens County, November 18, 1861. He is of Scotch-Irish descent. Moved, with his parents, to Walhalla in 1872, where he was educated at Newberry College. He began the study of law in the office of Keith and Verner, in 1880, but did not press his study to admission to the bar. He was married, in 1882, to Bertha A. Schroder. Early in life, took an active interest in politics. He was elected secretary of the County Convention of the first Farmers' Movement, in 1884, in his twenty-second year. He was appointed internal revenue storekeeper, under the first administration of President Cleveland, in 1886. He was promoted on his official record, to chief clerk, in the office of collector of internal revenue, in Columbia, where he remained until removed by Harrison. In 1890, he returned to Walhalla. Was elected secretary of the Democratic County Convention, and has been repeatedly re-elected ever since. He was elected county chairman, in 1892, and to the House of Representatives, at the head of the delegation, in 1894 and in 1896, after two of the most memorable campaigns ever made in the county. He was appointed, by Speaker Jones, a member of the Ways and Means Committee. Took an active part in the deliberations of the House, and secured the enactment of general and local measures. He was appointed by Speaker Gary, on the special committee, to examine the office of State Treasurer and other State offices, in 1896; and on the Legislative Committee to examine the State Dispensary, in 1897. He declined to enter the race for the House, in 1898, and was again made county chairman. In 1900, he entered the race for clerk of the court, against three worthy competitors, and was elected by a handsome majority for a term of four years. He is the third clerk of court, in Oconee's official calendar, in the thirty-two years since the formation of the county.

BURROUGHS, FRANKLIN AUGUSTUS.—Born April 16, 1872, at Conway, South Carolina. Graduated at Burroughs High School, in 1890; then attended Bingham School at Asheville, North Carolina, for two years. Married Iola Buck, January 16, 1895, daughter of Captain Henry L. Buck. Clerked in office of Waccamau Line of steamers; then was captain on one of these for a year and a half. Bookkeeper for Burroughs & Collins after its incorporation in 1895. He was elected vice-president, and on the death of his father, in 1897, was elected to fill the position of secretary and treasurer, in addition to that of vice-president of Burroughs & Collins Company. Elected president of the Conway & Seashore Railroad, at its organization. He personally superintended the construction of the road, which was completed and accepted last January. President of the Horry Tobacco Warehouse Company, Conway, South Carolina. Served two terms as alderman of the town of Conway. Trustee of the Burroughs High School, and also of the board of the Conway School District.

BURWELL, HENRY WARD.—Pastor of the Presbyterian Church at Bennettsville, South Carolina. Son of W. A. and Sallie H. Ward Burwell. Born in Franklin County, Virginia, November 2, 1865. He is of Scotch-Irish descent. When he was small his parents moved to Georgia. He graduated at Emory College, in 1887, and at the Theological Seminary of

Columbia, in 1890. Is now doing post-graduate work at Chicago, to be completed in 1902. Married Mary E., daughter of Dr. D. R. Anderson, July 12, 1893. Has been pastor of the Presbyterian Church at Sanford, Florida, and Fairview, South Carolina.

BUTLER, FRANCIS WILKINSON PICKENS.—Eldest son of General M. C. Butler and Maria Calhoun Pickens. Born December 8, 1858, at Edgewood, the residence of Governor F. W. Pickens, near Edgefield Court-house, South Carolina, where his father lived while Governor Pickens was in St. Petersburg as minister under Buchanan. Went through the sophomore class at Wofford College. Graduated in medicine, in 1882. Served thirteen months at old Roper Hospital; six months in Polyclinic, New York City; and three years in United States army, as assistant surgeon. Has been practicing twenty years. Married Lillian, who was a daughter of Captain Iredell Jones, of Rock Hill, South Carolina, and granddaughter of Governor Adams, of South Carolina. He is now county physician and chairman of Board of Health of Edgefield. Acted as assistant surgeon in United States army, from 1888 to 1893; served in Texas, Indian Territory, Colorado, and Kansas; and was too old to ask for a commission. Resigned from the army after the death of his brother, Captain William Butler; returned to his native home, and took charge of his father's plantation. After about six months on the plantation, his preceptor, Dr. J. W. Hill, the leading physician in Edgefield, urged him to accept a partnership, which lasted only six months. After this dissolution of partnership, he practiced alone till January, 1900, when he formed a partnership with Dr. J. F. Pattison, of Edgefield County. Dr. Butler has paid special attention to fever, the most prevalent disease in South Carolina. Has written several papers for the South Carolina Medical Association of which he has been a member for a number of years. Dr. Butler practiced his profession in the city of Columbia for three years, where he was appointed city physician.

BUTLER, MATTHEW CALBRAITH.—Son of Dr. William and Jane Perry Butler. His mother was a sister of both the

Commodores Perry of the Navy. Was born March 8, 1836, near Greenville, South Carolina. Attended the academy at Greenville, under the supervision of Dr. McNutt and Mr. Leary, until 1849. In 1851, attended Mr. Galphin's Classical School, in Edgefield, South Carolina. Prepared for college at Edgefield Male Academy, and entered the South Carolina College, in 1854. Left college, in the summer of 1856, to read law; and in December, 1857, was admitted to the bar. Married Miss Maria Calhoun, daughter of War Governor F. W. Pickens, of Edgefield, South Carolina, February 24, 1858. Elected to Legislature from Edgefield County, in 1860. Entered the Confederate service as captain of Edgefield Hussars, in June, 1861. Was promoted to major and assigned to the command of the four companies of cavalry, attached to the Hampton Legion, in July, 1861. Appointed colonel of the Second South Carolina Cavalry, when that regiment was organized, in August, 1862; appointed brigadier-general of cavalry, in June, 1863, and major-general, in September, 1864. Again elected to Legislature from Edgefield, in 1866, and delegate from that county to the several tax-payers' conventions during reconstruction period. was one of the committee appointed to visit Washington, to remonstrate with authorities, during Grant's administration, against the outrages and villainies of Radical reconstruction. Elected to United States Senate, in 1877; remained eighteen years in that body. Resumed practice of law, and supervision of plantation after defeat for the Senate. Appointed major-general of volunteers in the United States army, May, 1898, for the war with Spain. Commanded Fourth Division Second Army Corps, until September, 1898, when ordered to Cuba on the commission with Admiral Sampson and Major-General Wade, to superintend the evacuation of that Island by the Spanish army. Remained in Cuba until July, 1899; and, as a member of the Commission, received the island from the Spanish General, Castellanos. Returned to Washington, arriving there January 10, 1899. Was soon, thereafter, appointed a member of the court-martial that tried Commissary-General Eagan. Applied to be mustered out as soon as the sentence of the court was promulgated. The order was issued, taking effect April 15, 1899, and he is now living as a private citizen of Edgefield, South Carolina.

BUTLER, THOMAS BOTHWELL.—Born January 11, 1866, near Santuc in Union County. Son of Dr. and Mrs. P. P. Butler; and nephew of General M. C. Butler, and the late Governor T. B. Jeter. Was educated in the common schools of Union County, and at the South Carolina College. Soon after graduation, opened up an office at Union, South Carolina, where he practiced law until 1897, when Cherokee County was formed. After leading the fight for its formation, moved to Gaffney; and is now engaged in a large and lucrative law practice under the firm name of Butler & Osborne. Member city council of Union, two terms. He has been prominent in every measure calculated to advance the interests of Gaffney and Cherokee counties since taking up his residence there. He was elected to the House of Representatives from Cherokee County, in 1900, receiving the largest vote ever given a candidate from that county. Married Annie Wood, daughter of A. N. Wood, Gaffney, South Carolina, November 7, 1899.

BYNUM, FRANK LYLES.—Lawyer of Newberry, South Carolina. Son of John Thomas Bynum of Richland County, who married Miss Margaret F. Worthey of Newberry County. Graduate of the Newberry College. He was admitted to the bar in 1892, and immediately formed a copartnership with Honorable George S. Mower, under the style of Mower & Bynum, of which firm he is now a member. Is not married.

CALHOUN, C. F.—President of the Bank of Barnwell. Son of James Y. Calhoun and Jeannette Flowers. Born November 11, 1853, near Appleton, South Carolina. Attended the common schools and the Eastman Business College, Poughkeepsie, New York. Married Minnie H., daughter of W. B. Warren, October 31, 1880. He was a planter until 1887, when he was elected cashier of the Bank of Barnwell, and, in 1897, succeeded General Johnson Hagood as president. President of the Barnwell Business League, and mayor of the town.

CALHOUN, JOHN CALDWELL.—Eldest son of Andrew Pickens Calhoun, and grandson of the distinguished South Carolina statesman, John C. Calhoun, whose wife was Floride, daughter of John Ewing Calhoun, United States Senator for South Carolina in the Seventh Congress. Born near Demopolis, Marango County, Alabama, July 9, 1843. The origin of the family has been distinctly traced back to the reign of Gregory the Great, and connects with the Earl of Lexon in Scotland. On his mother's side his lineage goes back to the reign of William the Third. The first ten years of his life were spent on his father's plantation in Alabama, and the next six years at Fort Mill, South Carolina, with the noted educator, Rev. John L. Kennedy, as instructor in a little pine log school-house, called Thalian Academy. In the fall of 1860, at the age of seventeen, he entered the South Carolina College, as a sophomore; and the following spring he volunteered to Confederate army in a company of cadets which arrived in Charleston at the bombardment of Fort Sumter. After the cadets were disbanded, he joined the Hampton Legion, and was appointed color-sergeant. He was discharged on account of his youth, and, returning home, organized a cavalry company of one hundred and sixty men, and was on his way to the front one month after his discharge. His company was assigned to Adam's Battalion, afterwards merged into the Eighth Regiment, South Carolina Cavalry, under command of Colonel D. H. Rutledge, one of the regiments composing General M. C. Butler's Brigade. Under this command he served until the end of the war, when he returned to Fort Hill. After the war, and the death of his father, he undertook the support of his widowed mother, and the education of his young brothers, Andrew, James and Patrick; and sisters, Margaret and Lucretia. In 1866, he moved to Alabama, and entered into a copartnership with James R. Powell, at Montgomery, for the purpose of colonizing ne-

groes in the Yazoo Valley, Mississippi, to work plantation
lands on the co-operative plan. This proved successful, and
he disposed of his interest to his partner, in less than a
year, for $10,000. This experiment was repeated in Arkan-
sas on a much larger scale, and resulted in the removal of
over five thousand negroes from the Carolinas, Georgia, and
Alabama, to the Mississippi Valley. During fourteen years
he carried on agricultural operations, under the co-operative
tenantry system, very successfully. He organized the Calhoun Land Company and the Florence Planting Company, being president of both. In 1884, he disposed of his plantation
interest at a surplus net profit of over $100,000; and located
in New York City to enter the greater field of finance. He
organized a syndicate to refund the debt of Arkansas, and
soon became prominent in Wall Street. He inaugurated a
combination to acquire control of the Richmond Terminal
Railroad, which afterwards absorbed the Richmond and Danville and East Tennessee Railway system. He also led the
movement to obtain control of the Central Railroad and Banking Company, of Georgia; became a leading director, vice-
president, and chairman of the finance committee; also a director in the Richmond & Danville Railroad, and West Point
Terminal Company, so that, in 1891, he had a dominating influence of nine thousands miles of railway. He was elected a
member of the Manhattan Reform, Loyal, New, and other
clubs in New York City, the Metropolitan Museum of Art,
and the New York Geneological and Biographical Society.
He was one of the originators of the Southern Society of
New York, of which he was president for many years. In
1883, was a delegate from Arkansas to the Louisville Cotton
Exposition; was vice-president of the convention which pe-
titioned Congress for the improvement of the Mississippi
River; was a member of the World's Fair Committee of
one hundred, of New York; and was also one of the originators of the Sons of the American Revolution Society. In
1897, was appointed ambassador to France, by the Sons of the
American Revolution. Was one of the committee of five having charge of the reception to greet Admiral Dewey on his return from Manila. At present is the principal owner of the

Baltimore Coal Mining and Railway Co., controlling the cannel coal fields of New Brunswick. In 1870, was married to Linnie, only daughter of David Adams, of Lexington, Kentucky, a grand niece of Richard M. Johnson, once vice-president of the United States. His eldest son, James Edward Calhoun, was commisioned commissary of subsistence of volunteers by President McKinley, in the Spanish-American War, and was assigned as an aid-de-camp to General M. C. Butler. He hauled down the Spanish flag at Trinidad, Cuba. and hoisted the American in its place.

CALVERT, ARCHIBALD BOLAN.—Son of W. W. and Martha (Leonard). Born in Reidville, South Carolina, May 31, 1857. He attended the Reidville Male Academy until prepared to enter Wofford College, October, 1876. Graduated June, 1880. Read law in the office of Evins and Bomar, Spartanburg, and was admitted 1881. He served two years as a trial justice in the city of Spartanburg. He was elected mayor of the City of Spartanburg in October, 1893, and is now serving his fifth term. Was appointed United States Commissioner in 1884, which office he still holds.

CANNON, ELIHU WILLIAM.—Farmer. Born October 3, 1841, at Darlington, South Carolina. At the time of the breaking out of the war between the States, he was attending the North Carolina Military Institute at Charlotte, North Carolina, but was discharged to join the Confederate army, in 1861, enlisting in the Hartsville Light Infantry, Company G, Ninth South Carolina Volunteers, under Colonel Blanding, as private. While in the Ninth Regiment he was elected second sergeant, and third lieutenant. Later, he reorganized and enlisted in Company E, Sixth South Carolina Regiment, Captain J. L. Coker; and Colonel John Bratton was elected first lieutenant, and was in command of company at the battle of

Frazier's Farm, January 30, 1862, had his leg broken and was captured; half hour later, was recaptured and received a wound through the hip and other foot. He commanded a Red Shirt Club, in 1876; converted it into a cavalry company, in 1877; offered service to Governor Hampton, before he was acknowledged governor, and enrolled as part of volunteer troop of the State. Took the prize, offered by the Darlington and Cheraw Fair Companies, for the best-drilled cavalry company, in 1877. He was elected to the Legislature, in 1878, and again in 1880. Appointed treasurer, in 1882; served three years; and, in 1888, again elected to the Legislature. Married Miss M. Loulie Law, daughter of Colonel T. C. Law, on November 23, 1870.

CANTEY, MORGAN SABB.—Born April 7, 1844, in Clarendon County, South Carolina. He attended the common schools of the neighborhood, and Summerton Academy. He was twice married, first to Lilly F. Ragan, December 18, 1870; second, to Mrs. Belle Richbourg, February 1, 1888. He was chosen presidential elector for 1901. He is also one of the most successful farmers of his county.

CAPERS, ELLISON JR.—Was born in Greenville, South Carolina, May 9, 1869. Son of Bishop Capers. Attended the city graded schools, in Greenville, South Carolina; and, from there, went to the Greenville Military Institute, then in charge of Captain John B. Patrick. While there he was so successful that, upon Captain Patrick's endorsement, he was chosen to assist Professor Cook, of Furman University, who had been employed by the D. Appleton Company to correct and verify the proof of Appleton's Arithmetic, then being gotten ready for the press. After a year's clerking, Mr. Capers entered Furman University, and took a high stand in his class. The following year he procured a school in the northern part of Greenville County, conducted it satisfactorily, and had made his arrangements to teach it another year, when his father received and accepted a call to Trinity Church, Columbia. Acting upon his father's advice, he gave up this school, and entered the University of South Carolina. He taught school in Clarendon County three years, after which he procured a position in the railroad shops in Colum-

bia, where he worked for a considerable time. He then secured a school in Richland County, where he taught with
great satisfaction. It was while thus employed that he became a candidate for county superintendent of education, and
was elected over the former school commissioner, Mr. Sylvester. He was president of the Richland County Teachers
Association. Before his term as county school commissioner
expired, he was elected principal of Winyah Graded School,
at Georgetown, South Carolina, which position he is now
successfully filling. Married Carlotta Manigault Benbow, on
June 9, 1892.

CAPERS, FRANCIS F.—Eldest son of Bishop Capers. Was
born June 5, 1861, in Charleston, South Carolina. Of French
and Irish ancestry. His earlier schooling was had in Greenville. He spent three years at the Charlotte Military Institute, Charlotte, North Carolina, and one year at the University of the South at Sewanee. He was married on the 27th
of January, 1885, to Miss Emmola Keels. For several months
after leaving the University of the South, he was ticket agent
at Greenville, South Carolina, for the Richmond and Danville Railroad. He has been engaged in the banking business
in Greenville, for the past twenty years, first as bookkeeper
for the National Bank, and then as secretary and treasurer
of the Piedmont Savings and Investment Company.

CAPERS, JOHN G.—United States district attorney. Was
born in South Carolina, April 17, 1866.

He is a prominent lawyer, residing at
Charleston; and is at this time (1901)
United States district attorney for
South Carolina. He is a son of the
greatly beloved "Soldier Bishop" of
South Carolina: the Right Rev. Ellison Capers, D.D., an ex-Confederate
brigadier-general. Captain Capers'
mother was Miss Charlotte Palmer, of
St. Johns, Berkeley, and her mother a
Miss Marion, a near relative of General Francis Marion. Captain Capers
has four brothers: Frank F., a prominent business man and
6

banker of Greenville, South Carolina; William T. and Wal-
ter B., Episcopal ministers; and Ellison, Junior, a college
professor, prominently identified with the work of public
school education in South Carolina. The older sister, Mary
Videau Marion, is the widow of Captain Charles B.
Satterlee of the United States Army, who died on duty in Honolulu,
during the Spanish-American War. The other sister, Lottie
Palmer, lives in Charleston, and is the wife of Dr. William
Henry Johnson, of that city. Captain Capers' wife was Miss
Lilla Trenholm of South Carolina, a daughter of the late
Frank Holmes Trenholm, and a grand-daughter of George Tren-
holm, who was secretary of the treasury in President Jeffer-
son Davis' Cabinet, during the Civil War. They have two
daughters, Charlotte Palmer Capers and Frances Trenholm
Capers. Captain Capers was educated at the South Carolina
Military Academy, and has been, a number of years, a promi-
nent citizen, and a captain in the State Militia.

CAPPELMANN, JOHN D.—Son of Eimer Cappelmann, one
of the founders of the German Colonization Society that
founded Walhalla, in 1850. John D. Cappelmann was born at
Walhalla, South Carolina, July 24, 1857. Left Newberry College at the age of fourteen, on account of ill health, being
then in freshman class. After three or four years of work,
took up the study of law, with Colonel William C. Keith and
John S. Verner, at Walhalla, South Carolina. Moved to
Charleston, in October, 1879; admitted to the bar, in 1880; and
is at present a member of the firm of Simons, Seigling &
Cappelmann. Represented Charleston County two terms in
the Legislature, and declined to make the race again. Member of German Artillery, and served several years as lieutenant. Married Miss Julia Pieper, daughter of the late William Henry Pieper, of Walhalla, South Carolina, October,
1882.

CARLISLE, HOWARD BOBO.—Born January 28, 1867, at
Spartanburg, South Carolina. Son of John W. Carlisle.
Family on mother's side, among early settlers of county.
Entered Wofford College in October, 1881, and graduated in

June, 1885, taking medal. Studied law one year with Wofford & Jennings, and then entered law department of Vanderbilt University. Graduated from there in 1887, taking Founder's Medal for best stand in law department. Immediately on becoming of age, was appointed trial justice, and held this position for six months, when he was appointed Master for Spartanburg County, in January, 1889. Held this position for four years. Then entered law firm of Carlisle & Hydrick. Upon the withdrawal of Mr. Hydrick, the firm became Carlisle & Carlisle, county attorneys and attorneys for National Bank. Married, March 16, 1892, Miss George F. Adam.

CARLISLE, JAMES HENRY.—President of Wofford College, Spartanburg, South Carolina. Was born in Winnsboro, Fairfield County, South Carolina, May 4, 1825. Son of Dr. William Carlisle, a native of North Ireland, who came to America in 1818, and settled at Winnsboro, South Carolina. He was a physician, and practiced for thirty years; died in 1866. The subject of this sketch, "as a beardless youth, half advanced," entered the South Carolina College as a sophomore, February 1, 1842, after having attended the common schools of his native town, Winnsboro, Fairfield County, South Carolina. His parents having moved to Camden, he received his training for college in that historic town, his teachers being Professors McCandlass, Hatfield and Major Leland. During his course at the South Carolina College, Dr. Robert Henry was in charge of the language department, and Dr. Lieber in political economy and civil law. These men afterwards became illustrious in educational work. Dr. James H. Thornwell, then a young man, was chaplain, and just entering on a career that was destined to influence the church, the State and the South Carolina College. Lieber, Henry, and Thornwell — all great men — were the teachers of a man who stands higher as an educator than either. Dr. Carlisle grad-

uated, in 1844, as the second-honor man of his class. The
first-honor man was General P. H. Nelson, who was killed
at the battle of the "Crater." Having second-honor, it fell
to his lot to deliver an English oration. His subject was
the poet Shelly, then dead a dozen years. This oration attracted much attention, and justified the predictions of his
friends and comrades that he would make his mark in the
world as a great orator. Dr. Carlisle went from the college
to the schoolroom and, soon after graduating, was made principal of the Odd Fellows' Institute, in Columbia. This position he held for four years. In 1848, he went to the Columbia Male Academy, and five years afterwards, when Wofford College was established at Spartanburg, South Carolina,
he took the chair of mathematics. Since 1854 the history of
Wofford College and this great man have been inseparably
linked. He has been offered many positions of greater emolu-
ments and higher honors, but he has turned his back on them
all, preferring to remain with the college of his church. He
has at different times taught mathematics, astronomy, ethics,
civics, and the English Bible. He is the author of a very fine
text-book on astronomy. The honors that have come to him
have come unsought, as he is always reticent, modest and
unassuming. He is, perhaps, the best posted man in the
State, on the history of South Carolina, her people, and her
great men. He was elected a member of the First General
Conference of the Methodist Church, South, to which laymen
were admitted; and has been elected to each succeeding one.
He was also elected to several ecumenical conferences.
He was a member of the Secession Convention, and a
representative in the last Confederate Legislature, 1863-1864,
which are the only political offices he ever accepted. In
1875, he was made president of Wofford College, which position he still holds.

CARLISLE, JOHN WILSON.—Born in Fairfield County,
South Carolina, May 14, 1827. Graduated at the South Carolina College, in 1849; taught school several years, and while
teaching at Lancaster Court-house, South Carolina, read law
with Minor Clinton. Admitted to the bar, in 1854; moved to

Spartanburg, South Carolina, in 1855, and began the practice of law. February 5, 1856, he married Louisa, daughter of Honorable Simpson Bobo, and entered the firm of Bobo, Edwards & Carlisle. In 1861, assisted in raising company, Forest Rifles, T. Stobo Farrow, captain; David R. Duncan, first lieutenant; John W. Carlisle, second lieutenant. This company was a part of the Thirteenth Regiment, South Carolina Volunteers, Gregg's Brigade, Hill's Division, Jackson's Corps, Army of Northern Virginia. He was first promoted to first lieutenant and then to captain, which position he held at the surrender of Appomattox. His company engaged in some of the hottest battles of the Confederate War. The company was organized with one hundred and twenty-two men, twenty-six of whom were killed, and thirty-five wounded. After the war he resumed the practice of law. Was made a member of the Constitutional Convention of South Carolina, in 1865, and has served two terms in the State Legislature. He is still engaged in practicing law at Spartanburg, South Carolina.

CARLISLE, MARCUS LEE.—Pastor of Washington Street Methodist Church, Columbia, South Carolina. Born in Pendleton, South Carolina, October 13, 1863. Graduated from Wofford College, in 1883. Married Minnie M. Rast, February 17, 1887. Member of South Carolina Conference Methodist Episcopal Church South, stationed at Walhalla, from 1887 to 1890; Camden 1891 to 1894; Chester 1895 to 1896; Spartanburg Central Church from 1897 to 1900. The degree of D. D. was conferred on him by Wofford College, in 1901.

CARLISLE, MILTON A.—President of the National Bank of Newberry, South Carolina. Was born in Union County, South Carolina, September 7, 1841. A son of Thomas A Carlisle, and grandson of Rev. Coleman Carlisle, a pioneer Methodist preacher. Leaving the South Carolina College, where he was educated, he entered the Confederate army, and served in it until the surrender. In 1866, he moved to Mississippi, and entered the practice of law with his brother, James N. Carlisle, at Okolona, under the name of Carlisle & Carlisle. In 1874, he married Mrs. Rosa A. McMorries, a daughter of

Colonel John S. Renwick. Began the practice of law at New-berry, South Carolina, and continued until 1878. For seven years he was trial justice of Newberry County; chairman of Democratic party of same county four years, and, in 1898, was elected president of the National Bank of Newberry. He is also president of Carolina Manufacturing Company.

CARPENTER, ALFRED BAXTER.—He is in the drug busi-ness at Greenville. Was born July 20, 1857, near Piercetown, Anderson County. His ancestors came from Virginia, about 1790. He attended the common schools of Anderson and Oconee counties, and the high school of Williamston, taught by Professor J. M. Pickel. He was the organizer and founder of the firm of Carpenter Bros., at Greenville. He was also instrumental in establishing the first post-office at Pelzer, South Carolina, and was postmaster as long as he did busi-ness there. He married Miss Nannie C. Briggs, daughter of A. S. Briggs, of Greenville, on February 22, 1882.

CARR, JOHN LANE.—Editor of the "Greenwood Journal." Son of Charles F. Carr and Francis Spikes Carr. Was born at Cambridge, South Carolina, February 20, 1843. Limited education on account of having to leave college to enter the army. He joined the Sessions Guards, from Greenwood, South Carolina. Married Mary E. Gardner, on January 31, 1867. He is now engaged in teaching school, farming and editing the above-named paper.

CARRISON, HENRY GEORGE.—President of the Bank of Camden, which he was instrumental in establishing, in 1888. He is a son of George Carrison, of Columbia. Was born in that city, in May, 1851. Of Scotch-Irish descent. Acquired his education from the common schools. When quite young, served a short time as printer in Columbia. Removed to Kershaw County, in 1866, and to Camden, in 1871. Was en-gaged in clerking until 1876, when he became a partner of D. W. Jordan & Company. In 1883, Mr. Carrison became proprietor of the firm, and now does a large mercantile busi-ness. He is a large planter in Kershaw County. Warden of

Camden, in 1884, and mayor from 1892 to 1894; president of the Camden Cotton Mill from 1892 to 1895. Married Miss Margaret E. Jordan, daughter of Colonel Jordan, January 3, 1878.

CARROLL, EDWARD.—Son of B. K. Carroll. Distin guished as an educator and historical writer. Born July 31, 1838. Received his education under the instruction of his father, and at the Charleston College. Has made special study of South Carolina history. He has had charge of the Shaw School in Charleston, since 1881, with the exception of three years. He married Miss Frances J. Lartigue, August 15, 1860.

CARROLL, JOHN ERWIN.—Son of M. S. and Sara Neil Carroll. Was born September 14, 1868, at Brattonsville, South Carolina. Attended the common schools of York County and graduated from the University of Nashville, Nashville, Tennessee, in 1894. Elected county superintendent of education of York County, and re-elected, in 1900.

CARSON, JAMES A.—Pastor of Baptist Church at Saluda, South Carolina. Born in what is now Saluda County, June 7, 1850. Had no collegiate advantages whatever. Attended only the country schools. Maried Miss Josephine L. Deloache, December 24, 1881. He is also teaching in connection with his pastoral work.

CARTLEDGE, SAMUEL JACKSON.—Pastor of the First Presbyterian Church, Anderson, South Carolina. Was born at Bold Spring, Franklin County, Georgia, on May 9, 1864. A graduate of the North Georgia Agricultural College, Dahlonega, Georgia. Studied at Princeton Seminary, and the Columbia Theological Seminary. Married Reta Lamar Paullian, in March, 1900. He supplied churches in Gainesville and Washington, Georgia.

CARY, JAMES P.—Is a lawyer at Pickens, South Carolina. Was born April 27, 1858. Spent his boyhood in the country working on a farm; and attended the county schools of the neighborhood. Entered Adger College at Walhalla, in 1877, and remained in that institution three years. Received several prizes during his college course, for superior scholarship; represented the literary society, to which he belonged, on five successive occasions in public oratorical contests; and graduated with first honor, in the summer of 1880. During the years of 1881 and 1882, Mr. Cary taught school, and edited a newspaper, at Greenwood, studying law at the same time. In December, 1882, he was admitted to the bar. In April, 1883, he located at Pickens, where he has been ever since, giving his entire attention to the practice of law. He is the attorney for the Southern Railroad, the Pickens Railroad, the cotton mills, banks and most of the leading enterprises of his county, besides having a fine general practice.

CARY, JOHN CURTIS.—President of the Lockhart Cotton

Mill. Was born in what is now Oconee County near the site of the old Pickens Court-house, on July 10, 1848. John C. Cary was reared on a farm in Oconee County, and was prepared for college in the Thalian Academy, taught by Rev. J. L. Kennedy, a distinguished educator of that time. He served six months in the Confederate army in the latter part of 1864, holding the rank of second lieutenant of Company I, First Regiment of South Carolina Militia. He was then but sixteen years of age. He served with the same command until the close of the war, then re-entered the Thalian Academy where he remained until August, 1866. During the year 1867, he was a student under Professor W. J. Ligon, of Anderson. In 1869, he accepted a position with a corps of engineers surveying the line of the Blue Ridge Railroad. This occupied his attention until 1872, when he entered the employ of a railroad concern, as bookkeeper and paymaster, which position he held for a year. In the spring of 1873, he was

ı

employed by the Savannah and Memphis, in the engineering
department, but the money panic of that year compelled a
suspension of work.   In 1874, he helped to survey a railroad
from Greenville to Asheville, North Carolina.   In 1876, he
was made the agent for McFadden and Bros., of Philadelphia,
Pennsylvania, and Liverpool, England.   He was the agent of
South Carolina and   northeastern Georgia   for more   than
fifteen years.   In 1893, he sold one of his water powers to
Charleston capitalists, and engaged with them to superintend the erection of a cotton mill thereon, which was completed early in 1894.   In March, 1894, he commenced nego-
tiations with the president and director of Lockhart, a company organized for the purpose of buying this property on
Broad River in Union County, and erecting thereon a cotton
mill.   The mill was completed, in 1895, at a cost of over one
half-million dollars.   In November 1895, he was elected president and treasurer, and has held this position ever since.
In 1899, he organized the Lockhart Railroad Company, and
was elected president and treasurer of the same, and had it
in running operation by June, 1900.

CATHCART, ROBERT SPANN JR.—Physician of Charleston, South Carolina. Son of Colonel W. R. Cathcart and
Mary Elizabeth Kelly. Born at Columbia, South Carolina,
September 25, 1871. Of Scotch-Irish ancestry. Attended private schools of Columbia, and graduated from South Carolina
College, in 1890, with degree of Ph.D. In 1893, obtained his
degree of M.D., from Medical College of South Carolina, at
Charleston. Married Miss Catherine Julia Morrow, of Birmingham, Alabama, January 5, 1898. Served in city hospital
one year after graduation and also as city physician four
years. Was assistant professor of clinical surgery, in Medical College of South Carolina. Member of Medical Society,
and State Medical Association of the Carolinas and Virginia.
Also of American Association and Gynaecological Association.

CATLETT, GIBSON.—Publisher, writer, and illustrator of technical and industrial literature. Born at Catlett, Virginia. Of old Virginia family. Educated in private neighborhood school, and at Staunton, Virginia. When twenty years of age went to New York City and worked as bookkeeper, cashier, manager, etc., with various concerns, improving with each change. Leaving the desk, for his health, he worked as city solicitor for advertising house and later traveled through eastern and middle-western cities. At the age of twenty-five, entered publishing business on his own account, and has brought many books and papers into print, including souvenir volumes for trade associations, hand books and manuals for employers and employees associations, illustrated technical books and pamphlets of industrial plants, and government departments, notably, among the latter, the United States Ordnance Department, and the Government Printing Office, both at Washington. He has prepared many illustrated industrial art editions of newspapers in the most progressive cities and towns of the country. In the "South Atlantic Seaboard," he has published illustrated editions of newspapers describing Guilford County, North Carolina, Spartanburg and Greenville Counties, South Carolina, and the State of South Carolina, the last being considered the most extensive newspaper edition ever issued.

CAUGHMAN, THOMAS H.—Elected sheriff of Lexington County in 1896, and re-elected to same office, in 1900, which position he is still creditably filling. He is a son of Captain P. H. Caughman of Lexington, South Carolina. Was born November 2, 1861, at Lexington, South Carolina. Common school education. He is also a prominent farmer of his section.

CAUTHEN, WILLIAM COLUMBUS.—Was born February 12, 1870, on Hanging Rock Creek, Pleasant Hill Township, Lancaster County, South Carolina. He is a son of Barksdale and Julia Robertson Cauthen. His father died when he was five years of age, leaving four children, of whom the subject of this sketch was the eldest. He worked on the farm until eighteen years of age, going to school about two months out of the year. At the age of twelve he met with an accident which brought on hip joint disease and rheumatism, from which he became a confirmed invalid at eighteen. He improved sufficiently to be able to use a wheel chair, and began looking around for something a man in his condition could do. He ran for the office of county treasurer, in 1898, stumped the county in a wagon, the opposition being that he was physically unable to perform the duties of the office. He succeeded in giving satisfaction, and was re-elected, in 1900, without opposition.

CHAFEE, WILLIAM GREGG.—Lawyer. Is the recently-appointed postmaster at Aiken, South Carolina. Was born January 29, 1866, at Kalmia, near Aiken, South Carolina, then in the county of Edgefield. Graduated from the South Carolina College in 1886. Was mayor of the city of Aiken, 1892 and 1895. Was the founder and first owner of "Greenwood Index." Captain of Tenth Regiment, United States Volunteer Infantry, in the Spanish War. He was Senator Butler's secretary, from 1886 to 1887. Not married.

CHAPMAN, JAMES A.—President of the Inman Cotton Mill. Was born at Spartanburg, South Carolina, February 7, 1863. Son of Robert Hett and Belle Fort Chapman. Entered Wofford College, October, 1879; graduated in June, 1883. Graduated in law at Harvard University, in 1886, with the degree of LL.B. After graduation he entered the law office of Cary & Whitridge, New York City, and in October of the following year was admitted to the bar in that city. He practiced law in New York until September 1890, when he moved to Middlesborough, Kentucky, and formed the firm of Chapman & Nicoll, and, in March 1893, the firm of Chapman & Sampson. These firms enjoyed a large and lucrative practice, representing the English interests that were developing the town of Middlesborough and the adjacent territory. In April, 1899, he returned to Spartanburg and continued the practice of law until November, 1900, when he organized and built the Inman Cotton Mill at Inman, South Carolina, and was elected president and treasurer. Mr. Chapman married Rachel B. McMaster, of Winnsboro, South Carolina, on the 22d of October, 1887.

CHAPMAN, SAMUEL D.—Treasurer of Pickens County. Was born in that county in 1861. His education was acquired principally in the country schools. Began merchandising at Easley, in 1883, and continued until 1898. Then moved to Greenville, South Carolina, where he was engaged in the same business. Afterward went to Pickens, and continued the mercantile business until elected to the position he now holds.

CHAPPELL, JOHN HENRY.—Appointed magistrate of Newberry County, in 1900. A son of Thomas Henry and Ann Chappell. Born near Chappell's Depot, Newberry County, on the 19th of May, 1855. Attended the common schools of his county, and three years at the Newberry College. Married Mary Price, February 4, 1884. He was chief of police and special detective of Newberry, South Carolina, before being elected magistrate, which position he now so ably fills.

CHASE, JEROME P. HON.—Former mayor of Florence, South Carolina. He was born at New Market, Tennessee, on the 28th of July, 1838, being the second of thirteen children. His parents removed to Laurens County when he was only three years of age. Eight years later, the family took up their residence in Washington, District of Columbia, and it was in that city that he received the greater portion of his scholastic training. At the age of twenty-one, engaged as telegraph operator in South Carolina. Continued in this occupation until the outbreak of the war, when he offered his services to the Confederacy as "free fighter," his delicate health not permitting him to join the regular army. For eighteen months he bore his share of the conflicts with bravery and faithfulness. At the end of that time, he became a military telegraph operator, and later, was placed in charge of a large forage district in the quartermaster's department, in which he continued for a year and a half. After the war, Mr. Chase went into mercantile business, at Florence, South Carolina, but after two years he turned his attention to real estate, and subsequently added insurance. In 1878, he was sent to the Legislature; and, in 1880, declined re-election. One year later was chosen to fill a vacancy in that body, and while a member, introduced and secured the passage of a bill preventing freight trains from running on Sunday. He is president or a director in most of the stock comapnies of Florence. In 1866, married Miss Hettie McLeod, daughter of Napoleon McLeod, of Clarendon County, South Carolina.

CHASE, JOHN ALEXANDER.—Son of John P. and Maria B. (Brunson) Chase. Born in Darlington District, now Florence County, February 22, 1868. Of English and French-Huguenot descent. Attended the common schools and schools in Nashville, Tennessee. Married Miss McMakin, of Raleigh, North Carolina, November 8, 1900. He is engaged in the mercantile business at Florence, South Carolina. Member of board of water commissioners of Florence.

CHESWELL, WILLIAM EARNEST.—President of the Cheswell Cotton Mills of Westminster, South Carolina. Was born at Newmarket, Rockingham County, New Hampshire, on November 11, 1858. He is a graduate of the Newmarket High Schools. His manufacturing training was received in the New England States. He came to White Hall, Georgia, from Canada, in December, 1888, accepting the position of superintendent of the Georgia Manufacturing Company. In the following year he was elected mayor of White Hall, Georgia. January 1, 1894, he was appointed superintendent and manager of the Courtenay Manufacturing Company of Newry, South Carolina. He planned, built, and equipped the Cheswell Mill personally; and was elected president and treasurer, at its organization. Now fills the position of president, treasurer, and general manager of the same. He was director and cashier of the Oconee Savings Bank, and was for four years a magistrate of Oconee County.

CHILDS, WILLIAM GILLON.—President of the Bank of Columbia, South Carolina. Son of Lysander D. Childs and Mary Hoke Childs. Born in Lincolnton, North Carolina. Graduate of the Virginia Military Institute. Married Alice Gibbes Childs September 2, 1872. Was president of a railroad. Lieutenant for years in Governor's Guards, and adjutant of Palmetto Regiment.

CLARK, ADOLPHUS JONES.—Editor of the "Lancaster Enterprise." Was born in Chatham County, North Carolina, July 15, 1852. Attended the common schools, Beaumont Academy, Mount Vernon Academy, and Bank Spring Academy of Chatham County, and two years at Furman University. Taught school several years in Chester. In 1881, accepted the principalship of Franklin Academy at Lancaster, South Carolina. Taught five years, then went into the Life and Fire Insurance business. In 1891, helped establish the "Lancaster Enterprise," and from that time to this has been editor of same. He is now conducting the insurance business in connection with the paper, and is manager of the job printing department of the Enterprise Publishing Company. Married Cynthia A. McNeill, January 19, 1879.

CLARK, EDWARD BAILEY.—Superintendent of the Columbia Phosphate Company until 1899. Resigned this position to accept the one he now holds as general manager and treasurer of the Columbia Electric Street Railway and Power Company. He is a son of Washington A. and Virginia M. Clark. Born December 31, 1871, at Columbia, South Carolina. Studied two years at the South Carolina College, and entered Lehigh University in class of 1895, studying mechanical engineering. He is unmarried.

CLARKSON, GERARDUS FLOYD.—Pastor of the Methodist churches of Seneca and Walhalla. Was born September 6,

1868, at Manning, South Carolina. Took Bachelor of Arts degree at Wofford College, in 1891, and pursued studies for one year, in Biblical department of Vanderbilt University, 1895 to 1896. Married Miss Annie E. Kennedy, of Williamsburg County, South Carolina, November 19, 1896. Taught school for one year at Sally, Aiken County, South Carolina. Joined the South Carolina Conference Methodist Episcopal Church South, in December, 1892; and has supplied various charges since that time.

CLAYTON, WILLIAM FORCE.—Member of the Florence bar. Born at Athens, Georgia, August 17, 1843. Moved to Washington City when he was six years old, but left Washington, in 1861. His education was obtained from the common schools. He had an appointment to the United States Naval Academy when war broke out, gave it up, came South, and received his diploma on the battle field. Married Miss Lizzie Brown, December 22, 1869. Entered the Confederate States service, as midshipman, in 1861; served until May 4, 1865. Was promoted to passed-midshipman, and participated in several fights. After the war closed, he took up farming and school teaching, and commenced the practice of law at the age of forty-nine. Was a member of the Constitutional Convention, of 1895. A member of the State board of education for four years. Resigned that office, in 1900; and is at present devoting his whole time to the practice of law.

CLEVELAND, JESSE F.—Born February 7, 1847, in the town of Spartanburg, South Carolina. Attended Wofford College until 1864, when he entered the army. After the war, read medicine with his father, Dr. R. E. Cleveland, and entered the South Carolina Medical College, graduating at the Jefferson Medical College in Philadelphia, in 1869. Practiced in Spartanburg and surrounding country for eighteen years, when he retired to attend to his private business. Is director of the National Bank of Spartanburg, of the Arkwright and Glendale cotton-mills, of the Produco Oil Mill, the Limestone Lime Company, and president of the Tucapau Cotton Mill. Is largely interested in agriculture and manufacturing. Married Miss Caro V. Zimmerman, of Glenn Springs, in June, 1873.

CLEVELAND, JOHN BOMAR.—A prominent and influential business man of Spartanburg. Is a native of that city. Was born November 9, 1848. He is a graduate of Wofford College. After finishing school he studied law in the office of Evins & Bomar, a leading firm of Spartanburg. In 1871, he was admitted to the bar, forming a partnership for the practice of law with Major D. R. Duncan, and for ten years, this firm did a very successful business. In 1880, Mr. Cleveland dissolved his connection with this firm, and turned his attention to other business. For the past ten years, he has done a private banking and brokerage business, in which he has met with great success. He was a delegate to the National Convention in Chicago, in 1884, and nominated Grover Cleveland for president. Director in the National Bank of Spartanburg, Fidelity Loan & Trust Co., Arkwright, Whitney, Tucapau, Saxon, Enoree and Spartan Mill cotton factories. Vice-president of the National Bank of Spartanburg. President of the Lime Stone Springs Lime Company, Home Water Supply Company, Whitney Manufacturing Company, and the Charleston and Western Carolina Railroad. A trustee of Wofford College, and, also, of Converse College. For several years one of the trustees of the city schools, and a prime mover in establishing the graded school system in his native city. He was married, in 1871, to Miss Georgia A. Cleveland. His reputation among business men is very high, and, socially, he enjoys the highest esteem and respect of his fellow citizens.

CLIFTON, JESSE ALEXANDER.—Pastor of the Methodist Church of Sumter. Son of Jesse C. Clifton and Mary Walker. Born in Chester, South Carolina. Of Scotch-Irish descent.

His father served in the Confederate army. Educated in the Ebenezer High School of York County, under Professor Mathew Elder, and at the University of Virginia. Married Mary, daughter of Dr. W. J. Hicklin. Joined the Confederate army in Company D, First South Carolina Volunteers, Hampton's Brigade, Army of Northern Virginia. Served as courier and scout. For thirty-two years he has been a minister of the gospel. Delegate, twice, to the general conference of the Church. Degree of Doctor of Divinity was conferred by Rutherford College, North Carolina, in 1893.

COGBURN, WILLIAM BENJAMIN.—Elected clerk of the court for Edgefield County, in 1900, for the term of four years, his predecessor having held the office two terms. Son of Simon and Sarah Cogburn. Born at Meeting Street, Edgefield County, South Carolina, September 1, 1856. His education was limited, only that afforded by the country schools. Remained on the farm until fifteen years of age, then went to work for May & Stevens at Meeting Street, as clerk in store. Afterwards filled position as bookkeeper. Married Miss Lizzie L. Lott, on November 27, 1879.

COGGENSHALL, JAMES ROLAND.—Member of the Legislature from Darlington County. He is a son of Peter C. and Nancy (Wild) Coggeshall. Born near Florence, South Carolina, January 6, 1866. Of Welsh and English ancestry. Graduated at the South Carolina College, in class of 1890. Married Miss Carrie Duncan, of Union, South Carolina, in April, 1899. Taught school at Society Hill, and was admitted to the bar, in 1892. Practiced law two years at Florence, and remaining time at Darlington.

COGSWELL, JULIUS ELISHA.—Captain of Washington Light Infantry of Charleston, South Carolina. He is a son of Harvey and Mary (Keller) Cogswell. Born in Columbia, South Carolina, May 13, 1865. Ancestors descended from the Pilgrim Fathers of New England, The Palatine Germans of Orangeburg, South Carolina, and the French Huguenots, of Charleston. Graduated from South Carolina College in 1886, and from Georgetown Law School, Washington, District of

7

Columbia in 1888. Not married. City hospital commissioner, in 1893. Elected, by Legislature, registrar of Mesne Conveyance, in 1893, re-elected, in 1898. He is now practicing law, and is registrar of Mesne Conveyance. His father was Confederate Government printer and furnished the Government bonds and money. His works were carried to Columbia, for safety, and hence his residence there.

COHEN, ASHE D.—Son of Dan. D. Cohen. Born in Charleston, South Carolina, May 28, 1838. Obtained education from public schools of Charleston, South Carolina. Married Miss Miriam Hart, on November 8, 1865. Was in Confederate war as lieutenant in Palmetto Rifles; afterwards, as private in Company D, South Carolina Cavalry till war closed, under the command of General A. P. Butler. After the war, resumed the practice of law in Charleston.

COHEN, WILLIAM CALEB.—Banker and manufacturer of Darlington, South Carolina. Born near Society Hill, South Carolina, June 8, 1839. Was educated in the Society Hill Academy and the South Carolina College, graduating from the latter in December, 1859. In 1861, entered the Confederate service as sergeant Company F, Eighth South Carolina Volunteers. Subsequently, assisted in the organization of Company M, Eighth South Carolina Volunteers, as first lieutenant, and afterwards became captain of the company. He was wounded and disabled, at Gettysburg, and on the retreat made prisoner at Williamsport, Maryland, and so remained, until February, 1865. Studied law and was admitted to the bar, in 1867. Abandoned practice, and life has been devoted to farming and merchandising at Society Hill, South Carolina. In 1884, assisted in organizing the Darlington Manufacturing Company, being elected president and treasurer until 1900. Since 1885, he has been a resident of Darlington, South Carolina, and in 1887 was elected State Senator from that county, and re-elected, in 1878 and 1882. At present he is vice-president of the Bank of Darlington. He was twice married, first to Mary E. McIver, January 25, 1869, and, second, to L. V. McIver, February 24, 1885.

COKER, JAMES LIDE.—Born at Society Hill, South Carolina, January 3, 1837. He was educated at St. David's Academy, the South Carolina Military Academy, and at Harvard University, where he studied chemistry and botany. March 28, 1860, was married to Miss Susan Stout, of Alabama. In the fall of 1860, organized the Hartsville Light Infantry; as captain, he commanded that company in several battles. He was in command of his company at Fredericksburg, Blackwater, and Suffolk, and was specially mentioned in orders, by General Jenkins, for conduct in these campaigns. He was wounded very severely at Lookout Valley, Tennessee. He was borne from the battlefield to a private house where he had to remain for six months. In the meantime the enemy occupied the country and he fell into their hands, but was afterwards paroled and sent through the lines as disabled and unfit for active service. Early in 1864, he was promoted to major of the Sixth South Carolina Volunteer Infantry. He succeeded in business in Hartsville; and also in Charleston, where he belonged to the firm of Norwood & Coker, cotton factors, from 1874 to 1881. In 1882, he was made president of the Darlington National Bank which was very successful under his administration. He was the first president of the Darlington Manufacturing Company. Built a short railroad to Darlington. He, with his eldest son, established the Carolina Fiber Company, at Hartsville, South Carolina, and it is successfully manufacturing pulp and paper from native woods. He is also president of the Southern Novelty Company. Has organized the Welch Neck High School, and contributes largely to its support.

COLCOCK, FRANCIS HORTON.—Lawyer. Son of Charles J. Colcock and Lucy Frances Horton. Born at Huntsville, Alabama, June 19, 1855. Of English, Scotch-Irish, and Welsh descent. Education obtained under private tutors. Graduated from Union College, Schenectady, New York, with degree of Civil Engineer, in 1877. Married Mary Robert Jones, August 4, 1880, daughter of Colonel Seaborn Jones, of George's Station. Read law in office of General James Connor, of Charleston, and admitted to the bar, in 1879. Practiced several years in Beauford, Hampton, and Barnwell. Served in the United States Engineer Office, in Savannah and elsewhere. Taught at Porter Military Academy of Charleston, from 1886 to 1894; and is now teaching at South Carolina College.

COLEMAN, WILLIAM.—Engaged in a banking business at Whitmire, South Carolina. Was born April 15, 1875, near Flint Hill, Goshen Hill Township, Union County, South Carolina. Attended Wofford College in the fall of 1891, and Harvard University in the summer of 1895 and 1897. Studied a few months at the University of North Carolina, to prepare for the bar examination, and was admitted to the bar, in February of 1898. Married Miss Evelyn K. Coleman, June 6, 1900. Was engaged in the practice of law, for a short time, in Charlotte, North Carolina. Since then, he has been looking after farming interests, and investments of different kinds. He is president and treasurer of Glenn-Lowry Manufacturing Company; also of Whitmire Oil and Fertilizer Company.

CONNORS, CHARLES THORN.—Editor of the "Lancaster Review." Was born in Lancaster County, South Carolina, January 7, 1855. Son of the late W. M. Connors who was a member of the Lancaster bar. He attended the public schools of Lancaster, Kings Mountain Military School of Yorkville, and the University of the South, Sewanee, Tennessee. Was admitted to the bar, in February, 1876, formed a partnership with General Joseph B. Kershaw, and was associated with him until his elevation to the bench. Was a member of the Legislature, from 1886 to 1890. For a number of years was a member of the county board of examiners. He is secretary and treasurer of the board of trustees of the Lancaster Graded Schools. Was for several years an officer in the State militia with the rank of major.

Married Miss Nell R. Tompkins, of Binghamton, New York, February 28, 1876.

COOK, HARRY TOLIVER.—Professor of Greek, in Furman University. Was born at Millway, Abbeville District, South Carolina. Attended private schools and Furman University. He taught in the Patrick Military School for nine years. Alderman of the city of Greenville two terms. County superintendent of education through Tillman, Evans and Ellerbe terms.

COOK, JOHN AMOS.—Son of Eliza M. and Nathaniel Cook. Born in Chesterfield County, South Carolina, April 27, 1866, near Lynches River. Parents moved to Lancaster County when he was about one year old. His education was limited to a few months at the public schools. Married Miss Miranda C. Hitton, on January 26, 1888. After marrying, bought a small farm and continued to farm, until taking charge of the auditor's office, to which position he was elected, in 1896. Re-elected in primary of 1898, without opposition, and re-elected, for the third term, in primary of 1900, on the first ballot, over two prominent competitors, with a majority of 534 votes.

COOPER, ERNEST.—Principal of the Presbyterian High School of Columbia, South Carolina. Born January 29, 1877, near Charlotte, Mecklenburg County, North Carolina. Eldest son of Charles C. and Theodocia C. Kendrick. Of Scotch-Irish descent. Attended the Charlotte Graded Schools; one term at Clemson College; and graduated at the South Carolina College, taking a special course in languages. Clerked in Charlotte. While taking course in languages, served as assistant in the Presbyterian High School of Columbia, South Carolina. Served as editor of the "Carolinian," the college journal, and represented the society in the interstate debate.

COOPER, ROBERT ARCHER.—Lawyer. A member of the Legislature from Laurens County. A native of that county. Born at Waterloo, June 12, 1874. Had the advantage of the country schools, and one year at the Jones High School. Taught school four years. Married Miss Eugenia Machen, on March 22, 1899. Was appointed magistrate, to fill out unexpired term of J. W. Peterson, on November 13, 1899. Is now serving his first term as a member of the Legislature. Admitted to the bar, in 1898. Practiced one year with Colonel J. L. M. Irby; and after the latter's death, he formed a partnership with Colonel H. Y. Simpson, of Laurens. He is attorney for the Charleston and Western Carolina Railroad.

COOPER, WILLIAM (STAGGERS).—Was born August 23, 1852, in Williamsburg County, South Carolina. He being the only grandchild, his grandfather offered to adopt him. His parents consented and his name was changed by the Legislature to William Cooper. He attended school near his home, under Rev. James B. Gilland and Rev. Hugh Strong, near Maysville, South Carolina. Then attended King's Mountain Military School, Yorkville, under Colonel Coward. He then went to the University of Virginia, but on account of death of grandfather was compelled to return home. After this he read law in the office of James F. G. Richardson, of Sumter, South Carolina; but finally gave it up and engaged in farming and merchandising. His grandfather, Colonel William Cooper, fought in the War of 1812, and represented his county in the Senate. Married Miss Esther A. Daniel, February 28, 1878. He was postmaster for eighteen years, and census enumerator in last census. Was captain of the Williamsburg Light Dragoons, in 1876 and 1878. Member of Legislature two sessions, and is now filling the office of county superintendent of education of Williamsbury County.

CORNELSON, GEORGE H.—Proprietor of the Orangeburg Cotton Mill. Born in Ottersberg, near Brennee, Germany, December 7, 1842. Acquired education from the High Schools of Germany. Married A. M. Holman, January 21, 1869. Mayor of Orangeburg, from 1868 to 1870. Built the city waterworks in 1889. General merchant, from 1868 to 1900, in Orangeburg.

CORNWELL, JOHN ELIE.—Son of John Bennet and Alice Stone Cornwell. Born October 30, 1861, at Chester, South Carolina. His great-grandfather came from Cornwellshire, England, and great-grandmother from Wales. His father represented Chester County, in the Legislature, one year. Graduated from Greenville Military Institute, and took a course in Bryant and Stratton Business College, Baltimore, in 1882. Has since taken a course in veterinary medicine, and is practicing same. On October 27, 1886, he married Miss Corrie Virginia Calvin. He was employed as book-keeper two years, and as teller in Bessemer City Savings Bank eight months, Bessemer, Alabama. Has been sheriff of Chester County four years.

COSGROVE, JAMES.—A member of the House of Representatives, of Charleston County. His present term will expire in 1902. Was born, August 26, 1861, in Charleston, South Carolina. Married Miss Mathilda, daughter of W. C. Forsythe, of Charleston, South Carolina. He is chairman of the committee on banking and insurance, and member of the ways and means committee, privileges and elections, and military committees. He paid special attention to the drainage of the low lands of the State, and is one of the largest real estate and insurance dealers of Charleston.

COTHRAN, THOMAS PERRIN.—Lawyer of Greenville, South Carolina. A son of James S. and Emma C. Cothran of Abbeville, South Carolina. Was born in Abbeville, South Carolina, on October 24, 1857. His earlier schooling was received from the high schools of Abbeville, and he graduated from the University of Virginia, in 1878. He is assistant division counsel of the Southern Railway. He married Ione, daughter of W. Joel Smith, of Abbeville, on January 6, 1886.

COTHRAN, WILLIAM COULTER.—Member of the Greenville bar. Was born, August 28, 1872, at Abbeville, South Carolina. He attended the high school at Abbeville, and entered the South Carolina University, in 1890. Began work in railroad service as general agent of Blue Ridge Railroad, resigned and studied law. Admitted to the bar, May 20, 1897. He is a member of the law firm of Cothran & Cothran.

COVINGTON, FURMAN P.—Son of F. and Eranda (Chappel) Covington. Born, May 31, 1859, in Richmond County, North Carolina. Obtained education from the common schools and Wake Forest College, North Carolina. Graduated from the Charleston Medical College, in 1885. Married Fannie H. Townsend, February 22, 1882. President of the board of health of Florence. Member of the State Medical Association. Member of the board of trustees of the Southern Baptist Theological Seminary.

COX, WILLIAM BROWN.—Graduated in medicine, March, 1890, and has practiced that profesion continually, since in Landsford, Chester County, and in the city of Chester, South Carolina. Born, November 26, 1867, at Landsford, Chester County, South Carolina. Son of Dr. D. M. Cox, who practiced medicine for nearly forty years in the eastern section of Chester County. His earlier training was obtained from the public schools of Lancaster, South Carolina. Later attended Kings Mountain Military School, Wofford College, University of Kentucky, and the Southern Medical College, Atlanta, Georgia; also, New York Polyclinic, New York City. Married Miss Willie M. Cross, October 8, 1890. Member of South Carolina Medical Association. Several times member of State democratic conventions, and now one of the commissioners of the South Carolina Interstate and West Indian Exposition, Charleston, South Carolina.

COX, WILLIAM FRANKLIN.—Son of George W. and Martha M. Cox, of Belton, Anderson County, South Carolina. Was born October 12, 1855. Attended the Patrick schools in Greenville, and one year at Furman University. Taught school at Belton, eight years; and at same time, held the position of trial justice. In 1886, he was elected probate judge and held the position eight years. In 1895, organized the Excelsior Oil and Fertilizer Company, and is now manager and president of same. In 1899, he organized the Cox

Manufacturing Company, of Anderson, of which he is president and treasurer. Trustee of Baptist Theological Seminary at Louisville, Furman University, and the graded schools of Anderson. Director of Merchants and Farmers Bank, and secretary of the board. Has been alderman of the town of Anderson for two years. Married Miss Anna, daughter of Dr. W. J. Dargan, of Greenville, South Carolina. June 21, 1892.

CRAIG, CLARENCE LEANDER.—County superintendent of education of Oconee County. Was born at Stewarts, Pickens County, South Carolina, April 4, 1872. Attended Furman University. Married Miss Ada Brown, April 19, 1898. Was ordained to the Baptist ministry, in 1893, and has since supplied several churches.

CRAIG, NILES ALEXANDER.—He was engaged in mercantile business at Ora, South Carolina, until 1899, when he built the Roller Flour Mills at Greenwood, South Carolina, of which he is president. He was born in Laurens County, near Enoree River, June 21, 1871. In early boyhood, attended the old field schools, and the Laurens Male Academy, completing his literary course at the Presbyterian College, Clinton, South Carolina. Mr. Craig was happily married to Miss Mollie E. Hunter, daughter of Dr. J. P. Hunter, January 24, 1900. He is also secretary and treasurer of the Greenwood Hardware Company.

CRAIG, THOMAS BROOKS.—Pastor of Fountain Inn and other churches of the neighborhood. Was born, June 26, 1856, in Laurens County, South Carolina. His primary schooling was received from the Reidville Academy. Later he attended Davidson College, North Carolina, then entered Columbia Theological Seminary, and remained two years, also spent one year in Union Seminary, New York; and one summer at Chautauqua, New York. He married Miss Maggie E. Anderson, of Fairview, South Carolina, in October, 1882. Was the winner of the oration medal in college. He has supplied churches in various portions of the State, at

Liberty Springs, Port Royal, Ninety-Six, Hopewell, Fountain Inn, New Harmony, and Dorroh.

CRANE, ARTHUR ERNEST.—Pastor of the Baptist Church at Camden, South Carolina. Was born in London, England, December 10, 1875. Educated at Thornton Academy, Saco, Maine, and graduated from the Theological Seminary, Chester, Pennsylvania, in June, 1900. Married Miss Sara Rebecca Qudale, of Camden, South Carolina, February 20, 1901.

CRAWFORD, EDWARD ALEXANDER.—Sheriff of York County eight years. Son of James D. and Mary D. Crawford, (nee Gill). Born in Chester County, near Fishing Creek, July 3, 1830. Only a common-school education. Was twice married, first to Miss Henrietta E. Lindsay, in 1858. His second wife was Miss Mary E. Scoggins, whom he married February 27, 1866. Entered the Civil War, in 1861; joined Company K, Seventeenth South Carolina Volunteers. Was made captain of the company and remained so until the surrender at Appomattox. Elected a county commissioner, in 1898. He is also a prosperous farmer.

CRAWFORD, SAMUEL LEVI.—Son of Peter C. and L. A. M. Crawford. Born June 9, 1865, ten miles from Bonneau, Berkeley County, South Carolina. Of Scotch and French ancestry. Good practical education obtained from the common schools. He is a merchant, notary public, postmaster and is interested in the real estate business. Married September 22, 1886.

CREECH, FRANK HENRY.—Now serving his second term as sheriff of Barnwell County. Born near Allendale, Barnwell County, South Carolina. Son of Richard M. Creech and Maria J. Bailey. Good common school advantages. Entered the Confederate service at the age of fifteen, served until the battle of Fort Harrison, when he lost the use of his right arm, also wounded at Lookout Mountain, in 1863. Married twice. First wife was Susie E. Cuter, second wife Miss C. L. Oeland of Spartanburg. Captain of the Gary Rifles, in 1876. Knight of Honor, and Good Templar. President of the Interdenominational Sunday-school Convention of Barnwell County. County commissioner, in 1875. Elected colonel of the Barnwell County Regiment, by the United Confederate Veterans.

CREWS, THOMAS B.—Editor and proprietor of the "Laurensville Herald." He was born in Rutherfordton, North Carolina, January 7, 1832. Educated principally in the common schools, and in a printing office. He married Miss Eugenia E. Hance, October 21, 1856; and Miss Celia Balew on November 10, 1870. He was a member of the Legislature, and also of the Senate. He was appointed postmaster at Laurens under Cleveland's administration. He was president of the South Carolina State Press Association, seven years. Served in the war between the States as first lieutenant, commanding Company A, First South Carolina Cav_ alry, Hampton's Brigade, Army of Northern Virginia.

CRITTENDON, STANLEY S.—Son of Dr. John Crittendon of Hartford County, Connecticut, and Sarah M. Stanley, of North Carolina. Was born in Greenville, February 22, 1829. Was educated at the old academies in Greenville, with three years at school in New Jersey. In 1855, he married Miss Eliza J., daughter of Colonel Henry Lynch. Went to the war, in 1861, as first lieutenant Company G, Fourth South Carolina Volunteers. Was appointed adjutant on the field of First Manassas, in place of General Sam Wilkes, who was slain in that battle. At the reorganization at Yorktown, he was elected first lieutenant of his company, and again appointed adjutant of the battalion. Was wounded at Seven Pines, and while on furlough appointed, by Governor Pickens, lieutenant-colonel of the Third Regiment South Carolina Reserves, then forming for services on the coast. At the expiration of his time with that regiment, joined the Cavalry, command of General M. W. Gary, and served on his staff until the close of the war. Was elected three terms, to the House of Representatives, and one term to the State Senate, serving continuously, from 1870 to 1880. In 1871, he was married to Mrs. Sarah A. Bedell, of Columbia, South Carolina. Was appointed postmaster, at Greenville, by President Cleveland, serving five years. He assisted General Ellison Capers in organizing the Confederate Veterans of the State, and succeeded him to the command of the Division of South Carolina, which position he resigned, in 1895. He is now farming, and doing occasional literary work.

CROMER, GEORGE BENEDICT.—Born in Newberry County, October 3, 1857. His early education was obtained in the common schools, and preparatory department of the Newberry College, graduating from the latter with first honor, in June, 1877; took the honorary degree of A.M., from the same college in 1879. He was twice married, first to Miss Caro J. Motte, October 11, 1883; and on November 27, 1890, to Miss Harriet S. Bittle. He was, from 1877 to 1879, a teacher in the preparatory department of Newberry College, then elected professor of Latin, history and political science, in the same college. Mr. Cromer was admitted to the bar, in 1881, and was mayor of Newberry, from 1886 to 1890. He was elected president of the Newberry College, in November, 1895; assumed the duties of the office, January 1896, and still holds this position.

CROSSON, D. M.—Was born at Prosperity, Newberry County, South Carolina, September 29, 1858. His father was of Scotch-Irish descent, and his mother German or Dutch. His father, John F. P. Crosson, graduated, before the war, at Erskine College, and was regarded as a classical scholar, and made quite a reputation as a writer and teacher; but in his latter years devoted his entire attention to his large farming interest. Dr. Crosson was reared upon the farm, and is of an agricultural turn of mind and is a scientific man. His early education was obtained from the common schools of the community, and from the Prosperity High School. He afterwards attended Erskine College three years, where he made a very good stand, and being a member of the Euphemean Literary Society, made quite a reputation for himself as a debater. After leaving college, he began the study of medicine, and after reading for over a year, attended lectures in the South Carolina Medical College, Charleston. Afterwards graduated from the University of Tennessee, Nashville, with first honor, over a large class, and delivered the valedictory. After completing his medical course, he located at Lewiedale, South Carolina, where he remained ten years. Then moved to Leesville, South Carolina, where he is regarded the leading physician and surgeon of his county. Dr. Crosson was married to Miss Sara C. Bodie, September 27, 1883. He is regarded as a fine financier, and is the largest and most successful farmer in Lexington County, and one of the largest in the State. Served eight years in succession on the county Democratic executive committee, for the most time being chairman, and declined to serve longer. He has frequently been called upon to represent his county and district in various agricultural and political meetings. In 1899, by a large majority, was elected to the State Senate. While in that body, by his financiering and executive ability, he succeeded in enacting such bills, as to get his county clear of debt, a reputation it had not enjoyed since the war. He was nominated, and urged to make the race to fill the unexpired term of the late Congressman Stokes; but, owing to his professional duties, declined. He takes great interest in educational matters, and is trustee and physician of Leesville College.

CROUCH, BEN W.—Son of Noah and Sallie E. Crouch. Born August 11, 1868, in Saluda, formerly Edgefield County, South Carolina. Attended the old field schools, and completed junior class at Wofford College. Married Miss Daisy Norton, daughter of Dr. E. Norton, of Conway, South Carolina, in November, 1898. Taught school three years after leaving college. The summer, of 1895, was devoted to the formation of Saluda County. Elected first clerk of court of new county of Saluda, and admitted to the bar, in 1900. Was clerk of suffrage committee, during Constitutional convention of 1895. He is now engaged in the practice of his profession, at Saluda, South Carolina.

CRYMES, FURMAN JARVIS.—Dentist for the Connie Maxwell Orphanage, at Greenwood, South Carolina. Born at Williamston, Anderson County, South Carolina, March 17, 1869. Prepared for college at the Williamston Male Academy, and entered Furman University. At the age of sixteen he commenced the study of dentistry under his father. Graduated from the Pennsylvania College of Dental Surgery, and is now practicing his profession at Greenwood, South Carolina. He is first vice-president of the South Carolina State Dental Association.

CULP, JOHN RIPLEY.—Son of John and Sarah Jordan Culp. Born, October 19, 1829, near Landsford, Chester County, South Carolina. He attended the old field schools, until fourteen years of age. He was lieutenant, major and colonel of the Twenty-seventh Regiment South Carolina Infantry, before the Civil War, for a term of eight years. Entered the service as captain of Company A, Seventeenth South Carolina Volunteers, and was promoted to the offices of major and lieutenant-colonel respectively. Was in nearly all the battles of any consequence, in which his regiment was engaged. Was wounded at Second Manassas. Was captured April 1, 1865, and imprisoned on Johnson's Island, remained until the 26th of July, when he was released. Married Frances N. Ragsdale, on April 30, 1856. Postmaster at Rossville for twelve years, and now serving third term as county supervisor.

CULP, THOMAS GIBBONS.—Born in the Panhandle Section of Lancaster County, June 9, 1832. Ancestors were German and English. Thrice married, his present wife being Miss Augusta Cunningham, whom he married January 19, 1881. Only a common English education. Magistrate eight years; elected county commissioner, in 1882; served four years. In 1896, elected county supervisor, and served two terms. Chairman board of trustees of Fort Mill High School.

In partnership with his brother, he established a wagon factory and successfully conducted same, until 1858, when the plant was destroyed by fire. After this misfortune, Mr. Culp engaged in railroading. Pursued that occupation for about ten years, when he again settled down to private business in Fort Mill, dealing in machinery, sawing lumber, etc. In 1881, he was elected trial justice, and held the office eight years. During the Civil War, he was detailed to do mechanical work on the railroads of the South, and remained until 1868.

CUNNINGHAM, GEORGE IRVIN.—Son of Abner and Celia Stevens Cunningham. Born in Monroe County, Tennessee, September 8, 1835. Ancestors fought in the Revolution. Good English education, obtained from common schools. At age of seventeen, he removed to Charleston and engaged in cattle and butchery business, which business he is still carrying on. Alderman of city during Reconstruction Period, and mayor, in 1873. Chairman of county board of commissioners, from 1872 to 1879. Appointed United States Marshall, in 1889; served until 1894. President of Charleston Waterworks Company and other enterprises. Postmaster of Charleston, since 1897. Has always been a Republican. Has the confidence and respect of the people.

CUNNINGHAM, WILLIAM JOSEPH.—Son of Joseph A. Cunningham. Born, April 25, 1852, in Lancaster County, South Carolina. Ancestors were Scotch-Irish. His education was obtained from Kings Mountain Military Academy. Married Miss Mary E. Dunlap, September 25, 1873. Farmed from 1872 to 1882. Merchandised in Lancaster, from 1883 to 1891, and has succeeded in both these undertakings.

DABBS, EUGENE WHITEFORD.—Postmaster at Goodwill, South Carolina. A native of Darlington, South Carolina; was born on April 15, 1864. Studied at home, until twelve years of age, and a few months at the public schools. Then entered the South Carolina Agricultural and Mechanical College of Columbia, South Carolina, at its organization in 1850; but death of his father, J. Quincy Dabbs, brought college career to a close two months later. Married Alice Maude McBride, on February 7, 1893. Helped organize, and was secretary and treasurer of Sumter County Agricultural Association, 1884 and 1887. Charter member and corresponding secretary of Sumter County Alliance, from 1888 to 1891. President of Sumter County Democratic executive committee. One of the trustees of the public school.

DAGNALL, RICHARD ROBERT.—Born in Augusta, Georgia, March 17, 1838. He is a son of Elbert H. Dagnall, and Martha Brown. His father is ninety years old, and lives with his daughter in Atlanta, Georgia. He fought in the Indian War in 1836, and also in the Confederate army. The subject of this sketch was educated at the Cokesbury Conference School. He was licensed to preach, in 1857; and admitted on trial, in the South Carolina Conference the same year. He is now in charge of the Pickens Circuit. Married Mary E. Hellams of Laurens County, November 20, 1867.

DANIEL, DAVID WISTAR.—Born in Laurens County, South Carolina, May 23, 1867. Educated in the primary schools of his county, and graduated at Wofford College with the degree of A. B., in 1892; he was selected junior debater of his class, literary editor of the journal, member of the S. A. E. fraternity. Took a special course at the University of Chicago. He was for a while principal of the Hebron High School, Marlboro, Central High School, and the Batesburg Institute. District department Grand Chief Templar of I. O. G. T. He was elected assistant professor of English, at Clemson College, South Carolina, in 1898.

DANIEL, WILLIAM WELLINGTON.—President of Columbia Female College. Son of James W. Daniel and Eliza Anderson. Entered the preparatory department of Newberry College, in 1874; graduated in June, 1879. Taught school several years after graduation. Married Alice R. Aull, August 29, 1883. Joined the South Carolina Conference, Methodist Episcopal Church, South, in 1883, served on a circuit, and was then sent to Chester, Newberry, Florence, Washington Street Church Columbia, South Carolina, and Anderson. Received degree of A. M., in 1882, from Newberry College. In 1899, degree of D. D. conferred by same college.

DANTZLER, CHARLES GLOVER.—Lawyer. Born March 9, 1854, near St. Matthews, Orangeburg County, South Carolina. Attended Mt. Zion Institute, Winnsboro, Kings Mountain Military School at Yorkville, and graduated at Wofford College, in 1875. Married Laura A. Moss, December 12, 1876. Member of the Legislature, from 1886 to 1890. He is now practicing law at Orangeburg.

DAVANT, CHARLES, M. D.—Son of R. J. Davant, a prominent lawyer of his time. Was born at his father's home, Beaufort District, on April 7, 1839. He is descended through two lines from the French-Huguenots. His preparatory training was confided to the care of F. W. Fickling, and Leroy F. Youmans. At the age of sixteen he entered the South Carolina Military Academy, where he remained two years. Then he pursued his studies in Furman University, Greenville; immediately after which, he began the study of medicine, and graduated from the Charleston Medical College, in 1861. He entered the army as assistant surgeon of the Third South Carolina Cavalry. In November, 1862, he married Mary, the eldest daughter of Captain W. M. Bostick. He was one of the foremost supporters of Hampton, in 1876. In November, 1887, he again married Mary, daughter of Colonel Thomas J. Pickens, of Pendleton, South Carolina. In the practice of his profession has been successful in a marked degree, giving special attention to surgery and malignant fevers.

8

DAVIS, HENRY CAMPBELL.—Principal of the High School of Columbia. Second son of Professor R. Means Davis, and Sallie LeConte, daughter of the late Joseph LeConte, professor of geology in the University of California. Graduated with distinction, from the South Carolina College, in 1898. Attended the three State summer schools for teachers. Principal of Bear Creek School, from 1898 to 1899. Principal of the Blufton School, from 1899 to 1900, and of the Lancaster Graded Schools, from 1900 to 1901, Member of the county board of education, and instructor in the county institutes of Richland County.

DAVIS, JAMES E.—Was born on September 17, 1856, in Barnwell, South Carolina. He is a son of the late Colonel James L. Davis, a large planter. Served Barnwell District, as clerk of court, two terms, from 1852 to 1859. He read law in the office of Honorable James Aldrich, and after standing a most creditable examination, was admitted to the bar, December 13, 1880. In the spring of 1881, he went to Barnwell, and opened up an office for the practice of his profession. Married Miss Mary Ella Bronson, daughter of the late Edward A. Bronson, the founder of the "Barnwell Sentinel," January 28, 1886. He is now serving his first term as solicitor of the Second Circuit.

DAVIS, JAMES QUENTIN.—Was born at Buckhead, Fairfield County, South Carolina, March 23, 1851. Now resides in Winnsboro, South Carolina. His earlier education was obtained from Mt. Zion College, Winnsboro, and the Kings Mountain Military College, at Yorkville, South Carolina. He was a student in the South Carolina College at the time that that institution passed into the hands of the negroes, during reconstruction times. Appointed special agent by Governor Hampton in 1878, also county treasurer in 1873, which office he held continuously, until 1891. President of the Fairfield Savings and Loan Association. Cashier of the Peoples Bank; and also of the Winnsboro Bank at the consolidation of the Peoples Bank and the Winnsboro National Bank. Treasurer of the Fairfield Loan and Trust Company. Director of the Fairfield Cotton Mill. He was at one time co-editor of the "News and Herald." Delegate to County State, and Congressional Democratic conventions. Elected a trustee of the South Carolina College, in 1898; re-elected by the Legislature, in 1900. Married Miss Beckie Pagan, daughter of Major James Pagan, of Chester, South Carolina.

·DAVIS, JOE CABELL.—Son of Ashley L. and Sallie (Cabell) Davis. The latter is a daughter of General Benjamin W. S. Cabell, of Virginia. Born at Lunenberg, Court-house, Virginia, July 31, 1857. He attended the Danville High School, Berkeley and Everett Military Academy, Danville; and University of Virginia. Studied physics under Doctors W. C. and J. R. Cabell. Married Miss Lucy Brantley, Butler, Georgia, August 3, 1898. He was general Southern and Western agent, of the Boston Tobacco Works, South Boston. Assisted Dr. William C. Cabell, as state manager in Mutual Reserve of New York. Started in insurance business as special agent for North Western Life Insurance Company; remained as such two years; then went with Mutual Reserve of New York, as inspector for Southern and Western States, after which he was promoted to the position he now holds. Office in Greenville.

DAVIS, ROBERT MEANS.—Eldest son of Isabella Harper and Henry C. Davis, whose grandfather, Dr. James Davis, came from Maryland, in 1874, to Laurens County. Prepared for college by private tutors, and at Winnsboro, South Carolina, and graduated from South Carolina University. Taught one year in Kings Mountain Military School. Graduated in law at South Carolina College, in 1872. Edited the "Winnsboro News and Herald," from 1873 to 1882, except in 1876, when he was on the staff of the "Charleston News and Courier." Secretary of Democratic executive committee in

Hampton County, in 1876. Became principal of the Mt. Zion School, in 1877. Organized the first graded school, supported by special tax, outside of Charleston, and other schools adopted the system which is now one of the most important educational features of the State. He was elected to the chair of history and political science in the South Carolina College. Taught in the first State institute in Spartanburg, in 1880. President of the South Carolina Teachers Association for a number of years. Member of the county board of examiners for Fairfield County several years. Member of State board of education, from 1882 to 1890. Member of the South Carolina Historical Commission. Married, June 3, 1877, Sallie LeConte, daughter of Dr. Joseph LeConte.

DAVIS, WILLIAM C.—Son of James E. and Anna M. Davis. Born, February 12, 1870, upon the farm of his father, near Manning, South Carolina. Graduated from Citadel, in 1889, at age of nineteen. Read law with Honorable James F. Rhame one year, going to University of Virginia. In 1891, admitted to practice in Virginia courts. Upon returning home, formed partnership with James F. Rhame, Esquire, which continued until breaking out of Spanish-American War. Captain of Manning Guards, taken into Spanish-American War as Company D, Second South Carolina, of which he was captain. Judge advocate of the Seventh Army Corps, in Cuba. Member of House of Representatives, from 1894 to 1898; member of judiciary committee of House. Director in Manning Oil Mill. First lieutenant of Company A, at the Citadel, and won medal for being best drilled man in the corps. Married Clara J. Huggins, daughter of Dr. Huggins of Manning, South Carolina, May 17, 1894. His father was clerk of the court of Manning sixteen years.

DEAN, ALVIN HENRY, JR.—Is now serving his second term from Greenville County in the State Senate. Was born near Duncans, in Spartanburg County, March 22, 1863. He acquired his education from the high schools of Spartanburg and at Furman University; also took a course at Vanderbilt. He was married, in 1886, to Miss Lida Byrd, who died in

1894. He married Miss Sarah Preston of Virginia, in August, 1898. His first position was that of alderman of the city of Greenville. Elected to State Senate, in 1896, and re-elected by a large majority, in 1900. Engaged in the practice of law.

DEAN, GEORGE ROSWELL.—Was born in Anderson County, South Carolina, January 25, 1844. He attended Furman University, and graduated from the Citadel, at Charleston, in class of 1865; but the class did not receive their diplomas until after the war. He was married, in 1868, to Hattie Camp, daughter of the late William Camp. He moved to Spartanburg County, in 1871. Taught school, and read medicine at the same time, at Belton, South Carolina, from 1865 to 1867. Graduated from the Jefferson Medical College, in 1868, and has since been actively engaged in the practice of his profession. He is a member of the Southern Surgical and Gynaecological Association, American Medical Association; Philadelphia County Medical Association. He is assistant surgeon of the Southern Railway. Ex-president of the Medical Society of South Carolina.

DeBRUHL, MARSHALL PRINGLE.—Born in Abbeville, South Carolina. He attended the private schools of Abbeville until fifteen years of age. He was for two years a clerk in drug store. Married Miss Kate C. Calhoun, who died, October 22, 1900. Has been a member of the House of Representatives, since 1898, and is now actively engaged in the practice of law at Abbeville, South Carolina.

DeHAY, ARTHUR HAMILTON.—Son of Robert H. DeHay and Sarah A. McCants. Born, November 17, 1857, at St. Johns Parish, now Berkeley County, South Carolina. Of Scotch and French descent. Only a good common school education. Married Miss Sallie J. Winter, daughter of D. McCants Winter, of Berkeley County, September 26, 1880. In early life, clerked a short time. Taught school, several sessions, in Berkeley County. Elected county superintendent of education, in 1892, re-elected, in 1894. Member of

State constitutional convention, in 1895. Again elected county superintendent of education, in 1896. In 1899, deputy sheriff of Berkeley County, and re-elected county superintendent of education, in 1900, which position he is filling at present.

DENDY, STILES PLUMER.—Was born in Pickens District, now Oconee County, South Carolina, May 28, 1839. He was a son of Captain James H. Dendy, a native of Laurens County, who for sixteen years served as ordinary of the old Pickens District. Major Dendy spent his boyhood days on the old Dendy homestead in Oconee County. He received his earlier schooling in the country academies; and, in 1859, entered the Thalian Academy. In the fall of 1859, he entered the Pendleton Male Academy, where he completed his preparatory course under Professor W. J. Ligon. In the early part of 1861, he entered the freshman class of the South Carolina College, at Columbia, and attended one session. The war having come on, a company of cadets was organized, in the college, of which he became a member. They asked and received permission to go to Charleston during the bombardment of Fort Sumter, but took no part in it, after which they returned to college and continued their studies until July, 1861. They did not return to college, but most of them entered the Confederate army. S. P. Dendy assisted in the organization of Company C, Second Regiment, South Carolina Rifles, in which he became first lieutenant. The regiment became a part of Jenkin's Brigade, Hood's Division, Longstreet's Corps, Army of Northern Virginia. It was mustered into service November 2, 1861. The regiment was first ordered to James Island, where it was placed under command of Colonel James L. Orr. Major Dendy served in this company until the close of the war. He was twice promoted; first to captain and second to major, serving in the latter capacity the last two years of the war. From the war he returned home and took a brief review of his literary studies from a country academy. In 1867, he went to Carnesville, Georgia, where, for a year and a half, he taught a classical school, and at the same time pursued the study of law, under Judge John B. Estes. In the fall of 1868, he entered the law department of the University of Virginia where he remained two years. Returning to his home in Oconee County, he was admitted to the bar at Walhalla, in 1870. Soon after his admission to practice he was elected probate judge, and was twice re-elected, serving three terms of two years each. On November 2, 1871, he was joined in marriage, with Miss Alice E. Sitton, of Pendleton, the daughter of John B. Sitton, Esquire. After retiring from the office of probate judge, he devoted his time wholly to the practice of law, until 1880. In that year he was elected to the State Legislature, serving therein two years. Major Dendy is a prominent Mason, having taken both the chapter and council degrees, and has been senior warden of the grand lodge of South Carolina.

DENDY, WADE JAY.—Editor of the "Clinton Gazette." Was born in Laurens County, January 21, 1859. Only the advantage of the common schools of the country. Remained on farm until of age, then went into the printing business. He established the "Clinton Gazette," in 1888, and is now editor and proprietor of same. He represented his county in the Prohibition Convention, at Columbia, in 1891, and was a member for one year of the State Executive Committee.

DERHAM, JOHN PICKENS.—Was born in Horry County, April 10, 1861. Of Irish descent. He attended the common schools of Horry County, one and a half years, and spent a year and a half at the Bingham schools of North Carolina. Married Miss Loula J. McGoughan of Fair Bluff, North Carolina, January 30, 1894. He was appointed school commissioner of Horry County, in 1887 and 1888; county auditor, from 1888 to 1891; then elected to State Senate in 1892, and served until 1896. Elected comptroller-general, in January, 1898, by general assembly, and won a second term before the people, in the campaign. He is still filling this position.

DERRICK, GEORGE A.—Son of Levi and Louisa C. Derrick. Born October 19, 1854, in Lexington County, South

Carolina. Attended the common schools up to twelve years of age, and since that time his advantages have been limited. He is a farmer, public land surveyor, and notary, and during year 1895, was trial justice for District Number 1, of Lexington County. He is now auditor for Lexington County, elected in 1898, and re-elected, in 1900, having strong opponents each time. Has been especially successful in this office. Married Miss M. Della Smith, November 19, 1876.

DERRICK, JASPER S.—Engaged in mercantile business at Leesville twenty-five years, he being considered the pioneer merchant of the town. He was born near Leesville, Lexington County, South Carolina. Of German parentage. Only the advantage of an old-field school. Entered the Confederate army early in 1861, joining J. M. Steadman's Company. Afterward colonel of the Fifth Regiment. Re-enlisted for the war, joining the Palmetto Sharp Shooters. He was a sergeant in Captain J. A. Lee's Company. Slightly wounded at Gaines' Mill, and painfully wounded at Frazier's Farm; lost left hand at Battle of Sharpsburg. Elected tax collector of Edgefield County, in 1863, and served as tax collector and auditor, until put out by the Radicals, in 1868. Served as treasurer, from 1868 to 1878, and from 1898 to 1900.

DERRICK, JOHN S.—Elected county superintendent of education for Lexington, September 11, 1900. Son of Walter F. and Amanda E. Derrick. Born August 15, 1872, in Lexington County. Attended common schools in early life; then entered Newberry College in fall of 1892, finishing, in 1897, with degree of A.B. Attended Georgia-Alabama Business College, and graduated in Commercial department, August, 1899. Taught three years after graduation.

DIAL, NATHANIEL BARKSDALE.—Son of the late Captain Albert Dial, who was one of the most prominent men in Laurens, and president of the Peoples Bank at the time of his death. N. B. Dial, the subject of this sketch, was born in Laurens County, April 24, 1862. He attended the Richmond College, Vanderbilt University, and graduated in law, at the University of Virginia. He was married on November 4, 1883, to Miss Ruth Mitchell. He was three times elected mayor of Laurens. He is president of the Enterprise Bank, and is engaged in the practice of his profession, also.

DIBBLE, HENRY MONTGOMERY.—President of the Bank of Aiken. Born in Marshall, Michigan, October 12, 1859. Attended the public schools of Marshall, and graduated from Cornell University, in 1882. Studied law at Grand Rapids, Michigan. President of the Carolina Light and Power Company. President of the Aiken Improvement Society, and the Aiken Library Association. Treasurer of the Aiken Cottages. Owner of the Vale of Montmorenci, dairy farm, situated seven miles from Aiken, which has nearly one hundred and fifty thoroughbred jerseys, the largest herd of jerseys in the State.

DICK, ALEXANDER COLCLOUGH.—Physician. Son of Dr. Leonard White Dick, who was assistant surgeon Twenty-third Regiment South Carolina Volunteers, Confederate States of America, and who practiced medicine in South Carolina after the war, until his death, in 1882. His mother was Leonora Ida Colclough. He was prepared for college at the Fort Mill Academy, at Fort Mill, South Carolina, graduating from Davidson College, in 1883. Read medicine under Dr. Paul M. Barringer, at Davidson College, during the summer of 1887. Attended medical lectures at University, of Virginia, in 1887 and 1888. Graduated from the medical College of South Carolina, in March, 1889; served at the city hospital. Married Clara Peel Russell, of Baltimore, Maryland, September 15, 1897. He is now practicing medicine and surgery at Sumter, South Carolina.

DICKSON, MICHAEL CALVIN.—Was born near Pendleton, Anderson County, South Carolina,
January 27, 1841. He is a son of
Thomas Dickson, who, with his brother, Rev. Michael Dickson, an eminent
divine of the Presbyterian faith, moved
from Abbeville County to Pendleton,
in 1840. His mother was a daughter
of General Scott of Revolutionary
fame. He was educated in the Pendleton High School under the instruction of the noted Professor W. J. Ligon. Was prepared to enter Davidson College, when he responded to the
call in defense of his country, entering the Fourth Regiment
South Carolina Volunteers, Company C, commanded by Captain John C. Calhoun. He was elected lieutenant, and served
during the entire four years. He never missed an engagement that his command participated in, from the First Manassas, until within nine days of the surrender, where, at the
battle of Fayetteville, North Carolina, when Hampton's
Cavalry surprised Kilpatrick, he was severely wounded in
the arm and hip. After the close of the war he merchandised six years, in Pendleton. He is now engaged in agricultural pursuits, and owns several large plantations. Married Miss Gilkerson of Laurens County in 1875, whose grandmother was Miss Calhoun, a first cousin of John C. Calhoun.

DOAR, JOHN WALTER.—Son of John W. and Emma C.
Doar. Born at Georgetown, South Carolina, September 11,
1870. Of French and English ancestry. Obtained education from public schools of Georgetown, Winyah Indigo Society, and the Richmond Business College of Savannah.
Married Miss Elizabeth Sheppard Black, April 16, 1901. Began newspaper and printing business at Georgetown, in 1884.
Moved to Columbia, in 1886, and was employed on "Columbia
Daily Register." Moved to Augusta, in 1894, then was with
Richards and Shaver's printing establishment five years. In
1900, returned to Georgetown and engaged in newspaper

work with C. W. Wolfe. Bought out "The Outlook," and formed a stock company, and he is now editor and manager. One of the orators at Labor day celebration, in Augusta, in 1899.

DOAR, JOSIAH.—Editor of the "Georgetown Times," the oldest paper in the State. Born August 20, 1850, on the Santee. Education limited, only that obtained from the common schools and the printing office. Married Ella Blain Russell, of Augusta, Georgia, February 11, 1879. He held the office of sheriff twelve years, and postmaster five; county chairman several times. Delegate, twice, to national Democratic Conventions. Was injured for life, in the late negro riot, by the accidental discharge of a rifle in the hands of a raw recruit.

DONALDSON, THOMAS QUINTON.—Born in Greenville County, on the 27th day of August, 1834. He is of Scotch-Irish ancestry. Until he was sixteen years of age, he lived on his father's farm and attended such schools as the country then afforded, when not engaged in farm work. At about the age of sixteen, he left home to attend a classical school at Williamston, South Carolina, which was taught by Mr. Wesley Leverett, a most excellent teacher, who numbered amongst his pupils such men as Governor Joseph E. Brown, of Georgia, Governor James L. Orr, of this State, and others who afterwards became distinguished. Under the tuition of this excellent man, for three years, Mr. Donaldson acquired a good knowledge of the English, Greek, and Latin languages, and mathematics. After leaving this school he taught school himself for a short while, and on the third day of March, 1853, entered the law office of Charles J. Elford, where he read law. Was admitted to practice by the Supreme Court in Columbia in the fall of 1855, in a class of fifteen. He practiced in partnership with his former law preceptor, until 1861. In April, 1861, he joined the Butler Guards, and entered the army in Virginia, where he served until May, 1862, when failing health compelled him to retire. During his term of service he was a participant in the first battle of Bull Run, and a number of skirmishes. Soon after returning home he was appointed, without solicitation, collector of the war tax for Greenville County, and discharged the duties of that office to the entire satisfaction of the people, until the close of the war. In 1865, he was a candidate for the lower house of the Legislature, but failed of election by forty votes out of a poll of several thousand. From this time, until 1872, he devoted himself to the practice of his profession, and by diligence and faithful attention to the interests of his clients, built up a large and lucrative practice, which he has since enjoyed. In 1872, he was nominated by the Democratic county convention of Greenville County, as a candidate for the State Senate, and at the ensuing election was chosen for that office over his Republican competitor by a large majority. After serving four years in the Senate, he declined a re-election and resumed the practice of the law. He was chairman of a committee of thirty-six gentlemen, appointed by a mass meeting of citizens, to conduct the canvass for a subscription of $200,000 to the Air Line Railway, which was voted by the county of Greenville by an overwhelming majority. He was the first president, and laid the cornerstone of the Huguenot Plaid Mills. Is a director in three or four of the largest cotton mills in the county, and a stockholder in all of them, with one or two exceptions. He was one of a commission of three, appointed by the Governor, to revise the tax laws of the State, and has been chairman of the board of trustees of the graded schools of the city of Greenville, for the past ten years. He has been a member of the Baptist Church, since 1854. Was married to Miss Susan B. Hoke, in November, 1859; and has four children, two sons and two daughters, one of his sons is practicing law in partnership with him, and the other having graduated from the United States Military Academy at West Point, is now a captain in the United States Cavalry.

DOUGLASS, ALEXANDER SCOTT.—Of Scotch-Irish descent. Born in Fairfield County, South Carolina, December 25, 1833. His parents were both natives of Fairfield Dis-

trict, South Carolina. His grandfather was, Alexander Douglass who came to South Carolina from Ireland about 1790;
his maternal grandfather, John Simmons, came to South
Carolina from Pennsylvania, in 1879. After securing his
primary education in the neighborhood schools, he entered
the sophomore class of Erskine College, Due West, South
Carolina, and graduated in 1853. Then studied law under
Governor B. F. Perry, Greenville, South Carolina, until 1854,
when he took the full law course at the University of Virginia. Was admitted to the bar in December, 1855. He was
twice married, his second wife being Miss Sallie McCants,
whom he married, in 1878. In 1856, he settled in Spartanburg, South Carolina, and, in co-partnership with John H.
Evans, edited and published the "Spartanburg Express," until he went into the Civil War, in 1861, as second-lieutenant
of Company C, Thirteenth Regiment South Carolina Volunteers, which belonged to Greggs, afterwards McGowan's Brigade, Hill's Division, Jackson's Corps, Army of Northern
Virginia. He was promoted to first-lieutenant, which position he held until the surrender at Appomattox. While a
citizen of Spartanburg, was a member of the State Democratic Convention, of 1860. After the close of the war, he
commenced the practice of law at Winnsboro, South Carolina,
and is now in copartnership with his son, W. D. Douglass.
Represented Fairfield County in the Legislature, from 1882
to 1883. Was a member of the board of directors of the
Winnsboro National Bank, from 1874, until it was connected
with the Winnsboro Bank. Is now a director in that institution. He was also attorney for the Winnsboro National
Bank, from 1886 to 1896, and is now holding that position
with the Winnsboro Bank. A director of the Fairfield Cotton Mill. He is an elder in the Presbyterian Church, at
Winnsboro, and has been superintendent of the Sunday-
school, since 1866.

DOUGLASS, WILLIAM DAVIS.—Engaged in the practice
of law at Winnsboro, South Carolina. Son of A. S. Douglass.
Born March 20, 1866, in Winnsboro, South Carolina. After
receiving preparation at Mt. Zion Institute, Winnsboro, South

Carolina, and Fort Mill Academy, Fort Mill, South Carolina, he entered the South Carolina College, and completed the course, in 1887. In 1888, he was elected tutor of Latin and Greek in his Alma Mater, and studied law, graduating with highest honors. Prior to his election as tutor, in the South Carolina College, he was a teacher in Mount Zion School, Winnsboro. Married Miss Floride P. Dwight, October 24, 1894. He was editor of the "Winnsboro News and Herald," from 1889 to 1901. Was nominated by anti-Tillmanite faction for House of Representatives in 1892; led his ticket but was defeated by about seventy-five votes. Has never been a candidate for public office since. He practiced his profession at Winnsboro, in copartnership with his father. Admitted to bar, in 1889.

DOYLE, THOMAS C.—Physician. Son of Patrick Doyle, of New York State, and Rachel Dukes. Born March 16, 1866, in Orangeburg, South Carolina. Graduated from Pio Nono College, Macon, Georgia, in 1884, and from the medical department of the University of Maryland, in 1889. Married Winifred Lanigan, of Charleston, South Carolina, in 1894. Alderman of the city of Orangeburg, from 1895 to 1901. Member of the board of commissioners of public works, from 1898 to 1901. Mayor of Orangeburg, elected September, 1901.

DRAFTS, GEORGE SEBASTIAN.—Probate judge of Lexington County, since 1898. A son of Michael Drafts. Born May 31, 1844, at Lexington Court-house, South Carolina. Ancestors were of German descent, and among the early settlers of Lexington County. His father died in the Civil War, as a prisoner. Only that training obtainable from the county schools. Married Miss Emeline L. Wheeler, December 5, 1867. Has been a farmer all his life. County commissioner of Lexington one term, 1882, and sheriff three successive terms, from 1883 to 1896. Served in Civil War as private, in Company F, Fifth Cavalry Regiment in General Butler's Brigade. Was in battle of Cold Harbor and other battles around Richmond, Petersburg, and the Wilderness.

DRAKE, CHARLES MILES.—In the mercantile business in Charleston, South Carolina. Son of Miles and Anna McIver Drake. Born at Charleston, South Carolina. Father was for many years a prominent merchant in Charleston. He is of Scotch-Irish descent. Educated at Fordham College, New York. Married Miss Lizzie M. Galvin, of Boston, Massachusetts. After leaving college went into business with his father and has continued to the present time. The business was established by his father, in 1850.

DRAKE, JOSEPH B.—Son of Miles and Anna Drake, of Charleston, South Carolina. Born September 14, 1859. Educated under Professor Brown, and in the High School, under Virgil C. Dibble. Connected with firm of M. Drake & Son, until 1892, then merchandised in Orangeburg, three years, returning to Charleston, in 1895, to become president of the Drake-Innes Shoe Company. He is now associated with the wholesale shoe firm of H. Drake & Son.

DRAKEFORD, JOSEPH SYDNEY.—Was born near Camden, in Kershaw County, South Carolina, August 31, 1870. His father was Joseph J. Drakeford, of Kershaw County, who served as a soldier of the Confederacy from the commencement to the end of the war between the States, being captain of Company C, Twenty-second South Carolina Volunteers, when Johnston surrendered at Goldsboro. His mother was Miss Laura Haile, also of Kershaw County. His antecedents were among the earlier settlers of Virginia, and removed to South Carolina, in 1741, from Fairfax County. His father's family removed to Fort Mill, in the eastern portion of York County, in the spring of 1874, where the father died in 1883, leaving him the oldest of six living children. Received less than three years schooling, but that, under Colonel A. R. Banks, has left an indelible impress. Thrown early upon his own resources, at the age of sixteen, while engaged as clerk in the postoffice at Fort Mill, he bought a small printing press, and commenced a work that he has followed since. In 1887, he started the "News," the first paper published at Fort Mill. For three years this was continued. In 1890, went to Rock Hill and worked several months for the "Herald," principally as printer. In December of the same year went to Charlotte, North Carolina, as job printer for the Blakey Printing House; and later, when the business was incorporated, became one of the four stockholders. Sold his interest there, in 1893, and, in August of that year, moved to Yorkville, where he bought the plant of the defunct "York Enterprise" and started the publication of "The Yorkville Yeoman," of which he is yet the editor. Was married March 30, 1892, to Miss Eugenia M. Miller, of Santa Barbara, Sao Paulo, Brazil, South America, and to them a number of children have been born.

DREHER, ERNEST S.—Superintendent of the public schools of Columbia, South Carolina. Born July 25, 1866, in Lexington County, South Carolina. Bachelor of Arts graduate of Roanoke College, Salem, Virginia, in 1888; Master of Arts degree from same college, in 1893. He has never married. Taught one year as principal of the Mount Tabor School, of Newberry County. In 1889, he went to Columbia, and taught three years, in the Laurel Street School for boys; promoted to principal of same, and, at the expiration of three years, was elected to the position he now holds.

DUCKETT, THOMAS JACOB.—Sheriff of Laurens County. Born, in that county, January 4, 1842. Son of Thomas Duckett and Narcissa Dillard, daughter of Major James Dillard, of Revolutionary fame. He had only the advantage of an old field school. He was among the first to volunteer in the war between the States and joined as a private Company I, Third Regiment of South Carolina Infantry, which was one of the original parts of Bonham's Brigade, which afterwards became so distinguished for its valor under the leadership of Brigadier-General J. B. Kershaw. Elected lieutenant while at hospital from wound received in Battle of Wilderness and commanded his company until the close of the war. Has been three times married; his present wife was Mrs. Edna Workman. Elected county school commissioner to fill unexpired term, in 1894. Elected to the position he now holds, in 1900.

DUKES, JOHN WILLIAM HAZELWOOD.—President and general manager of the Orangeburg Street Railway Co. Son of Sheriff John Dukes and Sophia Johnson. Born July 14, 1858, in Orangeburg County. Of Irish and Dutch descent. Ancestors were early settlers of South Carolina. Good English education obtained from the common schools. Married Lucia B. Lowman, of Aiken County, November 25, 1879. He is now interested in farming and stock raising. Mayor of Orangeburg ten years.

DUNCAN, D'ARCY PAUL.—Secretary of the county board. Son of Professor David Duncan and Amanda Peamond, of Virginia. Attended Wofford College until the partial closing of this institution, in 1863. He was appointed a cadet in the Citadel Academy, Charleston. Served in the Confederate War with the cadet corps until the close of the war. He was twice married; his first wife died in 1876; he then married, in 1881, Miss R. M. Richardson, daughter of Congressman I. M. Richardson, of Sumter, South Carolina. Chairman of the county commissioners of Union County, from 1876 to 1880; president of the agricultural society, six years, from 1882 to 1888; appointed railroad commissioner, in 1882, and served until 1894. Secretary of the National Alliance four years, and for eight years manager of the Alliance Exchange.

DUNCAN, DAVID R.—Lawyer. Was born at Randolph-Macon College, Mecklenburg County, Virginia, September 27, 1836. He received his early education at Randolph-Macon College, in which his father was a professor, where he graduated. He at once came to Spartanburg, whither his father had removed, in 1854, and taught the Odd Fellows High School, as its first teacher, one year. He read law in his leisure hours, and at the age of twenty-one was admitted to the bar. Has since been engaged in the practice of his profession. In August, 1861, he entered the service of the Confederate army as first-lieutenant of Company C, Thirteenth South Carolina Volunteers. Upon the re-organization of the regiment he was made captain of the company. He

9

served in this capacity until the spring of 1864, when he was promoted to the rank of major. At the close of the war, he resumed his law practice. In 1865, he was elected a member of the lower house of the State Legislature, re-elected in 1870, and in 1872, was elected a member of the State Senate, serving in that body four years. In August, 1875, he was elected president of the Spartanburg and Asheville Railroad Company, and served as such four years. This was the first railway built across the Blue Ridge, in South Carolina. In 1880, Major Duncan was elected solicitor of the Eighth Circuit, and served eight years, being re-elected, in 1884. Married July 9, 1856, to Miss Virginia, daughter of William and Martha Nelson. He is a Royal Arch Mason, an Odd Fellow, and a Knight of Pythias. He is a director of the Spartan Mills and is connected with numerous other corporations in the county.

DUNCAN, JOHN T.—Lawyer. Born in Newberry County, South Carolina, September 18, 1862. He acquired his education under Thomas Duckett, of Liberty Hill. Graduated, with degree of A. M., from Furman University, and degree of L. B., at South Carolina College, in 1896. Married Louise, daughter of Hon. D. H. Tomkins, February 19, 1895. Elected as a representative for Newberry County, in 1892, and again, in 1894. Chief Clerk of Secretary of State, 1894, 1895 and 1896. Began the practice of law, in 1897, at Columbia, associated with his brother-in-law, Frank G. Tompkins, until October, 1901; but is now alone. Secretary of the Farmers' Convention of 1890.

DUNCAN, THOMAS CAREY.—Son of Bishop W. W. Duncan and Medora (Rice). Was born July 5, 1862, in Union County, South Carolina. After attending the county schools, he entered Wofford College, from which institution he graduated in 1881. On September 10, 1885, he married Fannie A. Merriman. He commenced merchandising in Union, in 1881, and developed great ability along this line. He soon came to be recognized as one of the best business men in upper South Carolina. Turning his attention to cotton manufacturing, he was mainly instrumental in the establishment of the Union Cotton Mills, in 1893. He was elected as a member of the South Carolina Legislature in 1892, and served one term. He has been president and treasurer of the Union Cotton Mills since its organization. He organized the Buffalo Cotton Mills of which he is also president and treasurer. These two mills together operate 3,700 looms, and 134,000 spindles. They have been among the most successful mills in the State, their success being in a large measure due to the untiring energy coupled with sound business judgment of Mr. Duncan.

DUNCAN, WATSON BOONE.—Pastor of the First Methodist Church of Laurens, South Carolina. Was born on March 19, 1867, in York County, South Carolina. After the training received in the common and high schools, he graduated from Wofford College, the Polytechnic College, and Erskine College, receiving his A. M. degree from the last-named institution. After teaching for some time, he decided to enter the ministry, and joined the South Carolina Conference, in December, 1887. Is a member of various committees and boards. He was a delegate to the General Missionary Conference, in New Orleans, in May, 1901. For several years the Sunday-school lessons for the "Southern Christian Advocate" were prepared by him. He is the author of several booklets, and of a volume known as "Twentieth Century Sketches," containing biographical sketches of the members of the South Carolina Conference. Married, February 6, 1889, to Miss Lizzie, daughter of Dr. H. H. Huggins, of Manning, South Carolina.

DUNKIN, WILLIAM HUGER.—Clerk of the court of Charleston County. Was born in that city, on March 24, 1861. He graduated from Professor Sachtleben's School, in June, 1875. One year afterwards, in July, 1876, he entered an insurance office as clerk, but is now conducting the same business on his own account. He was elected superintendent of education of Charleston County for three successive terms, resigning to accept the office he now holds. He was

married, in 1886, to Miss Eunice Martin, daughter of Colonel
W. A. Martin, of Barnwell County, South Carolina. Grandson of late Chief Justice Dunkin, of South Carolina. Elected
clerk of court in 1900.

DuPRE, JULIUS H.—Cashier of the Farmers' Bank of
Abbeville, South Carolina. Was born in Lowndesville, South
Carolina, November 8, 1857. Attended the public schools,
and was one year at Wofford College. Married Miss Josephine Hill on the 5th of February, 1880. He was elected alderman of the city of Abbeville, four times. Is a notary public and is in the fire insurance business.

DURANT, CHARLTON.—Member of firm of Wilson &
Durant, attorneys, at Manning, South Carolina, since admission to bar, in 1897. He is a son of E. C. Durant, and Miss
Virginia Tinsley. Born in 1874, at Bluffton, Georgia. Ancestors were French, Scotch and Irish. Only the advantage
of a free school education. Has never married. Served in
Express service, from 1890 to 1894.

DURANT, DAVID E.—A member of the Legislature from
Sumter County. Born July 26, 1841, at Lynchburg, Sumter
County, South Carolina. Received his early education in
the common schools of his county, and afterwards spent
two years at the Cokesbury High School. Read medicine in
the town of Camden, and prepared for first lecture, but was
deprived of further medical education on account of the war.
Entering the service with Company E, Sixth South Carolina
Volunteers, as third-sergeant. Was wounded at Gaines'
Mill, June 27, 1862, and discharged from further service.
Was magistrate at Bishopville two years; elected clerk and
treasurer of the town four years. He is a very successful
farmer. Married Miss S. A. Carnes, November 13, 1862.

DURHAM, DAVIS COLEMAN.—President of the Gilreath,
Durham Company, of Greenville, South Carolina. Son of
David N. and Esther R. Durham, (nee Coleman). Was born
September 11, 1867, at Shelby, North Carolina. He attended

the Shelby High School, and the Greenville Military Institute under Captain J. B. Patrick. On September 12, 1894, he was united in marriage with Miss Stella Ferris, of New York State.

DURST, WILLIAM LOWNDES.—President and treasurer of Greenwood Cotton Mill. Was born at Kirkseys, Edgefield County, South Carolina, August 31, 1843. Education limited, only that of old-field school. His first wife was Louise Devore, whom he married, in 1873. He married Annie Cothran, in 1898. Served in the First Regiment of South Carolina Volunteers, at Appomattox, on the 9th of April, 1865.

EARLE, FORT SUMTER.—Mayor of Columbia, South Carolina. Son of Thomas Earle and Caroline Leaphart. Born in Hurtville, Alabama, August 26, 1865. Attended the Columbia Male Academy under Governor Hugh S. Thompson, six years, then entered South Carolina College, and graduated in 1885. Married Margaret Olive Miller, November 6, 1894. Followed railroad surveying one year; then entered drug business, in which he has since been employed. Alderman of city, from 1892 to 1900; mayor pro tem, from 1898 to 1900. Has been elected commissioner; member of board of county supervisors; and also county board of equalization.

EARLE, GEORGE W.—Was born in Pendleton, South Carolina, September, 1836. Good English education. Graduated from the Medical College, at Charleston, in 1858. Practiced medicine until the outbreak of the war. Then was in service four years. Was wounded at the battle of Williamsburg, in Virginia. Since the war he moved to Pickens, where he has been actively engaged in the practice of medicine, and in the drug business. Several years president of the Medical Society of Pickens County. He married Miss Janette Breazeale, of Belton, South Carolina, in October, 1874.

EARLE, JAMES IRBY.—A son of Dr. J. W. Earle and Eliza Keith. Was born June 30, 1862, in Oconee County. Moved to Greenville, in 1868. Was prepared for college at Patrick High School, and graduated from Furman University, in 1882. Read law in the office of Wells & Orr, and was admitted to practice in 1884, at Greenville, where he still resides.

EARLE, JULIUS RICHARD.—Practicing law at Walhalla, South Carolina. Was born near Hollands, Anderson County, South Carolina, November 4, 1863. He graduated from the South Carolina College. Was twice married; first to Miss Lula Perry Hix; and later, to Miss Eva Merritt. Represented Oconee County in the Legislature two terms. Was a member of March convention, 1890, and approved nominations. He is the publisher and editor of the "Oconee News."

EARLE, MARSHALL DELPH.—A member of the faculty of Furman University. Was born in Greenville, South Carolina, August 7, 1871. He graduated from Furman University, in 1889, with the degree of Master of Arts. Afterwards a student at Cornell University; University of Wisconsin; and the University of Cambridge, England. For two years, he has filled the position as professor of mathematics in the South Carolina summer school for teachers.

EARLE, THOMAS KEITH.—Son of Dr. J. W. and Eliza A. Earle. Was born at Old Pickens, November 17, 1863. His ancestors were of English and Scotch descent. He attended the private school of Professor J. P. Carlisle, and graduated from Furman University in the class of 1884; with Master of Arts degree. After leaving college he read law in the office of Wells & Orr of Greenville, and was admitted to the bar, in 1886. At present he is a member of the firm of Heyward, Dean & Earle.

EAVES, HAVELOCK.—Born April 25, 1870, at Bamberg, South Carolina. Educated at the Kings Mountain Military Academy and at the South Carolina Military Academy, grad-

uating from that institution, in 1900. Married Emily Eva
Riley, daughter of Captain W. A. Riley, of Bamberg, South
Carolina, November 19, 1898. He was given the position as
freight and passenger agent of the South Carolin Railroad,
and also of the Southern Railway at Bamberg, South Carolina. Mr. Eaves was elected captain of the Bamberg
Guards, in 1896. When the war broke out between this
country and Spain, this company volunteered their services,
with Mr. Eaves as their captain, and the company became a
part of the First South Carolina United States Volunteers.
When the second call for volunteers was made Governor
Ellerbe appointed him senior-major of the Second Regiment,
which was the only part of the South Carolina Volunteers
to see foreign service during the Spanish-American War.
Was summary court officer of the regiment during his entire
service.

EDMUNDS, NICHOLAS WILLIAM.—Pastor of the First
Presbyterian Church, at Sumter, South Carolina. Born September 23, 1831, in Richland County, South Carolina. He is
a son of R. R. Edmunds and Ann Vaughan Marshall. Attended Mt. Zion College, under I. W. Hudson, and graduated,
in 1852. Then entered the Seminary at Columbia. Married
Mary Claudia Leland, daughter of Rev. A. E. Leland, May
23, 1853. Taught eight years at Limestone, Barhamville,
South Carolina, and the Sumter Institute. Held State commission as chaplain, preaching at hospital and camps. Afterwards pastor at Ridgeway and Hartsville. Took Bachelor
of Arts degree from South Carolina College, in 1852. The
degree of Doctor of Divinity conferred by Davidson College,
North Carolina, in 1890.

EDMUNDS, SAMUEL H.—Son of the Rev. N. W. Edmunds
and Mary Leland Edmunds. Born May 28, 1870, on the Edmunds plantation, fourteen miles east of Columbia. Educated at Davidson College, North Carolina, graduating, in
1890. Winner of declaimer's medal; selected by the faculty
to deliver one of the orations at the graduating exercises of
his class; and chosen by the Eumenean Society, as valedic-

torian of the class of 1890. Since graduation he has been engaged in educational work, as principal of the Sumter Graded School, head master of the high school at Rock Hill, and, since 1895, superintendent of schools in Sumter. He has conducted, and assisted in the conduct of, summer schools, in ten different counties, and this summer, 1901, will be principal of the State Normal School for colored teachers. Married, December 24, 1896, Miss Ella Champian Davis, of Camden, South Carolina, grand-daughter of Chancellor DeSaussure and Bishop Davis of South Carolina.

EDWARDS, JOHN ODAM.—Probate judge of Berkeley County, since 1894. He is a son of John Odam Edwards, Sr., and Sarah Elizabeth Dennis, of Charleston, South Carolina. Born February 9, 1864, at Moncks Corner, South Carolina. The advantage of the public schools, until grown. Then attended night school in Charleston. Married Duella I. Whaley, April 12, 1885. Taught several terms in the public schools of Berkeley County. For six years connected with the Fernoline Chemical Company, of Charleston and New York. Afterwards read law under Mr. W. Moultrie Gourdin, of Charleston, and under Senator Dennis of Berkeley County. Admitted to bar, in 1893. Member of the W. O. W., Masons and Knights of Pythias. Has twice represented Cleveland Lodge Number 39 in Grand Lodge of South Carolina.

EDWARDS, ROBERT LEE.—Practicing physician of Darlington, South Carolina. Son of A. F. and Elizabeth S. Hart. Born January 19, 1871, at Palmetto, Darlington County, South Carolina. Of Welsh and English ancestry. He attended the Florence Graded School, and the South Carolina University. Graduated from the University Medical College of New York City, May 1, 1894. Married Jennie Covington, May 15, 1900. After leaving college, located at Hagerstown, Maryland, and remained there until March, 1897, when he removed to Darlington, South Carolina. Member of the Pee Dee Medical Association, State Medical Association, and of the Medical Society of the Carolinas and Virginia. Local surgeon of the Atlantic Coast Line Railroad, and the Darlington Guards.

EDWARDS, THOMAS HARTWELL.—Assistant superintendent of Connie Maxwell Orphanage. A native of Darlington. Was born April 14, 1865. His preliminary education was obtained under Captain J. B. Patrick, at Greenville, South Carolina. Twice he attempted a college course, but was interrupted on account of ill-health, a third attempt was made at Furman University, but death of father caused him to return home. In 1890, he married Miss Anna Eliza Wallace. He was at one time postmaster, and pastor of two churches, he has supplied churches in Sumter and Darlington counties.

EDWARDS, THOMAS LEE.—Master of Saluda County, since September, 1900. He is a native of Saluda, then Edgefield County. A graduate of Centennial College. Married Miss Mary Bell Plunkett, December 28, 1894. Is one of the most successful farmers of his section.

EFIRD, CYPRIAN M.—Born December 18, 1856, in the Fork Section of Lexington County. The foundation of his education was laid in the Pine Ridge Academy of Lexington County. In 1874, he entered Newberry College, Walhalla, graduating therefrom, in 1877. Married Carrie Boozer, on December 28, 1882. Was elected State Senator, from 1892 to 1896. A member of the County Convention of 1895. Also chairman of the State Democratic Convention, of 1894. He is now a trustee of the college from which he graduated, treasurer of the Theological Seminary of the Lutheran Church of the South. He was offered the position of State Reporter, in May, 1895, resigning the position of State Senator, in March, 1896, to accept that position which he now holds. Being admitted to the bar, in 1882, has since been actively engaged in the practice. In 1897, he formed a copartnership with F. E. Dreher, and the firm is still engaged in practice at Lexington, South Carolina.

EGAN, GEORGE W.—Was born in Charleston, South Carolina, in 1836. Having served out his apprenticeship, as a house carpenter, at the age of twenty-two, he went into business for himself as a contractor and builder.

He won the confidence and esteem of his fellow citizens, which they attested in various ways, having elected him twice to represent them in the Legislative Halls, and as one of the commissioners of the Charleston Orphan House. His latest work, the contract made with the United States government to deepen Charleston Harbor, by building stone jetties at the entrance, has been successful, and has benefited the trade of Charleston, the water on the bar having been thereby increased, from eighteen to twenty-three feet. In 1897, he purchased one of the finest rice plantations in the State, and has turned his attention to that field of labor. He is president of the Southern Coast and River Navigation Company; a director in the Miners and Merchants Bank, and sole owner of Accommodation Wharf, in Charleston. He is vice-president of the Hibernian Society, and a member of the German Friendly Society.

ELFORD, JOSEPH MARSH.—Clerk and treasurer of the city of Spartanburg, South Carolina. Born in Charleston, South Carolina, February 21, 1822. Good English education, obtained from the common schools. Married Elizabeth A. Elford, in April, 1848. He was magistrate and trial justice thirty-eight years. Chairman of the board of county commissioners. Clerk of board of county, six years. Practiced law thirty-five years. Grand Master of the I. O. O. F., Deputy Grand Master of A. F. M. Assistant quartermaster in Confederate War. Warden, in Church of Advent (Episcopal), and vestryman, over fifty years. He is also engaged in the real estate and insurance business.

ELLIOTT, THOMAS KETCHIN.—President of the Winns-boro Bank. Was born in Fairfield County, South Carolina, near Winnsboro, on October 8, 1855. Graduated, with honors, from the Virginia Military Institute, at Lexington, Virginia, in 1875. In the fall of that year, he was given the position as teller in the National Bank of Winnsboro. Three years later, he was made cashier, and in 1896, he was promoted to the position he now holds. He is also president of Fairfield Cotton Mills.

ELLIOTT, WILLIAM.—Member of Congress. Was born in Beaufort, South Carolina, September 3, 1838. Was educated at the College of Beaufort, Harvard University, and the University of Virginia. Was admitted to the bar in Charleston, 1861. Entered the Confederate War, and served as an officer throughout the war. In 1866, was elected a member of the South Carolina Legislature, and intendant of Beaufort. A delegate to the Democratic convention in St. Louis, in 1876 and 1888. Was appointed Democratic presi_dential elector for the State, in 1880. Has been a member of Congress for six consecutive years.

ELLIS, CHARLES WILEY.—A member of the firm of Ellis & Pope, wholesale grocers, of Greenville. Son of William J. and Dorothea Ellis, of North Carolina. Was born December 7, 1869, in Gaston County, North Carolina. His early schooling was acquired from the high schools of North Carolina, and later he took business course, at the Oak Ridge Institute. When eighteen years of age, he took a position to travel for a tobacco company, remaining with them, until 1898, at which time he went to Greenville, and engaged in merchandising. He married Miss Stella Hutchison of Gaston County, North Carolina, on October 20, 1897.

ELLISON, ARCHIBALD HENSON.—Was born in Anderson County, near Belton, South Carolina, on December 22, 1839, and reared in Pickens County. His education was acquired from the country schools. On December 22, 1869, he was united, in the holy bonds of matrimony, to Martha A.,

daughter of the late W. D. and Margaret Steele.   In 1857,
he went to Rockingham, North Carolina, and engaged in the
manufacture of tobacco, continuing this business until 1861,
at which time he volunteered in the Confederate service,
joining Captain Westfield's Company F, Second South Carolina Regiment, Hampton's Cavalry. Served during a greater
portion of the war, in Virginia, and was engaged in many
hard battles; but fortunately never received a wound. His
company was disbanded in North Carolina, after Lee's surrender at Appomattox. After the war, he engaged in the
saw mill and lumber business, until 1882. He is now a
prosperous farmer in Oconee County.

ELMORE, EDWARD CARRINGTON.—Son of the late Edward C. Elmore, of Columbia, South Carolina. Treasurer of
the Southern Confederacy. Grandson of Benjamin T. Elmore, who commanded the Richland Volunteers in the Semi-
nole War and who was at one time comptroller-general of
South Carolina. His mother is a daughter of Major J. Starke
Sims, of Union County. Through his father's mother, who
was a daughter of Judge Joseph Brevard, of Camden, he is
related to the noted Brevard family of North Carolina, who
were prominent signers of the Mecklenberg Declaration of
Independence, and to the Kershaws of Camden. The first
one of the Elmore family to settle in this State was John
Archer Elmore, of Prince Edward County, Virginia, a soldier
of the Revolution, under General Greene. He was twice
married, first to Miss Saxon, of Laurens County; afterwards
to Miss Martin, of Abbeville; and his descendants have been
prominent in public life in this State and Alabama. The
subject of this sketch was born in Alabama, and spent several years of his early life in that State. For the past fourteen years, he has been a teacher in the high schools of this
county, having previously taught in Union County. He now
occupies the position of superintendent of education of Spartanburg County, having been appointed to that position, to
fill a vacancy caused by the death of Joseph M. Ballenger.

EMANUEL, PHILIP ALBERT.—Lawyer. Born at Brownsville, Marlboro County, South Carolina. Attended the Brownsville School; also the Military School, at Hillsboro, North Carolina. December 24, 1868, he married Amelia Josephine Wilson, at Ravenwood, Johns Island, South Carolina. In 1877, he was admitted to the bar at Aiken, where for nearly twenty-five years, he has been practicing his profession. He has devoted a great deal of his time to the development of Kaolin, in Aiken County. He has invented and patented a process for reducing alumina from clays. Largely through his work, the mines have increased from fifteen to twenty, to sixty or seventy-five thousand tons annually shipped therefrom. He is now mayor of the town of Aiken.

ENSOR, JOSHUA FULTON.—Was born in Butler, Maryland, in 1834. Received early education in the common schools of Maryland. Attended several institutes in Pennsylvania, and graduated at the University of Maryland, in 1862. Married Miss Henrietta Kemp, in November, 1862. First-lieutenant United States Army, in Civil War; appointed surgeon with rank of major. In 1868, medical purveyor for Freedman's Bureau, in South Carolina. In 1870, appointed surgeon-in-chief of South Carolina Hospital for Insane, at Columbia, resigning therefrom, in 1878. Chief inspector and surveyor Port of Charleston, in 1879 and 1882; then appointed general deputy collector, internal revenue service for South Carolina. In 1894, he resigned and resumed practice of medicine in Columbia. In June, 1897, he was appointed postmaster at Columbia, by President McKinley, which position he now holds.

EPPS, JOHN LAW.—Son of John M. and E. H. Epps. Born January 25, 1848, near Whitmires. Ancestors came from Wales and Ireland. Early educated in the common schools and at St. John's High School, Spartanburg. Later entered the Hillsboro Military Academy, in 1864. In that year received an appointment to the South Carolina Military Academy at Columbia, and remained there until the burning

of Columbia by Sherman. He married Miss Mary, daughter
of Dr. G. W. Glenn, of Newberry County, April 20, 1876.
Most of his life has been spent on the farm, with the exception of a few years that he spent in town as clerk. He
served as trial justice for several years. He has also taught
school in Newberry County for some time. He was elected
treasurer of Newberry County, in 1900, and still holds the
position.

ERCKMANN, HARRY LOUIS.—Member of the law firm
of Burke & Erckmann, of Charleston, South Carolina. He is
a son of Charles G. and Sarah E. Erckmann. Born in
Charleston, South Carolina, January 18, 1878. He is of German and English ancestry. He attended the public and private schools of Charleston; was three years at Charleston
High School, and graduated from Charleston College, in
1898. Admitted to bar in December, 1899. Private instructor in families in afternoons, while reading law in office of
Burke & Lord.

ETHEREDGE, ALVIN.—Was born in that portion of Eage-
field which is now Saluda County, Sep-
tember 8, 1861. Dr. George M. Etheredge, his father, practiced medicine
in the Red Bank Section, with Dr.
William Mobley. He was assistant
surgeon in the Confederate army, and
only lived to see the close of the war,
dying in 1866. Alvin Etheredge attended school at the Graniteville
Academy; graduated from the Richmond Academy, Augusta, Georgia, in
1878; then entered Furman University, Greenville, graduating in the
class of 1881. Afterwards he spent two years in Massachusetts, studying civil and electrical engineering. Was on
railroad work both in South Carolina and Georgia, several
years. Built the first long distance, distributive plant for
light and power, in the Southern States, at Cotton Shoals,

on Little Horse Creek, transmitting electricity to Aiken, South Carolina, a distance of about ten miles. This plant was built in 1891, and was the pioneer of its kind in the South. He made strenuous efforts for the formation of Saluda County, and worked more strenuously still, possibly, for the location of the county seat near Red Bank Church, where it now is, it being as late as 1896, in primeval forest. Was chairman of the commission whose duty it was to survey the new county of Saluda, and locate the county seat, and was the first mayor of Saluda. The Etheredges are of English descent, and from Oxfordshire, England. Among those to whom James, King of England, granted the Charter of Virginia, in the year 1609, was one George Etheredge, Gentleman, who was the first of the name in this country and settled at, or near, Fairfax Court-house, Virginia. Several of the family came to South Carolina about the year 1750, and to Samuel Etheredge, was granted a tract of land in South Carolina, September 23, 1754, in Craven County; and a second grant was obtained, in 1772, on waters of Red Bank Creek, Colleton County, which land is now owned by Alvin Etheredge. August 22, 1883, he married Jenny Hammond, of Worcester, Massachusetts, who is one of the descendants of William Hammond, of London, County Kent, who married Elizabeth Penn, sister of Admiral Sir William Penn, and an aunt of William Penn the Quaker. From these are also descended the family of Governor Hammond of South Carolina.

EVANS, BARNARD BEE.—Third son of General N. G. Evans and Ann Victoria Gary. Was born on the 14th of September, 1865, at Cokesbury, Abbeville County, South Carolina. President of the South Carolina Mutual Fire Insurance Company, and manager of the Union Mutual Life Insurance Company. First assistant Money Order Bureau, Department of Post, Havana, Cuba, 1899, under American occupation. Government appointed him junior warden, and one of the organizers of the first English speaking lodge of Masons, in Cuba, at Havana. Major of the first South Carolina Brigade. He has always been prominent in local and State politics. He is now practicing law at Edgefield, South Carolina.

EVANS, JAMES DR.—Was born in Marion, South Carolina, September 12, 1831. He was educated at the South Carolina Military Academy. From there, went to Arkansas, as a civil engineer, afterwards being appointed, by the governor, as State engineer in charge of the levees, This position he held until 1859, when he decided to study medicine, and went to the University of Pennsylvania. He was graduated from there, in 1861, and immediately entered the Confederate States service, first in the hospital, and then as surgeon in the front; served until the close of the war. After the war, he returned to South Carolina, and settled in Marion County, removing to Florence, in 1878. He is a member of the South Carolina Medical Association, and was elected president. In 1888, he was elected a member of the State board of health, and in 1894, elected secretary of that body, which position he still holds. Member of the American Medical Association and the Southern Surgical and Gynaecological Association. Elected a member of the American Social Science Association.

EVANS, JOHN GARY.—Was born at Cokesbury, in Abbeville County, South Carolina, on the 15th day of October, 1863. He was the second son of General Nathan George Evans and Ann Victoria Evans (nee Gary). Nathan George Evans was born at Marion, South Carolina, on the 15th of September, 1827. He entered Randolph-Macon College, in Virginia. Was subsequently appointed a cadet at West Point, by John C. Calhoun; then United States Senator from South Carolina. He graduated from West Point, in 1848, and was shortly afterwards made a captain in the Second Dragoons. He gained renown as an Indian fighter, and was awarded a sword by the State of South Carolina for gallantry in the batte of Wichita. In this fight General Evans killed the Indian Chief in a hand to hand combat, capturing his head-dress used as a flag, and the bow and arrow and spear. After Carolina seceded, Captain Evans offered his services to his State. He was made a colonel, and, before the first battle of Manassas, a brigadier-general. At the First Manassas, he distinguished himself at the defense of Stone Bridge, holding in check, with his small force of five thou_ sand men, the entire Division of McDowell, numbering over seventeen thousand; this action saved the day to the Confederates. He was the hero of Balls Bluff or Leesburg, and for his gallantry in this battle, was thanked, a second time by his State; and awarded a gold medal by the General Assembly, the only one of its kind ever presented. He died, in 1869, leaving his widow and four children, all of whom now reside in South Carolina. Ann Victoria Gary, the mother of John Gary Evans, was born at Cokesbury, Abbeville, County, South Carolina, on the 15th of September, 1837. She was the daughter of Dr. Thomas R. Gary, a distinguished and representative citizen of the county, and Mary Ann Porter who was a descendant of John Knox and kinswoman of John Witherspoon, the signer of the Declaration of Independence. Both branches of this family are distinguished for their prominence in political and business. affairs of South Carolina. The Evanses, Garys and Witherspoons having been represented in every war of the United States, and having been members of every important convention of South Carolina. John Gary Evans attended the Cokesbury Conference School, a celebrated preparatory school for the old South Carolina College. He afterwards went to Union College, Schenectady, New York, entering the class of 1883. He was elected class president, in his junior year, and was the youngest member of his class by several years. Upon the death of his distinguished uncle and guardian, General Martin W. Gary, Evans left college just before his graduation, and entered the law office of his uncle Major William T. Gary, at Augusta, Georgia. In 1887, he opened an office at Aiken, South Carolina, for the practice of law. In 1888, he was elected a member of the Legislature, from Aiken County; and again returned, in 1890. He was identified with all the important measures before that body, and introduced a bill repealing the old Civil Rights Law which was intended to humiliate the white people of

10

the State by the carpet-bag government. He introduced
the resolution calling a Constitutional Convention. In 1892,
he was elected to the State Senate, from Aiken County, for
the term of four years; but served only two, having received
the nomination of his party for governor, in 1894. He was
elected to succeed Governor Tillman, and his administration
was a stormy one, as the Dispensary Law, which he had
fathered while a member of the Senate, was being fought
most bitterly by the opposition. An effort was also made
to set aside the law, calling a Constitutional Convention,
and the United States courts were appealed to by the Republicans and the opponents of the Dispensary Law. Judge Nathan Goff took great pleasure in granting an injunction
against the governor and State officials which brought forth
from Governor Evans a scathing denunciation of the Judge
and his allies, and the statement that "The Constitutional
Convention would be held, Judge or no Judge"; and it was
held, and South Carolina elected Governor Evans president
of the Convention. This Constitution has been attacked by
the Republican party for the reason that it disfranchised
the negro; but the Supreme Court of the United States sustained it; and its practical operation and effect has been to
disfranchise 200,000 ignorant negro voters, and to place the
State forever in control of the intelligent, and property-own-
ing citizens. Governor Evans was opposed to the waging
of the War against Spain, but after it was declared by Congress, he offered his services to the president in any capacity he might see fit to accept them. He was commissioned
a major, and assigned to duty as inspector general on the
staff of Major Keifer, of General Lee's Seventh Corps. Upon
reaching Cuba, Major Evans was detached from the Seventh
Army Corps, and attached to the staff of Major General Wm.
Ludlow, governor of the department of Havana. He assisted
in organizing the civil government of Havana and instituted
the first court, on the Island, formed upon American ideas
and principles. Upon the expiration of his term, he returned to South Carolina, and is now engaged in the practice of law, at Spartanburg, South Carolina. On the 15th
of December, 1897, he married Emily Mansfield Plume,

daughter of Honorable David S. Plume of Waterbury, Connecticut, an influential manufacturer and banker as well as statesman. Governor Evans has a daughter, Emily Victoria, born August 10, 1899. He is a member of the Spartan City and Elks Clubs of Spartanburg, the Commercial Club of Augusta, the Waterbury Club of Waterbury, Connecticut, and the Union College Alumni of New York.

EVANS, NATHAN GEORGE.—A prominent member of the Edgefield bar. Was born March 14, 1861, at Cokesbury, Abbeville County, South Carolina. He attended Wofford College, preparatory to entering Union College, Schenectady, New York. He was a member of the House of Representatives from Edgefield County, 1899 to 1900; and mayor of the town of Edgefield four years. Read law, under General M. W. Gary and Judge Earnest Gary. Was admitted to the bar, in June, 1884, and practiced at Edgefield under the firm name of Gary & Evans. The firm was dissolved by the election of Judge Gary to the bench, and Mr. Evans has continued the practice alone. Married Elizabeth Walker, September 25th, 1901.

EWART, WILLIAM CAMERON.—Pastor of Associate Reformed Presbyterian Church, in Lancaster, South Carolina, and also Shiloh. Son of R. Knox Ewart. Born September 19, 1864, at Huntersville, North Carolina. Attended the Huntersville High School until prepared for college. Entered Erskine College, taking theological and literary courses at same time. Married Miss Lucia W. Reid, October 19, 1892. Most of boyhood was spent on a farm, or as clerk in a village store.

EZELL, SAMUEL BRYSON.—Merchant at Spartanburg, South Carolina. Son of Rev. John S. Ezell. Born February 8, 1847, near Algood Post-office, six miles northwest of Limestone Springs, in Spartanburg County. He was reared on a farm. Attended the neighborhood schools. He entered the service of the Confederacy, July, 1864, joining Company D, Second Battalion South Carolina Reserves, and was appointed battalion guide with rank of sergeant. He spent the first half of 1867, in the New Prospect Academy, and the lat-

ter half of the year in teaching a school at Algood Seminary.
In the summeh of 1868, he was appointed deputy sheriff of
Spartanburg County, under Sheriff John Dewberry. He held
this position until the fall of 1872, when he resigned to enter
Wofford College. In June, 1875, was graduated from that institution. On August 11, of the same year, was married to
Laura Maxwell, of Spartanburg. About the first of 1876, he
embarked in the mercantile business in Spartanburg, which
he has pursued until the present. Director in Central National Bank, Spartanburg Savings Bank, and the Home Building and Loan Association, of Spartanburg. For a number
of years trustee of the city school. He is, at present, on
the board of trustees of Limestone College, and Converse
College. He is a member of the First Baptist Church of
Spartanburg, which he has served in various capacities, including those of clerk, deacon and superintendent of the
Sunday-school, for the past twenty-five years. He usually
attends, as a delegate, the county, State and national conventions.

FAISON, JULIUS ALEXANDER.—Practicing physician at
Bennettsville. Son of W. W. and Elizabeth A. Faison. Born
at Faison, North Carolina, April 15, 1850. Lived in North
Carolina, until 1894, when he removed to Bennettsville, South
Carolina. Educated under private tutors, and at Trinity
College, North Carolina, and graduated in medicine from the
Jefferson Medical College, Philadelphia. Married Laura J.
Keer, of Sampson County, North Carolina. Assistant physi-
cian at the Hospital for the Insane, at Raleigh, from 1894,
to 1897. Taught school and kept books before beginning
the practice of medicine. Member of the American Medical
Association of the North Carolina Medical Association, and
also of the South Carolina Medical Association.

FANT, HANDY BRUCE.—Senior partner of the grocery
firm of H. B. Fant & Son. Was born in Chattooga County,
Georgia, on April 11, 1846. His parents returned to South
Carolina while he was an infant. He attended the Anderson Military School during the Civil War, and after the war,
went to the Anderson High School taught by Messrs. Hillhouse and Sloan. Married Eugenia Mary Carlisle, June 22,

1871. He was agent of the Blue Ridge Railroad, at Anderson, during the latter years of the Civil War. Was conductor on train between Columbia and Greenville, several years. In 1870, entered the agency office, at Anderson, under his father, who was then agent, and, in 1873, he succeeded him, as agent, and held that position until 1891. In the year 1878, he was licensed to preach the gospel, by the Anderson Baptist Church. In 1884, he was ordained; and since that time has been pastor of various churches, but at present has no charge.

FANT, JOHN A.—President of the Monarch Cotton Mills of Union, South Carolina, since its organization. He is a son of David J. Fant. Was born April 22, 1857, at Santuc, Union County, South Carolina. Attended school until sixteen years of age, and then began clerking, afterwards became bookkeeper. In 1883, he went into business, on his own account, with a capital of one thousand dollars, and in twenty years has accumulated a fortune of about one hundred thousand dollars. He is a director in the Merchants and Planters Bank at Union; of Union Oil Mill; and of Union Cotton Mills, since organization of each. He was three times elected mayor of Union. Chairman of board of trustees of Union Graded Schools; also, of Furman University, Greenville, South Carolina, and of the Greenville Female College. He is president of Building and Loan Association of Union, South Carolina. He married Miss Ora Wilkes, of Union, on the 27th of April, 1881.

FEATHERSTONE, CLAUDIUS CYPRIAN.—At present engaged in the practice of law, at Laurens, South Carolina. He was born in that county on December 1, 1864. His education was acquired under the instruction of Professor W. J. Ligon, at Anderson, South Carolina. Married Miss Lulu, daughter of Rev. J. D. Pitts, of Laurens, South Carolina, October 10, 1893.

FICKEN, JOHN F.—Served in the House of Representatives, as a member from Charleston County, seven successive terms, and resigned, in 1891, to accept the position as mayor of Charleston, which position he held for one full term of four years, and declined re-election. He was born, on the 16th of June, 1843, in Charleston, South Carolina. Obtained his education from the public schools of Charleston, and graduated from the College of Charleston. Subsequently studied at the University of Berlin, Germany. Served in the Confederate army. Was admitted to the bar, in 1868, and has practiced continuously since. Was a member of the board of commissioners, of the South Carolina Institution for the education of the deaf, dumb, and blind. Trustee of Newberry College, and also of the Medical College of the State of South Carolina. Vice-President of board of trustees of the College of Charleston. Is one of the directors and also of the general council of the South Carolina Interstate and West Indian Exposition.

FINLEY, DAVID EDWARD.—Congressman. Was born at Trenton, Arkansas, February 28, 1861.

Since September, 1865, has resided in York County, South Carolina. Was educated in the schools of Rock Hill and Ebenezer, South Carolina, and the South Carolina College. Served two years as a member of the House of Representatives of South Carolina, and elected to the Senate, in 1892, to 1896. Was chairman of the Committee on Ways and Means. Was a member ·of the Judiciary Committee, and chairman of the Finance Committee. Since 1890, has been a trustee of the South Carolina University. Was elected to the Fifty-Sixth Congress without opposition.

FISHBURNE, FRANCIS CHALMERS.—Son of Robert Fishburne and Harriet Chalmers. Grandson of General Wm.

Fishburne, of Revolutionary fame, who was general in
command of Charleston, during the War of 1812. F. C. Fishburne was born in Charleston, October 8, 1849. Of Scotch
descent. Obtained education in city schools of Charleston,
Military School at Athens, Georgia, and Mount Zion College,
of Winnsboro, South Carolina. He entered the service of
the Confederacy, in 1864, Company H, Fifth Regiment Cavalry, Butler's Brigade; and remained until the close of the
war, being the youngest of six brothers in the field. Married Miss Susan C. Neyle, daughter of Colonel Charles F.
Neyle, December 19, 1872. After the close of the war he
engaged in rice planting. For about twenty years engaged
in mining phosphate rock, and met with much success.
Vice-president of Georgia Chemical Works, at Augusta, and
Pon Pon, South Carolina. Took an active part in the campaign of 1876, in Colleton County. In 1878, elected to House
of Representatives from Colleton County. Appointed clerk
of the court of Charleston County. Owns a controlling interest in the Atlantic Woodenware Company, and is now
president and treasurer of the company. Was on the staff
of General B. H. Rutledge of the Fourth Brigade Militia, during Hampton's administration, with rank of major.

FLOYD, JOHN.—Born at Darlington, South Carolina, on
the 20th day of January, 1836. He is
a son of the late Captain W. J. Floyd,
of Darlington, South Carolina, and a
grandson of Buckner Floyd, of Virginia. His early education was obtained in the common schools of the
county, and later attended St. John's
Academy, Darlington, South Carolina.
He volunteered as a soldier in the
Confederate war, and was third sergeant in the Darlington Guards. After the surrender of Fort Sumter, the
company disbanded, and several new
companies were raised, by volunteers, from the old. Among
the companies raised, was the Darlington Rifles, John Floyd

was first-lieutenant, and when the resignation of Captain J. W. Norwood was tendered, he was promoted to captain. He was several times wounded, and at the "blow up" on the Crater, he was officer of the day, of his regiment, the Eighteenth South Carolina Volunteers, and was knocked down, and covered up with earth and debris. Extricating himself from the debris, he, with the assistance of Adjutant Sims and Lieutenant Anderson, gathered as many men (about fifty) as could be spared from the regiment, and threw them in the breach and held the lines for twenty minutes, in a hand-to-hand fight, against fearful odds, until General Elliott could rearrange his lines for defense. At least half of the men had been killed before they got to the Cross Ditch, the latter having already been occupied by Colonel Elliott's troops. After the war, was married to Miss Fannie A. Bland, and went into the mercantile business. He has held many offices of trust. Was elected to the Legislature, from his county, in 1898 and 1899. Now lives in Darlington, where he was born and raised.

FLOYD, L. WASH.—Son of J. N. Floyd and Louise Anderson, of Newberry County. Born on the 23d of December, 1860, in the western portion of Newberry County. He attended the local schools, and remained two years at Patrick Military Institute; after which, he took a six months' course at the Bryant and Sadler's Business College, Baltimore, Maryland. Married Miss Ola Clark, October 23, 1889. He was engaged in the mercantile business from 1888, to 1899, under the firm name of Floyd & Purcell. He is president, treasurer, and manager of the Newberry Oil and Fertilizer Company, a director of Building and Investment Company of Newberry, a director of Commercial Bank, and the Land and Security Company, Newberry, South Carolina. He built and owns the Newberry Telephone Exchange, the Prosperity Exchange, and the Clinton Telephone Exchange, Clinton, South Caroline.

FOLK, HENRY CALHOUN.—Master in equity of Bamburg County. Born December 4, 1859, at Forks Store, Colleton County, South Carolina. Attended the common country schools, until the age of fourteen, then entered Wofford College, graduating therefrom, in 1880. Won the Kappa Alpha gold medal for the best essay in an intercollegiate contest; elected annual debater, and received several class honors. Married M. Elizabeth Weissinger of Blacksburg, South Carolina, April 12, 1883. Since graduation has been engaged in mercantile pursuits, and farming at Bamberg, South Carolina. Prominent in the organization of Bamberg County, and has been chairman of the Democratic Convention, since its organization. Member of the Legislature, two terms, from Barnwell County. Has served Bamberg, as alderman, and mayor, and secretary and treasurer of the Commissioners of Public Buildings. Trustee of the Carlisle Fit: ting School and vice-president and director of the Bamberg Cotton Mill. Was chairman of the board of commissioners to effect a division between the old County of Barnwell, and the new County of Bamberg, and performed his duty to the satisfaction of all concerned.

FOOSHE, JAMES FRANKLIN.—Editor of the Carolina "Teacher's Journal," four years. Son of James Fuller and Mary Fuller Fooshe. Born at Coronaco, South Carolina, November 11, 1871. He attended Wofford Fitting School four years; then entered Wofford College, graduating, in 1892, with Bachelor of Arts degree. Took Master of Arts degree, in 1893. Taught school eight years after graduation, the last two years, as assistant principal of the Mount Zion School, Winnsboro. He is also editor of the "News and Herald," of Winnsboro. Appointed a commissioner of the South Carolina and West Indian Exposition, of Fairfield County. Also secretary of the Fairfield Agricultural Society.

FORD, RUFUS.—Pastor of the Baptist Church at Bennettsville, South Carolina. Son of E. B. and Anna J. Herring Ford. Born August 22, 1852, in Marion County, South Carolina. Of English and Scotch descent. Attended Wake Forest College, North Carolina, and then took the course at the Southern Baptist Theological Seminary, at Louisville, Kentucky. Married Miss Hattie Temple, of Wake County, North Carolina, April 6, 1880. After leaving college in 1878, settled in Marlboro and supplied a country church. From 1890, to 1895, pastor of a church at Newberry, North Carolina. For several years, he was chairman of the board of trustees, of the Marlboro Graded Schools, and corresponding editor of the "Pee Dee Advocate."

FORRESTER, ELDRED JOHN.—Pastor of Baptist Church, at Greenwood, South Carolina. A native of Hampton County. Born on November 14, 1853. Graduated from Furman University, with the degree of Bachelor of Arts, in 1876; and graduated from the Southern Baptist Theological Seminary, in 1878. Has been pastor of churches continuously since, and is now pastor of the Greenwood Church. Degree of Doctor of Divinity conferred by Furman University, in 1893. Author of a book on "Distinctive Baptist Principles." Married Miss Margaret L. Dargan, January 6, 1885.

FRASER, THOMAS BOONE.—Member of the Legislature, from Sumter County. Son of Judge T. B. Fraser and Sarah M. McIver. Born June 2, 1860, at Sumter, South Carolina. Prepared for college by W. T. Rhame, and graduated from Davidson College, in 1881. Read law under his father, and admitted to the bar, in 1883. Married Emma Edmunds, daughter of Rev. N. W. Edmunds, D. D., December 16, 1886.

FREEMAN, ROBERT LAWRENCE.—Born near Red Hill, in Marlboro County, South Carolina, January 1, 1871. Worked on a farm, and attended the country schools, and the Marlboro Graded Schools, at Bennettsville, from 1886, to 1889. Entered the Wake Forest College, North Carolina, in the fall of 1890, and graduated, in 1894. One of the graduating speakers, in 1894. Taught school after leaving college, and was elected county superintendent of education, in 1896. Served two terms, and was elected to the House of Representatives, in 1900. He is also a surveyor. Since

May, 1900, has been editor and publisher of the "Pee Dee Advocate." Published the "Marlboro School Bulletin," in 1899 and 1900. Member of the house education committee.

FRETWELL, JOSEPH JOHN.—President of the Peoples Bank, at Anderson, South Carolina. Was born near Anderson, March 21, 1850. Attended the old field schools until sixteen years of age. Later was under the instruction of W. J. Ligon, who taught in Anderson, South Carolina. Married Mary C., daughter of Sylvester Bleckley, January 21, 1879. Manager of the firm of Bleckley, Brown and Fretwell. President of Furman's Oil Mill, and the Building and Loan Association of Anderson. He was connected, in business, with Sylvester Bleckley, for more than twenty years.

FRIDAY, JAMES MARION.—A minister of the Methodist Episcopal Church South. Was born February 18, 1855, cn Cedar Creek, Upper Richland County, South Carolina. Graduated at Wofford College, in 1879. Studied for the ministry, and has had charge of various churches. Is now pastor of the Methodist Church, at Clinton, South Carolina. Married Miss Rabb, from Fairfield County, on December 23, 1880.

FROST, FRANK RAVENEL.—Son of Elias Horry and Frances Ravenel Frost. Was born at Society Hill, South Carolina, October 17, 1863. His father was a large merchant of Charleston. F. R. Frost's earlier training was received from private schools in Charleston, and Sewanee, Tennessee. He was fitted for college under private tutors, at Cambridge, Massachusetts; and graduated from Harvard University, in 1886, with degree of A. B. Read law in the office of Smythe and Lee, of Charleston, and was admitted to the bar, in 1888. He is at present a member of the firm of Smythe, Lee and Frost. He is also a member of various boards, political, charitable, and otherwise. Trustee of Porter Military Academy. During Spanish-American War, he held a captain's commission, in the Third Regiment, United States Volunteer Infantry.

FROST, JOHN D.—Assistant adjutant and inspector general of South Carolina. Was born six miles from Columbia, South Carolina, February 11, 1871. Attended the Graded and High Schools ot Columbia, and graduated from the South Carolina Military Academy, at Charleston, in the class of 1891. Married Miss Mary Irvine Davis, of Paris, Kentucky, on November 28, 1900. Bookkeeper and cotton buyer, from 1891, to 1898. Appointed regimental adjutant First South Carolina Volunteer Infantry, in Spanish-American War, May 3, 1898. Promoted to major, October 21, 1898. Mustered out, November 10, 1898, at Columbia, South Carolina. He is a cotton buyer, and receiver for Olympia, Granby and Richland Mills, of Columbia. Colonel Frost is an ardent military man, and his friends predict for him still greater honors as such.

FURMAN, CHARLES MANNING.—Professor of English in Clemson College. Was born in Darlington County, South Carolina, July 8, 1840. Son of Rev. J. C. Furman, D. D. He was educated at the high school of Charleston, and Furman University, from which institution he was graduated, in 1859. Read law, in Charleston, until May, 1861. Then enlisted in Palmetto Guard, Second South Carolina Volunteers (Kershaw's Regiment). Served in Virginia, from Bull Run to Sharpsburg; transferred to an artillery company on the coast, in December, 1862; elected lieutenant in Company H, Sixteenth South Carolina, in July, 1863. Soon promoted to captaincy. Served, until the war closed, with Army of the West, under Bragg, Johnston, and Hood. After the war, he engaged in teaching, one year, in Maryland, and eight years at Bethel College, Kentucky. He returned to South Carolina, in 1877, and practiced law, in Greenville, until elected to the position he now holds. He was appointed assistant

United States district attorney, under Cleveland's administration, in 1886.

FURMAN, JOHN H.—President of the Sumter County Agricultural Society. Was born March 19, 1824, near Coosawatchee, Beaufort County, South Carolina. Son of Samuel Furman, D. D., a noted scholar and educator, of his day. Was educated by his father, and accompanied him to Europe, where he passed several years in the city of Edinburgh. Upon returning to America, he determined to pursue the study of medicine, and graduated from the Charleston Medical College, in 1845. He had a large practice, and succeeded so well in combating that fell disease of a newly settled country, bilious remittent fever, that he was given the sobriquet of the "Fever Wizard." His health failing, he partially withdrew from practice, and returned to Sumter County, South Carolina, and engaged in farming. After the war, when the Order of Patrons of Husbandry spread like a tidal wave through the State, he built up "Cavalry Grange," the banner grange of middle Carolina, and was for three consecutive terms, its master. Also master of the Pomona Grange, of Clarendon County. He was one of the organizers of the Agricultural and Mechanical Society, of South Carolina. He was twice married; first, to Miss Eliza Carter, in 1845; then to Miss Susan Emma Nestor, of Sumter, South Carolina.

FURMAN, McDONALD.—Son of Dr. John H. and Mrs Susan E. (Miller) Furman. Born March 1, 1863, in the Privateer Section, of Sumter County, South Carolina. His early education was obtained in the common schools of the neighborhood. He then entered the Greenville Military Institute, remaining there, until 1882, when he entered the South Carolina College. While there was one of the editors of the college magazine. He is a member of the Southern Historical Association, of South Carolina, and the Historical Society. Has several times been a member of the County Democratic Conventions. He is the originator of the Columbia, South Carolina, Centennial, held in 1891, and the

George Bancroft Centennial, held in 1900. Mr. Furman is an author, and lecturer on historical subjects. Never married.

GADSDEN, CHRISTOPHER. S.—Third vice-president of the Atlantic Coast Line, Savannah and Florida Railroad, and superintendent of Charleston and Savannah railroad thirty-four years. He was born, August 15, 1834, in Summerville, Colleton County, South Carolina. Attended private schools taught by his father, Rev. Philip Gadsden. Graduate of South Carolina Military Academy, 1852. Chairman of board of visitors of South Carolina Military Academy. Alderman of the city of Charleston for eighteen years. Married Miss Florida I. Morrall, in May, 1861. Began life as a rodman in engineering corps of Northern Ohio and Great Northern Railway.

GADSDEN, JOHN, M. A.—Professor of history and economics in the College of Charleston, South Carolina. He was born in Summerville, South Carolina, May 31, 1833. He is a son of Rev. Philip Gadsden and Susan Branford Hamilton. On his father's side, he is a great-grandson of General Charles Gadsden, of Revolutionary fame, and by his mother, a grandson of Paul Hamilton, governor of South Carolina in 1804, and secretary of the navy under Madison. He was prepared for the College of Charleston by his father, in 1849; but by advice of his uncle, Bishop C. E. Gadsden, transferred, in 1851, to the College of St. James, Maryland. There he was graduated with the honor of his class, in 1853, and retained, till 1856, as principal of the grammar school there. Returning to his native State, in 1856, he married, April 14, 1857, Miss Julia E., daughter of the late John Boyle. From his graduation to the present time he has been continuously engaged in teaching first at the College of St. James; then in private schools, until 1867. After that, principal of what is now the Porter Military Academy, from 1867 to 1885, and from 1889, to 1893, headmaster of the Grammar School, Sewanee, Tennessee. He is, at present, professor of economics in College of Charleston. In the intervals noted above, he conducted his own school, modeled after the classical schools once so popular in Charleston.

GAGE, GEORGE WILLIAM.—Son of Robert J. and Martha
(Williams) Gage. His ancestors were of Scotch-Irish descent, and came to Union County, from Pennsylvania, about
1802. George W. Gage was born in Union County, South
Carolina, near Fair Forest Creek, February 4, 1856. His
early training was acquired from the public schools, graduating from Wofford College, in 1875. Entered the law department of Vanderbilt University, September, 1879, completing
the course in June, 1880, taking Founder's medal for law.
Before entering Vanderbilt University, he was engaged in
banking in Charleston three years, removed to Chester, in
1878, where, in 1880, he was married to Miss Janie Gaston,
daughter of Captain J. Lucius Gaston, of Chester County.
Member of the Constitutional Convention of 1895, and the
Legislature, in 1897 and 1898. Elected circuit judge, in 1898,
which office he still holds.

GALLOWAY, WILLIAM LEONARD.—Practicing physician
of Darlington County. Son of Isaiah and Eliza Hudson Galloway. Born at Lydia, Darlington County, South Carolina,
June 28, 1841. Of Scotch-Irish descent. Ancestors settled
in that county, about 1800. Education was acquired from
the common and high schools and from Memphis Medical
College, where he graduated, in 1869. Married Desdemonia,
daughter of James Jacobs, of Georgetown, South Carolina,
September 30, 1869. Member of the city board of health
several years; surgeon to board of pensioners in this county,
since pension law was established. Entered the Confederate army, April 15, 1861, as private in Company F, Eighth
South Carolina Volunteers. Served in said company, until
February, 1862; then, when company was re-organized, in
1862, he was elected lieutenant of Company M, Eighth South
Carolina Volunteers. Served in that company until July,
1862, when he lost his right foot, at Malvern Hill. He is
still practicing medicine at Darlington.

GALLUCHAT, MINOR CLINTON.—Son of Joseph Gallu-
chat, of Clarendon County, and Rebecca Gill, of Lancaster
County. His grandfather was Joseph Galluchat of South
Carolina Conference, the only one of that name who ever

came to this country. He was a French-Huguenot from St. Domingo, landed at Charleston, South Carolina, in 1796; left only one son, Joseph, father of Minor Clinton Gullachat. The subject of this sketch was born March 6, 1856, at Lancaster Court-house, South Carolina. Had the advantage of the common schools, and one year at Wofford College. Read law, and was admitted to the bar in 1882. Elected to Legislature in 1900. Member of city executive committee, 1890 and 1892. Has been in nearly all Democratic conventions since, from Clarendon County. Married Miss Thomasia Woodson Thompson, of Orangeburg, South Carolina, January 31, 1878.

GAMBLE, WILLIAM GADSDEN, M. D.—Practicing physician of Kingstree, South Carolina. Second son of J. P. Gamble and Martha J. Graham. Born near Gourdins, in Williamsburg County, South Carolina, in 1869. Obtained education from private schools, one year at Citadel, Charleston; and graduated from South Carolina College, in 1891, with degree of B. S. Graduated in medicine from Charleston Medical College, in 1894. Married Cornelia Boyd Gourdin, February 14, 1895.

GAMEWELL, JOSEPH AUGUSTUS.—A native of North Carolina. Born at Rutherfordton, January 3, 1850. He entered Wofford College, and graduated, in June, 1871. He has devoted his life to the profession of teaching. Was for one year, principal of the Green Brier High School, Kentucky, and also principal of the High School for boys at Mount Sterling, Kentucky. Since 1875, he has been connected with Wofford College, first as principal of the preparatory department, and later, as professor of Latin. He was married, on the 17th of September, 1879, to Julia Adelaide, daughter of Dr. J. A. McDowell, of Asheville, North Carolina. He is now filling the chair of Latin in Wofford College.

GANTT, ROBERT JOSEPH.—Son of T. Larry and Telitha Anna (Johnson) Gantt. Born in Elbert County, Georgia, April 8, 1872. Received his earlier education at Mason Academy, Lexington, Georgia, and in public schools of Athens, Georgia. Graduated from University of Georgia, with degree of Bachelor of Engineering 1893. Accepted a position in government service, in Washington, District of Columbia, and while thus engaged, graduated at Georgetown College, with the degree of Bachelor of Law, 1896. Removed to Spartanburg, and entered firm of Ravenel & Gantt, attorneys at law. Elected to Legislature, from Spartanburg County, 1898, and served one term. Appointed member of commission to complete South Carolina State House, 1900.

GARDNER, GEORGE WILLIAM.—Son of Dempsey and Elizabeth Gardner. Was born in Orangeburg County, August 5, 1851. Graduated at Furman University, Greenville, South Carolina, in 1876; and at the Baptist Theological Seminary, 1878. He has had in charge several churches in this State, Georgia, and Mississippi. The degree of Doctor of Divinity was conferred, in 1893. He is managing editor of the "South Carolina Baptist." A member of the firm of Pittman & Gardner, publishers and owners of the "South Carolina Baptist" and the "Greenwood Journal" of Greenwood, South Carolina. He married Miss Sudie Shelor, January 18, 1898.

GARLINGTON, ERNEST A.—Was born at Newberry, South Carolina, February 23, 1853. He entered the University of Georgia, in 1870. Left this institution, in 1872, to accept an appointment to the United States Military Academy, from which institution he graduated, in 1876, receiving his commission as second-lieutenant, June 15, 1864, and assigned to the Seventh Cavalry. Hearing that busy work was expected on the frontier, he at once joined his regiment and was engaged in the campaign against the Ney Percey Indians. He was promoted to first lieutenant, June 25, soon after joining his regiment, and served as adjutant of the

Seventh Cavalry, from June, 1877, to November, 1881. He was sent on the Arctic expedition for the relief of Greely, in 1883; but the expedition was a failure, in consequence of the destruction of the vessel, the Proteus, in an ice pack. After the Proteus was crushed by the ice, the party journeyed eight hundred miles in open boats, in the Arctic seas, before they were rescued by the Yantic, the naval vessel accompanying the expedition. He was made captain, in 1891; and, in 1895, was appointed major and inspector general, by President Cleveland, and assigned to duty in Washington, District of Columbia. During the Spanish War of 1898, he was inspector general of Cavalry Division of Cuba, and took an active part in battles around Santiago. In 1899, he was sent to the Philippines as inspector general of the Department of the Pacific and Eighth Army Corps. He was made colonel, in March, 1901. Is, at present, serving as inspector general Division of the Philippines stationed at Manila. Was awarded a medal of Honor for distinguished gallantry in action against hostile Indians, on Wounded Knee Creek, South Dakota, December 29, 1890, where he was severely wounded. Married Miss Anna Buford, of Rock Island, Illinois, August 17, 1886.

GARY, EUGENE BLACKBURN.—Associate justice of the Supreme Court of South Carolina. Born at Cokesbury, South Carolina, August 27, 1854. After attending the schools at that place until 1872, he entered the South Carolina College, and graduated in the classical branches. At the age of eighteen, he began the study of law under his uncle, General Mart W. Gary, of Edgefield. Was admitted to the bar a few weeks after attaining his majority. After graduating at the South Carolina College, he taught school, for one year, at Hodges. He began the practice of law, at Abbeville, South Carolina, where he continued until 1894, attaining a front rank in his profession, being engaged in nearly every case of importance tried in Abbeville and the surrounding counties. In 1881, when General Carlos J. Stolbrand contested the election of the Honorable D. Wyatt Aiken for Congress, Mr. Gary represented Colonel Aiken, and succeeded in seating his client. He was for many years county chairman of the Democratic party in Abbeville County, his election being unanimous. He was a member of the State Democratic Executive Committee for several years. He served one term in the Legislature, and there gained an enviable reputation. His work on the floor of the House calling him the next year to become lieutenant governor of the State, to which office he was re-elected. While serving in his second term as lieutenant governor, he was elected associate justice of the Supreme Court, in which capacity he is now serving his State with dignity and ability, having just been re-elected. He married Miss Eliza Tusten, a direct descendant of the Honorable Benjamin Tusten, member of the first Colonial Congress of New York, whose son Benjamin, was a colonel in the Revolutionary War. Colonel Benjamin Tusten was killed while leading his regiment in the fight for American independence, and his brave deeds are commemorated by a monument erected by the public at Boshen, New York. Justice Gary's mother was Miss Mary Carolina Blackburn, a lineal descendant of William Blackburn, a hero of the battle of King's Mountain. His father was Dr. F. S. Gary, an eminent physician, who held many positions of trust. On his father's side he is a lineal descendant of John Witherspoon, who was born near Glasgow, Scotland, in 1670, and suffered persecution during the time of the Stuarts. John Witherspoon was a grandson of Mrs. Lucia Welch, the grandmother of John Knox, who married a lineal descendant of Robert Bruce, of Scotland. He is a member of very distinguished family in this State. His only brothers are Judge Ernest Gary, judge of the Fifth Circuit, and Honorable Frank B. Gary, who was for many years speaker of the House of Representatives. His only sister is Mrs. James M. Eason, of Charleston.

GARY, FRANK BOYD.—Born at Cokesbury, on the 9th of March, 1860. His early education was obtained in the Cokesbury Conference School. Afterwards entered Union College, Schenectady, New York, where he remained for three years, graduating, in 1881. Married Miss Maria Lee

Evans, January 6th, 1897. He was elected to the House of Representatives, in 1890, serving continuously until 1901, but was not a candidate for re-election. He held the position as speaker of the House, upon retiring; was also a member of the Constitutional Convention of 1895. He is trustee of the city schools of Abbeville, South Carolina. A member of the board of trustees that located and built Winthrop College at Rock Hill, South Carolina. He holds the position as high priest of Hesperian Chapter Number 17, Royal Arch Masons and past master of Clinton Lodge Number 3, Accepted Free Masons. Is also a member of Columbia Commandery Number 2, Knights Templars, and of Oasis Temple of Shriners, at Charlotte, North Carolina.

GASQUE, ELI H.—Son of Henry and Harriett Porter Gasque. Born May 8, 1834, at Marion, South Carolina. Only a common school education. Twice married, first to Sarah C. Shaw; his second wife was Sarah F. Foxworth, of Marion, South Carolina, whom he married in 1883. Entered the Confederate War, May, 1861, as private, joining the Eighth Mississippi. Promoted to first-lieutenant in the army of Tennessee. In most of the battles, fought under Bragg, Hood and Johnston. Twice wounded. After the war closed, went into the mercantile business in Marion County. In 1870, moved to Marion Court-house, where he is still engaged in this line of business. Served as alderman and mayor of the town more than two terms. Secretary and treasurer of various corporations of the town and county. High priest of Marion Chapter, Royal Arch Masons, three terms; and worshipful master of Clinton Lodge Number 60, Accepted Free Masons, four years. Grand office in the Grand Chapter of South Carolina, several years, reaching as high as grand high priest. Steward in the Methodist Church for twenty-five years, and district steward eleven years.

GASTON, ARTHUR LEE.—Vice-president of Commercial Bank of Chester, South Carolina. Son of T. C. Gaston. Born August 14, 1876, at Chester, South Carolina. Ancestors were Scotch-Irish. Graduated with Bachelor of Arts

Degree from Davidson College, North Carolina. Studied one year, at University of Virginia, law, logic and literature. Read law under Judge Gage, and was admitted to bar, in 1898. Practiced under firm name of Caldwell and Gaston. Appointed first-lieutenant Company D, First South Carolina Volunteer Infantry. Member of House of Representatives of South Carolina.

GEER, BENNETT EUGENE.—Son of Solomon M. Geer and Mary (Holmes) Geer. Was born in Broadway Township, Anderson County, South Carolina, June 9, 1873. He was educated at the Neals Creek Academy, Anderson County; Belton High School; and graduated from Furman University, in 1896, with the degree of Master of Art. Took course at University of Michigan and University of Wisconsin. He is instructor in Greek and mathematics, at Furman University Preparatory School. Assistant professor of Latin in Furman University and professor of English. He married Miss Rena Rice, of Belton, South Carolina.

GEER, JOHN MATTISON.—Son of Solomon M. and Mary E. Geer. Was born near Belton, in Anderson County, May 15, 1858. Early educated in the common schools. Was two years at the University of Tennessee, at Nashville. He taught school a few terms, in early manhood; and, in 1881, engaged in the mercantile business, at Belton. He was connected with the cotton department of the Piedmont Manufacturing Company ten years, until he accepted the position of president and treasurer of the Easley Cotton Mills, which position he still holds. Married Miss Ella W. McGee, daughter of G. W. McGee, of Belton, South Carolina, November 21, 1888.

GEIGER, CHARLES B.—Physician at Manning, South Carolina. Son of Franklin J. and Anna E. Geiger. Born June 19, 1867, in Lexington County, South Carolina. His parents removed to the St. Matthews Section of Orangeburg County. He attended the country schools; and worked on the farm, and attended the public schools a few months during the winter. He prepared himself, by studying at night, to enter the South Carolina Medical College, in 1889, graduating therefrom, in 1892. Served one year as house physician and surgeon in St. Francis Xavier Infirmary, of Charleston. He then moved to Manning, South Carolina, where he has since resided, and practiced his profession.

GENTRY, JOHN JOSEPH.—Probate judge of Spartanburg County. Born June 15, 1866. in Spar-

tanburg, South Carolina. He took part in the campaign of 1876, and rode in the Democratic Red Shirt Procession, in the company with James Franklin, colored, an old negro who took charge of him on those occasions. He studied under Misses Mary and Mattie Gamewell; then attended the Academy taught by Mr. R. O. Sams, now superintendent of the graded schools of Gaffney. Graduated from Wofford College, in 1888, with degree of Bachelor of Art. He was a member of the Preston Literary Society. He then spent one year in the office of his father, who was sheriff; and at the same time studied law under the direction of Messrs. Bomar & Simpson. In the summer of 1899, took the summer law course at the University of Virginia, under Professor John B. Minor, and afterwards spent one year in the law department of that institution. In the summer of 1890, he went to Van Buren, Arkansas, where he formed a partnership with Messrs. Sandels & Warner. After spending one year in Van Buren, he went to Fort Smith, Arkansas, where he opened an office. Remained there until 1891, when he decided to locate in Spartanburg. In 1892, he was a candidate for master against H. B. Carlisle, the incumbent of that office, Mr. W. L. Tinsley and L. R. Hill. In this race, Mr. Gentry was defeated, and Mr. Hill elected. Mr. Gentry was then appointed trial justice, and held that position two years, being then elected to the position he now holds. Four years later, he was re-elected. He has been a member of the law firm of Mooney, Gentry & DePass, and is now senior member of the firm of Gentry & Depass. Member of the First Baptist Church of Spartanburg, a Mason, a Knight of Pythias and I. O. Red Man. In college, he was a member of the Preston Literary Society, chief marshall, and on annual debate in junior year.

GEORGE, SAMUEL B.—Clerk of the court of Lexington County. Born at Laurel Falls, near Lexington Court-house, July 27, 1871. Son of E. J. George and Beadia (Taylor) George. Attended school at Lexington, and completed the study of surveying under Professor Paul T. Brodie, now of Clemson College. December 19, 1892, he was appointed official deputy clerk of the court under H. A. Spann, and this position he held eight years. In the primary election, held August 28, 1900, he was elected clerk of the court of Lexington County. Although opposed by three men in this race, he received 1,911 votes out of the 3,027 cast. He is the twelfth clerk of the county since the court-house was moved from Old Granby, in 1819. He married Olga O. Hendrix, December 29, 1896.

GIBBES, ALEXANDER MASON.—Son of Major W. H. Gibbes, of Columbia. He was born December 11, 1877, at Columbia, South Carolina. He attended the graded schools of Columbia and spent a short time at the South Carolina College. At seventeen years of age, he left college to assist in the machinery business of W. H. Gibbes & Company, and in a few years became manager. By his robust business acumen he has developed an immense trade; and though a modest young man, working in his own sphere, he is, at the age of twenty-three, regarded as one of the soundest business men in the Capital City.

GIBBES, JAMES GUIGNARD.—Was born January 6, 1829, in Columbia, South Carolina. Graduated from the South Carolina College, in 1847; took a special course in mathematics and engineering at the South Carolina Military Acad-

emy, in Charleston. His first wife was Mary E. Mc-
Cullough, of Mobile, Alabama, whom he married on April
17, 1856. Married Mrs. Gilchrist, formerly Miss Waller, of
Greenwood, on August 8, 1870. In 1852, elected chief engineer of very important road in New Orleans, called the New
Orleans, Opelousas and Great Western, being the first road
built west of the Mississippi, now part of the Southern Pacific. Left there, in 1854, to build the Columbia and Augusta Road, which was not finished until after the war.
Was employed by Mr. Plant to build several lines in Florida
and Georgia after the war. About 1887, he was made chief
engineer of Pensacola and Mobile Road, now owned by the
Louisville and Nashville. During the Civil War he was sent
to Europe by the Confederate government, to negotiate a
Confederate cotton loan (associated with James Spence, the
English financial agent), in which he succeeded. He attended the marriage of the Prince of Wales. Colonel Gibbes
enlisted, but was immediately detailed to take charge of
his Saluda factory in order to make cloth for the Confederacy. He advanced one and a half million dollars in Confederate money, equivalent to $70,000 in gold, to Union of-
ficers confined in the State Lunatic Asylum, at General Win-
der's request to help the Confederacy. Not one single dollar of this money was ever repaid. Drafts given him by the
prisoners on their friends at home, were repudiated and ig-
nored. Was made mayor of Columbia the day after that
city was burnt by Sherman, holding office two years. Was
appointed collector of internal revenue, 1865 and 1866. In
the campaign of 1876, and 1880, he divided his time between
South Carolina and Florida, on the stump for the Democracy. Went to Florida, in 1870, to build railroads, and moved
back to Columbia, in 1890, and has been State land agent
ever since. He has put on the tax books a million acres of
land, that had been utterly unknown to the State, as its
property. At the time of the Civil War Colonel Gibbes was
enormously wealthy. He literally contributed millions to
help the Confederacy, and as much again in gifts and un-
secured loans, to private parties. In peace, politics, and
war, he has rendered South Carolina service.

GIBBES, ROBERT WILSON.—Physician. Was born in Quincy, Florida, August 20, 1872. He is a son of Colonel James G. Gibbes. Graduated from the South Carolina University, in 1892, and the South Carolina Medical College, in 1895. Married Ethel Dole Andrews, of Woodworth, Wisconsin, November 29, 1900. He is an honor-graduate of the South Carolina Medical College. Resident physician, Charleston City Hospital, from 1895 to 1896. He then located in Columbia, and enjoys a very large practice. He is third of a line of distinguished physicians of the same name.

GIBBES, THOMAS HASKELL.—Cashier of the Bank of Columbia. Born November 17, 1850, at Columbia, South Carolina. Graduated from the South Carolina College, in 1870. Married Eugenia Talley, December 2, 1873. Teller of the Central National Bank seventeen years. Alderman from Ward Two. Treasurer of the Columbia Newberry and Laurens Railroad Company. Mayor pro tem of the city.

GIBBES, WADE HAMPTON.—Merchant. Born in Columbia, South Carolina, April 3, 1837. Prepared for college, by James H. Carlisle. Remained one year and a half, at the Arsenal in Charleston, preparatory to entering West Point, where he graduated, in June, 1860. On November 14, 1860, he married Jane Allan. Resigned as lieutenant in United States army December 20, 1860. On the day that South Carolina seceded, was appointed lieutenant of the South Carolina Regulars; resigned to go to the army in Virginia. Served with Wise, in West Virginia, as major of artillery, Confederate States of America. Served as commander of conscript camp at Columbia part of 1861, then with Kirby Smith, in Kentucky; one year as commander of the post at Wilmington, North Carolina, and with Longstreet's corps, as major of artillery, from the Wilderness to Petersburg. Desperately wounded, and surrendered with Lee's Army at Appomattox. County treasurer of Richland, ten years; postmaster four years and a half. Director in Central National Bank twenty-one years. Member of the city council.

GIBBES, WADE HAMPTON JR.—State agent of the Equitable Life Insurance Company stationed at Columbia. Son of Alan Mason and Jane Gibbes. Born in Columbia, South Carolina, October 14, 1861. Acquired his education from the Carolina Military Institute, and South Carolina College. Married Heloise Weston, January 3, 1896. Formerly proprietor and manager of the supply business of W. H. Gibbes & Co. County chairman of Richland County, and member of the sinking fund commission of land.

GIBSON, HIRAM A. H.—Magistrate at Walhalla, South Carolina. Was born in Pickens District, now Oconee County, on the 17th of May, 1832. His educational advantages were limited; attended the old field schools, and one year under the instruction of O. H. P. Fant. Was appointed trial justice, in 1877, by Governor Hampton. Was coroner, and served as sheriff for about eleven months. Was trial justice about fourteen years, and was mayor, of Walhalla, two years. He was admitted to the bar, in January, 1880. Served in the Confederate War, from April 1, 1862, to close of the war, as a member of Company B, Second South Carolina Rifles. Married Miss Catherine T. Jaynes, January 13, 1856.

GIGNILLIAT, GEORGE WARREN.—Son of N. P. and Charlotte Gignilliat. Was born in Darien, McIntosh County, Georgia, January 17, 1854. His father was a large rice planter in Georgia. His ancestors were French and Swiss Huguenots, who settled in South Carolina, in 1685. His early training was received from the public schools of Marietta, Georgia. Later attended the University of Virginia, at Charlottsville, and was graduated from the University of Georgia, in 1873. Married Miss Sue Lawrence, on June 16, 1880. Was bookkeeper, four years, for Roswell Manufacturing Company, at Roswell, Georgia. Since then he has been engaged in mercantile business at Seneca, South Carolina. He is a director of the Roswell Manufacturing Company, at Roswell, Georgia.

GILLARD, PHILIP PORCHER.—Entered the Confederate service as a member of the Palmetto Guard, of Charleston, South Carolina, on the 12th of March, 1861. Was stationed at Stephens Iron Battery, Morris Island, at the fall of Fort Sumter, 1861, and went with that company, which became I, Second South Carolina Regiment, to Virginia. In December, 1861, he was elected second-lieutenant of Company E. Seventh South Carolina Battalion, Hagood's Brigade; and made captain of that company, May 23, 1863. In 1864, was appointed commander of the Sharpshooters, Hagood's Brigade, and held that position until the close of the war. He was born at Providence, Sumter County, South Carolina, August 6, 1843. He attended the Wellington School of Abbeville County, the Kings Mountain Military Academy, at Yorkville, South Carolina; also the Arsenal, at Columbia, South Carolina, and the Citadel, Charleston, South Carolina. He was elected trial jutice of his county in 1877, and 1880; supervisor of Registration and treasurer of Sumter County, from 1886, to 1891. Member of the board of education of Sumter County, from 1894, to 1898. Postmaster of the city of Sumter, in 1894. Married Miss Rachel Baker Jackson, on December 19, 1867.

GILLIAM, REUBEN FERDINAND.—Son of Dr. Reuben Sims Gilliam, and Ann (Humphries) Gilliam. Was born in Union County, South Carolina, December 25, 1873. He attended several schools, Beaufort College, Seven Island School, Virginia, and graduated from Eastman Business College and University of South Carolina. Bachelor of Arts graduate from Stanford University, California. Admitted to the bar of California. He is superintendent of the graded schools of Abbeville, and has been member of the county board of education, since 1897. Was appointed a joint manager of dormitories at Stanford University in junior year.

GILLILAND, ROBERT JAMES.—Son of James Gilliland of Laurens County, who practiced medicine in that county forty years. Ancestors were of Scotch-Irish descent. The subject of this sketch was born at Pickensville, South Carolina, July 30, 1860. He attended Newberry College, until fourteen years of age; then was in the drug business, at Easley, three years. Entered Adger College at Walhalla, South Carolina, in 1878; left there in his junior year, and commenced the study of medicine at Easley. Graduated from the medical department of the University of Maryland, in 1884. He enjoys probably the most lucrative practice of any physician in Pickens County.

GILREATH, JEFFERSON DAVIS.—Sheriff of Greenville County. Was born, March 5, 1861, at Chick Springs, Greenville County, South Carolina. His ancestors were of Scotch-Irish descent, and his father was sheriff of Greenville County twenty-four years. He was educated at the Gowensville Academy and Furman University. Was united in marriage, to Miss Maria Anderson, of Tennessee, family formerly of Spartanburg County, South Carolina, on December 28, 1888. He is a member of the firm of Gilreath, Durham, & Co., and was also deputy sheriff of Greenville.

GLENN, JAMES PERRY.—Born in Laurens County, May 1, 1844. His parents emigrated from Scotland. Was educated at Thalian Academy under the tutorship of that noted educator, Rev. John Leland Kennedy, whose school in the upper part of Anderson County, just before the Civil War, was the pride of the State. Married Miss Hettie A. Smith of Anderson County, in 1876. Was elected to the House of Representatives, in 1888, and served one term. Elected to the State Senate from Anderson, in 1890, which position he held until 1894. Was a member of the board of regents for the State Hospital for the Insane, in 1896; and a member of the State Constitutional Convention, in 1895. Taught school for five years, beginning in 1870. Is now engaged in farming. He was elected to the Legislature from Anderson County before the Reform Movement swept the State. Was elected to the State Senate as an advocate of the Clemson Agricultural College, but was not a candidate for re-election.

GLENN, JOHN LYLES.—Son of Dr. E. L. and Louisa (Carter) Glenn. Born in Chester County, South Carolina, April 26, 1858. Attended the common schools of Chester and York counties. Graduated from Wofford College, June, 1879. Took the law course at Vanderbilt University, and admitted to the bar, in November, 1881. He was intendant and trial justice of the town of Chester. Chairman of board of trustees of the public schools, and chairman of the commissioners of public works. Elected to Constitutional Convention, 1895, and elected State Senator, in 1898, without opposition. Director in Exchange Bank of Chester, and a trustee of Wofford College. Is interested in farming and is still practicing law at Chester. Married Miss Alice Hall, 26th of April, 1883.

GOGGINS, JOHN CALHOUN. Clerk of the court of Newberry County. A native of that county, born February 17, 1853. Attended the common schools, in early boyhood, and the preparatory schools in the Molohon Section of county for two years. Then entered Furman University, Greenville, South Carolina, graduating therefrom, in 1876. Two years later, he married Miss Mary Adelle Long. He has recently moved to the town of Newberry, for the purpose of securing better educational advantages for his children. He was elected city clerk and treasurer, in 1899; and re-elected, in 1900; and, in the fall of that year, he was elected to the position he now holds.

GOLDSMITH, WILLIAM JR.—Actively engaged in the real estate and insurance business, in Greenville, South Carolina. Was born in that county. His education was acquired under the instruction of Professor J. B. Patrick. He was grand chancellor Knights of Pythias, one year. Married Miss Janie Wright, of Woodruff, Spartanburg County, on December 16, 1886.

GONZALES, AMBROSE ELLIOTT.—President and general manager of the State Company at Columbia, South Carolina. Was born, May 29, 1857, in St. Paul's Parish, Colleton County, South Carolina. His education was acquired from private schools. At sixteen years of age, he went with the Charleston and Savannah Railway, and the Southern Express Company, as railway agent and telegrapher, at Grahamville, South Carolina. Then planted for two years. From 1881, to 1885, he was with the Western Union and Postal Telegraph Companies, in New York and New Orleans, as operator and manager. Went with the "News and Courier" as general traveling agent, until fall of 1889; then for one year he was secretary of the department of agriculture at Columbia. In 1890, he helped organize the State Publishing Company, taking the position of general traveling agent, until March, 1893.

GONZALES, NARCISO GENER.—Editor "The State." Columbia, South Carolina. Born August 5, 1858, at Edingsville, Edisto Island, South Carolina. Second son of Ambrosio Jose Gonzales, a native of Matanzas, Cuba, who with Narciso Lopez, began the struggle for Cuban independence in 1848, being one of the junta of five members who declared the independence of the island, adopted the present Cuban flag, and organized the first filibustering expedition under Lopez, of which he was second in command, with the rank of brigadier-general. He was the first Cuban wounded in battle for the independence of the Island, at Cardenas, May 20, 1850; was exiled and under sentence of death. In 1856, he married Harriett Rutledge, youngest daughter of the Honorable William Elliott, of Beaufort, South Carolina. Served in the Confederate army as colonel and chief of artillery for the department of South Carolina, Georgia, and Florida, under Beauregard, Hardee, Pemberton and others, surrendering at Greensboro, North Carolina. In charge of the artil-

lery of Johnston's army in 1865. N. G. Gonzales was taught
at home until ten years of age, and at fifteen attended a
private school in Virginia for one year. Received no other
education, his family being ruined by the war. Worked as
a laborer on a farm in Virginia and for several years at the
family homestead plantation in Colleton County, South Carolina. In 1875, studied telegraphy, and from the summer of
that year, until the summer of 1876, was employed as telegraph operator at Varnville, Hampton County, South Carolina. In 1876, he organized the first Democratic club on the
line of the Port Royal Railroad, and was a campaign correspondent for the "Charleston Journal of Commerce," the
straight out Democratic organ of that time. In the fall of
1877, obtained a position as night operator for the Atlantic
and Gulf Railroad (now the Plant System) at Savannah,
Georgia, whence, a year later, he was transferred to the post
of operator and railroad clerk at Valdosta, Georgia. He left
this place, in June, 1880, on invitation of A. B. Williams,
whom he had met in the campaign of 1876 and who had
then just assumed charge of the "Greenville Daily News,"
to serve as local reporter for that paper. August 5, 1880,
he began his service with the "Charleston News and Courier," as its regular correspondent, at Columbia; and continued in that position until October, 1881, when he was
sent to Washington, to act as its special correspondent in
the exciting year following the death of President Garfield.
Reported the Guiteau trial and execution, and the long session of the Forty-seventh Congress, for "The News and Courier." In August, 1882, was transferred to Charleston, and
placed on the editorial staff of the "News and Courier,"
with the understanding with Mr. B. R. Riordan, one of the
owners, that he was ultimately to become editor of that
paper. But, after a few months, owing to a disagreement
with Captain Dawson, was again sent to Columbia, where,
in 1883, he organized the "News and Courier Bureau," and
continued in charge of its news and business departments
until the election of B. R. Tillman as governor, in 1890, reporting, besides, all the State campaigns and many famous
trials in different parts of South Carolina. His personal and

political antagonism to Governor Tillman indisposing him
to have such relations with the executive as the policy of the
"News and Courier" required, he resigned his position on that
paper, to take effect upon the close of the administration of
Governor Richardson. His purpose now was to leave the
State, and seek a newspaper opening in the Hawaiian Islands, to which he was attracted; but being urged to remain and become editor of a daily newspaper in Columbia,
representing the views of the opponents of Tillman, he
agreed to do so, and with his brother, Ambrose E. Gonzales,
secured the capital necessary to start "The State," of which
paper he was elected editor and manager. He purchased
the plant, selected the force, and organized the office; and
the publication of "The State" began February 18, 1891. His
supervision of the business department lasted for two years,
but his control of the editorial policy of the paper has continued throughout its existence of more than ten years.
Mr. Gonzales has held no public office. His interest in the
cause of Cuban independence moved him, soon after the
beginning of the Revolution of 1895, to offer his services
to the insurgents in the field; but they were declined, on
the ground that he could be of greater aid to the cause in
his editorial position. Before the breaking out of the war
of the United States with Spain, he sought the means of
taking part in it on Cuban soil; but, being disappointed in
other plans for getting to the front, he went to Tampa a
few days after war was declared, and was there appointed
first-lieutenant on the staff of General Emilio Nunez, of
the Cuban army, then preparing an expedition for the relief of General Maximo Gomez in Central Cuba. This expedition could not get transportation until June 20, when it
sailed from Tampa in two steamers, the Florida and Fanita,
with a convoy, the Peoria. It took two weeks to make a land-
ing. After being repulsed at two points, by the Spaniards,
the expedition disembarked, July 3, at Palo Alto on the
south coast of Cuba, a few miles west of the central trocha;
and the next day General Gomez was found and relieved.
After six weeks of extreme hardships and privations, cam-
paigning northward along the trocha, during which he par-

ticipated in one fight, an attack on the fortified town of Moron at the northern end of the trocha, Mr. Gonzales, learning on August 17, that the war was over, procured his discharge, and embarked for home in an expeditionary schooner, which, after various adventures, reached Key West, September 1, 1898. Married Miss Lucy Barron, of Manning, South Carolina, November 14, 1901.

GONZALES, W. E.—News editor of "The State." Son of General Ambrosio Gonzales. Born April 24, 1866, at Charleston, South Carolina. Attended the Kings Mountain Military School, and South Carolina Military Academy, at Charleston. Married Sara C. Shiver, February 2, 1887. Columbia correspondent of the "News and Courier," from 1884, to 1888. Governor's secretary, from 1888, to 1900. Adjutant of independent battalion, during Spanish-American War, from May 4, to August 23. Captain of Second South Carolina, from August 23, 1898, to April 30, 1899.

GOODING, WILLIAM JAMES.—Native of Hampton County South Carolina. Was born on the 9th of November, 1835. Has lived in Hampton County, formerly a part of Beaufort County, all his life. His ancestors came to America from England, and originally settled in New England, a branch of the family coming South about the beginning of the Eighteenth Century. He attended the common schools of the county, and for a short time, Professor W. I. Ligon's School at Sandy Run, Lexington County, South Carolina. Entered the South Carolina Military Academy, at the Arsenal, in Columbia, South Carolina, in 1854. In October of that year, his father died, which necessitated his return home to assist his mother in the management of the farm, and caring for his younger brothers and sisters. He has been a close student, and has kept himself well to the front in all matters of public interest, being prominent in every movement which had for its object the elevation and improvement of the condition of the people. He married, on the 4th of September, Miss Elizabeth A. Terry. He was adjutant and afterwards lieutenant-colonel of the Twelfth Regiment Infantry South Carolina Militia, from 1855, to the beginning of the Civil War. Was elected to the House of Representatives from Prince William's Parish, Beaufort District, in 1858 and 1860, and, when first elected, was the youngest member of the House. Captain of Company D, Twenty-fourth Regiment South Carolina Volunteer Infantry, in 1862. Resigned, and enlisted in Company D, Eleventh South Carolina Volunteers, in 1863. Was made second lieutenant in that company. He was badly wounded, and incapacitated for further field service. Was engaged, however, in the assessment and collection of the Confederate war taxes, for Beaufort District, until the surrender of Lee and Johnston, in April, 1865. Sheriff of Beaufort District, in February, 1866; held that office until the advent of the Negro government, in 1868. Governor Hampton appointed him county treasurer of Beaufort County, in 1877, which position he resigned when Hampton County was established, and became treasurer of that county for one term, declining re-appointment. A member of the State Democratic Committee. He was elected, without his consent, a delegate to the Constitutional Convention of 1895. He is a regent of the Hospital for the Insane. He is a farmer.

GORDON, DAVID ERWIN.—Son of John A. Gordon and Sarah A. Watson. Born, October 2, 1831, near Kingstree, Williamsburg County, South Carolina. Ancestors were among the early settlers of Williamsburg County, and came from Scotland. Early education obtained from common schools of the county. Graduated from Davidson College, North Carolina, with second honor, in 1853. Married Miss Esther J. McKnight, of Williamsburg County, in 1854; and June 10, 1869, married Miss Mary H, daughter of John Nettles, of Sumter. He is a planter. Has been magistrate of Williamsburg County about twenty years. He is now proprietor of the Gordon House, at Lanes, South Carolina. Entered the Confederate service, as a private, in an infantry company, Colonel J. D. Blanding's Regiment, General D. R. Jones's Brigade. Afterwards entered General M. C. Butler's Cavalry, and served with him, in Virginia, until the war closed. He was promoted to captaincy of a cavalry company, which position he held until the war closed. In June, 1864, he was captured and imprisoned at Point Lookout, and removed to Fort Delaware. While there he was selected as one of the officers to be retaliated upon, by being placed between the Federal and Confederate batteries, upon Morris Island, near Charleston, where he remained under fire, for nearly two months. He was then taken from there to Fort Pulaski, near the mouth of the Savannah River, and there retaliated upon for the treatment of the Andersonville prisoners; was fed on rotton corn meal two months. He reached home July 2, 1865.

GORDON, JOHN FRANCIS.—County supervisor of York County. Was born, June 1, 1862, in Chester County, South Carolina. Removed to York County, in 1873. Education was obtained from the common schools. Remained on a farm until twenty-one years of age, then traveled for Sewing Machine Company, and later, the American Bible Society. Then accepted a position as clerk, which he held for three years. Married Mary C. Youngblood, on January 12, 1888. After marriage, he went into the farming business; and, in 1900, entered the race for county supervisor, and was elected in the second race over six competitors.

GORDON, MYRAN W.—Preacher. Pastor of the Baptist Church at Abbeville, South Carolina. Son of Jackson and Sarah A. Gordon. Born, March 16, 1866, in Davies County, Kentucky. Obtained education from Masonville High School; Scearces College, Shelbyville, Kentucky; and Bethel College, Russellville, Kentucky. Twice married. His first wife was Hulda Sawyer, of Kentucky, whom he married, in 1888. Married Miss Margaret Amos, of Spartanburg, South Carolina, May 16, 1900. Has supplied churches in Camden, Georgetown, and Chester.

GOUGH, JOHN OLIVER.—Pastor of the Baptist Church at Manning, South Carolina. Was born in Yadkin County, North Carolina, December 18, 1867. He is a son of Stephen G. Gough who was wounded in the Civil War and died soon afterwards. Is a graduate of Wake Forest College; and was elected debater, to represent the college and its literary society, during his senior year. He was chosen pastor of the Baptist Church at Manning, January 1, 1894, the first and only church he has ever served. During his ministry, the church has grown to be strong and influential. In 1895, under his direction and leadership, a new church building was erected, which would be a credit to a much larger place.

GOWER, ARTHUR GAILLARD.—Son of Thomas C. and Jane (Williams) Gower. Was born, October 14, 1861, at Greenville, South Carolina. His father was prominent in establishing the first manufacturing interests in Greenville. He was compelled to stop school while in the freshman class at college. Has been three times married, his last wife being Miss Rosa Waldrop, of Richmond, Virginia, whom he married on October 30, 1895. He was messenger for the Southern Express Company for four years, and clerked for Gower & Riley four years. Was a partner of T. C. Gower & Son four years; and of Gower & Speights, with whom he is now connected, six years.

GRAHAM, HARRY MALCOLM.—Youngest son of the late Winchester Graham, of Barnwell, South Carolina. Born at Augusta, Georgia, Sepember 27, 1865. He was educated at the Richmond Academy, at Augusta, Georgia, and took a law course at the University of Virginia. He graduated in bookkeeping at the age of sixteen. Married Miss Jennie Lawton Kirkland, daughter of Dr. W. F. Kirkland, of Barnwell, South Carolina. He was for eighteen years, bookkeeper and credit man for J. D. Copeland, of Bamberg, South Carolina. Admitted to the bar in 1895. Licensed to practice in the United States Court, in 1899. Was elected first probate judge of Bamberg County, which position he resigned in order to move to Greenwood County to practice law. He is now representing Greenwood County in the Legislature. He is attorney for many strong corporations, including the Carolina Trust Company, The Abbeville Savings and Investment Company, and the American Surety Company, of New York. He is also a member of the firm of Crowder & Graham, real estate dealers, at Greenwood.

GRAHAM, THOMAS ADDISON.—Auditor of Greenwood County. Was born near Cokesbury, Abbeville County, January 10, 1857. Prepared for college at the Cokesbury school, entered Wofford College in 1874, and graduated with second honor. He married Miss Zolacus S. Rothrock, in July, 1879. Elected to the Legislature in 1890; elected again in 1896; and resigned, in spring of 1897, to accept his present position.

GRAY, WILLIAM L.—Merchant of Laurens. Was born on a farm in Laurens County, on the 7th of March, 1856. In 1872, he entered Wofford College, from which he graduated, in 1876. After graduation he taught school three years, the last two of which he was principal of the Laurensville Male Academy. In connection with his work as teacher, he read law; and was admitted to the bar, in 1878. He retired from the practice of law, in 1881, and devoted his whole attention to merchandising. He is the prime partner in three different firms. Mr. Gray is a stockholder and director in the Peoples Loan and Exchange Bank, also in the Oil & Fertilizer Company, of Laurens. He holds the same relation to the Building & Loan Association, and is one of the owners of the Ware's Shoals Water Power Company, of Laurens County. He is a member of the board of trustees of Wofford College. He has been twice married, his second wife being Miss Mary, daughter of Dr. Dunklin, of Laurens, South Carolina, whom he married, December 17, 1895.

GRAYDON, WILLIAM NORWOOD.—State Senator from Abbeville County. Son of S. E. Graydon and Susan (Dunwoody) Graydon. Born at Cokesbury, South Carolina, on December 11, 1860. He was educated at the Cokesbury Conference School. Studied law, and was admitted to the bar at Abbeville, South Carolina. He carried up to the Supreme Court the case of Aultman vs. Rush, in which it was first decided that a married woman could not give a mortgage to secure her husband's debt. He married Ada L. McMillan, January 11, 1890.

GREEN, EDWIN LUTHER.—Assistant professor of English languages in the South Carolina College. Son of A. H. Green and L. V. Fisher. Born in Milton, Florida, December 13, 1870. His great-grandfather, John Green, moved from Abbeville District, South Carolina, to Georgia, in 1800; and from there to Alabama. Served several times in the Legislature, and constitutional conventions of Alabama. Graduated, with degree of Bachelor of Arts, from Washington and Lee University, and with degree of Doctor of Philosophy, from Johns Hopkins University, in 1897. Taught two years in Washington and Lee University; private schools and Central University, Richmond, Kentucky. Member of the Phi Beta Kappa Society. Author of a "School History of Florida," which is used in the schools of that State. He is unmarried.

GREENE, WILLIAM PINCKNEY.—Son of James H. Greene, and Elvirah T. (Bowie). Born in Abbeville County, November 24, 1873. Prepared for college in Erskine College Preparatory School, entered freshman class Erskine College, in 1889. Graduated in 1893, taking highest stand in class. Taught school two years. Read law in office of Ernest Moore, at Lancaster, South Carolina, 1895. Admitted to the bar, December, 1895. Practiced law with W. C. McGowan, at Greenwood, 1896, under firm name of McGowan & Greene. Removed to Abbeville, 1897, on death of Mr. McGowan; and formed partnership with McGowan's former partner, William Henry Parker. Practiced law at Abbeville since then. Member of firm of Parker & Greene, attorneys for National Bank of Abbeville, Farmers' Bank of Abbeville, Abbeville Cotton Mills, local attorneys for Charleston and Western Carolina Railway.

GRESHAM, GEORGE THOMAS.—Pastor of several Baptist churches in Williamsburg and Sumter Counties. He was born in King and Queen County, Virginia. Obtained early education from private schools near his home, and attended two sessions at Richmond College, Virginia. Then graduated from Southern Baptist Theological Seminary. He has been twice married; his second wife was Miss Mabel M. Beckham, whom he married February 10, 1897. Taught school at Yorkville, Gaffney, and other places. Recording statistical secretary of the Baptist State Convention, from 1894 to 1897, when sickness prevented his attending the convention.

GRIER, BOYCE HEMPHILL.—Son of Rev. R. C. Grier, D.D., of Due West, South Carolina. He is a native of that town, having been born on November 8, 1861. His father was for many years president of Erskine College, and his older brother, Dr. William Grier, lately deceased, was president, for more than twenty-five years, of the same institution. His education was obtained from Erskine College and the University of Virginia. Graduated from Erskine Seminary, in 1887. Taught school a short time. Married Miss Susie M. Lee, on July 28, 1891, at Due West, South Carolina. Was pastor of Mount Zion Associate Reformed Presbyterian Church, in Lincoln County, Missouri. Has been pastor of Tirzah and Yorkville Churches seven years. He is at present a useful minister of the gospel. Has recently received a call to the church at Ora, Laurens County, South Carolina, which he has accepted.

GRIER, JAMES ELMORE.—Son of Rev. Lemuel A. and Sara M. J. Munnerlyn. Born, November 13, 1861, in Georgetown County, South Carolina. Ancestors were of Scotch-Irish and were among the early settlers of the lower Pee Dee section of South Carolina. Attended the neighborhood schools and Wofford College. Married Mary E. McNeill, December 12, 1882. Clerked a few years. Member of the South Carolina Conference.

GRIER, PAUL LIVINGSTON.—Son of Rev. R. C. Grier, D.D., and Barbara (Moffat) Grier; father for many years president of Erskine College. He was born in Due West, South Carolina, April 28, 1864. His primary training was received in the town schools of Due West, South Carolina. He graduated from Erskine College, with first honor, in 1884. After graduation he taught in the country, near Covington, Tennessee, then in the preparatory department of Erskine College for two years. He was also principal of one of the public schools in Washington, District of Columbia, one year; at which time he was elected to the chair of mathematics in Erskine College, which position he still holds.

GRIFFIN, VINCENT.—Judge of probate for Greenwood County. Was born near Whitehall, Abbeville County, September 30, 1837. His early training was received in the common-schools of Barrattsville; later attended Mount Pleasant, and the High Schools at Cueryton, Edgefield County. His second wife was Miss Bond, whom he married in 1886. He was magistrate of Abbeville County. Joined Company F, Second South Carolina Volunteer Infantry, under Colonel J. B. Kershaw; during the remainder of the war, was in Company G, Second South Carolina Volunteers, Colonel T. J. Lipscomb, formerly commanded by General M. C. Butler.

GRIFFITH, DAVID JEFFERSON.—Superintendent of the South Carolina Penitentiary. Son of  Alle Griffith and Sarah Banks, of Lexington County, South Carolina. Born in Newberry County, December 31, 1844. Ancestors were English and Scotch-Irish, with a trace of German. They were the early settlers of Lexington and Newberry Counties. Education was obtained in the country schools of Lexington County. On July 27, 1865, he married Sadie A. Lewie, daughter of Samuel Lewie, of Lexington. He joined the Confederate army at the breaking out of the war and was captain in Company C, First South Carolina Regiment. He was in many of the battles of that war, notably Chickamauga, Knoxville, Bean Station, The Wilderness, Spottsylvania, Cold Harbor, Petersburg, and was present when Johnston surrendered at Greensboro. After the war he engaged in farming, and was often called upon to represent his county in offices of honor and trust. He was for several terms senator from Lexington, and was serving in this capacity when called to succeed W. A. Neal as superintendent of the penitentiary, which position he now holds. He was voted a gold watch by the readers of the "Columbia State," which was offered to the most popular legislator, in 1897, defeating the next highest competitor, H. C. Patton, many thousand votes. He presented to the local chapter of the Daughters of the Confederacy a sword which was consigned to him by a dying Federal officer on the field at Gettysburg, July 2, 1863. He was placed in charge of the management of the penitentiary and the State farms, by a very flattering vote, and has been conspicuously successful in the management of this institution and of the State's property. He was re-elected without opposition.

GRIFFITH, HARRISON PATILLO.—Born in Laurens County, February 25, 1837. Was educated in the common schools of the neighborhood, and Furman University. Was for fifteen years president of the Cooper Limestone Institute. At present is professor of English in Limestone College. Author of the "Life and Times of John G. Landrum," and "Personal Recollections of the Battle of Chancellorsville." Editor of the "Gaffney Ledger." Volunteered August 15, 1861. Engaged in several battles around Richmond. Wounded in the leg at Gettysburg; desperately wounded at the Wilderness, May 5, 1864, and attempted to return to duty, but was unable to do so. Married Miss Amanda P. Sanford, January 22, 1861. He was principal of the Woodruff High School for eight years. Was captain of Company E, Fourteenth South Carolina Volunteers, McGowan's Brigade.

GRIST, LEWIS MASON.—Editor of the "Yorkville Enquirer." Was born on Cane Creek in the southern part of

Spartanburg County, South Carolina, on the fourth of November, 1831. L. M. Grist's father was a printer, and came to Yorkville, South Carolina, on the 10th of April, 1833, to follow his trade. In May, 1840, L. M. Grist was put to work in his father's printing-office, and is still so employed. When he took this position, he had but little education; could read a little by carefully and laboriously spelling out the words. His wife's name was Frances Vienna Vise, whom he married, in Oxford, Alabama, on the second day of July, 1854. In August, 1861, entered the army, as first lieutenant, and later was captain of Company A, Twelfth Regiment South Carolina Volunteers, until severely wounded in the elbow of the right arm at the second battle of Manassas, on the 29th of August, 1862. He did not serve in the field any longer, but continued in the Confederate service until the Confederate War came to a close. He was the first publisher of the "Yorkville Enquirer," the publication of which was commenced in January, 1855, by John L. Miller and Samuel W. Melton. In March, 1858, he bought out Melton and Miller, and has continued as proprietor up to the present. Never sought public office.

GUESS, JAMES BARRIE.—Merchant. Was born, November 7, 1859, and was reared in Denmark, South Carolina. Received his preparatory education, in the common schools of his native village. Entered the South Carolina Military Institute, at the age of fourteen, and graduated, in June, 1879, with the rank of cadet captain. After graduation he entered a general mercantile and planting business, with his father, Dr. S. D. M. Guess, under the firm name of S. D. M. Guess & Son. He was connected with the Militia of South Carolina for seven years, from 1879 to 1886, in both the infantry and cavalry service, as captain commanding efficient companies. Elected to the House of Representatives from Barnwell County, in 1886; re-elected in 1888, serving two terms in that body, and taking an interest in the welfare of the State. He was married to Hattie Ramelle Wroton, in October, 1880, who died, in 1882. He was again married to Miss Sallie S. Mitchell, of Batesburg, South Carolina, in August,

1884. He is a great church-worker, having served his church as trustee, steward, and Sunday-school superintendent, which position he has held for fifteen years.

GUEST, C. M.—Son of S. M. and H. J. Guest. Was born at Merrittsville, Greenville County, South Carolina, July 27, 1865. Education limited. Had only the advantage of the country schools of the period. Married Mary E. Hallan, April 14, 1895. He is an architect, and has designed several mills and public buildings.

GUNTER, FELDER B.—Practicing medicine, and engaged in drug business at Saluda, South Carolina. Born, October 21, 1869, in Aiken County, South Carolina. Education obtained from common schools, and from Baltimore Medical College, where he graduated in medicine in 1893. Married Miss Carolina Gunter, November 6, 1894.

GUNTER, U. X.—Assistant attorney-general. Was born at Batesburg, Lexington County, December 5, 1870. He studied in the high schools of Batesburg. Later entered the South Carolina College, graduating in 1892. Went to Aiken to practice law, and there entered partnership with the Honorable O. C. Jordan, and, later with the Honorable John Gary Evans, who, when elected governor, appointed Mr. Gunter his private secretary. At the expiration of Governor Evans' term, he was elected clerk of the Claims Committee of the House of Representatives, and this work completed, he moved to Spartanburg to practice law. For several years he has been secretary and treasurer of the State Democratic executive committee. Soon after moving to Spartanburg, he was appointed magistrate, which office he resigned to accept the position of assistant attorney-general, in the fall of 1898, under attorney-general Barber. Was reappointed by General

Barber's successor, General G. Duncan Bellinger. In 1896, he was commissioned major on the staff of Brigadier-General Stoppelbein, and later was appointed judge advocate general on the staff of Governor McSweeney, which position he now holds.

GUY, WILLIAM O.—County treasurer of Chester County. Was born in that county, on October 31, 1854. He attended the old field schools at Bullocks Creek, York County, South Carolina, up to Ku Klux time, in 1871. Then was two years at Rutherford College, Burke County, North Carolina. He was appointed treasurer of Chester County, in 1896, to fill an unexpired term, and has been re-elected ever since. He took an active part in redeeming the State from Radical rule, in 1876. Married Miss Martha C. Blair, on April 8, 1874.

GWYNN, ANDREW KEENE, REV.—Rector of St. Paul's Catholic Church, Spartanburg, South Carolina. Was born June 12, 1871, in Baltimore, Maryland. His parents came to Spartanburg when he was only four years old. His early training was received from private schools of Spartanburg. Attended Wofford College three years, and graduated from the St. Charles College, Maryland. Spent two years in Europe. Finished Theological studies at St. Mary's Seminary, Emmilsburg, Maryland. Ordained to priesthood by Right Rev. Bishop Northrop in July, 1895, and was appointed to the Aiken Missions. He is also rector of Greenville Catholic Missions.

HAERLOOP, HENRY.—Born in Vegsak, Germany. Attended the high school. Was president of the Farmers Basket Company. President of the German American Building and Loan Association. President of the Columbia Banking and Trust Company.

HAGOOD, WILLIAM MILLIKIN.—He was a prime mover in organizing the Easley Oil Mill Company, in 1890, of which he is secretary and treasurer. He is a son of J. E. Hagood of Pickens County, who has been a clerk of the United States Circuit Court for thirty years. W. M. Hagood was born in Pickens County, on December 29, 1850. Attended the common schools of that day. He married Miss Kate, daughter of the late John B. Cleveland, of Spartanburg, South Carolina, November 6, 1873. He is engaged in the mercantile business at Easley. In 1891, he organized the Easley Bank, of which he is president. Is vice-president of Easley Cotton Mill. Director of Peoples Bank; also F. W. Poe Manufacturing Company, at Greenville, South Carolina.

HAILE, COLUMBUS CURETON.—Probate judge of Kershaw County for the past eight years. He was born in that County on Hanging Rock Creek, January 17, 1824. He obtained a good English education from the country schools, and finished at the academy in Camden, South Carolina, taught by John A. Leland and Leslie McCandless, about 1843 and 1844. He then took a course in surveying under Thompkins Higday. He was major of the Twenty-second South Carolina Militia, and was promoted to lieutenant-colonel just before the breaking out of the Civil War. Raised a volunteer company, Company G, of the Second South Carolina Volunteers Regiment, Colonel James B. Kershaw's command, in April, 1861. After the reorganization volunteered again, and, with the assistance of Colonel John C. Evans, raised another company, and joined Colonel H. L. Benbow's Twenty-third Regiment to fill out a company that was about killed out. Mr. Evans was appointed captain, and Mr. Haile first lieutenant. This regiment distinguished itself at the battle of the Crater, Petersburg, Virginia, July 30, 1864. Mr. Haile was in command at the close of the battle, and charged the enemy out of the Crater at the time General Mahone came to his aid and charged on the left of the Crater. After the war, in 1876, he raised a company of cavalry, composed of men from Kershaw and Lancaster counties, near the battle-field of the Revolution on Hanging Rock, fought by General Sumter. This company escorted Hampton in his campaign meetings, at Camden and Lancaster, in 1876; and after the election and Hampton became governor

of South Carolina, the company was disbanded. Married
Miss Mary Ann E. Williams, March 29, 1849.

HAILE, J. E. W.—Physician at Kershaw, South Carolina, and surgeon of the South Carolina and Georgia Railroad for past four years. Born at Flat Rock, South Carolina,
July 14, 1859. Son of Dr. A. J. Haile, of Atlanta, Georgia.
Attended the common schools of South Carolina and Ala-
bama, and took a special course at the Herbert Institute,
Vincentown, New Jersey, before entering the Medical College. Has twice been elected mayor of the town of Kershaw, since which time has been a member of the board
of health. Appointed one of the board of examiners of
Lancaster County, by the governor, in 1890. Graduated at
University of Pennsylvania, in 1880, and from the Atlanta
Medical College, in 1882. Took postgraduate course at New
York Medical College and Hospital, in 1898. For two years
vice-president of the South Carolina Pharmaceutical Association.

HAILE, JAMES ROCHELLE.—Born in Kershaw County,
South Carolina, May 20, 1857. Son of the late James Lawrence Haile, who, with his family, moved to Jackson County,
Alabama, in 1859. He was educated in the common schools
of his County. Having had the misfortune to lose his father
during the war, and his family being permanently scattered,
he returned to his native State, penniless and almost an invalid. After working on the farm for three years, he secured a position as clerk in a store, at Fort Mill, South
Carolina, and by close attention to business, he was in a few
years made manager of the largest mercantile establishment in the town. On the 26th of May, 1884, he married
Lulu Shropshire Conly, of Kershaw County, South Carolina.
He has always been greatly interested in the political welfare of his State, and has served erveral times both as president of the local Democratic Club, and as a member of the
County executive committee; he was also a trustee of the
Fort Mill High School. In 1891, he moved to Charlotte,
North Carolina, where he accepted a position as bookkeeper

and cashier of one of the largest wholesale grocery firms in that city, which position he filled for six years. On account of ill health, returned to York County, and conducted a mercantile business in Fort Mill. Has since retired to his farm near Fort Mill, and has recently been elected a member of the House of Representatives, which office he still holds. He is commander of the local camp, Sons of Confederate Veterans.

HALL, WILLIAM THOMAS, REV., D. D.—Professor in the Theological Seminary, at Columbia, South Carolina. Was born on December 5, 1835, in Rockingham County, North Carolina, where the town of Reidville now stands. His preparatory studies were directed by his father at home; and, at the age of eighteen, he was graduated, with distinction, from Davidson College. Pursued theological studies at the seminary at Columbia, South Carolina. Began to preach the gospel, in 1858, at Lancaster, South Carolina. Served the Presbyterian Church, at Canton, Mississippi, for ten years; and for nearly two years, he served as chaplain of Walthall famous Mississippi Brigade in the army of Tennessee. In 1872, he became pastor of the First Presbyterian Church in Lynchburg, Virginia. Served that church for nearly twenty-three years, and, in 1895, he was called to fill the position he now has. The degree of Doctor of Divinity was conferred by the Southwestern University at Clarksville, Tennessee, in 1871.

HALLMAN, SAMUEL THOMAS, REV.—Editor "Lutheran Visitor." A native of Lexington County. Was born September 3, 1844, but is at present located in Newberry, South Carolina. Had the advantage of only the common schools of the time; he decided to enter Newberry College, but remained only a short time, leaving to enter the army. He joined Company K, South Carolina Volunteers, in Twentieth Regiment. Was engaged in several battles near Charleston, and went to Virginia, in 1864, in Kershaw's Brigade; served as private, until 1864, and then as corporal. Returned to Charleston in spring of 1865, and took further part in defense of Charleston. He returned to college in November, in 1866, graduated from the Theological Seminary, and entered the ministry, in 1868. He was for eight years, secretary South Carolina Lutheran Synod; served three years as its president. Edited "Ladies' Missionary Journal." Editor of the "Lutheran Visitor" six years. On Newberry College board over twenty-six years, and its secretary. The degree of Master of Arts and Doctor of Divinity conferred by Newberry College. Married first Miss S. J. Wingard; and second, Lillie L. Brown.

HALTIWANGER, JACOB BENJAMIN.—Son of William and Sarah Proctor. Born in Edgefield County, South Carolina, December 3, 1858. Attended a country school near Ninety-Six. Taught school one year, after which he was variously employed, until he arrived at the age of twenty-six years. He was married to Miss Caroline H. Brown, of Anderson, South Carolina, February 5, 1885. Until 1893, was engaged in farming. Since then he has held the position of county auditor of Edgefield County, which office he now holds.

HAMEL, JOHN WILLIAM.—Parents both came from Germany. He was born in Charlotte, North Carolina, June 18, 1861. Attended private schools of Charlotte, North Carolina, up to the age of twelve. The remainder of his education was obtained by personal effort, without aid of instructors. Married Miss Mollie J. Clark, October 25, 1882. In 1893, entered Lancaster post-office as clerk, and, in 1891, was appointed postmaster at Kershaw, South Carolina, April 1, 1891. Served four years. Editor and publisher of the "Kershaw Era," since July 1, 1891. Member of Lancaster Town Council, and clerk and treasurer of town, 1890 and 1891. Magistrate at Kershaw, South Carolina, 1894 and 1898. Member from Lancaster County of the Working Committee of "The Forty," 1895. Member of Constitutional Convention of 1895, from Lancaster County. Member of Fifth Congressional District Prohibition Campaign Committees, 1900.

HAMER, THOMAS COOK.—Lawyer. Resides in Bennettsville, South Carolina. He is a son of B. F. and Sue Cook Hamer. Born at Bennettsville, South Carolina, January 23, 1868. Of English and Scotch descent. Obtained education from the common schools, and graduated in law at the South Carolina College, in 1891. After graduation, formed a partnership with Judge C. P. Townsend, which copartnership still exists. He is also interested in farming. In 1889, he was appointed bill clerk of the House of Representatives. Held this position until 1899, when he was elected clerk of the House, which position he continues to hold. In December, 1900, was apointed lieutenant-colonel on Governor McSweeney's staff.

HAMILTON, JOHN ANDREW.—Engaged in the insurance business. Son of Captain James Hamilton and Martha Jane Hanna. Born June 16, 1835, at Charleston, South Carolina. His father was born in Edinburg, Scotland, and served with Commodore Perry at Lake Erie, War of 1812. His mother was born in Liverpool, England. Completed the course at the Charleston High School; took private course in Germany. Entered merchandising in 1858. His first marriage was with M. Perryclear, of Beaufort, South Carolina. Two years after her death, he married Miss Mary Bee, daughter of Rev. T. H. Legare. He married a third time, to Miss S. McCall, second daughter of Rev. T. H. Legare. He settled in Orangeburg, in 1865. Treasurer and alderman six years; vice-commander of the Confederate Veterans. President of Associated Charities. President of local board of Jeff Davis monument. Volunteered as sergeant in the First Regiment of Rifles, acting as commissary on James Island; purchasing officer for Johnson's command. Surrendered with him, in 1865. He took part in the battles of Fort Sumter, sinking of gunboat George Washington, Bee's Creek, and others.

HAMMOND, FRANK.—Was born July 22, 1852, at Tipton, Cedar County, Iowa. His father was a native of New Hampshire, and his mother of Maine. He was educated in the graded schools of his native town. Moved to Greenville,

13

South Carolina, November, 1869. He is president of the Home Building and Loan Association, The Peoples Bank, the Mountain City Land and Improvement Company, The Carolina Loan and Trust Company; vice-president of the Greenville Fertilizer Company, of the Paris Mountain Land Company, of Brandon Cotton Mill, and also the Greenville Savings Bank. He is a director of the Glenns Spring Railroad, Carolina, Knoxville & Western Railroad; Piedmont Savings and Investment Company; Peoples Bank; the F. W. Poe Manufacturing Company; Brandon Cotton Mill; Paris Mountain Land Company; The Mountain City Land and Investment Company; Bank of Laurens, South Carolina, and the Gaffney Land and Improvement Company. Ruling Elder of the Second Presbyterian Church, Greenville. Married Miss Mary B. Caine, December 12, 1877.

HAMPTON, WADE.—One of the grandest, most honored and respected men in South Carolina to-day, is Wade Hampton. He was  born in Columbia, South Carolina, in 1818. Graduated from the University of South Carolina, and afterwards studied law, but with no intention of practicing. He served in the South Carolina Legislature in early life, but the greater portion of his time was devoted to his plantation interests in South Carolina and Mississippi. When the Civil War opened, he entered the service of his State as private, but soon raised a command of infantry, artillery and cavalry which was known as Hampton's Legion, and which achieved great distinction. At Bull Run, six hundred of his infantry held for some time the Warrenton road against Keys' corps, and were sustaining Bee when Jackson came to their aid. In the Peninsula campaign they were again distinguished, and at Seven Pines lost half of their number, Hampton himself receiving a painful wound in the foot. Soon after, he was made brigadier-general of cavalry, and assigned to

Mr. J. E. B. Stuart's command. In the Maryland and Pennsylvania campaigns, of 1862, and 1863, he took a very active part, and at Gettysburg was thrice wounded. It is stated that twenty-one out of twenty-three field officers, more than half the men of Hampton's Command, were killed or wounded in this battle, August 3, 1863, Hampton was made major-general. In 1864, after several days, he gave Sheridan a check, at Trevillian's Station, that broke up a plan of campaign, which included a junction with Hunter, and the capture of Lynchburg. In twenty-three days he captured over three thousand prisoners, and large quantities of war material, with a loss of nineteen men. He was made commander of Lee's Cavalry, in August, with the rank of lieutenant-general, and, in September, struck the rear of the Federal Army at City Point, bringing away four hundred prisoners, two thousand four hundred and eighty-six beeves. Soon afterward, in another action, he captured five hundred prisoners. In one of these attacks, he lost his son. Hampton was then placed in command of General Joseph J. Johnston's Cavalry, and did good service in retarding the advance of Sherman. After the close of the war, he engaged in farming. In 1876, he was nominated for governor, against Daniel H. Chamberlain, and was re-elected, in 1878. He lost a leg by an accident, and while his life was despaired of, he was elected to the United States Senate as a Democrat. General Hampton married, in early life, Margaret Preston, daughter of General Francis Preston; and on her death, took for his second wife, a daughter of Senator McDuffie. Elected to the United States Senate, in 1879, and was succeeded by Irby, in 1891.

HANAHAN, PEYRE GAILLARD.—Organized the Carolina Portland Cement Company, March 5, 1900. Is secretary and manager of same at present. He is a son of Joseph S. Hannahan. Born at the Ray Place, Richland County, South Carolina. His father was captain of Washington Light Infantry during latter part of Civil War. John Gaillard, speaker of United States House of Representatives, for thirty years, was his great-great-grandfather. He attended the Porter

Military Academy of Charleston, South Carolina. He was married to Miss Sarah Blake Rhett, on October 9, 1899. He was engaged as clerk, and afterwards as salesman, for a cement house, before organizing the above firm. On the board of directors of the Charleston Young Men's Christian Association.

HANNAHAN, RALPH B.—Son of R. B. and A. D. Hanahan. Born October 27, 1860, at Edisto Island, South Carolina. His ancestors are of Irish descent, but came to this country from England. His literary training was received from Mount Zion College, Winnsboro. He graduated from the Charleston Medical College, in 1886. He was a druggist at Winnsboro, for a while; and after graduation, spent one year in the city hospital at Charleston. He was presented a medal by the city of Charleston, for services during the earthquake of August 31, 1886. Married Miss H. E. Bratton, daughter of Dr. J. R. Bratton, of Yorkville, South Carolina.

HARBY, HORACE.—Merchant. Son of A. J. Moses and Octavia Moses. Born in Sumter, South Carolina, January 6, 1846. Attended the local schools until sixteen years of age. Went to Hillsboro Military Academy a few months. Served in the Confederate army until the close of war. Married Emma H. Solomons, April 1, 1870. Held the position as alderman and mayor of the city of Sumter.

HARDIN, EDWARD KING, M. D.—Practicing medicine at Batesburg, South Carolina. He is a son of Peter and Rebecca Hardin. Born October 12, 1851, in Chester County, South Carolina. Graduated at Wofford College, in 1873; and completed medical course at the University of Maryland, in 1885. Married Miss Ida E. Clinkscales, March 4, 1875. Taught school ten years after graduation.

HARDIN, NOAH WEBSTER.—Member of the bar at Blacksburg. Born at Antioch, York County, South Carolina, May 5, 1857. His grandfather filled many positions of trust and confidence, and was a member of the State Legislature over thirty years. Education was obtained from the common and high schools of the county. Read law under Honorable W. C. Black, and was admitted to the bar, in 1888. Mayor of Blacksburg, and agent of the Southern Railway Company, and counsel for the city of Blacksburg. He is now city attorney of Blacksburg, South Carolina; attorney for the South Carolina and Georgia Railroad Company, attorney for the Bank of Blacksburg, and Cotton Seed Oil Mill.

HARDIN, PETER LAWRENCE.—Born at Bascomville, Chester County, South Carolina. His earlier training was obtained from the public schools of the neighborhood, and later attended Cokesbury High School. He was a member of the March Convention, of 1890, and in that year was elected to the Legislature. Nominated Hampton for re-election to the United States Senate. Has been elected to the House of Representatives twice, and is now a member of that body. Several years chairman of Chester County Democratic Executive Committee. Is now engaged in farming.

HARDIN, WILLIAM HENRY.—President of the Chester Mercantile Company, president of the Cheraw and Chester Railroad, and now serving his second term as mayor of the town of Chester. He was born August 19, 1831, in Chester County, South Carolina. Education was obtained from country schools and the Cokesbury Institute. Married Miss Rebecca, eldest daughter of Dr. Thomas W. Moore, in 1858. Was a member of Company I, Sixth Regiment South Carolina Volunteers, Bratton's Brigade. Merchandised twenty-three years in Chester, and is at prent engaged in insurance business.

HARMAN, GODFREY M.—Son of Reuben Harman. Born at Lexington, South Carolina, June 4, 1845. His father held many positions in Lexington County and was postmaster over forty years. Educational advantages were very good up to the Civil War, when, between the age of fourteen and fifteen years, books were laid aside for guns and bayonets.

and at the call of Governor Pickens, he enlisted in Company O, First South Carolina Regiment, comanded by Colonel Maxcy Gregg. Was messenger of General M. L. Bonham, at Manassas; discharged on account of being under age. Re-enlisted in the Thirteenth Regiment, transferred to the Twentieth, and served on the coast of the State, around Richmond and Petersburg, and in the valley of Virginia. After returning from the war, attended school for a short while, and as there was an opening in Lancaster for a newspaper, he started the publication of the "Lexington Dispatch." He was burned out, April 24, 1884, by a fire which originated in a building opposite his office; but he resumed its publication just as soon as he could, after the fire. Married Miss Pauline L. Boozer, daughter of Judge Lemuel Boozer, November 24, 1866. Has never held any public office except that of magistrate.

HARMON, GEORGE THOMAS.—A member of the South Carolina Methodist Conference, and pastor of Buncombe Street Church, Greenville, South Carolina. Was born at McCormick, Abbeville County, in April 12, 1850. He was united in marriage to Miss Margaret L. Seibels, December 17, 1873. He has been appointed presiding elder of several districts in South Carolina.

HARPER, COLUMBUS EVANS.—Left the farm, and moved to Honea Path, in 1871, and has there been engaged in the ginning business and the operation of other machinery. Mr. Harper was born April 23, 1849, near Honea Path, Anderson County, South Carolina. Educational advantages were not of the best, being only those obtainable from the country schools of that time. Mr. Harper was married to Miss Mary J. Clinkscales, January 25, 1872. He was intendant and member of the town council of Honea Path several years. Never aspired to any political position, though frequently urged to do so by his friends, but always declined, preferring to avoid politics. He is still interested in farming and live stock business.

HARPER, THOMAS JEFFERSON.—Born in Greene County, East Tennessee, January 7, 1845. Married Miss Emma M. Blood, in 1867. Educated in the common schools of Greene County. Moved to Greenville, South Carolina, in 1857. Enlisted in Campbell's Battery of Artillery, and served until the fall of 1862; then served in Second South Carolina Kershaw's Regiment, Company I, Palmetto Guards, until close of war. Began business, in 1868, in Columbia, and for fourteen years has been farming and conducting a dray and coal business in Columbia. Member of the city council, since 1892. Vice-president of the Gregory-Rhea Mule Company, of Columbia.

HART, GEORGE WASHINGTON SEABROOK.—Son of Dr. Oliver James Hart. Born at Rockville, Wadmalaw Island, South Carolina, July 27, 1851. Removed to Yorkville, in March, 1874. Attended the common schools only. Married Ellen A. Hackett, June 6, 1877. Has never sought a political office. President of the Loan and Savings Bank of Yorkville, from 1889, to 1900. United States commissioner for ten or fifteen years. Lawyer, since 1874. He is attorney for the South Carolina and Georgia Extension Railroad Company, especially as to its business in South Carolina.

HART, JAMES ELLIOT.—Son of W. C. Hart, whose ancestors were English and Scotch. He was born March 5, 1868, in the Meeting Street Section of Edgefield County. His education was obtained from the schools of Edgefield County. He took a business course at Eastman Business College, Poughkeepsie, New York, in 1887. He began clerking in the dry goods store of his uncle, Alvin Hart, when thirteen years old, and in 1891, became junior partner of the firm of Alvin Hart and Company. In 1896, after the death of Alvin Hart, bought out the business, and has been running it successfully since. Married Miss Zillah L. LaGrone, November 12, 1891.

HART, JAMES FRANKLIN.—Member of the bar of Yorkville. South Carolina. Son of John Hart and Elizabeth

(Grier) Hart. Born February 13, 1837, in Union District (now County), South Carolina. Attended the common schools until 1854, when he entered the Citadel Academy, graduating in November, 1857. His first wife who was Miss Janie Ratchford, died in 1883; and in 1900 he married Mrs. Rebecca C. Grier, of Cheetham County, Virginia. Entered the service of the Confederate army, in 1861, as lieutenant in Washington Light Infantry, Charleston; became captain, in November, 1861. Transferred to Hampton's Cavalry Corps, as horse artillery, in 1862, known as Hart's battery. Major of Horse Artillery Battalion, 1864. Lost a leg at Burgess Mills, in October, 1864. Began practice of law, at Yorkville, in 1868. Appointed one of the three commissioners, in 1881, to revise and codify Statute Laws of the State, C. H. Simonton and William H. Parker, the other two. Elected Senator from York County, in 1882, to fill unexpired term of I. D. Witherspoon, who had been appointed judge. Retired from politics, in 1885, and has since devoted himself entirely to his law practice.

HARTZOG, OCTAVIUS BOWEN.—Son of S. J. Hartzog, of Bamberg, South Carolina. His ancestors came from Germany and settled in Bamberg District, about 1702. He was born at Bamberg, South Carolina, April 9, 1872. His father merchandised at Bamberg for about twenty years. His education was obtained from the public schools of his native town, and Furman University. Graduated from the Atlanta College of Pharmacy, in 1894. He is a great-grandson of James T. Overstreet who represented South Carolina in Congress. Mr. Hartzog married Miss Roselle, daughter of J. M. Waddill of Greenville, South Carolina, November 22, 1899. Taught school a few years in Barnwell County. Since 1894, has been engaged in the work of pharmacist at Greenville, and is at present a member of the firm of Lewis & Hartzog, druggists at Greenville.

HASKELL, ALEXANDER C.—Was born in what is now Abbeville County, on September 22, 1839. In early years he was educated at home under private instructors and at about the age of fifteen attended school for a time in Charleston. In 1865, he entered the South Carolina College at Columbia, from which institution he was graduated, in 1860, with the second honor of his class. In 1861, Mr. Haskell enlisted as a private in Company D, First Regiment South Carolina Volunteer Infantry, under the command of Colonel Maxcy Gregg. The original term of enlistment for the regiment was six months, at the expiration of which time it was reorganized and Mr. Haskell was appointed adjutant, which rank he held until November, 1861. At that time he was appointed chief of staff, a position he held until the death of General Maxcy Gregg, in 1862. In March, 1864, Mr. Haskell was given command of the Seventh Regiment of South Carolina Cavalry with the rank of colonel, and he continued in this capacity until the surrender at Appomattox. At the battle of Cold Harbor he was badly wounded, in May, 1864, and still carries the ball. He was also wounded and left on the field for dead at Darbytown, near Richmond, October 7, 1864. Returning from the army at the close of the war, Colonel Haskell commenced teaching school at Abbeville, at the same time he was engaged in the study of law. In December, 1865, he was admitted to the bar, and in the same year, was elected to the Legislature, serving two years. He continued teaching and practicing law, until 1867, when he was elected judge of the district court at Abbeville. But he resigned this position in September of the same year, to accept a professorship of law, in the South Carolina College. In December, 1868, he was requested by the State Democratic Convention, to be an elector in the presidential contest between Grant & Seymour, the acceptance of which called for his resignation as professor of law in the South Carolina College. At the close of the campaign, Colonel Haskell opened a law office in Columbia, and in the following year, formed a partnership with Joseph D. Pope, which lasted until December, 1877. Was chosen associate justice of the Supreme Court of South Carolina, a position he held for two years. He was elected for a term of four years, but resigned to accept the presidency of the Charlotte, Columbia and Augusta Railroad, an office he held until December 1889. He was also president of the Columbia & Greenville Railroad. President of the Loan and Exchange Bank of South Carolina. From 1887, to 1889, he was one of the government directors of the Union Pacific Railroad, and was chairman of the committee which reported to the government the best method of dealing with that road. In 1876, he was chairman of the State Democratic Executive Committee. At its close, he was chosen to represent the State at Washington, to secure the recognition of General Hampton as governor of South Carolina. He married Rebecca C., daughter of John Singleton, of Richland County. In 1870, he was again married to Alice V. Alexander, of Washington, Georgia.

HASKELL, JOHN C.—Was born in Abbeville, South Caolina, October 4, 1842. Was educated at home until 1859, when he entered the South Carolina College. There he remained until 1860, when he enlisted in the Confederate army, and was appointed second lieutenant in Company H, Regular Artillery. In December, 1861, he was appointed an aide on General Joseph E. Johnston's staff, which position he held for only a short time. He was wounded at Gaines' Mill, which resulted in the loss of his right arm. In the battle of Fredericksburg, in December, 1861, his horse was shot under him, and in falling he was so injured that he was compelled to return to Richmond. In 1863, he was given the command of the North Carolina Artillery, and served under General D. H. Hill, during the winter campaign in that State. He joined General Longstreet's Corps and was assigned to the command of a battalion, thus serving until the close of the war, having been in the meantime promoted to the rank of colonel. Returning from the army, he married Miss Sarah, daughter of General Wade Hampton. Went immediately to Mississippi, where he engaged in the occupation of a planter for seven years. In 1877, he took up his residence in Columbia, and was soon after elected to the State Legislature. Has been elected several times since. He is practicing law in Columbia, and was counsel for several railroads, but gave up that line of practice, in 1890.

HAY, JAMES THORNWELL.—Son of Samuel H. Hay and
Mary S. Hay. Born in Columbia, South Carolina, April 28,
1847. His father was pastor of the Presbyterian Church at
Camden, South Carolina, from 1851, to 1879. His education
was acquired at home, and in the public schools of Camden.
In 1864, he joined the Confederate service, in Fifth Battalion
South Carolina Reserves, and served until the close of the
war. In 1866, he began the study of law in the office of General J. B. Kershaw, afterwards judge, and was admitted to
the bar, in February, 1868. From 1873, to 1878, was associated with W. D. Trantham, as editor and proprietor of the
"Camden Journal." In that paper, and on the stump, advocated the straight out movement, of 1876. From 1880, to
1882, was a member of the House of Representatives, of
South Carolina, from Kershaw County, and represented that
County in the Constitutional Convention of 1895. Has also
been a member of the Senate, since 1896. Is a member of
the Senate committee on Judiciary, Corporation Privileges
and Elections and Rules, and Charitable Institutions. Chairman of Committee on Penitentiary. Member of the Legislative committee of 1899, to investigate the affairs of the
State penitentiary upon the retirement of W. A. Neal as
superintendent. He is still actively engaged in the practice
of law. Married Miss Josephine, daughter of W. Oakman, of
Augusta, Georgia, on December 7, 1876.

HAYNES, LAWSON BEDFORD.—President of Leesville
College, South Carolina. Prominent in the cause of Prohibition, Young Men's Christian Association, and other religious work. Son of Rev. H. M. Haynes. He was born at
what is now known as Glendale, South Carolina, July 9,
1850. His parents were natives of North Carolina. Prepared for college by Rev. S. A. Weber and J. Emory Watson, entering Wofford College in class of 1872. Married Miss
Janie Frances, daughter of Rev. Thomas H. Herbert, January 13, 1881. Taught Pacolet High School, Spartanburg
County, 1872 and 1878. Connected with the publishing house
of Walker Evans and Cogswell Company, and editor of the
"Southern Educational Monthly" from 1879, to 1881. Elected

to the chair of mathematics in Columbia Female College, from 1881, to 1888. Since that time he has been president of Leesville College.

HAYNSWORTH, HUGH CHARLES.—Acting professor of economics and philosophy in Furman University. Was born May 27, 1875, at Sumter, South Carolina. His ancestors, on both sides, came from England prior to the Revolution. Graduated from the Sumter Graded Schools, in the first class sent out from that institution, and graduated with the Bachelor of Art degree, from Furman University, in 1895. He was principal of the Pendleton Street Graded School, of Greenville, South Carolina. Assistant in the Boy's High School, of Montgomery, Alabama.

HAZARD, WALTER.—Was born at Georgetown, South Carolina, December 25, 1859. He prepared for college in Winyah Indigo Academy, Georgetown. Entered Princeton College, in 1873, where he graduated, in 1877, with the degree of Bachelor of Arts, delivering the belles letters oration. He studied law with Honorable R. Dozier, and was admitted to the bar, in 1881. In 1880, he founded the "Georgetown Enquirer," which he published until 1889, when he sold out, in order to get more time for the practice of law, which was making increasing demands on his attention. In 1882, he was elected a representative from Georgetown County, and served a term. In 1884, he was renominated, but defeated by F. W. Macusker, Independent, in consequence of local dissatisfaction as to his course on the stock law. In 1884, he declined the nomination for solicitor in the convention in which there was a deadlock over the names of Gilland, Dargan and Beard; was renominated, and re-elected to the Legislature, in 1888, and again, in 1890. He was opposed to Governor Tillman, and attended all anti-Tillman conferences, but would not countenance a split in the party. He retired from the Augusta convention, with the delegates from Sumter, Richland, Fairfield, Beaufort and Charleston; and was a member of the advisory committee appointed by the July conference of anti-Tillman Democrats, and assisted in the preparation of the address issued by that committee to the people of the State. He is connected with all important local enterprises, one of the promoters of the Georgetown and Western Railroad, which first brought Georgetown into close connection with the world; and was made one of the trustees for the bondholders of that road.

HEATH, ALLEN CLAUDE.—Son of A. W. Heath, of Waxhaw, North Carolina. Was born March 23, 1879, at Curetons Store, North Carolina. His father was a merchant of that place. Education was obtained from the high schools of Oxford, North Carolina. He is now holding the position of secretary and treasurer of the Heath-Bruce-Morrow Company, of Pickens, South Carolina.

HEMPHILL, JAMES CALVIN.—Editor of the "Charleston News and Courier," of Charleston, South Carolina. Was born at Due West, Abbeville County, South Carolina, May 18, 1850. He was the son of Rev. W. R. Hemphill, D. D., many years a professor of Erskine College. James C. Hemphill was educated in the village schools, and at Erskine College, Due West, South Carolina, from which he was graduated, in 1870. In 1871, he taught school three months in Kentucky, after which he returned to South Carolina and engaged in journalism as editor of the "Abbeville Medium." In 1880, was offered a position on the staff of the "News and Courier," and, in 1882, was placed in charge of the news bureau of that paper, at Columbia. In 1885, he was made city editor, and from time to time acted as managing editor during the absence of Captain Dawson, in Europe and elsewhere. After the death of Captain Dawson, in March, 1889, he was made manager and editor-in-chief of the "News and Courier," which position he has since filled.

HEMPHILL, JOHN J.—Was a member of Congress from the Fifth District of South Carolina. He was born at Chester, August 25, 1849. Has always lived in his native town. Attended school until 1866, when he entered the South Carolina University, from which he was graduated, in 1869. He then began the study of law, and was admitted to the bar in the fall of 1870. He was nominated by the Democrats for the Legislature, in 1873, 1874, but was defeated. In 1876, he was renominated by the same party and held that position, until 1880, when he was elected to Congress.

HEMPHILL, ROBERT REID.—Was born in Abbeville, South Carolina, May 3, 1840. He enlisted June 8, 1861, at Richmond, in the Seventh South Carolina Volunteers, as a private. Acted as orderly, for General M. L. Bonham, deceased, at the first battle of Manassas. June 25, 1862, he was transferred to Orr's Rifles; and was made sergeant major, in 1864. In that rank, he served in most of the battles in Virginia, until the end of the war. He was imprisoned at Baltimore six weeks. He graduated with first honor at Erskine College, in 1859. Was married to Miss Eugenia Cornelia Brewton, of Spartanburg County, April 6, 1870. He was a member of the House of Representatives, from 1876, to 1880, and from 1884, to 1886. In that year he was elected to the State Senate, and served until 1894. He was also elected clerk of the Senate. Member of the Constitutional Convention, of 1895. Appointed a member of the Legislative committee to investigate charitable and penal institutions— a part of the great fraud committee. Chairman of committee on education in Senate, and ex-officio trustee, of Winthrop, when founded. Represented South Carolina at the funeral of Jefferson Davis, in New Orleans, on committee from State Senate. Delivered an address at Nashville Exposition, on Tennessee Day; also delivered an address before National American Woman's Suffrage Association in Atlanta, Georgia, 1895. Introduced a bill into the Senate so as to change constitution in order that women might be allowed to vote. He is now editor of the "Abbeville Medium."

HENDERSON, BRYANT HILARY.—Son of William Henderson, who was a member of the Legislature four sessions, from Berkeley County. Born August 8, 1873. One year South Carolina Military Academy, and graduated from Wofford College, in 1895. Following year, 1896, completed the

law course, and admitted to the bar in that year. Member
of House of Representatives from Berkeley County, from
1897, to 1898. Practiced law at Fitzgerald, Georgia, one year,
and in 1899, practiced at Hot Springs, Arkansas. Returned
to South Carolina, in 1900, and is now practicing law at
Georgetown. Has never married.

HENDERSON, CALLOWAY KIRKSEY.—Merchant of Aiken, South Carolina. Son of George W. and Julia F. Kirksey, born April 20, 1844, near Trenton, in Edgefield County;
ancestors were Scotch-Irish and among the early settlers of
Edgefield county. Common school advantages; entered the
Confederate army at the age of sixteen, joining Company F,
Eighth South Carolina Infantry, Kershaw's Brigade, McLaw's
Division, Longstreet's Corps Army of Northern Virginia,
served until the close of the war. Married Mary E., daughter of Starling Burnett, of Edgefield County, November 14,
1866. Merchandised at Graniteville until 1876, then located
at Aiken. President and treasurer of the Aiken Industrial
Company, member of the board of trustees of Furman University and the Greenville Female College about ten years.
Member of city council several terms. He is also interested
in farming.

HENDERSON, D. S.—Born in Walterboro, Colleton County,

South Carolina, April 19, 1849. His
father's name was D. S. Henderson,
and his mother's Caroline R. Webb,
both of whom were natives of South
Carolina. Was educated in the local
schools and then entered the Charleston College, from which he was graduated, in 1870, with first honors. He
began the study of law in the office of
Simon and Seigling, Charleston, South
Carolina, remaining there one year and
a half. On leaving them he went to
Chester, where he taught school as
principal of the Male Academy, pursuing his law studies

during his unengaged hours. Admitted to the bar in 1872, and commenced the practice of law in Aiken, South Carolina, being one of the first attorneys to open an office for the practice of law in that city after the formation of a new county. Every volume of the Supreme Court reports, from 1872 to 1891, shows from one to six cases argued before the court, by Mr. Henderson or his partner. He has been a member of every State Democratic Convention in Aiken County, except two, since 1873. Was a delegate to the Chicago Convention that nominated Grover Cleveland for president, in 1884. Served six years, in the State Senate, from 1880, declining to serve longer on account of business. He was the author of the famous bill to prevent dueling in the State, and secured the adoption of the test oath proposed by the Legislature, to be taken by every State officer from the highest to the lowest, never to engage in a duel. He has been a trustee of the South Carolina College, the Presbyterian Theological Seminary, an elder in the Presbyterian Church, and president of the Aiken Institute. Married, in 1875, to Miss Ripley, a daughter of T. R. Ripley, of Atlanta, Georgia.

HENDERSON, FRANKLIN BETTIS.—President of the Peoples Bank of Aiken. Son of George W. and Julia Kirksey Henderson. Born near Trenton, Edgefield County, South Carolina, June 8, 1847. Good English education obtained from the common schools. Entered the Confederate army at age of fifteen, joining Company B, Nineteenth South Carolina Volunteer Infantry, Manigault's Brigade, Wither's Division, Army of the West. Married Margaret Platte, in November, 1873. Dry goods merchant at Graniteville, and then at Aiken for several years. President of the Bank of Aiken eight years. President of the Aiken Manufacturing Company two years.

HENDERSON, PERONNEAU FINLEY.—Lawyer. Son of Daniel Henderson of Aiken. Born in Aiken, South Carolina, November 29, 1877. Graduate of the Aiken Institute, and first honor man of Davidson College, delivering the philosophic oration, in 1897. He is unmarried. Won the prize given by the Pope Manufacturing Company for South Carolina, in an easy contest; subject, "Good Roads." Read law under Henderson Brothers, and was admitted to the bar, in 1898. Became a member of the present firm of Hendersons (successor to Henderson Brothers), in 1899.

HENDRIX, MATTHEW QUITMAN.—Son of John S. Hendrix. Born, February 19, 1858, near Lexington, South Carolina. Received primary education at Lexington High School; then entered Roanoke College, Salem, Virginia, in 1876. Graduated therefrom in June, 1881. In the fall of that year entered Rush Medical College, Chicago, Illinois, completing the course, in 1884. In 1888, he married Miss Jessie Hendrix. He was raised on a farm until sixteen years of age. Then taught until twenty-six. Has practiced medicine and surgery, at Lexington, since leaving school.

HENRY, JAMES KILLOUGH.—Born on the banks of Rocky Creek, September 8, 1856, in Chester County, South Carolina. Attended the school near Old Purity Church, and the schools in Chester. Prepared for Erskine College by his brother. Married Sarah Ella Hamilton, of Marrissa, Illinois, January 7, 1888, at Winnsboro, South Carolina. Taught school at various places and was secretary of the Agricultural and Mechanical Association three years. Member of the boards of directors of the Moffett Manufacturing Company and the Exchange Bank of Chester. Three years chairman of the County Democratic Committee, and re-elected for four years more. Elder in the Associate Reformed Presbyterian Church. Admitted to the bar, in 1883. Solicitor of the Sixth Judicial Circuit six years.

HERBERT, DANIEL OSCAR.—Lawyer. Son of Captain C. W. Herbert and Mrs. E. S. Goggans. Born in Newberry County, April 19, 1857. Of English descent, the Herberts having emigrated to New England before the Revolution, some of them coming to South Carolina, about 1790. Graduated from Wofford College, in 1878, with first honor, received

14

Master of Arts degree from same college, in 1879. Graduated, in law, from Vanderbilt University, in 1881. Married Julia S., daughter of A. M. Sally, of Orangeburg, in January, 1893. Admitted to the bar, in 1882. As United States Postoffice Inspector, traveled in the New England States, and on the Pacific Coast, from 1887, to 1890. Has been a member of the city council and county board of education. In 1898, he raised a company for the Spanish-American War, and served through the Cuban War as captain of Company C, Second South Carolina Volunteer Infantry, under Colonel Willie Jones, this regiment being a part of the Seventh Army Corps under General Fitzhugh Lee, lieutenant-colonel of the Second Regiment of State Militia. Attorney of the Peoples Bank of Orangeburg, of which bank he is a director.

HERBERT, HILARY A.—Former secretary of the United States Navy. Born in Laurensville, South Carolina, March 12, 1834. Attended school in Laurensville, until twelve years of age, then at Greenville, Alabama. He then went to the University of Alabama, and later, the University of Virginia. LL.D. of Tulane University of Louisiana. Married Ella B. Smith, April 23, 1867. He was captain, major, lieutenant-colonel and colonel respectively, in Confederate States Army. Representative in Congress from the Second District of Alabama. Member of the Social Science Association of Philadelphia, Economic Federation, Chicago.

HERBERT, WALTER ISAAC.—Son of Thomas J. and Harriet Boyce Herbert. Was born April 6, 1864. Entered preparatory department of Wofford College, in October, 1881, and graduated with Bachelor of Art degree, in June, 1885. He married Miss Constance Furman, June 26, 1889. Joined South Carolina Conference of Methodist Episcopal Church, South, in December, 1885; and served as pastor in Union, Cheraw, Laurens, Florence, and is now supplying the church at Newberry. Is also serving the church as treasurer of board of missions of the Conference, since December, 1895. He is a member of the board of the Epworth Orphanage, at Columbia, South Carolina, and a trustee of Cokesbury Conference School.

HERNDON, EDMUND LEE.—Elected to the State Senate, from Oconee County, in 1900. Was born near Tunnell Hill, Oconee County, June 16, 1864. He attended the public schools of the county, and went to Adger College; but was induced by Professor W. S. Moore to stand competitive examination for scholarship to the Citadel, and won scholarship over four competitors. Remained in that institution until 1885. Taught school two years. Read law under Colonel Keith and General John Sam Verner. Was admitted to the bar, in 1888, at Columbia, before the Supreme Court. He was trial justice at Walhalla, a number of terms; and coroner. Elected judge of probate, in 1894, and served until 1898, declining re-election. He has lost but one case before the Supreme Court since admission to the bar. Is now junior member of the firm of Stribling & Herndon, at Walhalla, South Carolina. He married Miss Clara V. Platt, of Aiken County, June 27, 1900.

HESSE, EARNEST CHRISTOPHER.—Clerked with the firm of W. W. Whilden & Company, cotton and naval stores. On death of Mr. Whilden, went into business for himself; and, in 1891, admitted W. H. Shingler as partner. Mr. Hesse was born January 16, 1863, at Charleston, South Carolina. Obtained an education from high schools of Charleston, and Carolina Military Institute, of Charlotte, North Carolina. Married Miss Julia H. Albers, April 20, 1892. He is also a cotton factor and commission merchant; president of Combahee Land and Rice Company; vice-president of German American Trust & Savings Bank. Director of Charleston Cotton Exchange.

HEYWARD, DUNCAN CLINCH.—Born June 24, 1864, in Richland County, South Carolina. Son of Edward Barnwell Heyward and Katharine Maria Clinch. Attended Cheltenham Military Academy, near Philadelphia, Pennsylvania, for three years, and afterwards Washington and Lee University, for the same length of time. In 1887, engaged in the planting of rice, in Colleton County. Has been in that business ever since. In 1897, was elected grand chancellor of the

Knights of Pythias of South Carolina; and in 1901, supreme representative of that order. Captain Troop F, First Regiment South Carolina Volunteer Cavalry. Married Miss Mary Elizabeth Campbell, of Rockbridge County, Virginia.

HEYWARD, JULIUS H.—Third son of Nathaniel and Eliza B. (Rhett) Heyward. Was born at Beaufort, South Carolina, July 4, 1849. Arthur Middleton was the great-grandfather of his mother, and Thomas Heyward, Jr., was a brother of his great-grandfather. He attended Beaufort Academy until 1861. Subsequently at Columbia Academy, until 1865, and spent the following year at the College of Charleston. Kept books in Savannah, from 1871, to 1878, and while so employed, studied law. Was admitted to the bar in 1878, and located in Greenville the following year. March 10, 1881, he married Elizabeth, only daughter of William Middleton. He was United States Commissioner. Standing master of United States Circuit Court, and referee in bankruptcy under present law.

HICKS, WILLIAM PINKNEY.—Auditor of Greenville County. Was born in Greenville County, July 14, 1862. The foundation of his education was laid in the common schools, and the East Gantt High School. Later took a business course at Greenville, South Carolina. He was united in marriage with Miss Alice E. LeMance, on October 8, 1891. He taught school a few years, then farmed, until 1892, at which time he was elected to the above position.

HIGGINS, CHARLES MOUZON.—Son of James and Elizabeth M. Higgins. Born June 15, 1863, at Sand Ridge, Berkeley County, South Carolina. Of Scotch-Irish descent. Attended the private school of Miss Mattie Gamewell, of Spartanburg, South Carolina, and Porter Military Academy, Charleston. Married Miss Minnie E. Mims, May 29, 1883. Elected supervisor of Berkeley County, in 1897; served two years; and elected auditor, in 1899.

HILDEBRAND, PRESTON T.—Lawyer. Son of Dr. Daniel L. Hildebrand and Mary Ann Sutton. Born May 23, 1866, in

Orangeburg County. Read law in the office of Judge James F. Izlar. Admitted to the bar, in 1877, and located at Orangeburg. County attorney several years. Elected solicitor of the First Circuit, in 1900, to succeed Solicitor Jervey. Married Cornelia Zimmerman, January 8, 1888. Former trustee of the Orangeburg Graded School.

HILL, L. T.—Practicing medicine at Abbeville, South Carolina. Was born in Edgefield County, May 12, 1852. His early education was received from the public schools, and Edgefield Academy. Took one course at the South Carolina Medical College, Charleston, South Carolina. Graduated at the University of Maryland, in 1882. On October 11, 1876, he married Miss Fannie Johnson, of Edgefield County. He was engaged in the drug business and farming at Ninety-Six.

HILL, ROBERT EMMET.—Is now serving his second term as judge of probate for Abbeville County. Was born near Abbeville, South Carolina, January, 1839. He received his education from the public schools of the neighborhood, and at Erskine College, Due West, South Carolina. After leaving college, he spent several months traveling, principally in Scotland and Ireland. Soon after his return home, the war between the States came on, and, joining the Second South Carolina Rifles, he served with his regiment around the city of Charleston and vicinity, when by accident he was disabled for active service. Was thereupon assigned to duty under Major C. D. Melton, in which capacity he continued to serve until the close of the war. He has twice represented Abbeville County in the House of Representatives.

HINES, EDGAR ALPHONSO.—He is a practicing physician of Seneca, South Carolina. Was born near Goldsboro, North Carolina, November 19, 1867. His primary training was received in the graded schools of Wilmington, North Carolina. Graduated at the Medical College of the State of South Carolina, in 1891. Took a special course in chemistry, Clemson College, South Carolina, in 1895; and also a special course in diseases of women, at Johns Hopkins Hospital, in 1898. He married Miss Mary Woodbury, eldest daughter of General James W. Moore, of Hampton, South Carolina, July 25, 1894. He was president of Hampton County Medical Association, in 1892. Secretary of Oconee Medical Association. Member of the American Medical Association, Mississippi Valley Medical Association, and the South Carolina Medical Association. Medical examiner for New York Life Insurance Company, Mutual Life of New York, and Knights of Honor. He was sent as commissioner to the General Assembly, Atlanta, Georgia, in 1900.

HIOTT, DAVID WESTON.—Son of Arthur and Helen Hiott. Was born in Colleton County, South Carolina, June 24, 1852. He attended the common schools of the country, and the Walterboro High School. Later pursued theological studies at the Southern Baptist Theological Seminary, in Greenville, South Carolina. He married Miss Ella E., daughter of Captain Thomas W. Martin, of Anderson, South Carolina, August 8, 1876. Has since supplied churches in Georgia and South Carolina. He was moderator of Piedmont and Beaverdam Association, in South Carolina. Was grand chaplain of Grand Lodge of Masons of South Carolina, for seven years.

HOLLEMAN, JOSEPH WHITFIELD.—Farmer of Oconee County. Was born March 14, 1841, near Sandy Springs, in Anderson County, South Carolina. Removed to Pickens District; now Oconee County, in January, 1851. Has since that time resided in or near Walhalla, South Carolina. His education was acquired principally in the common schools. Volunteered in the war between the States, joining Orr's regiment. Was transferred to Company G, Twelfth South Carolina Volunteers, and served through the war with said company. His second wife was Sarah S. Sharp, whom he married on the 28th of December, 1865. Was at one time coroner of Oconee County. County treasurer seven terms. Judge of probate one term. Master two terms.

HOLMAN, WILLIAM ASHLEY.—Son of J. H. Holman and C. V. (Ashley) Holman. Born in Barnwell, South Carolina, October 7, 1856. Ancestors were English, and settled in this State, about 1710. Attended the common schools, and King's Mountain Military Academy three years, at Yorkville, under the control of Colonel Asbury Coward. Married Miss Isabel, daughter of James T. Aldrich, November 16, 1881. Admitted to bar, in 1885, and has practiced law continuously since. He removed to Charleston, from Barnwell, on August 1, 1898; and formed co-partnership with George S. Legare, in practice of law. Has never held office.

HOLMES, JOHN W.—Editor and proprietor of the "Barnwell People" over twenty-four years. He is a son of Joseph Holmes, of Fairfield County, South Carolina. Graduated from Wofford College, in the class of 1859. Member of the Wallace House. Unmarried.

HOOD, ABRAM DUBARD.—Supervisor of Fairfield County. He was born at Blythewood, Fairfield County, June 26, 1868. Ancestors were among the early settlers of the county. Had only the advantage of a common-school education. Has been a prominent farmer of his native county all his life.

HOOD, ISRAEL McDANIEL.—County auditor four years, of Chester County. Son of John and Elizabeth White Hood. Born August 22, 1846, in Chester County, South Carolina. Attended the old field schools, until sixteen years of age, then joined the First South Carolina Regiment, in 1862, serving until the surrender of the Confederate army. Married Miss Catherine Bradley, of Chester, February 5, 1873. He was in commercial business several years, but later was appointed supervisor of registration, which position he held for eight years.

HOOD, JOHN K.—Son of Professor William Hood and Mrs. Mattie McGaughrin Hood. Was born at Due West, South Carolina, in 1868. Graduated from Erskine College, in 1887. Was admitted to the practice of law, in 1890, and has since practiced his profession at Anderson, South Carolina. For nearly five years he was city clerk and treasurer, and in August, 1898, he was elected mayor of the city of Anderson. In August, 1900, he was elected city attorney. In 1895, he was married to Miss Sara Kennedy, of Due West. In 1892, he was elected to the chair of chemistry in the Washington City Schools, and resigned, in 1893, to accept the superintendency of the Summerton Institute at Bartow, Florida. He has since retired from teaching, and is now editor of the "Courier Informant," at Bartow, Florida.

HOOK, JOHN HILLIARD.—Was born in Orangeburg, South Carolina, April 8, 1870. Son of Judge J. H. Hook, formerly of Orangeburg County, but now of Clemson College. Entered the freshman class of Clemson College, in 1894; and graduated four years later. After graduation he was appointed by the Navy Department at Washington, District of Columbia, inspector of constructions on the coast of Florida, which position he held for two years, resigning to accept a position as instructor in his Alma Mater. He now resides at Clemson College. Married Miss Sara C. Brodie, of Lexington County, October 24, 1900.

HOOK, JOHN N., JUDGE.—Son of Dr. John H. J. Hook and Harriet N. (Culclasure) Hook.  Was born in Orangeburg County, South Carolina, August 23, 1844. He received the best academic education afforded by the county in his day. Spent three years in the Fall Branch Academy at Orangeburg, under the tuition of T. J. P. Walsh, who was a graduate of the University of Dublin, Ireland. Here he was prepared for the sophomore class at the South Carolina College; but his educational plans were broken up by the war. Although not subject to military duty, on account of his age, he enlisted in the Second Regiment of South Carolina Volunteer Artillery, which was stationed on James Island, and participated in many combats in the vicinity of Charleston. He had the honor to be one of the two hundred men, that, for two hours, held the Confederate works at Secessionville, against an overwhelming force of Federals, keeping the enemy in check until reenforcements arrived, and thus defeating a formidable attempt of the enemy on Charleston. Mr. Hook followed the fortunes of the Confederacy to the end, and at the battle of Averasboro a minie ball from the enemy struck him on the shoulder, near the neck, inflicting a slight wound. He participated also in the battle of Bentonville, where the sons of South Carolina nobly upheld the military honor of their gallant State. He was among those surrendered by General Joseph E. Johnston, at Greensboro, North Carolina, April 26, 1865. After the war, he devoted himself to farming and also found time to indulge a taste for study, kindled in his youth, along literary and historical lines. In 1893, he was appointed by the board of trustees, secretary of the South Carolina Experimental Station. Mr. Hook is also the judicial officer for the municipal corporation of Clemson College, the limits of which cover all territory included in a circle, formed with the college building as a center, with a radius of five miles. For the maintenance of order and the repression of crime within the limits of this district, he has, by special act of the Legislature, been clothed with all the powers of a city recorder. For the past eight years, his residence has been on the campus of Clemson College. Mr. Hook has developed more than ordinary power and eloquence as a public speaker. Assigned to duty by the executive committee in the political campaign of 1876, he won an enviable reputation in his native county as a speaker of force and eloquence. Since then, he has been called upon to meet many and varied demands of the platform. As to his success, the press correspondents write: Referring to an oration on the Fourth of July, Correspondent J. E. Penny writes: "Then the marshal introduced Lieutenant J. N. Hook, who had just been commissioned a lieutenant of the volunteer militia, by Governor Wade Hampton, and who was the chosen orator of the day. He held the audience spell-bound for nearly an hour, in an address, which for ornateness, conciseness and pathos would be difficult to surpass." Alluding to a speech delivered before the Calhoun Lyceum League of St. Matthews, South Carolina, editor J. B. McLaughlin of the "St. Matthews Herald" wrote: "After an appropriate introduction, Mr. Hook arose, and, in his own peculiarly eloquent style, held the audience as attentive listeners for fifty-eight minutes. His logic was faultless, his rhetoric unsurpassed, and the advice given was most timely and effective." Judge Hook was appointed by President Hartzog to deliver an address on industrial education, before the last Farmer's Institute at Clemson College. Professor Daniel, reporting for the press, said: "Next came Judge J. N. Hook on industrial education. His speech was a gem, abounded in historical allusions and economic statements in literary form, and was delivered eloquently and earnestly." These are a few of the many complimentary notices already published. Mr. Hook has twice been married, first on September 21, 1865, to Miss Susan M. Pou, who died January 27, 1891; and the second time, to Miss R. E. Miller, of Pendleton, South Carolina. He has five living children, all by his first marriage. One son, John H. Hook, a graduate of Clemson College, is now instructor in his Alma Mater. William N., his other son, is also a graduate of Clemson College, and is at present connected with the cotton-mill industry. The other children are H. Lula, Sue M., and Julia A. Miss H. Lula was a teacher in the Winthrop Normal and Industrial College for girls, until her recent marriage to Mr. L. A. Buckmyer, of Augusta, Georgia.

HOOK, MAXCY WILBUR.—Minister. Son of Edward E. and E. Jane Senn Hook. Born November 8, 1862, in Lexington County, South Carolina. Ancestors came from Holland, and settled along Saluda River, near Columbia. Attended the country schools and Lexington Academy, then went to Leesvilie College, finishing there, in 1885. Married Lena Johnson, September 9, 1891. Engaged in farming until he went into the ministry. Since joining Conference, he has served the following churches: Effingham, Ridgeway, Fairfield, and lower St. Matthews. He is now serving Bamberg Station.

HORNIK, M.—Born in Austria, in 1863. Common-school education in three languages. He is a widower. Engaged in retail business in this State, from 1882, to 1893. Since that time engaged in the wholesale dry goods business in Charleston, since 1893.

HORTON, JAMES EDWARD.—Postmaster at Belton, South Carolina. Was born August 8, 1849, near Belton, South Carolina. Married Miss Majors, on January 16, 1872. In 1898, commenced a mercantile business with his son, James A. Horton, the firm being John A. Horton and Son.

HOUGH, WILLIAM CLIFTON.—Son of M. J. and Esther A. Hough. Born October 28, 1867, near Fort Lawn, Chester County, South Carolina. Ancestors were of English and Scotch descent. Father was a lawyer and solicitor of the Chester Circuit at the time of his death. Education was obtained from Wake Forest College, North Carolina, and South Carolina College, Columbia, South Carolina. In early manhood on account of failing health, left college and farmed a short time. Taught school in Darlington County, and at Fort Lawn. Read law in his father's office, and was admitted to the bar, in 1890. Since then has been practicing law at Lancaster. Elected State Senator from Lancaster County, in 1898, and is still in office. Member of Governor's staff, ranking as lieutenant-colonel.

HOUGH, WILLIAM R.—County treasurer of Kershaw, which position he holds, after having been twice re-elected. Was born in the northeastern part of Kershaw County, near Timrod Post-office, South Carolina. Attended the old-field schools about two months out of each year, until he reached the age of fourteen, working on the farm and teaching in the meantime. Then entered the high school at Silver City, North Carolina, where he remained one year. He was elected supervisor of registration one year, then chairman of board of registration, during which time he was elected to the position he now holds. Married Miss Emma L. Lowell, on September 2, 1891.

HOUSEAL, WILLIAM PRESTON.—Editorial manager and publisher of the "Lutheran Visitor." Born July 30, 1856, at Newberry, South Carolina. Attended primary schools and preparatory department of Newberry College until sixteen years of age. Has had other advantages since, secured in a printing-office. Married Katie A. Rives, on June 16, 1881. Connected with newspaper business since 1878, and is now editor of the "Lutheran Visitor," the leading paper of the Lutheran Church, in the South.

HOWE, WILLIAM KENNEDY.—Son of Colonel James M. Howe and Malvina F. Kennedy. Born January 6, 1853, in Florence County, South Carolina. Of English and Irish ancestry. Attended the common schools of the County, and private tutorship under Professor Gay of Yale. Completed his education at Wofford College, then graduated from the Moore Business College of Atlanta, Georgia. Married Emmie C. Beckman, daughter of J. O. Beckman, of Charleston, February 1, 1852. He has been engaged in mercantile and banking pursuits all his life. For seven years he was connected with the First National Bank of Charleston. In 1900, organized the Commercial and Savings Bank of Florence, ot which he is president. He is also interested in farming.

HOYT, JAMES ALFRED.—Was born October 11, 1837, in Waynesboro, Virginia. Father, J. Perkins Hoyt, was a native of New Hampshire, a jeweler by trade, who came South for his health and located in Virginia. He married Miss Jane Johnson, of Virginia. Colonel J. P. Hoyt was a highly cultured man, and at one time edited the "Laurensville Herald" and the "Anderson Intelligencer." From Virginia, the Hoyt family moved to Clarksville, Georgia, where they lived a short time; and thence went to Laurens, South Carolina, where the subject of this sketch grew to manhood. At the

age of fourteeen, James A. Hoyt entered the office of the
"Laurensville Herald" as an apprentice. When he was eighteen years of age, he went to Anderson as foreman of the
"Anderson Gazette." One year later he was editor of the
paper, which position he held until August, 1860, when he
began the publication of the "Anderson Intelligencer." Colonel Hoyt was a member of the Palmetto Riflemen, a company organized at Anderson for service in the Confederate
War. His company entered the State service, in 1861, and
was present in some of the memorable fights, notably the
first battle of Manassas, the defense of the Stone Bridge,
and all of the principal battles of the Army of Northern Virginia, excepting Chancellorsville and Gettysburg. Colonel
Hoyt rose from the ranks as a private to become colonel of
his regiment, his promotion being "for gallant and meritorious conduct on the field." He was badly wounded, but
refused to leave the scene of action, and remained in command of his detachment until the end. His coolness under
fire was exhibited on many occasions. After the war, he returned to journalism. Was elected a member of the State
Democratic Executive Committee. Later he was made chairman of that committee; and, in 1890, when the Tillman
movement had swept over the State, carrying almost every
county, he was chairman of the National Democratic Committee. He has always been an organized Democrat, sup-
porting Seymour and Blair in 1872, and Greene against
Chamberlain, in 1874. In the early part of 1877, he was editor of the "Columbia Register," then the champion of the
unterrified Democracy. Two years later he purchased the
"Working Christian," which he changed into the "Baptist
Courier" and moved it to Greenville. This paper speedily
became one of the leading denominational papers of the
South. In 1885, Colonel Hoyt was elected president of the
State Baptist convention. Was re-elected to this position
for nine successive terms, when he declined to serve longer.
For twenty years, he was a trustee of Furman University,
and was once president of the Southern Baptist Convention.
In June, 1891, he sold the "Baptist Courier," expecting to re-
tire from journalism, but the ruling passion brought him back,

and in January, 1892, he bought the "Greenville Enterprise and Mountaineer," changed the name to its original form, "The Mountaineer," and became editor and proprietor, which position he now holds. He was a candidate for governor on the prohibition ticket, in 1900, but was defeated.

HUBBELL, JAMES T.—Was born in Norwalk, Connecticut, March 17, 1855. The son of John W. Hubbell and Nancy (Hoyt) Hubbell. Mr. Hubbell is a descendant of Richard Hubbell, who settled in New Haven in 1649, but afterwards removed to Fairfield, Connecticut. Received a common-school and academic education, and after reading law the statutory term, was admitted to the Connecticut Bar. While living in his native State, was a member of the Legislature, 1882-1883; clerk of the Borough of Norwalk, 1891 and 1893; mayor of the city of Norwalk, 1895; and associate judge of the town court of Norwalk, 1895-1897. In May, 1897, took up his residence in Greenville, South Carolina, where he has since lived, and engaged in the practice of his profession. In 1888, Mr. Hubbell married Miss Mary C. Clark.

HUCKS, J. JENKINS.—Son of James S. B. and Sarah (Jenkins) Hucks. Born at Georgetown, South Carolina, October 28, 1843. Educated at the Winyah Indigo Academy; at St. James Academy, at McClellansville; and in Charleston. Admitted to the bar, in 1868. Married Eugenia M. Michel, of Charleston, South Carolina. Lieutenant in the Confederate Infantry service, and lieutenant in the Fifth South Carolina Cavalry, Butler's Brigade, Hampton's Division, Army of Northern Virginia, from 1862, to 1865. Magistrate and trial justice twenty-five years; solicitor for Winyah Society; is now trial justice and city treasurer, and secretary to board of health. Practicing law, since 1869.

HUDGENS, WILLIAM AUGUSTUS.—Born at Honea Path, Anderson County, South Carolina. Son of Dr. Thomas A. Hudgens and Miss Ella Gaines. Born on September 26, 1878. He attended the Honea Path High School until fifteen years of age; then went to Wofford College, graduating there, in

1897, the youngest member of his class. In the fall of that year he was made principal of the school at Free State, Marion County, South Carolina. In 1899, he was elected Secretary and Treasurer of the Honea Path Oil Mill. Was teacher in the Anderson Graded School. Was the first volunteer from Anderson County during the Spanish-American War, elected corporal, in Company C, First Regiment, but rejected upon physical examination; afterwards elected captain of Company H, first regiment South Carolina Volunteer Infantry, which position he now holds.

HUDSON, JOSHUA HILARY.—Son of Dabney Hudson and Narcissa Cook. Born in Chester, South Carolina, January 29, 1832. Of English descent. Graduated from the South Carolina College, in December, 1852, with first honor. Married Miss Mary, daughter of Philip Miller, of Bennettsville, South Carolina, May 4, 1854. Taught school a few years, and then began the study of law at Bennettsville, South Carolina. In 1858, he served one term in the Legislature. In December, 1860, he was appointed reading clerk of the House of Representatives, and served until 1861. In January, 1862, he became a private in the Confederate army in the Company of Captain J. W. Thomas, Twenty-first Regiment South Carolina Volunteers. In April, 1862, became adjutant of the Ninth Battalion South Carolina Volunteers. In May, of the same year, he became major of the same battalion. In December, 1862, he became lieutenant-colonel of the Twenty-Sixth Regiment South Carolina Volunteers, which position he held until the war closed. In April, 1865, was severely wounded at the battle of Five Forks, in Virginia. After the close of the war, he taught school and then resumed the practice of law. On February 14, 1878, was elected judge of the Fourth Judicial Circuit, and remained in office until February, 1894. Then resumed the practice of law at Bennettsville, where he is at present so engaged. In December, 1897, and 1898, was chosen to preside over the State convention of South Carolina Baptists. Judge Hudson was for a number of years prior to 1870, a co-partner with Samuel J. Townsend, who was a very prominent lawyer of his day.

His only son, Dr. A. S. Townsend, is practicing medicine at Bennettsville.

HUDSON, WILLIAM AUSTIN.—Son of W. A. and Rosalie (McCann) Hudson of Greenville County, South Carolina. His father was a surveyor and real estate dealer. Ancestors were Scotch-Irish. W. A. Austin was born November 11, 1870, at Hudson's Mill, near Greenville, South Carolina. Earlier training received from common schools, was five years at Furman University, leaving college in 1894. Immediately thereafter, accepted a position with Lipscomb & Russell, as bookkeeper, holding same six years. In September, 1900, he bought out their retail business, and is still doing business in Greenville, under the firm name of Hudson & Jordan.

HUGER, WILLIAM HARLESTON.—Has been in charge of the Charleston Orphan House, since 1854. Dr. Huger was born May 20, 1826, at Charleston, South Carolina. Graduated from the South Carolina College, in the class of 1846. Studied medicine at the Medical College of South Carolina, at Charleston, and took his diploma in 1849. He then went to Paris, France, and spent two and a half years in the Hospitals and medical schools. Returned to Charleston, in 1857, and commenced the practice of medicine. When the Confederate War opened, he stood an examination before the medical board, passed, and entered the service as surgeon, remaining until the close of the war. Most of the time was in charge of the Confederate "Soldiers Relief" in Charleston. When yellow fever appeared in Wilmington, North Carolina, in 1864, he was ordered there, to look after the epidemic. He then returned to his hospital in Charleston, when the city was to be evacuated, and was ordered to take all the sick and wounded, who could bear transportation, to the town of Cheraw. The first train that left the city was under his care with five or six hundred sick soldiers. He reached Cheraw after several days, hopitals were opened, and the sick located and taken care of. Dr. Huger married Sabina Huger Lowndes, daughter of Mr. C. T. Lowndes, May 12, 1866.

HUGHES, EDWIN LEON.—Superintendent of the Greenville Graded Schools. Was born in Orange County, North Carolina, June 6, 1861. He pursued collegiate and pedagogical studies, and then took a special course in music and drawing. He has been very successful in teaching, and was principal of academy at Granite Falls, North Carolina, 1884; principal, afterwards superintendent, of graded schools at Reidsville, North Carolina, 1887, to 1892; and in that year he was elected to the position he now has. He is instructor and director in summer schools in this State, North Carolina, and Alabama, since 1889. Has been engaged in these schools, from one week to a month, in forty or more counties of these states, in some of the counties twice or thrice.

HUMBERT, JOSEPH BENSON.—Second son of Rev. John G. Humbert. Born near Knoxville, Tennessee, where his parents had recently moved from Beaufort, South Carolina. After a few years, they returned to South Carolina and located in Laurens County. Graduated at Wofford College, in 1860, and taught school for a few months. He assisted in the organization of an artillery company at Orangeburg, to serve in the Confederate States Army. He was elected second lieutenant, and afterwards first lieutenant, which position he filled until the close of the war, being principally engaged in the defense of Charleston. Honorable mention was made of his gallant conduct in the report of the commanding general. In 1884, he was married to Miss Emma Pooser, a daughter of Major George H. Pooser, of Orangeburg. He was elected to the Legislature, in 1876, and represented his County for four successive years. Has been connected with the State Agricultural and Mechanical Society for a number of years, and served as president, in 1887 and 1888. Was elected president of the Chattanooga, Knoxville and Western Railroad at its organization. He is a farmer, and has devoted his time to scientific and practical agriculture with success.

HUNT, COLUMBUS J.—Son of William J. and Sarah J. Hunt, nee Smith. Was born on a farm, in Anderson County, near Honea Path, South Carolina, on the 19th of November,

15

1853. In early life he worked on a farm, and attended the country schools; and later, attended a high school at Honea Path. In 1873, he went to Greenville, South Carolina, and clerked for Beattie & Company. Later, entered the dry goods business on his own account. In 1882, he closed out his business, and went to Laurens, South Carolina, and entered the law office of Benet & McGowan, and was admitted to the bar, in May, 1885. On February 20, 1886, he was commissioned and appointed, by Governor Thompson, one of the trial justices at Laurens, South Carolina; served two years. He continued to practice his profession at Laurens, until 1891, when he returned to Greenville where he is now practicing law. On the first of March, 1887, he was married to Elizabeth E., daughter of John L. and Mary R. Griffin, of Abbeville County, South Carolina.

HUNT, SAMUEL ARTHUR.—Son of Robert G. Hunt, of Pickens County. Was born December 24, 1872, at Dacusville, Pickens County. His ancestors setteled at Jamestown, Virginia, in 1607, and came to South Carolina just before the Revolution. Attended the common schools of his county, and took a business course from Kentucky University, at Lexington, Kentucky, in 1891. Married Miss Lillian E. Werts, daughter of David B. Werts, of Newberry, South Carolina. Taught school one year. Elected auditor of Pickens County, in 1898; and is still holding that position.

HUNTER, JOHN PIERCE.—Was born in Lancaster County, October 8, 1855. He was educated at home schools. He was elected sheriff of his county, when twenty-five years of age, and filled the office for four consecutive terms, beginning in the fall of 1880. Resigned April, 1894, to take charge of the United States Marshal's office for the District of South Carolina, to which office he had been appointed by President Cleveland. He continued in this office until April 1, 1898. At the expiration of his term as marshal, he returned to Lancaster, his native home, and was again elected sheriff, in 1900. He was advised by many prominent Republicans to apply for re-election to the marshal's office, but would not consent on account of being a straight-out Democrat. His family has ·always been strong and influential in their County. His father served as sheriff for eight years. He married Mrs. Laura A. Hickson, daughter of Rev. Elias E. Frazer, on the 13th of January, 1881. She died at Mount Pleasant, South Carolina, in 1895, while Captain Hunter was serving as United States marshal. On November 3, 1898, he was again married, to Miss Florella Meynardie, eldest daughter of Rev. E. J. Meynardie, D.D., of South Carolina Conference.

HYATT, FREDERICK HARGRAVE.—Was born on a farm in Anson County, North Carolina, June 14, 1849. By hard work, accumulated enough money to give himself a fair education in the schools and colleges of that State. Entered the senior class at college, but did not graduate. Followed farming until 1884. Married Miss Lina S. Kendall, August 12, 1874. Took up life insurance in 1884, and was made superintendent of agencies for Valley Mutual Life Insurance Company, of Virginia, for North Carolina. His able work attracted the attention of other companies, and after filling a special agency for the New York Life, for several years, became general agent of the Mutual Life, of New York, for North and South Carolina, with headquarters at Columbia; which position he still holds. Mr. Hyatt has made a remarkable success, as an insurance man. He is president of the Eau Claire & Columbia Electric Railway, and has repeatedly been honored by the governor of South Carolina, with appointments of honor and trust. He is president of the Young Men's Christian Association, of Columbia; and to his efforts, is largely due the erection of the splendid Young Men's Christian Association building in that city.

HYDRICK, AUGUSTUS SALLY.—Physician. Son of Major J. H. Hydrick and Margaret Hilderbrand. Born November 11, 1849, in Orangeburg County. Of German descent.

Common and high school education. Graduated from the medical department of the University of South Carolina, in 1873. Married Henrietta, daughter of J. H. Livingston, January 21, 1874. In 1869, he went to Arkansas, and clerked at Pine Bluff two years, returned to South Carolina and taught school one year. City physician of Columbia, in 1875. Moved to Orangeburg, in 1876. Democratic County Chairman, several years. He is now serving fourth term as member of the city council. Chairman of board of health many years. Appointed surgeon in First South Carolina Infantry, during late war, but rejected on account of age.

IRVINE, WILLIAM H.—Son of Dr. O. B and Frances M. Irvine, of Greenville, South Carolina. On his mother's side, Dr. Daniel F. McMahan, Sr., came direct to this country from Cork, Ireland, and settled at Pinckneyville, then the county seat of Union County, buying the county court-house and a large body of land adjacent when the county-seat was removed from Pinckneyville to the present town of Union, South Carolina. The subject of this sketch was born in Greenville, South Carolina, August 9, 1854. He attended the schools of his native town, and graduated from Furman University in the class of 1875. He was married to Miss Eva Baker, daughter of Rev. W. E. Baker, who was for twenty-six years the pastor of the Presbyterian Church at Staunton, Virginia, on October 3, 1889. He read law under the late Chief Justice Simpson and Moore, of Greenville. Was admitted to the bar, in 1877, and has since practiced at Greenville. For four years he was a member of the firm of Stokes & Irvine. Subsequently, he practiced with Mr. J. A. Mooney, and later still for a year or two, with James V. Crosskeys. He represented Greenville, as city attorney, two years, while S. A. Townes was mayor, and he drafted the present city charter. He is now practicing law alone, devoting himself almost exclusively to civil business. Is a large lender of money for clients. He is one of the largest real estate owners in the County.

IZLAR, JAMES F.—Lawyer. Born in Orangeburg County, November 25, 1832. Son of William H. Izlar and Julia Pou.

Of Swiss and Scotch descent. His education was obtained in the schools of Orangeburg County up to his seventeenth year, when he entered Emory College, Georgia. Graduated in 1854, with first honor. After completing his collegiate course, he turned his attention to educational pursuits, and was thus engaged until 1855, when he began the study of law, under Col. Thomas J. Glover, who at that time was circuit judge. Admitted to bar, in 1858, opening an office at Orangeburg. He volunteered in the First South Carolina Volunteer Regiment for a period of twelve months, under the command of Colonel Hagood. Mr. Izlar then served as third lieutenant of the Edisto Rifles. At the end of the first twelve months, the Edisto Rifles were assigned to the Twenty-fifth South Carolina Regiment, commanded by Colonel Charles H. Simonton. Lieutenant Izlar was appointed captain of the Edisto Rifles, which command he held until the close of the war. In 1863, the Twenty-fifth Regiment went to Virginia, and participated in the battles of Coal Harbor, Wéldon and the trenches near Petersburg. He was imprisoned at Fort Columbus, on Governor's Island, New York, until his parolement, in March, 1865. In 1866, he resumed the practice of his profession at Orangeburg. In 1889, elected judge of the First Circuit. Elected State Senator; re-elected, in 1884, and again in 1888. Member of State Democratic Executive Committee sixteen years. Trustee of the South Carolina College. After the war, appointed brigadier-general of State troops, and, later, promoted to major general. Has been mayor of Orangeburg. Married Frances M. Lovell. Elected to Congress from the First Congressional District, in 1894, to succeed Honorable William H. Brawley, member of the Fifty-third Congress. Was not a candidate for re-election. Since, has resumed the practice of his profession at Orangeburg.

JACOBS, JAMES FERDINAND.—Editor of the "Southern Presbyterian." Eldest son of Rev. W. P. Jacobs. Born October 6, 1868. Graduated with the degree of A. B., from the Presbyterian College of South Carolina, with degree of Master of Arts from Princeton University, and from the Columbia Theological Seminary. Married, on September 9, 1891,

Miss Mary Elliott Duckett, of Clinton, South Carolina. He was financial agent of the Presbyterian College of South Carolina; professor of physiology and Biblical literature, in same institution. He has been the pastor of various churches, and has edited the "Southern Presbyterian," since 1898. Manager of South Carolina Religious Advertising Syndicate.

JACOBS, WILLIAM PLUMER.—Pastor of the First Presbyterian Church of Clinton, South Carolina. Founder and president of the Thornwell Orphanage, at same place. Was born in Yorkville, South Carolina, March 15, 1842. He graduated at the Charleston College, in the class of 1861; and at the Columbia Theological Seminary, in 1864, at the age of twenty-two. He was licensed to preach, in April, 1862, and was ordained in May, 1864. His first charge was the Presbyterian Church at Clinton, South Carolina, of which he has been the pastor for thirty-seven years. In 1886, he established a monthly magazine devoted to religion, education and charity, of which he has since been the editor and publisher. He was married on April 20, 1865, to Miss Mary J., daughter of James H. Dillard, of Laurens County. Mr. Jacobs is a Mason and a Good Templar. In politics, he is Democratic. In educational and charitable work, he is one of the best known individuals of the South. He is a member of the national conference of charities and corrections, and has often been a delegate to the prominent conventions of his church. For five years of his early manhood, he was a reporter on the staff of the "Charleston Courier," the Charleston Mercury," The "Daily Carolinian" of Columbia, and the "Southern Presbyterian" of Columbia. He was founder and president of board of trustees of the Presbyterian College of South Carolina. The degree of Master of Arts was conferred by Charleston College, and of D. D. by Erskine College.

JAMISON, ATHA T.—Superintendent and treasurer of Connie Maxwell Orphanage, at Greenwood. He was born March 5, 1866, at Murfreesboro, Tennessee. Attended the high schools at Union, and the University of Tennessee. He took the theological course at the Baptist Theological Seminary,

Louisville, Kentucky. Married Miss Emma C. Caldwell, on
October 3, 1889. He was general secretary of the Young
Men's Christian Association, at Charleston, South Carolina,
from 1885 to 1894. In 1895, he was called to supply the Baptist Church at Camden, where he remained until he assumed
charge of his present position.

JAYNES, ROBERT THOMPSON.—Son of Waddy Thompson and Della S. Jaynes. Born February 14, 1862, at Richland, Oconee County, South Carolina. Attended the common
schools of the county. September, 1879, entered the Sophomore class of Adger College; graduated, June, 1882, at the
head of his class. Studied law in the office of Wells & Orr,
at Greenville, and admitted to the bar in May, 1884. On December 22, 1886, he was married to Mattie C., daughter of
Rev. J. Steck, D. D. Has at all times declined election to
political office, and has given strict attention to the practice
of law. He located at Walhalla, South Carolina, for the practice of law, in 1885, in partnership with Colonel R. A. Thompson, which lasted until 1893. On January 1, 1895, he formed
a partnership with Joseph W. Shelor, under the firm name
of Jaynes & Shelor, which still exists. On April 1, 1887, succeeded the late Colonel W. C. Keith, as editor of the "Keowee
Courier," and is still connected with the paper.

JEFFRIES, WILLIAM.—Was born April 2, 1830, in what
was then Union District, on Thickety
Creek. He was educated at Limestone
College. Taught a few years after
graduation, and merchandised two
years. Was elected to the State Legislature, in 1858. In April, 1860, he
married Mrs. R. C. Farr, of Jonesville,
South Carolina. In March, 1862, he
went into the service in Company F,
Eighteenth South Carolina Volunteers, as private; being unable to
stand the march, in November afterwards, he obtained a discharge. Af-
ter resting awhile, he joined the Holcomb Legion of Cavalry,

Captain Frost. He was detailed with other men to come to South Carolina, to get up horses for the dismounted men, and on the way back learned that General Lee had surrendered. After the new constitution was adopted, in 1895, he, with other men, went to work to create a new County—the result was the forming of Cherokee County out of Spartanburg, Union and York Counties. After this was elected Senator from the new County. He is a director of the Gaffney Manufacturing Company; the Merchants and Planters Bank, of Union, South Carolina; and also of the First National Bank of Gaffney, South Carolina.

JENKINS, HAWKINS KING.—Engaged in practicing law, and rice planting. He is a son of Paul F. Jenkins, M. D., and Theodora Ashe B. King. He was born at Adams Run, South Carolina, May 23, 1859. Of English descent. The Jenkinses came to this country in 1720. His grandfather fought in the Revolution. Obtained education at Porter Military Academy. Married Josephine, daughter of Lewis Manigault. Taught private school in Aiken two years. Member of House of Representatives from 1888, to 1890; Senator from 1890, to 1894; member of House of Representatives, from 1898, to 1900. Read law in office of George W. Croft, at Aiken. Admitted to bar, in 1881, and located in Rock Hill, South Carolina. Moved to Yorkville, in 1883; and later to Mt. Pleasant, then the county seat of Berkeley County. Has been practicing law in that, and adjacent counties, ever since.

JENNINGS, ROBERT HENRY.—He was born near Jenkinsville, Fairfield County, February 6, 1839. He is a son of Henry Reid and Nancy Malinda (Robinson) Jennings. Obtained education from old field schools. Married Nancy Leonora Gibson, May 17, 1860. Began life as a blacksmith. Served throughout war; was third lieutenant Company G; James Battalion of Infantry. Was in the Virginia campaign in Drayton's Brigade. Was captured in battle, and confined in Fort Deleware. Was exchanged, and transferred to Kershaw's Brigade. Promoted to second lieutenant, then to first lieutenant. From July, 1863, was in command of his company in nearly all of the important battles fought by Longstreet's Corps, in Virginia and Georgia. Lost his left arm. July 28, 1864, in battle of New Market Heights, Virginia. Tax collector of Fairfield, from 1866 to 1868; county treasurer; clerk of the court, from 1888 to 1900. In 1900, elected state treasurer, which position he now holds. Member of board of finance of South Carolina Conference, Methodist Episcopal Church, and board of trustees of Columbia Female College.

JERVEY, JAMES WILKINSON.—Specialist in diseases of ear, eye, nose and throat. He is a son of Eugene P. Jervey, of Charleston, South Carolina. Was born in that city, October 19, 1874. He graduated as valedictorian of his class, from the high school of Charleston, in 1890. Entered the sophmore class of the South Carolina College in the fall of that year; withdrew in 1892. Entered the South Carolina Medical College the following year. Graduated in 1897. and went immediately to New York, taking postgraduate work in several leading hospitals there. Located in Charleston, but remained only a short time, having been elected to the chair of the ear, nose, and throat in Shirras Dispensary Clinic, in 1898. In the fall of that year, he went to Green-ville. He is special examining surgeon of the United States Pension Bureau. Member of the Greenville County Medical Society and the State Medical Society, and also the American Medical Association. He is a frequent contributor to the leading medical journals of the United States. Was city editor of the "Charleston Daily Sun" during part of 1896 and 1897. A frequent contributor under the nom de plume of "Jo Wilkes" to the various papers of the State. He married Miss Helen D. Smith, on October 26, 1899.

JERVEY, W. ST. JULIAN.—Member of Charleston bar. Son of William and Catherine Stevens Jervey. Born in Charleston, South Carolina, April 26, 1847. Graduated from the College of Charleston. Married Miss Mary Caroline Greene, of Columbia January 24, 1878. Wife since deceased.

He was solicitor of First Circuit. Member of National Democratic Convention of 1894, and of Constitutional Convention of 1895.

JESUNOFSKY, LEWIS NATHAN.—Manager of the weather bureau in Charleston, South Carolina. He is a son of Jacob Jesunofsky, a native of Berlin, Prussia, a Revolutionist, of 1848, who escaped to America with Carl Schurz and other German patriots. Was a wholesale merchant at Washington, District of Columbia. Lewis Jesunofsky, the grand father of Nathan, was a Polander by birth, and the son of a distinguished Polish general who gave up his life for his country. The subject of this sketch, Lewis Nathan Jesunofsky, attended the public schools of Washington, District of Columbia, Georgetown College, and Vanderbilt University, also Mattern German Academy and Emerson Institute. Has had charge of the New York, Cincinnati and Washington weather bureau offices. Was in charge of an important division of the chief weather bureau office, from 1879 to 1880, when he was associated with the present chief of the bureau, Professor Willis L. Moore. Has been connected with the weather bureau, since 1874. He has been in charge of the Charleston office since 1891. He performed meritorious service during the storm of 1893, for which he was promoted. He is a member of several scientific societies and fraternal orders, by one of which he has been selected as an honorary member, notably "Die Oesterreichische Gesellschaft fur Meteorologie" of Vienna, Austria. He is associate editor of several prominent journals, writing upon meterological and scientific subjects. Married Ida F. Jesunofsky, August 11, 1887, in New York City.

JOHNSON, CLARENCE EDWARD.—Superintendent of the Florence City schools. Son of Colonel David Johnson. Born at Meadow Woods, Union County, South Carolina. Grandson of Governor David Johnson, and also of Daniel Wallace, Adjutant General of State Militia, and member of Congress. Attended the Union Academy under Judge Townsend, and Professor Benjamin F. Bailey, now of Abbeville.

Graduated from the South Carolina Military Academy, in 1889; and from the South Carolina College with the degree of Master of Arts. Married Madeline G. Coates, of Charleston, South Carolina, February 15, 1896. He was assistant professor of English at the Citadel. Principal of the Columbia high school.

JOHNSON, DAVID BANCROFT.—Born at LaGrange, West Tennessee, January 10, 1856, where his father founded, and, until his death, was president of, LaGrange Female College. Professor Johnson's grandmother was born and raised in Laurens County, South Carolina. Graduated from the University of Tennessee, Knoxville, Tennessee, with the highest honors of his class, in 1877, with degree of A. B. In 1879, secured degree of A. M. from his Alma Mater. Among the various positions held, are assistant professor of mathematics, University of Tennessee, 1879, 1880; Principal Abbeville, South Carolina, Graded School, 1880, 1882; Superintendant and organizer of Columbia, South Carolina, city schools, 1883-1895. He was president of the State Teachers' Association, 1884-1888; vice-president National Educational Association, 1894; organized South Carolina Association of School Superintendents; established Columbia, South Carolina, Young Men's Christian Association, and was it president 1885-1894; chairman State Executive Committee Young Men's Christian Association, 1886-1895; member of State Board of Education, 1891-1892. Having demonstrated his executive ability and his thorough grasp of school organization and management, Professor Johnson was called to organize the city schools of Columbia, South Carolina, in 1883, and, in the course of a few years under his superintendence, a system of public instruction was evolved, which is an honor to the State and has been an example after which many of the larger towns and cities have modeled their schools. To meet the requirement for better teachers to introduce these better methods, Professor Johnson, aided by the Peabody board and under the auspices of the board of school commissioners of Columbia, established, in 1886, the Winthrop Training School for Teachers. The Legislature of the State first established scholarships in this school for the training of teachers, and, afterwards, in 1891, adopted it as a full State institution; and, enlarging and broadening it, named it the Winthrop Normal and Industrial College of South Carolina, which is now located at Rock Hill, South Carolina. Professor Johnson has been the president of Winthrop College since its organization.

JOHNSON, JOHN.—Born in Charleston, South Carolina, December 29, 1829. He was educated in the private school of Mr. C. Cotes, and being very ambitious he determined to spend two sessions at the University of Virginia. There he won a gold medal for the best contribution to the college journal, and also the valedictory of the Jefferson Society. Married Miss Floride Cantey, of Camden, South Carolina, on December 20, 1865. He was for ten years a civil engineer. Having later decided to enter the ministry, began preparations, and studied at Camden, South Carolina, under Bishop Thomas F. Davis, when the war between the States broke out and prevented him from completing the course at that time. He enlisted in the army, and was first lieutenant, captain, and major of engineers, while being in active service at Savannah, Charleston, and Wilmington. He was engineer-in-charge during the bombardment of Fort Sumter. He was ordained to the ministry in 1866, and assumed charge of Grace Church, Camden, South Carolina. Went to Charleston, 1871, to become assistant rector of St. Phillips Church; afterwards became pastor of the church and holds this position at the present time. He is the author of a book, "The Defense of Charleston Harbor," including Fort Sumter and the adjacent islands. The University of the South at Sewanee, Tennessee, has conferred upon him the degree of Doctor of Divinity; and the College of Charleston, L. L. D.

JOHNSON, JOSEPH TRAVIS.—Congressman from the Fourth District of South Carolina, from 1901, to 1903. Born at Brewerton, Laurens County, South Carolina, February 28, 1858. Son of Benjamin and Mary J. Johnson. Graduated from Erskine College, in 1879. Married Sarah Anderson, of Laurens, South Carolina, July 30, 1890. Admitted to the South Carolina bar, May 30, 1883. Has since practiced at Laurens and Spartanburg, South Carolina.

JOHNSON, OSCAR EDWARD.—Has been engaged in the insurance business since 1870. Mr. Johnson was born December 25, 1853, at Charleston, South Carolina. His earlier education was obtained from the private and high schools of Charleston, and, later, from the College of Charleston. He was twice married. First to Miss Lila Boozer, of Newberry, South Carolina, who died in 1887; and, in 1889, to Miss Maude Boozer, of Newberry, South Carolina. Vice-president of Charleston board of fire underwriters from 1892, to 1896; and president from then, until the present time. Went into insurance business immediately after leaving college, and is still so employed, being senior member of the firm of Ravenel, Johnson & Robertson.

JOHNSON, WILLIAM ANDREW.—Was born near Galivants Ferry, in Horry County, South Carolina, February 21, 1866. His education was confined to the common schools of the neighborhood. He clerked some time, and from 1888 to 1900, he was traveling salesman for F. W. Wagener & Company, of Charleston, South Carolina. He married Miss Mollie Holliday, of Marion, South Carolina, February 15, 1894. In January, 1900, he organized the wholesale grocery house of the W. A. Johnson Company, at Columbia, South Carolina, of which he is now the president and general manager. He is a leading figure among the big Gervais Street merchants of Columbia.

JOHNSTON, PRESTON CORNELIUS, JR.—Son of Preston C. and Annie C. Johnston. Was born in Spartanburg, South Carolina, September 11, 1862. He received his education in the Reidville school, and the Pittsburg Institute, Texas. His father removed to Texas when he was seven years old, and remained there ten years. Preston C. Johnston was seventeen years old when he returned to his native State, and had the privilege of attending school only a few months after this time. He was for several years engaged in the lumber business. A short time before the county of Dorchester was formed, he removed to Reevesville, South Carolina, and was elected the first clerk of court of the new county. Is now serving his second term. He was twice married, first to Miss A. T. Minus, July 14, 1888; and second to Miss Louise King, in September, 1898.

JOHNSTON, SAMUEL ROBERT.—Son of James Johnston, of Fairfield County. Born April 27, 1830, near White Oak, Fairfield County. His father was a Revolutionary soldier. Ancestors came to this country from Antrem County, Ireland. Had only the advantage of the neighborhood schools. He was twice married; his second wife was Miss Jane Mc-Dowell, whom he married in November, 1879. Before the Civil War he was captain of the militia. Belonged to Company G, Sixth Regiment, South Carolina Volunteers, Bratton's Brigade, Longstreet's Corps. Served until the close of the war, at which time he was imprisoned at New Port News, Virginia, and was not released until July 4, 1865. He belonged to the Ambulance Corps, during the whole of the war. He has been engaged in farming all his life, until 1890, at which time he was elected probate judge, which position he still holds.

JOHNSTONE, A. P.—Engaged in the practice of medicine at Anderson, South Carolina. Was born on the 15th of September, 1847, in Chester County, South Carolina. Grandson of Chancellor Job Johnstone, of Newberry, South Carolina. Had only the advantage of such schools as were to be had during the war. Graduated in dentistry from the Pennsylvania Dental College, in Philadelphia, in 1874. His first wife was Essie Burress; and the second was Sallie A. Witherspoon, whom he married in 1900. He is secretary of Masonic Lodge; president of South Carolina State Dental Association. Taught in the dental department of Vanderbilt University.

JONES, ALLEN.—Treasurer of the Saxe-Gotha Mills, Lexington Manufacturing Company, Middleburg Mills, in Lexington County; and president of the Palmetto Mills, Columbia, South Carolina. He was born August 23, 1846, in Hillsboro, North Carolina. Removed to Columbia, South Carolina, in 1888. His earlier schooling was had from the common schools at Ebenezer, York County, until the war came on, in 1861. He volunteered with the State Guards for the defense of Charleston, in April, 1863; and was promoted to second-lieutenant. In January, 1864, he joined the Twelfth Regiment, Army of Northern Virginia. Was wounded in front of Richmond, and paroled after the surrender of Appomattox. He went into business at Rock Hill after the war, and served one term as mayor of that town. He is one of the foremost cotton-mill owners of the State. He was married to Miss Augusta Porcher, of Winnsboro, South Carolina, October 15, 1874.

JONES, CHARLES DE PASS.—Son of Ira B. Jones, associate justice of supreme court, South Carolina. Born February 2, 1876, in Edgefield County, South Carolina. Paternal ancestors are Scotch-Irish. Graduated from Franklin Academy, Lancaster, South Carolina, and Charlotte Military Institute, Charlotte, North Carolina. Graduated in law from South Carolina College, in 1898, and admitted to bar same year. Married Miss Lena Wilson, daughter of B. D. Heath, of Charlotte, North Carolina, October 17, 1900. Clerk of Judiciary Committee House of Representatives of South Carolina, in 1897 and 1898. After leaving college, returned to Lancaster, and that same year was elected probate judge. Still holding that position and practicing law at Lancaster.

JONES, CHARLES FOSTER.—Son of James T. Jones, of Hart County, Georgia. Was born in that county, September 19, 1857. His education was acquired from the old field schools. Went to Greenville County, in 1873, and clerked for a while. Afterwards organized the firm of C. F. Jones & Company, and is president and treasurer of it. Capital stock, $35,000. Mr. Jones married Miss St. Claire Webb, of Greenville County, May 29, 1897.

JONES, FRANK DUDLEY.—Pastor of the Aiken Presbyterian Church. Son of Dudley Jones and Margaret Erwin. Born in Arkadelphia, Arkansas, July 16, 1874. Of Scotch-Irish and Welsh descent. Graduated from the graded schools of Rock Hill, South Carolina, and with Bachelor of Art degree from Davidson College, North Carolina. Then took theological course from Seminary at Columbia. Married Rowena Gunby, of Columbus, Georgia, June, 1900. Taught school in North and South Carolina. Pastor of the church at Columbus, Georgia, two years.

JONES, IRA B.—Associate justice of the Supreme Court of South Carolina. Son of Charles M. Jones and Mary J. Neal. Was born in Newberry, South Carolina, December 29, 1851. His ancestors were Scotch-Irish. He received his early education in the Lutheran College of Newberry, going through the sophomore year. He then entered Erskine College, and graduated in 1870, at the age of eighteen. After leaving college, taught in Newberry and Edgefield Counties about three years, during which time, he studied law. Was admitted to the bar, in 1872, at once opening an office at Newberry. He also accepted the position as associate editor of the "Newberry Herald," holding same one year. In the fall of 1875, he moved to Lancaster, South Carolina. He was elected to the Legislature from Lancaster County, and enjoyed the distinction of being the only lawyer in the State who had no opposing candidate. Appointed chairman on the Ways and Means Committee. In 1886, he was appointed chairman of the Democratic Executive Committee for Lancaster County, and also of the Congressional Executive Committee for the Fifth Congressional District. June 25, 1875, he married Rebecca H. Wise, of Edgefield County. He was vice-president of the Constitutional Convention, of 1895.

JONES, IREDELL.—Son of Colonel Cadwalder Jones and Annie Isabella, daughter of James Iredell, governor of North Carolina. Born at Hillsboro, North Carolina, February 8, 1842. He was prepared for college at Mount Zion, Winnsboro, South Carolina, under General John A. Alston. Entered the South Carolina College, in the fall of 1858, leaving to join the Confederate army in 1861, serving four years, and surrendered at Greensboro, North Carolina. He was twice married, first to Ellen, daughter of Governor I. H. Adams, of South Carolina; the second time to Laura, daughter of R. P. McMahn, of Alabama. He was second lieutenant, in 1861, of the College Cadets; first lieutenant of the South Carolina Artillery, in 1862; private in Hampton Legion, in 1861, and wounded at the first battle of Manassas. For one year Intendant of Rock Hill. In 1880, he was elected to the South Carolina General Assembly, from York County. At present regent of South Carolina Hospital for Insane, and chairman of board of trustees of Rock Hill public schools.

JONES, JOHN FRANKLIN.—In politics Major Jones is a Republican, in all relations to national affairs. He was born September 9, 1846, in Springfield, Massachusetts. He is a great-grandson of Dearing Jones of Revolutionary fame. Graduated from Springfield High School, and then took a course in civil and mechanical engineering, and immediately entered upon the practice of his profession. At twenty-three, was in charge of the business of A. D. Briggs & Company. Personally identified with designing, and the construction of some of the most important plans of hydraulic and railroad work in New England. He was married September 6, 1871, to Isabella S. Deane, of New Hampshire. Before coming South, Major Jones was vice-president and general manager of the Hampshire Central and Western Railroad, resigning that position to accept that of chief engineer and superintendent of construction of the Charleston, Cincinnati and Chicago Railroad, which he built from Camden, South Carolina, to Marion, North Carolina. He built the railroad shops at Blacksburg, the iron works, fertilizer factory, acid works, the Cherokee Inn. Taking $4,000 town bonds, built a six thousand dollar graded school building, and set up the second electric light plant in the State. He has been a delegate to national conventions, political and civil. Major Jones is a Knight Templar, a Mason, and stands high in the order of Knights of Pythias.

16

JONES, J. L.—Born in Knoxville, Tennessee, March 14, 1828. His elementary training was received from Maysville College, under the presidency of Dr. Isaac Anderson. He then took a full course in science, literature, art, mathematics, and languages at Engineering and Horticultural College, Virginia, under the presidency of Dr. Charles Collins. Soon after graduation, he found his way to Georgia, where he became president of a flourishing institution in the city of Carrollton, at the age of twenty-two years. At the end of four years he was called to the presidency of the Southern Masonic College at Covington, which, under the auspices of the Grand Lodge of the State of Georgia, and under the management of Dr. Jones, had the largest patronage in the State of Georgia for a number of years. His reputation, as a college president, became so widely known that his students hailed from every State in the South except two. After the war he was elected president of the Methodist College at Columbia, which is the property of the South Carolina Conference. To resuscitate this institution, he performed a feat which is said not to be equaled. With many embarrassments to carry, he assumed all pecuniary responsibility for salaries and otherwise, and paid all bills without a single exception, taught ministers' daughters free of charge, and paid the college $2,000 yearly. Besides this he made for himself a larger salary than any other college man in the State. His career as a college president has been eminently successful. As to scholarship, it may be said that, as was his custom, he ably filled any department in a full college course, whenever circumstances required it. Married Miss R. J. Tomlinson, daughter of J. F. Tomlinson, a prominent citizen of Carrollton, Georgia, October 20, 1853, Bishop Pierce officiating. During the war, Dr. Jones was detailed as manufacturing and commercial agent for Georgia, in the state of Virginia. Many hundred thousand dollars passed through his hands, safely and wisely administered. In Covington, he was president of the college, president of the city railroad, and mayor of the city, all at the same time. He was three times elected mayor, and was offered the office indefinitely had he remained in the city. He is an architect to some extent, having constructed buildings which have been much admired, and have been copied. Dr. Jones is not an active politician. He has been a representative in important State conventions, and, in 1858, was a representative from Georgia to the great Commercial Convention held in Tennessee with delegates in full from every Southern State. Dr. Jones has delivered many lectures before colleges, societies and fraternities, and has lectured in nearly every town and city in the State of South Carolina. He has traveled quite a good deal, visited all the expositions that have been held in the last twenty-five years.

JONES, RICHARD HERBERT.—Preacher, pastor of the Abbeville Methodist Church. The son of Jesse Jones and Hannah Margaret Evans. Was born in Charleston, South Carolina, March 28, 1853. His father and grandfather were natives of Charleston. His mother was the daughter of Thomas Evans, a large rice planter of Georgetown. Educated in the public and private schools of Columbia and Charleston under such educators as Rev. F. W. Pape, Dr. W. H. Tarrantt, Henry P. Archer, and Joseph T. Caldwell. In early manhood, he entered the employ of Walker, Evans, Cogswell & Company, learning one branch of that business. Soon after attaining his majority, he determined to enter the ministry. Being unable to enter the Seminary, he took the course under Rev. John T. Wightman, D. D., who kindly directed the efforts and aspirations of a poor boy, so that, in 1876, he entered upon the active work of the ministry. Served on circuits, though for the past fifteen years has supplied some of the most important churches in the Conference. While he was pastor at Laurens, the handsome new church was erected. Trustee of Columbia Female College. November 16, 1880, married Miss Irene Palmer Venning, daughter of the D. Brainard Venning and Harriet Moore Wigfall, of Charleston, South Carolina, and a grand-niece of Rev. B. M. Palmer, the noted divine of New Orleans.

JONES, WILIE.—Was born in Hillsboro, North Carolina, October 7, 1850. Moved to York County, South Carolina, when five years of age. Had only an old-field schooling.

Married Miss Anna R. Caldwell, of Columbia, May 20, 1886. Has been with the Carolina Bank of Columbia, for thirty-two years, having held every position up to that of vice-president, which, with that of cashier, he now holds. Was for many years captain of the Old Governor's Guards. Elected colonel of Palmetto Regiment. For years he has been a leading figure among military men. Was appointed colonel of the Second South Carolina Regiment, in the Spanish-American War, commanding the only regiment of South Carolina soldiers that left this State to go on foreign soil, with the exception of the Palmetto Regiment. Colonel Jones is a self-made man. As a banker he has been signally successful. He is known all over South Carolina, and his popularity is universal. He has always shunned politics until recently; is now, and has been for several years, chairman of the State Democratic Executive Committee.

JONES, WILLIAM HATCHER.—Superintendent of the Barnwell Graded Schools. Son of Louis D. Jones and Louisa Flippen. Born at New Store, Buckingham County, Virginia, February 21, 1874. Ancestors were French-Huguenots. Prepared for college in the private and public schools. Entered the William and Mary College, in 1890. Graduated, in 1894. Won declaimer's medal. Married Laura M. Bellinger, of Barnwell County, July 26, 1901. Served as principal and superintendent of various schools in Virginia and South Carolina. In 1900, taught in the County school for teachers, and made an address at the National Educational Association, in Charleston. President of the Barnwell County Teachers Association. Vice-chancellor of the Barnwell Lodge Number 16, Knights of Pythias.

JONES, WILLIAM MONTAGUE.—Was admitted to the bar, in 1882, and began the practice of law in Spartanburg, South Carolina. Soon afterwards, formed a partnership with Arch B. Calvert. In 1885, he bought the "Spartanburg Weekly Herald," which he edited and published, until 1890, when he and J. C. Garlington founded the "Spartanburg Daily Herald." W. M. Jones is a son of Samuel B. Jones,

D. D., who was at one time president of Columbia Female College. He was born at Cokesbury, Abbeville County, South Carolina, June 10, 1859. Was prepared for college at the Columbia Male Academy, and was graduated from Wofford College with special distinction, in 1878. Received the degree of Master of Arts from the same college, in 1880. November 24, 1897, he was married to Mrs. Dora Fanning Heartt, of Durham, North Carolina. In 1893, he formed a law partnership with Judge George W. Nicholls, and has ever since practiced law in Spartanburg.

JORDAN, D. A. PARKER.—Born near Greenwood, South Carolina, August 24, 1851. Attended the best schools in the County, and afterwards received a full business course at Eastman College, Poughkeepsie, New York. Is unmarried. In 1868, he entered the mercantile business, in the town of Greenwood. Afterwards was connected with the firm of William Bryce & Company, of New York, which position he held for many years. In 1891, the City Bank was established at Greenwood, through his efforts, and he became president of that institution, which position he still holds. In 1896, he organized the Grendel Mills, and was elected president. The plant has been enlarged from time to time, and now has a capital stock of three hundred and fifty thousand dollars ($350,000). He has been president of the board of trade of the city of Greenwood for many years. Is a director of the Charleston and Western Carolina Railroad; a director of the Hartsville Cotton Mills; and is connected with numerous other business enterprises.

JORDAN, GEORGE EDWARD.—Son of Dr. R. H. and Martha (Robertson) Jordan, of Chester County, South Carolina. Ancestors were of Scotch and French descent who settled in Chester about 1840. His father practiced medicine in that county over thirty years. G. H. Jordan was born in Chester, July 9, 1861. Obtained a common school education. He has clerked a number of years, in Asheville, North Carolina, five and in Charlotte six. Engaged as machinist at Lowell, Massachusetts, six years. In 1900 he and W. Austin Hudson

bought out Lipscomb and Russell, wholesale and retail grocers, and have since that been running the business under
the name of Hudson & Jordan, Greenville, South Carolina.

JORDAN, WILLIAM GLOVER.—Was born in Winnsboro,
South Carolina, November 2, 1847. Attended the schools of
Rev. George Boggs and Rev. Josiah Obear, also Mount Zion
College. In 1864, received appointment as midshipman in
Confederate Navy, but as the sixteen-year-old boys were
"called out," preferred to go the field, and served from
November, 1864, to close of war, as second lieutenant of
Company H, Third South Carolina State Troops. Was
elected captain of the Gordon Light Infantry at its organization, in April, 1877, and continued as its captain until the
company was disbanded by Governor Tillman, in 1894, for
refusing to respond to call to participate in "Darlington
War." Served three terms as intendant of town of Winnsboro. Was elected teller of the Winnsboro National Bank,
in 1884, and now holds same position in the Winnsboro Bank,
the successor of the Winnsboro National Bank. Married December 11, 1878, to Miss Belle Gooding.

JOYNES, EDWARD SOUTHEY.—Was born at Accomac,
Virginia, March 2, 1834. He is a graduate of the University
of Virginia, receiving, in 1852, the degree of Bachelor of Arts,
and that of Master of Arts, the year following. He studied
at the University of Berlin, from 1856 to 1858. He married
Miss Eliza V. Vest, at Williamsburg, Virginia, December,
1859. From 1853, to 1856, he was assistant professor at the
University of Virginia. Professor of Greek and German at
William and Mary College, from 1858 to 1866. Professor of
modern languages and English at Washington and Lee University, from 1866 to 1875, then at Vanderbilt University,
until 1878; then at the University of Tennessee, until 1882,
when he was called to the South Carolina College, where he
is now professor of modern languages. The degree of LL.D.
was conferred on him by Delaware College, in 1875, and by
William and Mary College, in 1878. Dr. Joynes is eminent
as a lecturer on education, having promoted public and, es-

pecially, normal education largely in Virginia, Tennessee and South Carolina. He is well known as an author of text-books in French and German, some of which are very extensively used. He is one of the founders and first trustees of Winthrop College.

JUDSON, CHARLES HULLETTE.—Dean of the faculty, and professor of mathematics and astronomy, in Furman University. He was born in Monroe, Connecticut, April 20, 1820. His parents were of pure English stock. Dr. Judson's earliest education was obtained at the public schools of his native town. From this he was transferred to a high school for two years, and was then sent to New Haven to prepare for business. At the age of eighteen he professed faith in Christ, and though his parents were Methodists, he joined the Baptist Church, and was led to think of preparing for the ministry. Encouraged by his pastor, he entered Hamilton Literary and Theological Institute, now Colgate University. Here he enjoyed, for two years, the instruction of two illustrious educators. Having been compelled to leave Hamilton, for lack of funds, he spent two or three years in Washington, District of Columbia, and near Charlottesville, Virginia, teaching private schools and continuing his studies. He entered the University of Virginia, in 1843, and remained two years. In 1845, he taught mathematics in the Academy of William Burke, Richmond, Virginia. In 1849, he was elected to a professorship of mathematics and chemistry, in Anson Female College, North Carolina. In 1857, called to the chair of mathematics and mechanics in Furman University. From 1855, to 1894, treasurer of that institution; and from 1859 to 1898 held the same position in the Baptist State Convention of South Carolina. At one time president of Greenville Female College. Was offered the presidency of the Richmond Female Institute, in 1870, and again, in 1873. In 1847, he married Miss Emily T. Bosher, of Richmond, Virginia. Has twice been offered the presidency of Jackson College Alabama, but he chose to remain at Furman with less than half the salary offered elsewhere. Since 1880, a trustee of the Southern Baptist Thelogical Seminary. In

1884, the degree of LL.D. was conferred by Richmond College, Virginia.

KELLEY, JOHN ALEXANDER.—He is a son of Joseph J. and Ann J. (Campbell) Kelley. Born in Clarendon County, South Carolina, July 20, 1844. Graduated from South Carolina College, in 1868. Married Elizabeth B. Kelley, (nee Boyd), October 29, 1872. Taught school a few years, and then read law with Johnson & Johnson. Has practiced at Kingstree since 1877. Served one term in the House of Representatives. He is at present mayor of Kingstree.

KENNEDY, JAMES BOYD.—A member of Erskine College faculty, since July, 1900. Principal of fitting department. He is a native of York County, and was born September 6, 1871. He received his primary training in the county schools, the Yorkville Graded School, and private high schools. Entering Erskine College, in 1889. Took a post-graduate course at Johns Hopkins University, Baltimore, Maryland. Principal of Lowryville, South Carolina, High School; of Oak Hill, Alabama, High School; and of Yorkville, South Carolina, Graded Schools. He was also Principal of Coronaco, South Carolina, High School.

KENNEDY, MICHAEL FRANCIS.—Director in the Dime Savings Bank, of Charleston, South Carolina. Mr. Kennedy was born September 26, 1844, at Charleston, South Carolina. He obtained his education from the public and private schools of Charleston, principally B. R. Carroll's Academy. He was engaged as a printer in a newspaper office for a short time. In the war between the States, he served on the coast, both in State troops and Torpedo service, beginning as a member of the Jamison Rifles, under Captain T. G. Simons. Served four years in the Legislature, as a representative from Charleston County. Mr. Kennedy is now engaged in the real estate and brokerage business. Is secretary and treasurer of the Hibernian Mutual Fire Insurance Company, and president of several leading building and loan associations; State assessor, in Ward Four of city, and grand dictator of the Knights of Honor, of South Carolina.

KENNEDY, ROBERT McMILLAN.—Superintendent of the Camden Graded Schools. A son of Robert M. Kennedy, a native of Scotland, and for fifty years a prominent merchant of Camden, South Carolina. Was born September 24, 1866, at Camden, South Carolina. He is descended, on mother's side, from the early Quaker settlers of Camden, South Carolina. His early education was obtained from private instructors. Later he attended Shenandoah Valley Academy, under Dr. Minor, Winchester, Virginia. Then took a course at the South Carolina College, in 1882, and 1885, later a post-graduate course, in 1885, and 1887. Most of his life has been devoted to teaching with the exception of one year, as bookkeeper in the Atlanta National Bank. He was tutor in English and French at the South Carolina College, in 1885 and 1887. Superintendent of the public schools in Barnwell in 1887; at Edgefield in 1890 and 1892; and at Camden from 1892, to the present time. Takes a great interest in normal summer-school work.

KENNEDY, WILLIAM HENRY.—Born in Sumter, South Carolina. Obtained education from the country schools, and the Camden Academy. He resided in Charleston from the age of sixteen, until the beginning of the war. Went into service with Rutledge Mounted Rifles. Later, joined the South Carolina Rangers, Captain Zimmerman Davis. After serving here for some time, was detailed on important and special duty, and held this position until the close of the war. Member of the county Democratic Convention, from its organization until the present time. Chairman of the Democratic Convention from Williamsburg County, in 1876. He was a strong, straight-out, and rendered valuable service in those dark days. Captain of a large company from his section. Delegate to several Democratic conventions of the State. Member of the Legislature, but declined re-election.

He was merchandising at Indiantown, South Carolina. Interested in farming; but, in 1899, rented farm, and moved to Kingstree, where he is engaged in the mercantile business. Married Julia E., daughter of John E. Scott, of Williamsburg County, November 10, 1867.

KETCHIN, THOMAS HOGE.—Mayor of Winnsboro, South Carolina, since April, 1901. Son of Robert S. Ketchin. Born in Winnsboro, Fairfield County, South Carolina, July 27, 1856. His ancestors were Scotch-Irish, and Scotch. He obtained his education from Mount Zion Academy, Winnsboro, South Carolina. Married Miss Mary Shaw, September 23, 1879. After leaving school, he clerked for McMaster & Bruce until admitted to the firm. Since then has been engaged in the mercantile business. County chairman of the Democratic Executive Committee, from 1890, to 1894, and is now a member of the State Democratic Executive Committee. President of Winnsboro Creamery Company, and the Ketchin Mercantile Company. Vice-president of Fairfield Cotton Mills, and also of the Merchants Building and Loan Association. Served as school trustee six years, but resigned to accept his present position.

KEY, DANIEL WEBSTER, REV.—Pastor of Rutherford Street Baptist Church, Greenville, South Carolina. A native of Texas. Was born in Panola County, Texas, in 1854, but reared in Clinton, Tennessee. A graduate of Carson and Newman College, Tennessee. Spent two years at the Southern Baptist Theological Seminary, at Louisville. Has supplied churches at St. Matthews and Williston nearly eight years, also at Society Hill. Has had his present charge, since 1895. Degree of D. D., conferred by Carson and Newman College. Secretary of board of trustees of Furman University and Greenville Female College.

KILGO, PIERCE FLEMING.—Son of Rev. James F. and Catherine Kilgo. Born at Cokesbury, South Carolina, May 18, 1867. Graduated, with degree of A. B., from Wofford College, in 1888. Married Nettie B. Bethea, of Marion County, December 6, 1888. Joined the South Carolina Conference, in 1888. Has supplied churches at Lancaster, Green-wood, Cheraw, Williamston. Is at present, pastor of the Darlington Church.

KINARD, HENRY JEFFERSON.—Born in Newberry County, January 16, 1849. Entered Wofford College, in the fall of 1869; graduated, in 1873, with the degree of Bachelor of Science. Married Lillie M. Tucker, of Spartanburg County. He was elected to the Legislature from Abbeville County, from 1892 to 1897; and again, in 1900, to represent Greenwood County, it being formed from portions of Abbeville and Edgefield. He is now an enterprising merchant and farmer. Was a director in the Farmer's Bank at Abbeville, and is now a director of the Farmers and Merchants Bank at Greenwood.

KINARD, JOHN MARTIN.—John Martin Kinard was born at Kinards, Newberry County, South Carolina, May 17, 1862. His education was acquired at the Newberry College, and the South Carolina College, where he took a special course. He won the debater's medal given by the Clariosophic Society, at the latter institution. Married Miss Margaret Lee Land, of Augusta, Georgia, June 5, 1895. Was for ten years, clerk of the court of Newberry County. He was made president of the Commercial Bank of Newberry, at its organization, in 1896; and is now holding that position. Is also a director in the Newberry Cotton Mill, and president of the Newberry Knitting Mill.

KINSEY, JOSEPH C.—Son of Rev. Lewis and Martha E. Kinsey. Born February 13, 1873, at Bell's Cross Roads, Colleton County, South Carolina. He attended the Lexington Graded School, graduating in 1893; then attended the Lexington Normal School. After completing the course there, with honor, was actively engaged in school teaching, until 1900, when he was elected to the State Legislature. Married on March 25, 1898, Luander Jennet Vick.

KIRK, ROBERT JAMES.—Son of Honorable Philip C. Kirk, of St. Johns, Berkeley. Born January 25, 1859. Prepared for college by Joseph T. Caldwell, of Charleston, and graduated from the College of Charleston, in 1881. Married Miss Amelia C. Courtenay of Charleston, November 14, 1889. Probate judge of Berkeley County, from 1885, to 1893. United States consul, at Copenhagen, Denmark, from 1894, to 1897. Practiced law at Mount Pleasant ten years, from 1883, to 1893. Past Master of Lodge Number 95, Ancient Free Masons, and trustee of Porter Military Academy, Charleston. Has been associated in the practice of law, with Honorable M. Gaillard, since 1899.

KIRKLAND, THOMAS JEFFERSON.—Son of William L. Kirkland and Mary M. Withers. Born at Camden, South Carolina, May 9, 1860. Educated at the Camden Academy. Member of the State Legislature, from 1890, to 1894. Member of Senate, from Kershaw, 1894; resigned, in 1896. Chairman of the County Democracy, from 1898, to date. Attorney-at-law, having been admitted to the bar, in December, 1886. Has practiced his profession since, at Camden. He is now connected with Professor R. M. Kennedy, in compiling a complete "History of Camden," a field full of classic and historic interest, to be published in January, 1902.

KLUGH, JAMES COKE.—Circuit judge. Was born April 30, 1857, at Cokesbury, South Carolina. Son of Wesley C. and S. Catherine Klugh. His grandfather, Humphrey Klugh, came from Culpepper County, Virginia, and settled in Abbeville County shortly after the Revolution. His great-grandfather, Michael Klugh, served under Washington, from Valley Forge to Yorktown. His grandmother, Rebecca Eddins, wife of Humphrey, was also of Revolutionary ancestry, being the granddaughter of Colonel Daws of the American army, whose home was in Prince Edward County, Virginia. Wesley Klugh and three of his sons served in the Confederate army. He attended the common schools of his neighborhood, and was prepared for college at the Cokesbury Conference School Entered Wofford College October, 1874; graduated with degree of Bachelor of Arts, 1877, and Master of Arts, 1878. Taught for three years, the last as professor of history and political economy in Southwestern University, Texas. Entered law department of University of Virginia, October,

1880; and graduated with degree of Bachelor of Law, June, 1881. Was admitted to the bar in December, 1881, and at once began practice at Abbeville. He married, December 12, 1888, Frances Caroline, daughter of Honorable John E. Bradley, of Abbeville County. He was attorney for county comissioners, 1882-1885. In January, 1885, was unanimously recommended by the Abbeville bar for the office of master for Abbeville County, and was at once appointed by Governor Thompson. Held the office until February, 1897, when he resigned on being commissioned as circuit judge. In 1895, he was elected a delegate to the Constitutional Convention of the State, in which he served on the committees on Executive Department, Jurisprudence, etc. On January 29, 1897, he was elected by the General Assembly judge of the Eighth Circuit to fill the unexpired term of Judge Earle, who had been elected United States Senator. Was commissioned February 1, 1897, and the next day opened court at Florence. A year later, he was elected for the full term of four years. He was for many years a trustee of the Abbeville Graded Schools from their foundation. Was for eight years a member of the county board of education, and for four years a trustee of the estate of Dr. John de la Howe, which maintains a school for poor children. He served, for four years, as alderman of the city of Abbeville. Is a director of the National Bank of Abbeville, was a director and president of the Abbeville Cotton Mill during the organization of the company and the foundation of the mill, and has otherwise taken an active part in developing and advancing the interests of his city and county.

KLUGH, WILLISTON WIGHTMAN.—Assistant instructor in drawing, at Clemson College. Was born in Abbeville, now Greenwood, County, October 31, 1875. Was prepared for college at the Coronaco High School. Entered Clemson Agricultural College, 1893, graduating in the first class that was graduated from that institution. He has done special work at Cornell and Vanderbilt Universities. Taught in the Fitting School, at Clemson, one year, and was assistant instructor in wood and forge work.

KNIGHT, A. WILKES.—Editor and proprietor of the "Bamberg Herald." Born October 29, 1869, in Marlboro County. Attended the common schools of Bennettsville, at which place he lived until 1888, when he was sent to Manning, South Carolina, as printer on the "Manning Times." Lived there until 1891, when he went to Bamberg and worked on the "Bamberg Herald," getting out first issue of that paper. In 1892, went to Orangeburg, where he was employed in the job printing establishment of Berry & Howell, and for a while, temporary editor of the "Enterprise." Returned to Manning in 1892, and was employed on the "Manning Times" until 1893, when he moved to Sumter, to take charge of the "Sumter Herald," as local editor and business manager. In January, 1895, he and his brother, J. M. Knight, bought the paper. Married, in June, 1894, Miss Hennie Ingram Legg, of Manning. Commissioner of State elections for Bamberg County, and exposition commissioner for Bamberg County. Member of the board of directors of the Cotton Oil Company, of Bamberg.

KNIGHT, JOHN MARION.—Was born in Chesterfield County, South Carolina, November 18, 1866. Son of A. H. and Mary J. Knight. His parents moved to Bennettsville, South Carolina, when he was quite young. He attended the Bennettsville Academy, and then served as apprentice in the office of the "Marlboro Planter." Learned the printing business and afterwards studied at night, in preparation for college. He entered the South Carolina College, in 1884, remained two years; upon leaving college took the principalship of the Burroughs High School, at Conway, South Carolina. Taught at various places several years. Twice married.

KNOX, WILLIAM DUNLOP.—Was born in Chester County, South Carolina, five miles east of the court-house, March 8, 1847. Son of James Nesbitt and Nancy Dunlop Knox. His grandparents came from Ireland, about 1760. Educational advantages were such as the old field schools of the country afforded; attending school only when his services were not needed on the farm. On December 22, 1873, he was married to Miss Mary Camilla Rogers, of Indiantown, South Carolina. Member of Taxpayers Convention. Has held almost every office in the Masonic Lodge. Trustee in Davidson College, from 1886, to 1892. Took an active part in rescuing the State from radical rule in 1876. School commissioner of Chester County, from 1884, to 1892, and is at present county superintendent of education. He taught school in Indiantown and other places, in Williamsburg County, from 1871, to 1879, then returned to Chester where he continued to teach until elected school commissioner.

KOESTER, GEORGE RUDOLPH.—Internal revenue collector of South Carolina. Son of William Koester, of Germany, and Susannah Welles, of New Jersey. Born in Philadelphia, Pennsylvania, August 14, 1870. Raised in Charleston, South Carolina. Attended the public schools of Charleston, and Furman University, Greenville. Married Eleanora Browne, a daughter of Captain J. D. Browne, of Columbia, April 23, 1893. Reporter on "Charleston Sun" in 1888. In October, 1890, became reporter on the "Charleston World," and in 1891, became reporter on the "Columbian Register," next, night editor and then managing editor. Left "Register," and established the "Columbia Record," on April 26, 1897.   ?

KOHN, AUGUST.—Manager of the bureau of the "News and Courier," at Columbia, since 1892. Son of Theodore Kohn, of Orangeburg. Born, February 25, 1868, at Orangeburg, South Carolina. He attended the Sheridan School, of Orangeburg, and took the literary course at the South Carolina College. Won the debater's medal and graduated with degree of Bachelor of Arts. Was for a time connected with the "Carolinian," the college magazine. Soon after finishing college, accepted a position as reporter for the "News and Courier." War correspondent for the "News and Cou-

rier" from the First Regiment, during the Spanish-American
War. Secretary of the Charleston Exposition.

KOLLOCK, CHARLES WILSON.—Charleston, South Carolina. Son of Dr. Cornelius and Mary
Henrietta (Shaw) Kollock. Grandson
of Oliver Hawes Kollock. Was born
April 29, 1857, at Cheraw, South Carolina. Educated at the Cheraw Academy and at the Virginia Military Institute. He began to read medicine,
in 1877, in his father's office at Cheraw. Matriculated in the University
of Pennsylvania, department of medicine, in 1878; attended three courses
of lectures at that institution, and
was graduated in March, 1881. Also
attended eye and ear clinics in London and Paris, in 1884.
He was interne at the Philadelphia Hospital, Children's Hospital and Wills' Eye Hospital, Philadelphia, from 1881 to
1884, inclusive, and has been a practitioner in Charleston,
since 1885. He was ophthalmic surgeon to Charleston City
Hospital, 1891-1895; to the Shirras Dispensary, 1892-1895;
and has been lecturer on diseases of the eye and ear in the
Charleston Medical School, 1888-1895. Dr. Kollock is a member of the South Carolina Medical Association; of the Medical Society of South Carolina; of the American Medical Association; of the American Ophthalmological Society; of the
Society for the Assistance of Widows and Orphans of Medical Men; of the South Carolina Club; of the Charleston Yacht
Club; of the St. Cecilia Society; of the Charleston Library
Society; of the South Carolina Agricultural Society; and of
the Alumni and Greek Letter (A. T. Q.) Society of his Alma
Mater. He is the author of papers on "Rotheln," "Philadelphia Medical Times," 1882; "Jequirity," "Medical News,"
1883; "Peculiar Growth on Optic Disk," ibid., 1887; "Removal of Steel from Vitreous by Electro-Magnet," Transactions of the South Carolina Medical Association, 1885; report
of cataract cases, ibid., 1889-1891; "Eye of the Negro," "Trans-

actions of the American Ophthalmological Society, 1890-1892;"
"Further Observations on the Eye of the Negro," Transactions of the Pan-American Medical Congress, 1893; "Eyes of School Children," "Transactions South Carolina Medical Association, 1893;" "Wounds of the Eye, with report of Cases;" ibid., 1895. Dr. Kollock has made a special study of the eye of the negro. He was lieutenant of cavalry (Charleston Light Dragoons), South Carolina Volunteer Troops, 1886-1895. Married, November 10, 1885, Miss Gertrude E. Gregg, of Charleston, South Carolina. Their children are William Gregg, and Henrietta Shaw Kollock.

KROEG, ANDREW ALEXANDER.—Son of Andrew Kroeg and Bertha (Kloss). Born January 25, 1858, at Charleston, South Carolina. Ancestors of German descent. Attended the Charleston High School, and graduated from the Philadelphia College of Pharmacy, class of 1878. Married Miss Ida Bernadine Heins, in 1883. Engaged as drug clerk, until 1882, then went in business on his own account and continued until 1893. He is now engaged in the real estate and insurance business. Organized the Germania Fire Insurance Company, of Charleston, and is secretary and treasurer of same. Instrumental in organizing the Germania Building and Loan Association, alderman of Charleston four years. Organized the first chain-gang system in this State, in Charleston County, and chairman of board for management of convicts eight years. Member of park board of Charleston several years. Captain of Palmetto Guards. Chairman of committee and grand marshall of Fantastic Parade, during first gala week ever held in the city of Charleston. Past chancellor of Knights of Pythias Lodge of Charleston. Instrumental in organizing first uniform rank company of Knights of Pythias, in South Carolina, and captain of Palmetto Company Number 1, Uniform Rank Knights of Pythias several years. Afterwards elected lieutenant-colonel of same company. Member of examining board of Pharmaceutical Association ten years.

KUKER, JOHN.—Son of D. H. Kuker of Hamburg, Germany. Born in Hamburg, Germany, August 22, 1845. Com-

pleted the high school education in his native city. Studied
pharmacy. Came to New York City, in 1865, where he entered the employ of McKesson & Robbins, wholesale druggists. Married Miss Louise Lay, in August, 1870. From
New York, he went to Fernandina, Florida, from which place,
after remaining one year, came to Florence, and started in
the mercantile business. Intendant of town, and member of
city council eight years.

LADSHAW, GEORGE EDWARD.—Civil and hydraulic en-

gineer. Born at Drummondville, Upper Canada, now Dominion of Canada,
January 28, 1850. Son of Edward and
Elizabeth (Poulton). Ancestors have
been college-bred people for more
than four centuries, during which
time they have, and now hold, many
important positions in education,
science, church, and state, in Britain
and France. Attended the common
schools of native town and college in
Toronto, Canada. Served apprenticeship in architecture and civil engineer-
ing under John Ladshaw, grandfather. During apprenticeship was engaged on the Prospect Park suspension bridge,
Niagara River. Was several years in the oil country, Pennsylvania, and the far West, locating in this country, in 1875.
Designed and constructed the hydraulic structures for the
Pacolet Manufacturing Company, Number 1 Mill; and the
Whitney Manufacturing Company. Engaged with the Henrietta Mills, Rutherford County, North Carolina, as chief designing and consulting engineer and constructor. Still holds
same position with this corporation, which is one of the largest and wealthiest in the South. Holds same position with
the Spray Water Power and Land Company, Spray, North
Carolina. Reorganized two mills and built the largest finishing mill in the South at this place. Also Cooleemee Cotton
Mills, Cooleemee, North Carolina. Reorganized the power
development for the McAden Mills, McAdenville, North Caro-

lina. Also a number of smaller concerns, and numerous water power developments and steam power plants. Determined the rational principle of estimating stream discharge, from observations of the rainfall and subsurface measurements of permanent water level in the earth. Determined the increase in the rise of freshet water below a dam due to the mobility of water within and upon itself and the successful application of the principle to hydraulic development. Determined the theoretical limit of recession of fill in a stream due to an obstruction; of which several practical applications have been decided favorably by the courts. Explanation of these principles and other scientific data published in "Hydraulic Notes, 1900." Determined the magnetic elements of this section from local observations and charted the same, with the aid of Bessel's harmonic functions, as given by C. A. Schott, United States Civil and Geological Survey, for the use of surveyors in retracing old land lines. Determined the chordal error in magnetic formulae, as applied to long magnetic lines computed by co-ordinates. At present engaged in the construction and equipment of the Cliffside Mills, Cliffside, North Carolina. The Globe Cotton Mills, Augusta, Georgia, and the Jonesville Knitting Mills, Jonesville, North Carolina.

LAIRD, ELVIN ADDISON.—Superintendent of education of Orangeburg County. Son of Thomas Laird, of Lexington County and Martha Jefcoat. Born in Lexington County, November 15, 1865. Of Scotch-Irish descent. Graduated from the South Carolina Military Academy, as a beneficiary, having won the scholarship from Orangeburg County. Taught school a few years in this State and Tennessee; graduated from the Baltimore Medical College, in 1893. Married Essie Lou, daughter of J. Rhett Riley, April 21, 1895. Practiced medicine in Orangeburg seven years. Moderator of the Orangeburg Baptist Association, since 1897; and trustee of the Orangeburg Collegiate Institute.

LAKE, FRED U.—Son of E. H. and Jane (Abbott) Lake. Born in Westmoreland, New Hampshire. His parents came

South, when he was a mere child. Attended the Pittsboro Scientific Academy. Married Miss Hattie Parrott, February 20, 1876. Married his second wife, Narcie Fonvielle, June 20, 1899. Treasurer of the town of Florence several years. Clerk in a drug store, in Goldsboro, North Carolina; from there went to Boston. Located at Florence, in 1875, as partner of Dr. J. W. King, in drug business.

LANDER, SAMUEL.—President of Williamston Female College. Was born in Lincolnton, North Carolina, January 30, 1833. Graduated from Randolph-Macon College, Virginia, in 1852. The following year, he married Miss Laura Ann Mc-Pherson, of Lincolnton, North Carolina. His whole life has been devoted to teaching, having taught in Catawba College, Olin Institute, Randolph-Macon College, Greensboro Female College. Principal of High Point Female School, Lincolnton Female School. President of Davenport Female College, Spartanburg Female College, and, since 1871, has held the presidency of Williamston Female College. The degree of D.D. was conferred by Trinity College, North Carolina. Joined South Carolina Conference, in 1864, and has been elected to General Conference twice.

LANGSTON, WILLIAM JAMES.—Pastor of Pendleton Street Church, Greenville, South Carolina. A native of Laurens, South Carolina. Was born, March 22, 1854. A son of William H. Langston. Attended a boarding school taught by Rev. Z. L. Holmes, and the Clinton High School, taught by N. J. Holmes. Graduated at Furman University. Having decided to enter the ministry, graduated from the Southern Baptist Theological Seminary, in 1884. After leaving school he accepted the position as principal of the Mount Gallegher High School, in Laurens County, and at several other places. In 1884, he supplied the Bush River and Mt. Zion churches in Newberry County. In 1898, elected president of the board of Ministerial Education. Trustee of Furman University, the degree of Doctor of Divinity conferred by Furman University. His wife is Miss Nannie Finley, of Waterloo, South Carolina, whom he married in December, 1876.

LATHAM, JOHN THOMAS.—Mayor of Easley, South Carolina. Was born April 13, 1868, near Easley, South Carolina. Graduated from Furman University, in 1889. He is a prominent merchant of Easley, South Carolina. Not married.

LATHROP, ABIAL.—Lawyer. Son of John Lathrop and Elizabeth Moody. Born in Morganville, Greene County, New York, November 9, 1845. His father settled in Northern New York, in 1815. He is of English descent. Attended the common and high schools of Greene County, New York. Read law under Judge L. N. Bangs, of LeRoy, New York. Admitted to practice in the Supreme Court of Illinois, in 1870. Located at Rockford, until 1875, then came to Orangeburg, in 1876. Married December 31, 1878, Martha F. Heiidtman, a native of Charleston and of German parentage. United States commissioner from 1879 to 1889; United States attorney for South Carolina, from 1889 to 1893, and again, from 1897 to 1901. Member of the city council. Acted mayor, from 1893 to 1899, and is now holding same position.

LATIMER, ASBURY C.—Was born near Lowndesville, Abbeville County, South Carolina, July 31, 1851. Was educated in the common schools then existing. Removed to Belton, Anderson County, his present home, in 1880. Was elected chairman of the Democratic party of his county, in 1890; and re-elected in 1892. Has served as Congressman from the Third District, for four terms in succession.

LAW, JOHN ADGER.—Born in Spartanburg, South Carolina, September 30, 1869. Educated in the graded schools of Spartanburg and Wofford College, graduating in 1887. For two years a stenographer in Charlotte and Wilmington, North Carolina. In 1890, was given the position as bookkeeper in the National Bank, of Spartanburg. In 1891, was one of the prime movers in the organization of the Spartanburg Savings Bank, of which he was elected cashier, and the following year helped organize the Home Building and Loan Association, being made secretary and treasurer, now a director in both of the above institutions. In 1895, assisted in organizing the Central National Bank. In 1900, he organized and commenced building the Saxon Mill, as its president and treasurer, near Spartanburg, South Carolina. Has capital $200,000, ten thousand and eighty spindles and three hundred looms. Married Miss Pearl Sibley, of Augusta, Georgia, November 14, 1895.

LAW, THOMAS HART.—District superintendent of the American Bible Society, for North and South Carolina, eleven years, and is now field agent for North and South Carolina, Georgia, Florida, and Alabama. Was born, October 26, 1838, at Hartsville, South Carolina. He attended the common schools of his county, until fifteen years of age. Graduated at the South Carolina Military Academy with first honor, in 1859. Went at once to the Theological Seminary at Columbia, South Carolina, and graduated, in 1862. He was married, in March, 1864, to Anna E. Adger, daughter of the late William Adger of Charleston, South Carolina. He served as pastor of the Florence and Lynchburg, South Carolina Presbyterian churches for several years. Was chaplain of the Confederate army at Fort Caswell, North Carolina. He was evangelist of the Charleston Presbytery, for two or three years, and was, for seventeen years, pastor of the Spartanburg Presbyterian Church.

LAW, WILLIAM ADGER.—Banker. Was born in Hartsville, Darlington County, South Carolina, on December 26, 1864. After being prepared for college, by Dr. James H. Kirkland, now the chancellor of Vanderbilt University, he graduated at Wofford, in 1883. He taught in the Cape Fear Academy, Wilmington, North Carolina, until January 1, 1884, when he resigned to become official court stenographer of the Seventh Judicial Circuit of South Carolina. At the age of twenty-six, he resigned to become the first president of the Spartanburg Savings Bank, in 1891. He organized, and became

president of the Central National Bank of Spartanburg, in May, 1895. In 1900, he was elected vice-president of the American Bankers' Association, for South Carolina, and, in 1901, was elected the first president of the South Carolina Bankers' Association. He married, on December 4, 1889, Miss Lucy Lathrop Goode, daughter of Colonel Charles T. Goode, of Americus, Georgia.

LEE, LeROY.—Son of Henry B. and Margaret L. (Lynch) Lee. Born in the eastern part of Clarendon, what is now Florence County, May 21, 1875. Attended the country schools, and entered law office of Mr. F. M. Gilland, Kingstree, South Carolina, in 1893; and the South Carolina College, Columbia, in 1895. Graduated in class of 1898. Married Miss Eva C. Riser, of Newberry, South Carolina, July 12, 1900. Entered Anderson's Heavy Battery South Carolina Volunteer Artillery, on July 11, 1898. Honorably discharged October 16, 1898. He is now practicing law, at Kingstree, South Carolina.

LEE, RICHARD DOZIER.—A prominent member of the Sumter bar, and a native of that county. Born August 5, 1850. He is the youngest son of the late Colonel George W. Lee and Susan Dozier. Graduated from the South Carolina College, in 1867. After leaving school, he read law, and was admitted to the bar, in 1872. Is now practicing at Sumter. He was elected to the House of Representatives, from Sumter, in 1882, and served until 1885. A member of the State Democratic Executive Committee, from 1882, to 1901. Elected a member of the State Constitutional Convention, in 1895, and Democratic presidential elector in 1900. President of the Democratic Electoral College, in 1901. He was married, on April 22, 1875, to Miss Mary Dozier, only daughter of the late Honorable Richard Dozier, of Georgetown, South Carolina.

LEE, RUDOLPH EDWARD.—Son of Thomas B. Lee, the eminent civil and mechanical engineer. Was born in Anderson County, South Carolina, March 12, 1876. Was prepared for college in the Columbia Graded Schools, and graduated at Clemson, in mechanical and electrical engineering. Took special courses at Cornell, and Zanerian Art Schools, Columbus, Ohio. He married Mary Louise Egleston, of Winnsboro, South Carolina, on June 27, 1900. Upon graduation at Clemson, was elected tutor in mathematics. Was transferred to mechanical department, and is now in charge of drawing, at Clemson.

LENHARDT, RICHARD FRANKLIN.—President of the Easley Roller Mill. Son of Richard Lenhardt, of Pickens County, a prosperous farmer of Pickens County. His education was acquired principally from Adger College, at Walhalla, South Carolina. He is vice-president of Easley Bank, director of Easley Cotton Mill, and director and vice-president of the Easley Oil Mill. He is very much interested in farming. Not married.

LEVER, ASBURY FRANCIS.—Congressman from the Seventh District. Born January 5, 1875, near Spring Hill, Lexington County, South Carolina. Obtained primary education from the common schools. Graduated from Newberry College, with first honor, in 1895. At Georgetown University, in 1899. Taught school eighteen months. Clerk for Congressman J. William Stokes, five years. Served in State Legislature, one term, by the largest vote ever given a candidate, from that county. Made the race for Congress against four men, and won by a majority of 1,223. He is also engaged in farming. Not married.

LEVI, ABRAHAM.—Son of Moses Levi. Born in Manning, South Carolina, July 31, 1863. Attended primary schools of Manning; private schools New York city. Graduated in class of 1882, from Carolina Military Institute, Charlotte, North Carolina, with rank of captain, then became a student in the law department of University of Virginia. Graduated, in law, at the Albany Law School of New York, in 1884. Married Miss Kitty Isaacs, of Philadelphia, June 2, 1892. Admitted to the bar, in 1885, and has practiced law since in

Manning, South Carolina. For several months editor of the "Manning Times." Organized and elected president of the Bank of Manning, in 1889. Director in Manning Oil Mill and Illuminating Company. Captain of the Manning Guards, at its re-organization after the war. Elected major of the Fourth Regiment South Carolina Volunteers, which position he held for several years.

LEWIS, JAMES A.—Was born March 30, 1858, in Horry County, South Carolina. Attended the country schools, and the Mullins High School in Marion County. Married Miss Cora Huggins, January 10, 1883. Taught school three or four years after leaving school. Elected county auditor of Horry County, in 1892, and has been continuously re-elected since. Is now serving his fifth term as such. He is a Methodist, and has been a lay delegate to the annual conference for the past three years. Delegate to State alliances for about eight years, and is now trustee and stockholder for Horry County, in the State exchange.

LEWIS, JOHN JOSEPH.—Was appointed United States commissioner, in 1900. Was born at Pendleton, South Carolina, April 20, 1837. Attended the Pendleton Male Academy. Served in the Confederate War, first in Trenholm's Squadron, which was merged into the Seventh South Carolina Cavalry. After the war, he farmed until the Hampton Campaign opened, when he raised a company of "Red Shirts" and took an active part in redeeming the State from Radical rule. Elected clerk of the court, in 1876; and served until 1884, when he again turned his attention to farming. He has been twice married. His second wife was Miss Maggie G. Wilkinson, whom he married in December, 1882.

LEWIS, JOSEPH VOLNEY.—Son of J. W. Lewis, a lumber dealer of Charlotte, North Carolina. Was born September 14, 1869, in Rutherford County, North Carolina. He was prepared for college in the High Schools of Mooresboro and Forest City, North Carolina. Graduated from the University of North Carolina in 1891. Took post-graduate courses at

Harvard and Johns Hopkins Universities. He married Miss Margaret Herndon of Chapel Hill, North Carolina, on December 24, 1895. He was assistant in biology, University of North Carolina, 1888 to 1891. Employed in field work of United States Geological Survey, in 1891, and North Carolina Geological Survey, when not engaged in University work. He is professor of geology at Clemson, also instructor in physical geography at State summer school for teachers, at Winthrop College in 1900, and Converse College, in 1901. Member of American Institute of Mining Engineers, National Geographic Society, and American Bureau of Geography. Fellow of American Association for the Advancement of Science.

LEWIS, ROBERT AUGUSTUS.—President of the Bank of Belton. Was born near that place, on the 27th of March, 1859. His educational advantages were obtained from the Belton High School. Married Jessie J. Brazeale of Belton, South Carolina, October 19, 1882. He was mayor of Belton. Is a director in Belton Cotton Mills; Moneyrick Oil Mill, Pelzer, South Carolina; the Bank of Belton. Alderman of the town of Belton. Is interested in various other local enterprises. He is a large real estate owner, and was specially influential in the erection of Belton Cotton Mills, and the organization of the Bank of Belton.

LIDE, ROBERT.—Born November 25, 1871. Son of Rev. Thomas P. Lide, well-known Baptist minister of the State, and Martha Carolina Hawkins. Graduated at Wake Forest College, North Carolina, in 1892; and moved to Orangeburg, to study law, the following year. Was admitted to the bar, in 1894, and soon afterwards formed a partnership with B. H. Moss, under the firm name of Moss & Lide, which still continues. Was appointed United States commissioner, in 1895. Was for several years a member of the Orangeburg County board of education, and has creditably filled several other public positions of local importance. Was elected a member of the Legislature by a large vote, in 1900. Married Miss Ethel M., daughter of Dr. J. W. Lowman, in 1897.

MEN OF THE TIME.

LIDE, ROBERT WILKINS.—Son of Evan J. and Martha
Miller Lide. Born December 16, 1852, at Springville, Darlington County, South Carolina. Ancestors came from
Wales. Name formerly spelled Lloyd. Educated in the Darlington schools, Furman University, and the Southern Baptist Theological Seminary. Married Mrs. Annie Wilson,
daughter of Dr. F. E. Wilson, December 14, 1880. Has supplied several churches in Darlington County; the First Baptist Church in New Berne, North Carolina; First Baptist
Church, Charleston, South Carolina; and is now pastor of
the church at Darlington.

LIGHTFOOT, EDWARD MORRIS.—Pastor of the Orangeburg Baptist Church. Son of John and Ellen Lightfoot of
England. Born in Philadelphia, Pennsylvania, August 24,
1866. Attended the public schools of Philadelphia; literary
class of Dr. F. R. Moore of New York City; and Colgate University, but did not complete course. Ordained at Schaller,
Iowa, in 1892. Married May Pagan Lightfoot, of Brooklyn,
New York, September 1, 1887. Missionary to Iowa, from
1891 to 1893. Pastor of several churches in Pennsylvania.
State vice-president of Children Aid Society of New Jersey.
Moderator of the Burlington Baptist Association, in 1893;
and also of Clarion Baptist Association, in 1898.

LIGON, HENRY ARTHUR.—Druggist, of Spartanburg,
South Carolina. Born in Lexington County, South Carolina,
October 15, 1856. Attended the school of Professor W. J.
Ligon, at Anderson. Married Lucie Eoline Reed. Began
business as clerk for Benson & Sharp at Anderson, South
Carolina; then for Dr. E. E. Jackson, of Columbia, South
Carolina. Came to Spartanburg, in 1879, and opened a drug
store on his own account. Director in the Merchants and
Farmers Bank, and a trustee of Converse College and the
graded schools. President, Peoples Building and Loan Asso-
ciation.

LIGON, ROBERT EMMETT.—Born September 11, 1868, at
Anderson, South Carolina. Educated at the high school,

taught by his father, at Anderson, South Carolina. Married Miss Mamie Benson, on December 21, 1892. He held the position as clerk in a store and bank, from 1885 to 1889. He then had the position as bookkeeper at the cotton mill offered him. Held same until 1891, when he was made superintendent of the mill, in 1897, being promoted to secretary and manager of the Anderson Cotton Mill.

LILES, JOHN BELTON.—Son of Henry and Jane Brian. Born in Polk County, North Carolina, July 12, 1856. Moved to Spartanburg County, South Carolina, January, 1861. First school New Prospect. Attended Gowensville, and Wofford College one year, finishing the sophomore term. Married Miss Annie Dean, of Spartanburg, April 30, 1891. First position one year in a country store with Captain Copeland. In 1876, began merchandising in Spartanburg in heavy groceries and agricultural implements; continued this business until 1894. In 1890, was elected president and treasurer of Fingerville Manufacturing Company, a new cotton mill in the upper part of Spartanburg County. Has managed this enterprise all the time with reasonable success. First organization of this mill, 1280 spindles; present equipment, July 1, 1901, 9,000 spindles on two-ply yarn. Was manager of Spartanburg Opera House eleven years.

LINDSAY, SAMUEL.—A practicing physician of Winnsboro, since 1898. Son of William and Nancy (Stewart) Lindsay, who came to Chester from North Ireland, about 1860. He was born in Chester, South Carolina, September 29, 1873. He received his early training from the Chester graded school, then entered Bellevue Hospital Medical College, New York City, class of 1895; and graduated in 1898.

LINK, WILLIAM EDWIN.—Born in Abbeville County, December 19, 1831. Attended the public schools and the academy taught by Professor James L. Lesley. In December, 1852, he married Miss Louisa C. Harris. Clerked in Abbeville one year, taught school at Lower Long Cane one year, then decided to study medicine, and graduated in

March, 1859. He attended lectures in Charleston ,and Augusta. He volunteered as a private in the Civil War. After two years service he was appointed assistant surgeon, and held that position until the close of the war. Since the war he has devoted his whole time to the practice of his profession, and farming.

LIPSCOME, COLONEL T. J., SR.—Former mayor of Columbia, South Carolina. Was born in Abbeville County, South Carolina, March 27, 1833. Received his education in South Carolina College, and in the University of Virginia, at Charlottesville. From the latter he went to Philadelphia, and took a course in the Jefferson Medical College. Afterward returned to Charleston, where he graduated from the Medical College, in 1854. On leaving college he went to Paris, France, where he remained eighteen months, having previously spent three months in New York. After his return, he bought a plantation in Laurens County, and remained there three years. He then sold out and bought a plantation near Newberry, where he remained until early in 1861, when he volunteered to serve in the Confederate army, He was made second-lieutenant of Company B, Third Regiment of Volunteer Infantry, Colonel James Williams commanding. He was in the first Bull Run battle, and after that General Bonham took him on his staff as aide-de-camp. Served with him until the General was elected governor of South Carolina, in 1862, and then served on the staff of General J. B. Kershaw. Colonel Lipscome then raised a cavalry company and was made captain of it. His command was assigned to General Wade Hampton's command. At the battle of Stevensburg, he was made major, and soon after lieutenant-colonel. At Gettysburg, he was made colonel, and held that rank until the close of the war. After the war ended, he returned to his plantation near Newberry, and remained until 1867, when his home was burned, and he was driven from the premises by Radical element, losing all he had and being compelled to remain away three years. In 1870, he settled in Newberry, and went into the business of buying cotton, remaining there until 1878. He was then elected superintendent of the State penitentiary, and served for several years. He married, in December, 1861, Miss Hattie, daughter of William H. Harrington.

LITTLE, JOHN PRESTON.—Son of John W. and Eliza J. Little. Was born near Clinton, South Carolina, on the 26th of January, 1856. His education was acquired from the country schools, and one year at the Holmes Institute in Laurens. He married Eula F. Blakely, on December 27, 1877. For five years trustee of the Clinton Graded School. Engaged as salesman in M. S. Bailey's store five years. Merchandised six years, after which he resumed his position as clerk for M. S. Bailey. Appointed postmaster at Clinton, under Cleveland's administration, in 1893; re-appointed in 1896, and is still holding same.

LITTLE, JOHN WILLIAMS.—Son of James and Matilda Little. Was born near Clinton, Laurens County, February 10, 1832. Only the advantage of the common schools of that time. On March 31, 1853, he married Eliza J. Little. He has devoted his life to farming. Was elected county commissioner, in 1885 and 1886, and filled out unexpired term, in 1893. Volunteered, in 1862, joining Company B, South Carolina Cavalry, First Regiment. Surrendered at Greensboro, North Carolina.

LIVINGSTON, KNOX, COLONEL.—Attorney at Law. Was born in Madison County, Florida, January 1, 1850. He was educated at the University of North Carolina, and read law under Judge E. J. Vann, of Florida. Was admitted to the bar of that State by a special act of the Legislature, he being still a minor. He came to Bennetsville, in 1870, and continued the study of law under Judge Hudson. In September, 1870, he was admitted to the bar of South Carolina and immediately formed a partnership with Judge Hudson, the firm name being Hudson, Livingston and Newton. This copartnership continued until 1872, when Mr. Livingston withdrew and formed a partnership with Captain Harris Covington. He continued this partnership until the death of Mr

Covington, in 1876; since which time he has practiced alone, with the exception of one or two years as a partner of Mr. Townsend. He represented the defendants in the case of Steenberger versus the California Fruit and Yosemite Valley Railroad, in which the jurisdiction of the State courts, in matters of interstate commerce, was first judicially established. He has held the positions of warden, intendant and, after the town was incorporated, that of mayor, of Bennettsville. In 1883, he was elected to the Legislature. While a member of the House, Colonel Livingston was a member of the Judiciary Committee, and of Privileges and Elections, and took a leading part in the debate; and in forming the laws of these two sessions. He is a member of the board of trustees of the Marlborough public schools. In 1883, he was appointed on the personal staff of Governor Thompson, with the rank of lieutenant-colonel. In 1888, was elected as a delegate to represent the State at the first Southern Emigration Convention, which met at Asheville. He was also selected to receive on behalf of the State the diploma, presented by the Augusta exposition, for the best exhibit ever made by a State. Colonel Livingston was married in Columbia, South Carolina, on November 30, 1871, to Miss Ella A. Wells, the daughter of Jeth Wells. He is a member of the Knights of Honor.

LLOYD, EDWARD WILLIAM.—Son of William and Mary E. (Robb) Lloyd. Born in Charleston, South Carolina, June 26, 1830. Of Welsh descent. Obtained education in Charleston and Columbia. Twice married. City clerk of Florence. Deputy District Grand Master of Grand Lodge Ancient Free Masons. Captain of the Washington Light Infantry, Company B, in Twenty-Fifth Regiment South Carolina Volunteers, Hagood's Brigade, from 1861 to 1865, and commander of Pee Dee Camp 390 United Confederate Veterans at Florence. He is now magistrate for Florence County.

LOEB, LEE.—Was born in Branchville, South Carolina, August 28, 1848. At the age of fifteen came to Charleston, South Carolina, and entered the dry goods business of Louis

Cohen & Company, where he remained for seven years. He then opened business for himself, the firm being Cohen & Loeb, and was in business eight years. He then sold out his interest, and came into the firm of Louis Cohen. Married Mr. Louis Cohen's daughter. Vice-President and also director of a bank. President of several Building and Loan Associations. He is one of the largest real estate owners in Charleston.

LOGAN, JOHN ROWELL.—Is now filling his second term as sheriff of York County, having been re-elected in November, 1900. His parents were of Scotch-Irish descent, and on father's side fought in the Revolutionary war. Was born near Bethesda Presbyterian Church, in York County, on November 22, 1858. Lived there until 1897. His father D. J. Logan, first-lieutenant of the Seventeenth Regiment, South Carolina Volunteers in the Confederate army, was killed near Petersburg, Virginia, in 1864. He attended the old field schools of York County, until the age of sixteen, when he was compelled to go to work to support his widowed mother and sister. He has farmed, and operated a ginnery and saw mill, for eight years. Married Miss Sallie M. Moore, March 3, 1886.

LOGAN, W. TURNER.—Born Summerville, South Carolina, June 21, 1874. Removed to Charleston at an early age, and has resided there continually since. Graduated at the College of Charleston, class of 1895. Read law in the office of Honorable Joseph W. Barnwell, and also studied at the University of Virginia. Admitted to the bar, in 1895. Elected a member of the General Assembly, in 1900. Member South Carolina Society, Carolina Yacht Club, Commandant Camp Moultrie, United Sons Confederate Veterans. Secretary Alumni Association, College of Charleston; and member of other social organizations.

LONG, LORENZO D.—Was born February 12, 1846, on Buck Creek in Horry County. Moved near Conway, the county seat, in 1856. Attended the common country schools.

Volunteered, February 10, 1861, in the first company leaving the county. Was in eleven regular engagements. Slightly wounded twice. Captured March 29, 1865, in front of Petersburg, Virginia; taken to Point Lookout, Maryland. Released July 3, 1865, and reached home July 12. Now engaged in farming.

LORICK, PRESTON CAMPBELL.—Was born in Lexington, South Carolina, August 15, 1843. He was placed under the instruction of Robert Boyd at Cokesbury Academy. Married Agnes F. Dreher, of Lexington. Mr. Lorick is one of Columbia's solid business men, being one of the partners of the firm of Lorick & Lowrance.

LOWMAN, JACOB WALTER.—Vice-president of the Edisto Savings Bank. Son of Daniel Lowman, of Lexington County. Born March 11, 1837, in the Dutch Fork, of Lexington County, South Carolina. Attended the common schools, and read medicine under Dr. J. K. Kneece. Graduated from University of Georgia, 1858. Enrolling lieutenant Confederate States America, from 1863, to 1865, with Maj. H. A. Metetze. Member of the Legislature from Lexington County, from 1872 to 1874. Physician to North Carolina Industrial and Mechanical College, of South Carolina. Surgeon to Atlantic Coast Line. Director of Orangeburg Manufacturing Company. Examiner of the Knights of Honor, and numerous life insurance companies. Married Lodusky Rish, September 15, 1860.

LOWMAN, WILLIAM RICHARD.—Physician. Born in Lexington County, South Carolina, December 3, 1866. Graduated from the Mellichamp's High School, Orangeburg, South Carolina, in 1886, and also from the college of Physicians and Surgeons, Baltimore, in 1888. Took postgraduate course at New York Post Graduate Medical School, and New York Polyclinic, 1890 and 1891. December 27, 1891, he married Elvira Earle Izlar, niece of General James F. Izlar, and daughter of Judge B. P. Izlar. Ex-member and secretary of the South Carolina Medical Board of Examiners. Past mas-

18

ter of Shibboleths Lodge Number 28, Accepted Free Masons. Past high priest, Eureka Chapter Number 13, Royal Arch Masons, Knight Templar and Mystic Shriner. Surgeon of the Atlantic Coast Line. Lecturer on physiology and hygiene at the Orangeburg Collegiate Institute. Secretary of the board of trustees of the C. W. I. A. and M. College of South Carolina. President of the board of trustees of the Orangeburg Institute. Member of the National Science Association of America; American Medical Association; South Carolina Medical Association, and the Tri-State Medical Association. He is also medical examiner of numerous insurance companies.

LOWRANCE, WILLIAM BARR.—Was born in Rowan County, North Carolina, November 4, 1841. Attended the common schools, and was at the Military School of Morganton, North Carolina, when the war broke out. He entered the First North Carolina Regiment, Avery's Company, D. H. Hill's Division. Was twice married, first to Miss Mamie Cochran, daughter of Captain John Cochran of Cokesbury, South Carolina, and second, to Miss Bessie Green, of Columbia, South Carolina, in 1898. Served in the war, from Bethell, until surrender at Appomattox. Held variously, positions of lieutenant, adjutant of Thirty-fourth North Carolina, and captain in same regiment. Served with gallantry and distinction throughout the war. Served eighteen years as alderman of Columbia. He was one of the board of trustees that built the Columbia Canal. Member of the Legislature, from 1890 to 1892. Started business in Columbia, in 1868, succeeding Fisher & Lowrance. Is now the head of the firm of Lorick & Lowrance.

LUCAS, JAMES JONATHAN.—Born November 21, 1831, at Tiller's Ferry, Kershaw County, South Carolina. He was the eldest son of Dr. Benjamin Simons Lucas, an eminent physician and surgeon, who was educated in England. Graduated at the South Carolina Military Academy, Charleston, South Carolina, on November 28, 1851. After leaving school he engaged in the hardware business, in Charleston, South Carolina, which he continued until the war between the States. He was for seven years, captain of the Palmetto Guards, and trained that company for its distinguished service in the Confederate army. He was elected a member of the Legislature in October, 1856; and was the first graduate of the Military Academy, to attain that distinction. He was appointed aide-de-camp to Governor F. W. Pickens, December 31, 1860, with the rank of lieutenant colonel. He was commissioned major in the Confederate States army on June 6, 1861, and was placed in command of Lucas's Battalion, Heavy Artillery, which was composed of State and Confederate Regulars. The Stone Fortifications were commanded by Major Lucas until Charleston was abandoned in February, 1865. After the war he removed to Society Hill. He married, on November 21, 1861, Caroline McIver. Since the war, he has been engaged in cotton and tobacco planting, and wine making. He is now a member of the board of visitors of the South Carolina Military Academy, and of the Porter Military Academy. Is a director of the Atlantic Coast Line Railroad Company. He is the only South Carolinian in this great corporation. He was aide-de-camp to Governor Johnson Hagood, and was present as such at the unveiling of the Cowpens monument in Spartanburg, and the laying of the corner stone of the Yorktown monument, in 1881. He was selected with Colonel J. B. E. Sloan, of Charleston, to lead the Veterans at the unveiling of the monument to General Robert E. Lee, in Richmond, in 1890, by General Joseph E. Johnston. The veterans from South Carolina were placed in front and led the entire procession.

LUCAS, W. E.—President and treasurer of Laurens and Darlington Cotton Mills. Was born in Hartsville, Darlington County, South Carolina, November 16, 1864. He is a son of Dr. B. S. Lucas, a prominent physician of Darlington County. The boyhood of W. E. Lucas was spent in his native town, where he attended the country schools. He entered Wofford College, and completed the sophomore year at nineteen years of age. He then engaged in the cotton business at Columbia, South Carolina, in the employ of Ford Tally & Company, and at the end of one year, became a partner in that firm, and manager of its business in the eastern part of the State. He remained with them two years, when, in 1887, he entered the employ of Walker, Fleming & Sloan, prominent cotton merchants in Spartanburg. Remained with them one year as buyer. He then bought cotton one year for the Pacolet Manufacturing Company. During the year 1889, he constructed the Spartan Mills, at Spartanburg. These mills are among the largest and best in the South—the largest under one roof. Mr. Lucas is a stockholder in this institution. On August 1, 1890, the Morgan Iron Works were organized, with Mr. Lucas as president, and one of the leading stockholders. Member of the Greek letter Kappa Alpha fraternity. December 18, 1890, he married Miss Cora Cox, of Nashville, Tennessee. Is at present residing in Laurens, South Carolina.

LUNNEY, JOHN.—Son of William and Martha Lunney. Born in the north of Ireland, on December 12, 1838. Of French-Huguenot, English and Scotch-Irish descent. Was educated in the national schools up to the age of seventeen. Shortly afterwards, came to Philadelphia, Pennsylvania, where he studied medicine, graduating at the Pennsylvania University; in the spring of 1864. Has been four times married. His last wife was Annie F. Howle of Darlington. Soon after graduation he was appointed surgeon in the United States army, and served with the Second Army Corps, Hancocks', in Virginia, until the close of the Civil War. He was honorably discharged, and subsequently, without his solicitation was re-appointed a surgeon in the army, and served for a time on quarantine duty, on Hilton Head Island, later was sent to Darlington, where he acted as post surgeon three years. In 1868, he resigned his position in the army and located at Darlington. Was soon thereafter elected State Senator from the county. He also held the position as county auditor for about six years. He served as United States marshal, in taking the ninth census, and also as census-taker for Darlington, in 1875. Medical examiner for the Knights of Pythias; New York Life Insurance, and others. Has been president of the Darlington County Medical Association. He is now president of he Pee Dee Medical Association. Member of the American Medical Association. He took postgraduate courses at Paris, London, Edinburgh, and Belfast.

LYLES, JOHN WOODWARD.—Clerk of the court of Fairfield County. Son of Thomas W. Lyles. Was born in Fairfield County, on September 2, 1845. He was prepared for college at St. John School, Spartanburg, South Carolina. Entered the First South Carolina Cavalry, Hampton's Brigade, Army of Northern Virginia, and was with Johnston's army at the surrender. In 1866, he attended the South Carolina University. Was a member of the House of Representatives, also on board of directors of the South Carolina Penitentiary, and county chairman several terms. Married Miss Susan C. Morris.

LYLES, WILLIAM HAYNSWORTH.—Was born July 1, 1863, at Buckhead, Fairfield County, South Carolina. Educational advantages were limited to one year at Furman University Fitting School, and two years at Mt. Zion Institute, Winnsboro, South Carolina. Married Miriam Sloan, October 31, 1877. Member of the Legislature for one term. In the famous litigation for the possession of the Agricultural Hall property, he represented E. B. Wesley, and, after five years, the State surrendered the property and satisfied the mortgage which Mr. Wesley held. He is Division counsel of the Seaboard Air Line; general counsel, Columbia, Newberry and Laurens Railroad; solicitor for Bank of Columbia, and Granby and Olympia Cotton Mills, Columbia Land and Investment Company.

LYON, CHARLES J.—Son of Dr. H. T. Lyon, of Abbeville County. Was born at Abbeville Court-house, on November 4, 1865. The advantage of the public schools of his native town. He married Miss M. Elizabeth Wardlaw, February 7, 1887. Was elected sheriff of Abbeville County, in 1900.

McALLISTER, C. M.—A member of the firm of McAllister & Beattie, prominent merchants of Greenville. The senior member of the firm was born April 15, 1856. His education was obtained from the Walhalla Old Spear Academy, and the noted Hillhouse school at Old Pickens, and completed under the instruction of Rev. D. McMahon in the Oconee Store section. His parents settled in old Pickens district near Pickens Court-house in 1867. Just after leaving school he accepted a position with a firm in Charleston, and remained with them until 1886. In that year he moved to Greenville and commenced a dry-goods business as McAlister & Bentz, which existed until 1893, when he bought out Mr. Bentz's interest and formed the present partnership in 1894. He married Miss Virginia, daughter of Major Henry M. Earle, of Greenville, on the 21st of April 1881.

McARTHUR, WILLIAM FRANKLIN.—Born in three miles of Gaffney, South Carolina, May 17, 1844. Attended the Limestone Male Academy both during and after the war. Taught at Banner, Mississippi, from 1871 to 1877. Founded the Gaffney Seminary in 1877 and continued as co-principal till 1898. Served in the Civil War and was severely wounded twice, and made a prisoner. Was elected superintendent of education when the new county of Cherokee was formed, which position he still holds.

McBRYDE, JOHN THOMAS.—Pastor of Second Presbyterian Church of Spartanburg, South Carolina. He is a son of Rev. Thomas L. McBryde, A. M., D. D., who was born in 1817, and who was also missionary to China several years, going out in 1837. J. T. McBryde was born at Anderson, South Carolina, July 22, 1845. Graduated at the University of South Carolina, in 1868, and from the Theological Seminary at Columbia, in 1871. Married, December 26, 1871, Miss Francis Palmer Hutson, daughter of Colonel William

Ferguson, of Orangeburg, South Carolina. His second wife was Miss Sallie Chappell, of Fairfield County, whom he married May 21, 1895. On leaving the seminary was an evangelist of the Charleston Presbytery, then pastor at Aiken, Americus, Georgia, and at Marshall, Texas, ten years. Degree of Doctor of Divinity was conferred on him by Bishop College of Texas. At the second battle of Manassas his mess of eight men were eating breakfast just as the sun rose, and they asked each other, "How many of us will be alive when that sun sets this evening." That night John McBryde was the only one left. At the "Bloody Angle" at Spottsylvania, he was among the men holding an advanced position of the Confederate entrenchments. The Yankees had broken the line and gotten behind without these men knowing what had happened, and when one called to Mr. McBryde to surrender, he replied "I'll not do it." Struck in the face with the butt of a gun, his teeth broken with the blow, he became senseless and was dragged by the hair over the breastworks. With his wounds untended he was afterwards placed in the hole of a vessel, and kept there for more than forty-eight hours, under conditions of incredible hardship, and carried to Fort Delaware. The Confederates were infomed that there were one thousand and seven hundred prisoners upon this vessel. The men were crowded so thickly in this hold that they lay one upon the top of the other. Air could not circulate, the only ventilation was the hatch. They were given no water. Biscuits were thrown down through the hatch to those who happened to be within reach, as food would be thrown to dogs. Few men could eat; they were in the grasp of fearful seasickness, and in the throes of nausea; it was impossible for one man to get out of the way of another, so close was the pack. It was said that one hundred men died on the voyage. The survivors arrived at the prison in a state of horrible filth, and starvation. Upon the resignation of Dr. McBryde as pastor of the church in Marshall, Texas, suitable resolutions were drawn up expressing the regrets of the people at his departure; resolutions were also drawn up by the congregation of Greenville Church upon nis resignation as pastor.

McCAIN, JOHN IRENALUS.—Professor of Greek and German in Erskine College. Was born April 5, 1857, at Idaville, Tennessee. Received his early education at the Southwestern University (Presbyterian) in Tennessee, and at Erskine College at Due West, South Carolina, graduating from the latter in 1879 at the head of his class. For three years he taught school very successfully in Alabama, Tennessee, and North Carolina. In 1890 obtained leave of absence for the purpose of taking a special post-graduate course in Princeton University, graduating in 1892 with the Ph.D. degree, after which he was elected professor of English in Erskine College. Aside from this work he has had charge for several years of the senior literature of the Due West Female College, and has taught in various teachers institutes. For ten years a member of the State Board of Education. Married Miss Loula Todd, of Due West, South Carolina.

McCALL, JOHN GREGG.—Son of Moses S. and Mary E. Gregg McCall. Was born March 14, 1842, on Pee Dee River, in Darlington County. Prepared for college at the Mount Zion High School, Winnsboro, South Carolina; then entered the South Carolina College and remained until April, 1861. Volunteered and went to Virginia, joined the Second South Carolina Cavalry Regiment, and surrendered with Lee. Married Lida Inez Dargan, January 8, 1868. Several years mayor of Darlington. Is merchandising and has been all his life.

McCASLIN, ROBERT FOSTER.—The efficient sheriff of Greenwood County. Was born at Clear Spring, Abbeville County, September 4, 1836. Was prepared for college under J. L. Lesley, and graduated from Erskine College, at Due West, South Carolina, in 1857. A member of the Constitutional Convention in 1895. Was captain Company H. Nineteenth South Carolina Regiment, Manigault's Brigade. served in several battles. A member of the commission to locate the line of battle at Chickamauga. Delegate to the General Assembly of the Presbyterian Church at Chattanooga, Tennessee. He was married to Miss Rosalie Vincent Walker on June 13, 1878.

McCLINTOCK, E. PRESSLY.—Pastor of Thompson Street Church, Newberry, South Carolina. Was born at Ora, in Laurens County, South Carolina, June 11, 1845. Graduated from Erskine College in June, 1861. Served in the Confederate army in Hampton's Legion, and is now chaplain of the James D. Nance Camp of United Confederate Veterans. Graduated from Erskine Theological Seminary in 1869. The degree of Doctor of Divinity was conferred by Newberry College. Chairman of board of trustees of Erskine College. Married Miss Elizabeth Young, daughter of Professor J. N. Young, Doctor of Law, in May, 1870.

McCOLL, DUNCAN DONALD.—Son of D. D. McColl and Nellie Thomas. Born March 17, 1877, at Bennettsville, South Carolina. Received preparatory education at the Bennettsville Graded School. Graduated from the South Carolina College in June, 1897. Entered the senior law class in the fall of 1897, and received diploma and license to practice in June, 1898. Member of the Chi Psi Fraternity and the Euphradian Society. Took a leading part in athletics. Has never married. At present is practicing law in Bennettsville, South Carolina, under the firm name of McColl & McColl, which firm represents the Bank of Marlboro; Bennettsville Manufacturing Company and other enterprises. Is of Scotch-Irish and Welsh descent.

McCOLLOUGH, JOHN DEWITT.—Son of John L. McCollough, who graduated at the South Carolina College in 1815, was admitted to the bar and practiced law. John D. was born at Society Hill, South Carolina, December 8, 1822. Attended St. David's Academy in his native town, and was privately taught by R. D. Shindler and Rev. W. W. Wheeler. Graduated in 1840 from the South Carolina College. On June 29, 1842, he married Miss Harriet B. Hart. He was a planter on Pee Dee from 1842 to 1848. Removed to Columbia in 1847 to study for the ministry; taught school at Glenns Springs the following year. Ordained a deacon June 21, 1848, and minister at Spartanburg and Glenns Springs. Removed to Spartanburg in 1851 and opened a school for boys. Built the St. Johns School (now Converse College), and conducted a large school assisted by several able teachers. Since 1848 has been steadily engaged in ministerial, work principally in Spartanburg and Union counties. Moved to Walhalla in 1892. Was secretary of the Episcopal Council or Diocesan Convention thirty-three years. Deputy to General Convention from 1874 to 1889.

McCONNELL, HENRY E.—Practicing physician of Chester, South Carolina. Was born September 10, 1866, at McConnellsville, York County, South Carolina. Attended the common and high schools of McConnellsville. Studied medicine at South Carolina Medical College in 1888 and graduated from the medical department of the University of Maryland at Baltimore in 1890. Married Miss Mamie Russell Bailey on December 20, 1898. Worked in general mercantile store four years. Commenced practice of his profession at Kings Mountain, North Carolina, in 1890, then came back to McConnellsville and remained four years. Is now county physician and on board of health in Chester, South Carolina.

McCONNELL, THOMAS MAXWELL.—Pastor of the First Presbyterian Church of Greenville for nearly ten years. Son of William King and Esther Maxwell McConnell. Born July 13, 1851, in Washington County, Virginia. Ancestors on both sides were Scotch-Irish, and among the early settlers of Southwestern Virginia. Master of Arts graduate of King College, Bristol, Tennessee. A student two years at the Theological Seminary situated at Columbia, and the Union Theological Seminary of Virginia. Also attended Hampden-Sidney, now located at Richmond, Virginia. Married Miss Annie, daughter of Judge J. G. Wallace of Franklin, Tennessee, on October 1, 1879. Began his ministerial work in Tennessee; was pastor of Westminster Church in Nashville several years. The Doctor of Divinity degree was conferred by the Presbyterian College of South Carolina. Wrote Sabbath-school lessons for "Christian Observer" seven years. Author of "Last Week with Jesus" and "Day Dawn of Chris-

tianity," also "Eve and Her Daughters." He has also contributed several articles to papers and magazines.

McCORKLE, WILLIAM HART.—Probate judge of York
County since 1888, and has had no opponent for the office
since the first election. He was born August 25, 1821, at
Ebenezer, York County, South Carolina. Had only a common-school education. Married Miss Margaret L. Robinson,
February 15, 1849. Married a second time Mrs. E. M. Dixon,
August 16, 1860. She died December 4, 1884. Farmed until
nineteen years of age, and in 1840 began merchandising,
and when the war broke out raised a volunteer company,
Palmer Guards, Company A, Twelfth Regiment South Carolina
Volunteers. Left the regiment as lieutenant-colonel. After
the war began merchandising again, until July 1875. Served
eight terms as mayor of his town, Yorkville, South Carolina.

McCOWN, JOHN REESE.—Son of S. O. and S. E. (Gee)
McCown. Born September 30, 1862, at Indiantown, Williamsburg County, South Carolina. Of Scotch descent. Attended
the common schools, Darlington Male Academy, and graduated from the South Carolina Military Academy in 1886.
Married Lena Bostick February 14, 1891. Taught school two
years. President of the Florence County Farmers' Alliance.
Is county superintendent of education and a commissioner
of the Charleston Exposition.

McCOY, THOMAS.—Practicing physician of Laurens,
South Carolina. Was born on the 25th of December, 1831,
in Newberry County, near the town of Newberry. Had the
advantage of the common schools of the county, and
spent a year and a half at the Teamster High School in Mississippi. Graduated at the University of Tennessee Medical
College in 1855. Attended the Jefferson Medical College at
Philadelphia. Lectures at the Baltimore Medical College,
and the college of Physicians and Surgeons of New York,
and New Orleans Medical College. Married Mrs. Alberta
E. Young on December 27, 1858. He was assistant surgeon of the Confederate army for about three years. Volun-

teered in the First Regiment South Carolina Volunteers, General Gregg's Brigade, afterwards McGowan's. Served in battle of Gettysburg and was in charge of the sick and wounded of the First Regiment. Was captured and kept a prisoner at Fort Delaware fourteen months. Was in several other battles. After the close of the war returned to Laurens and commenced the practice of medicine.

McCRADY, EDWARD.—Was born in that city on April 8, 1833. Is a son of Edward McCrady, a distinguished member of the Charleston bar. Was prepared for college in private academies of Charleston and graduated from the Charleston College in 1853, and two years later was admitted to the bar. He married, on February 24, 1863, Mary Fraser Davie, daughter of Major Allen J. Davie. He took part in the military operations around Charleston, entering the State service as captain, in December, 1860. Served as such throughout the winter of 1860 and 1861. Was present at the bombardment of Fort Sumter. Entered the Confederate service as captain of the Irish Volunteers, an independent company raised under acts of Congress, "the first company raised for the war" in South Carolina. Was assigned to Gregg's (reorganized) First South Carolina Volunteers. Was promoted major and lieutenant of same. On account of wounds received was placed in command of the camp of instruction, Madison, Florida. After the war was appointed major-general State volunteer forces. Resumed the practice of his profession in October, 1865. Was elected to the Legislature from Charleston County in 1880. Served until 1890, and was the author of the State election and registration laws; also established a bureau of Confederate records in the adjutant-general's office, for the collection of rolls and records and other important measures. Elected a member of the Historical Society of South Carolina in 1857. One of the early members of the Elliott Society of Natural History. For some years a trustee of the Charleston Library Society; also of the Medical College of South Carolina, and is now president of the Historical Society of South Carolina. Received his honorary degree of Doctor of Laws from his Alma Mater in 1900.

He is the author of the History of South Carolina under the proprietary government 1670 to 1719 (1897), the History of South Carolina under the royal government 1719 to 1776 (1899), and the History of South Carolina in the Revolution 1775 to 1780 (1901). He has also written several essays on legal, political and historical subjects.

McCRADY, LOUIS DeB.—Was born in the city of Charleston, April 13, 1851, being the youngest child of Edward and Louisa Rebecca McCrady. On his paternal side his ancestry was Scotch-Irish, and on his maternal English and French Huguenot. Attended the public schools of Charleston. Entered the college of Charleston in October, 1866, and graduated March, 1870. He at once began the study of law in the office of his father and brother, and admitted to the bar April 13, 1872, since which time he has devoted his time to his profession. Married in October, 1882, Irene Shackelford. Has always taken a great interest in political matters, especially during the troublesome times of the reconstruction period, and in the reorganization of the Democratic party afterwards. He has never held any office. In 1865, at the age of fourteeen, he received an appointment as courier in the Confederate army, and at once started to join the army of General Jos. E. Johnston, but on the way learned of General Lee's surrender. He afterwards served in the militia of his State, finally retiring in 1888 as lieutenant commanding the first battalion of infantry.

McCREIGHT, EDWARD OSCAR.—Mayor of Camden, South Carolina, which position he has filled since April 9, 1900. He is a son of R. J. and M. H. McCreight. Born February 19, 1849, at Camden, South Carolina. Ancestors were Scotch-Irish. Had only a common school education. Served as alderman in 1879, and 1892. Has been engaged in the undertaking business at Camden thirty years. Married Miss Margaret E. Alexander on October 26, 1874. Has been interested in mechanical work since fourteen years of age.

McCULLOUGH, JOHN HENRY.—Practicing physician of Newberry, South Carolina. Was born at Newberry, Au-

gust 20, 1860. Attended the private schools of Miss Fannie
Levell, and Hartford Academy. Spent four years at the
Newberry College, after which he engaged in the mercantile
business for three years. Began the study of medicine under Drs. J. Gilder and S. Pope. In 1889 entered the University of Maryland, remaining one year; in 1890 entering the
Southern Medical College of Atlanta, Georgia, from which he
was graduated March 4, 1891, and has since been engaged
in the practice of his profession at Newberry, South Carolina.
On January 3, 1893, was married to Miss Hattie Laura Glover,
of Columbus, Georgia. Is a member of the Southern Medical Society of Atlanta, Georgia, and was county physician
for Newberry County four years.

McCULLOUGH, JOSEPH ALLEN.—Born September 9,
1865, in Greenville County. Son of Rev. A. C. Steppe. Was
adopted by his uncle, Colonel James McCullough, and name
was changed by act of General Assembly. Was educated at
Wofford College and the South Carolina College, finishing
both the academic and law courses in 1887. While a student
at the South Carolina College was chosen president of the
Clariosophic Literary Society, associate editor, afterwards
editor-in-chief of the College journal, assistant editor of the
"S. A. E. Record." City attorney of Greenville three years,
and a member of the House of Representatives from 1897
to 1900. He is the author of the act providing for special
courts, and other acts of public interest. Is president of the
"Club of 39" organized for the purpose of studying social,
political and economic questions. He quit politics of his
own accord and is now devoting all of his time to the practice of law. He has been asked by the faculty of Furman
University to take charge of the summer law school which
they propose establishing.

McDANIEL, JAMES HENRY GRACE.—Sheriff of Pickens
County. Only son of B. W. G. and Grace Jane McDaniel.
Was born November 28, 1847, in Greenville County, and lived
there until 1855, then moved to Charleston and remained
there until the beginning of the Civil War. Upon returning

to Greenville the call was made for boys of the age of sixteen to enter the army. He joined Company A., Captain James Anderson, Colonel Griffin's Regiment, First South Carolina Militia. His early training was had from the common schools of Charleston, and later he was under the instruction of Professor James O'Harelson. Married Miss Sallie J. Ligon, daughter of Colonel John T. Ligon, of Greenville County, on December 16, 1869. Was bookkeeper for the Reedy River Manufacturing Company, and later clerked in the Company's store, sold his farm in Greenville County and moved to Pickens, South Carolina, in 1883. Was elected sheriff of Pickens County in 1892, and has held the office ever since. Is the only man that was ever elected to the sheriff's office three times in succession.

McDERMOTT, JOHN ALEXANDER.—Son of Charles and Sallie (Floyd) McDermott, both of whom are of Scotch-Irish descent. Born March 26, 1860, at Floyd's Cross Roads, Horry County, South Carolina. Had good country school education. Was elected clerk of the court in 1892, and re-elected in 1896. Member of Constitutional Convention of 1895 and elected to State Senate in 1900. Married Miss Mary Vance Coleman, of Columbus County, North Carolina, March 2, 1892. At present he is farming and dealing in live stock. Previous to 1892 he was engaged in mercantile business.

McDONALD, CHARLES EDGAR.—Pastor of the Associate Reform Presbyterian Church, of Winnsboro, South Carolina, since 1892. Was born near Richburg, Chester County, November 23, 1859. Graduated from Erskine College, July, 1877, and from Erskine Theological Seminary June, 1881, and in September of that year was licensed to preach. Married Miss Maggie Harris of York County, South Carolina, December 23, 1886. Was pastor of Steele Creek Associate Reform Presbyterian Church, Mecklenburg County, North Carolina, from 1882 to 1892. Was moderator of the Associate Reform Presbyterian Synod of the South at its meeting at Due West, South Carolina, October, 1895. Editor of the Sabbath-school literature of the Associate Reform

Presbyterian Church since 1893. Editor of the woman's department Associate Reform Presbyterian published at Due West, South Carolina. Member of the South Carolina Historical Society, and life member of the American Bible Society.

McDOW, THOMAS FRANKLIN.—Son of Dr. Thomas F. McDow. Was born at Liberty Hill, Kershaw County, South Carolina, December 27, 1863. Graduated at Bingham School at Melbane, North Carolina, in 1882, and in the fall of 1883 entered the South Carolina College, but left before graduation. Chairman of Democratic Executive Committee of Lancaster County, mayor of Yorkville and member of the House of Representatives from York County. Actively engaged in the practice of law at Yorkville, South Carolina. Married Miss Mary Simmons Clarkson on December 27, 1893.

McDOWELL, WILLIAM LAWRENCE.—Editor of the "Camden Chronicle." Is a son of A. A. McDowell and was born at Westville, South Carolina, March 15, 1861. Had only a country school education. At the age of eighteen, entered the printing business in Columbia, South Carolina, and after working in various offices he established the above-mentioned paper, which has met with marked success. On June 16, 1890, he married Miss Elizabeth Cunningham Niles.

McELHANY, JOHN WATSON.—Elected mayor of Fort Mill in January, 1901. Born March 2, 1859, near Clay Hill, York County, South Carolina. Attended the country schools of the neighborhood. Policeman of Fort Mill four years, and magistrate eight years of the same place. Now engaged in livery, sale and feed business, and also a farmer. Married Miss Addie May Saville, August 15, 1878.

McFADDEN, SAMUEL EDWARD.—Junior member of the law firm of Glenn & McFadden of Chester County, South Carolina. Son of John C. and Margaret L. McFadden. Born December 7, 1869, at Chester, South Carolina. Ancestors were Scotch-Irish. His father, John C. McFadden, is now serving his second term as clerk of the court of Chester County, having been elected to that office in 1882. Completed the graded school course at Chester, South Carolina, and graduated from Bryant Stratton Business College, Baltimore, in 1886. Attended Furman University at Greenville, South Carolina, in 1887. Graduated therefrom with degree of Master of Arts in 1890. Taught in the Chester graded schools until 1892. Read law in the office of J. L. Glenn, of Chester, graduated in law at the South Carolina College in 1894, and has since devoted his time entirely to the practice of his profession. At college was a member of the Kappa Alpha Fraternity. President of Adelphian Literary Society at Furman and of Clariosophic Literary Society at South Carolina College, and debater of the respective societies at each place. Married Miss Ethel, daughter of Captain J. D. Means, a capitalist and financier of Chester, South Carolina, on November 14, 1900.

McFALL, WADDY THOMPSON.—Youngest son of Colonel John and Elizabeth Todd McFall. Born near Anderson, South Carolina, February 19, 1847. Education limited, the war having interfered. Elected county auditor in 1878, serving one term. Has several times been placed at the head of municipal affairs in his town. For a number of years worshipful master of Keowee Lodge A. F. M. Entered the Confederate army at the age of seventeen and served until the close of the war. In the fall of 1866 moved to Texas. In 1872 returned to Anderson, and has successfully engaged in the mercantile business since. Is also president of the Pickens Bank, which was established in 1898. Married Miss Vesta Mauldin, December 7, 1879.

McGAHAN, CHARLES F.—Physician at Aiken. Son of Thomas R. and Emma Fourgeand of Charleston. Born in Charleston, South Carolina, July 25, 1861. Is of French ancestry. Graduated from Georgetown College, District of Columbia, in 1881, and from Dartmouth Medical College in 1885. Studied in England, France and Germany. Head of the Aiken Cottage Sanitarium.

19

McGEE, HENRY PINCKNEY.—Son of Michael and Sophronia McGee. Was born October 25, 1850, at Level Land, in Abbeville County, South Carolina. Attended Long Cane and Meeting Street Academies of Edgefield County, and Furman University. In 1871 took a business course in Moore's Business College, in Atlanta. Since 1871 he has been engaged in mercantile work at Due West. Director in the Farmers' Bank of Abbeville, Bank of Greenwood, Greenwood Cotton Mills, Farmers Loan & Trust Company of Anderson. Has been a trustee of Furman University, and the Greenville Female College for about twelve years. Is also chairman of the executive board of Furman University. Married Miss Emma C., daughter of John McKay, of Greenville, South Carolina, on December 27, 1877.

McGHEE, GEORGE WASHINGTON.—Son of Burrel McGhee and Sara Hodges. Was born in Anderson County March 23, 1827. Educational advantages were limited. Married early in life to Miss Jane Brock. Was trial justice and later notary public. Was connected with the hotel business thirty-four years and merchandised and farmed up to a few years ago, when he retired from business. Served in the Confederate war, and surrendered at Appomattox on April 9, 1865.

McGHEE, SAMUEL HODGES.—Son of W. Z. McGhee, who was a prominent merchant at Hodges, South Carolina, for a number of years. Was born at Cokesbury, South Carolina, October 16, 1873. Prepared for college at the Cokesbury Conference School and Greenwood High School. Entered Wofford College and graduated in 1895. Took A. M. degree in 1896. Taught school several years in Marion County, and edited the "Greenwood Index" for two years. Studied law and was admitted to the bar in 1897. Is a member of the firm of Johnson, Welch & McGhee of Newberry and Greenwood.

McGHEE, WILLIAM ZACHARIAH.—Assistant superintendent of education. Son of W. B. and Sophronia Hodges.

Born February 6, 1872, at Cokesbury, Abbeville County, South Carolina. Graduate of South Carolina Military Academy with degree of Bachelor of Science, and South Carolina College with degree of Master of Arts. Is unmarried. Taught in public schools of South Carolina from 1892 to 1899.

McGOWAN, PATILLO H.—Son of Captain Homer L. McGowan. Born at Laurens, South Carolina, November 23, 1872. His great-grandfather, Thomas Farrow, of Spartanburg, was captain of the South Carolina Partisan Rangers during the Revolutionary War. His family moved to Spartanburg in 1881. Received his elementary education in the schools of Spartanburg and graduated in law from the South Carolina College in 1893. Continued his studies and completed his legal training at Charleston in the office of Ficken & Hughes and later moved to Atlanta, where he practiced his profession two years. In November, 1897, returned to Spartanburg where he has since remained in active practice. In 1898 was appointed by Governor Ellerbe magistrate for the city of Spartanburg. Has been twice re-appointed by Governor McSweeney to succeed himself. Married in May, 1894, to Miss Martha White Miller, of Richmond, Kentucky.

McGOWAN, SAMUEL.—Second son of Captain Homer L. McGowan and Julia (Farrow) McGowan. Was born at Laurensville, South Carolina, September 1, 1870. He obtained his education from private schools in Spartanburg. Attended Wofford College three terms and graduated from the South Carolina University in 1889, and the law class of 1891. He was admitted to the bar by a special act of the Legislature. He held a position with the South Carolina Railway at Columbia, the State Publishing Company, the "Columbia Record," and the "News and Courier." Previous to graduation in law, he was on the staff of "The Spartanburg Herald." Was appointed by President Cleveland while on the staff of the "News and Courier" to be assistant paymaster in the United States Navy. In 1894 promoted to passed assistant paymaster in 1895, and to paymaster in 1899. He is a commissioned officer with rank corresponding to that of captain in the regular army. He was placed on several different ships, but was assigned to duty at Port Royal, South Carolina, two years. In June, 1900, he joined the new battleship Kearsage, now flagship of the North Atlantic fleet, and was then transferred to the battleship Alabama.

McGOWAN, WILLIAM.—Lawyer at Spartanburg. Son of Dr. John McGowan and Sarah Lind-sey. Born near Bullocks Creek in York County, South Carolina, in 1867. His parents removed to Union County, South Carolina, when he was quite small. Acquired his education from the country schools and McArthur Academy, and graduated from the South Carolina College in 1885. Then began the study of law in the office of Colonel William Munro, of Union. Admitted to the bar in 1888. Elected school commissioner for Union County in the same year. Appointed first lieutenant in Johnson's Rifles in 1892. At the breaking out of the Spanish-American war the Johnson Rifles were ordered to Columbia by the Governor. Appointed First Lieutenant of Company E, South Carolina Volunteer Infantry. Went with the regiment to Chickamauga and was there detailed as recruiting officer. Afterwards rejoined regiment in Jacksonville, Florida. After regiment was mustered out in Columbia, opened up a law office in Spartanburg in co-partnership with Assistant Attorney-General U. X. Gunter. Was appointed United States Commissioner by Judge William H. Brawley in 1898, which position he still holds.

McINTOSH, JAMES.—Born of Scotch ancestry. Son of James H. McIntosh and Martha Gregg McIntosh, whose ancestors came from Scotland about 1750 and settled on the PeeDee River. Was born on February 27, 1838, at Society Hill, Darlington County, South Carolina. Graduated at the South Carolina College in 1857. Deciding to study medicine

entered the South Carolina Medical College at Charleston, South Carolina, and graduated in 1861. Was appointed assistant surgeon in South Carolina troops in 1861. Joined Company F, Eighth South Carolina Regiment, and served through the first campaign in Virginia, and participated in first battle of Manassas. He was twice married, first to Fannie Caldwell Higgins on November 25, 1862, second to Sara B. Rook, daughter of Major L. L. Rook, of Laurens County, on June 13, 1893. Was president of the Newberry Medical Society in 1870; president South Carolina Medical Association for two years, president Newberry Building and Loan Association, the Newberry Farmers Bank, a director in National Bank of Newberry, also Newberry Cotton Mill, and a trustee of Furman University.

McIVER, HENRY.—Was born near Society Hill, in Darlington County, South Carolina, September 26, 1826. The rudiments of his education were acquired in Cheraw, and he afterward entered the South Carolina College at Columbia, graduating in December, 1846. Upon returning home he entered the law-office of his father and was admitted to the bar in December, 1847. He at once entered into partnership with his father, which continued until the death of the former in 1850. At the time of his father's death he held the position of solicitor and his son immediately after was appointed by Governor Seabrook to fill the vacancy, and he held the office until December, 1850. He was reappointed to this office by Governor Manning in March, 1853, to fill the vacancy caused by the death of W. J. Hannee, who was elected to the office by the Legislature in March, 1850, and who died in March, 1853. He served in this capacity until 1865, when he was reconstructed out of office. In 1877 he was elected associate judge of the Supreme Court, which office he held until Chief Justice Simpson's death, when he was elected Chief Justice. He was a member of the Secession Convention which met in Columbia. He entered the Confederate service as second-lieutenant of Company A, of the Fourth South Carolina Cavalry, which constituted part of General Wade Hampton's command. He was promoted to the first-lieutenant and then to the captaincy which rank he held until the close of the war. He was twice severely wounded, on account of which he was compelled to return home. Judge McIver was married June 7, 1849, to Caroline H. Powe, daughter of Dr. Thomas Powe, of Cheraw, South Carolina.

McKINLEY, CARLYLE.—Employed on the staff of the "News and Courier" as editorial writer. He is a son of Charles G. McKinley and Frances C. Jackson, of Atnens, Georgia. Born November 22, 1847, at Newnan, Georgia. His mother's father was a professor in Franklin College, Georgia. Taught by private instructors, and graduate of Theological Seminary, Columbia. Married Elizabeth H., daughter of Campbell R. Boyce, Columbia, South Carolina, May 18, 1876. Taught in male academy from 1874 to 1875. Colum bia correspondent of "News and Courier" from 1875 to 1879 and Washington correspondent from 1879 to 1881.

McKINNON, JOHN FRANKLIN.—Son of Daniel and Sara McKinnon. Born in Jefferson County, Florida, July 25, 1855. Received preparatory education at Bingham School, and graduated from Davidson College in 1880. Married October 23, 1893, Mrs. Hattie Wyman. He was professor in Brainard Institute, Cranberry, New Jersey. Principal of Laurinburg Female Institute, Laurinburg, North Carolina. Principal of Aiken Institute, Aiken South Carolina, and president of Chicora College, Greenville, South Carolina. Entered the ministry of the Presbyterian Church in 1894. Served the Second Church in Augusta, Georgia, and at present pastor of Upper Long Cane, and Little Mountain churches in Abbeville County.

McKISSICK, ANTHONY FOSTER.—Electrical and mechanical engineer of the Pelzer Manufacturing Company. Son of Colonel I. G. McKissick. Born June 10, 1869, at Union, South Carolina. Graduated from the South Carolina College in June, 1889, with degrees of Bachelor of Science and Master of Arts. Superintendent of Congaree Gas & Elec-

tric Light Company until January, 1891, when he entered
Cornell University as a post-graduate student, receiving from
this institution the degree of Master Mechanical Engineer.
Elected professor of electrical engineering at the Alabama
Polytechnic Institute, Auburn, Alabama, in June, 1891. Resigned this professorship in July, 1899, to accept the position
of electrical and mechanical engineer of the Pelzer Manufacturing Company. In addition to this he is consulting engineer for various cotton mills. Member of the American
Institute of Electrical Engineers and the American Society
of Mechanical Engineers. On the death of D. A. P. Jordan
was elected president of Grendel Cotton Mills at Greenwood,
South Carolina.

McLAUGHLIN, DUGALD NEILL, D. D.—Pastor of Presbyterian Church at Chester, South Carolina. He was born in
Cumberland County, North Carolina, May 26, 1863. His
grandparents came from Scotland. Prepared for college at
Union Home School, Moore County, North Carolina, and
graduated from Davidson College in 1888. Studied theology
at Union Seminary, Hampden Sidney, Virginia. Has supplied
churches in North Carolina, and is now chaplain of the First
Regiment South Carolina Volunteer Militia. On July 24,
1894, he was married to Miss Fannie McFadden.

McLAURIN, JOHN LOWNDES.—United States Senator
from South Carolina. Was born at Red Bluff, Marlboro
County, South Carolina, May 9, 1860. Educated at the Bennettsville and Bethel Military Academy, near Warrenton,
Virginia. Swarthmore College, Philadelphia, Carolina Military Institute and the University of Virginia. Read law at
the last-named institute and admitted to the bar in 1882. In
1890 elected to the General Assembly of South Carolina.
Elected attorney-general the following year. Elected to the
Fifty-second, Fifty-third, and Fifty-fourth, and re-elected to
the Fifty-fifth. In 1897 appointed United States Senator by
Governor Ellerbe to fill the vacancy caused by the death of
Joseph H. Earle, and took his seat June 1. Elected for the
full term in the Senate.

McLAURIN, MILTON.—Practicing law at Bennettsville since 1877. Son of Daniel C. and Elizabeth Staunton Mc-Laurin. Born May 28, 1851, in Marlboro County, of Scotch-Irish ancestry. Attended the South Carolina University. Married Lena LeGette, November 15, 1876. Probate judge of Marlboro County since 1890. Was United States Commissioner ten years.

McLEES, JOHN LOGAN.—Pastor of the Presbyterian Church at Orangeburg. Son of Rev. John McLees and Sarah Cornelia McLees. Born in Greenwood, South Carolina, May 24, 1855. Prepared for college in the Academy at Greenwood, South Carolina, and graduated from Adger College in June, 1880. Graduated from the Theological Seminary in the fall of 1883. Licensed to preach at Johnson, Edgefield County, South Carolina. Married Annie L. Cornelson, of Orangeburg, February 2, 1892. Taught school two years in Brunswick, Georgia. His first pastorate was at Providence, North Carolina, then called to Charlotte, where he remained until 1889, when he accepted his present charge.

McLEOD, DANIEL MELVIN.—Son of Wm. J. and Amanda Rogers McLeod. Was born October 1, 1866, at Bishopville, South Carolina. His early training was received from the common schools of the neighborhood, graduating from Wofford College in 1890. Took theological course from Vanderbilt University in 1892. Is a member of the South Carolina Conference, and has supplied several churches. Married Miss Bertie Guyton on January 10, 1900.

McLEOD, FRANK HITTON.—Practicing physician. Born in Richmond County, North Carolina, February 26, 1868. Obtained literary education at Wofford College and King's Mountain Military Academy. Medical education was obtained at Nashville and New York. Has been alderman of the city of Florence, and school commissioner.

McLEOD, THOMAS GORDON.—Son of Captain William J. and Amanda Rogers McLeod. Born in Lynchburg, Sumter

County, South Carolina. Educated in the common schools of his county. Entered Wofford College in 1889; graduated in 1892. Has the honor of being the winner of every medal given by the Calhoun Society in 1891. Read law in the office of Purdy and Reynolds, Sumter, South Carolina, and for a short time at the University of Virginia. Admitted to the bar in 1896, but did not enter upon the practice of law immediately, on account of having to assume charge of his father's business. Was elected to the House of Representatives in 1900, receiving the largest vote ever given a candidate for this office in Sumter County. At present he is president and general manager of the W. J. McLeod Mercantile Company at Lynchburg, South Carolina.

McLIN, JAMES LINDSAY.—Was born August 12, 1849, near Moffattsville, Anderson County, South Carolina. Of Scotch-Irish descent. His primary training was received principally at the Moffattsville Academy. Took literary course at Erskine College, and the theological seminary at Columbia, South Carolina, and at Union Seminary, Virginia. He was brought up on farm and taught two years previous to entering college. Licensed by the Presbytery of South Carolina, and ordained by Harmony Presbytery as a minister of the gospel. Moderator of Harmony Presbytery in 1883. Filled the same office in Bethel Presbytery in 1890, and was a delegate from the latter Presbytery to the General Assembly at Dallas, Texas, in 1895. Supplied churches in Darlington and Kershaw counties nearly five years. Pastor of churches in Chester County over ten years, and in Anderson and Abbeville counties for the past five years. Married Miss Mattie Lee Beaty, of Winnsboro, South Carolina, May 11, 1892.

McLUCAS, JOHN D.—A leading citizen and public official of Marion, South Carolina. Was born in Marlboro County, January 14, 1838. He left home and went West when quite young, and was teaching in southern Arkansas when South Carolina seceded from the Union. Arkansas being slow to act he returned home and in February, 1861, enlisted in Company K, Eighth South Carolina Volunteers. This regiment was called into service April 14, 1861, and Mr. McLucas served as private until the spring of 1863 when he was appointed second-lieutenant, and in 1864 he was promoted to first-lieutenant, serving in this capacity until the close of the war. After the close of the war he studied law, and was admitted to the bar in 1866. He practiced until 1868 when he engaged in the mercantile business until 1881. During part of that time and until 1885 he published the "Merchant and Farmer," a newspaper at Marion, South Carolina, and the last two years of its publication at Laurens, South Carolina. His establishment having burned in 1885 he discontinued its publication and on returning to Marion was appointed master of equity in 1887. Was elected judge of probate of Marion County in 1888, and still holds both of the above offices. In 1876 was chairman of his county in Hampton campaign for governor, and in that year was also delegate to the Democratic National Convention which met at St. Louis. He has been twice married, first in 1868 to Miss Amanda Alford of Marion County, and again in 1871 to Miss Elnia Sherwood, of Wilmington, North Carolina. Lieutenant McLucas is major on the staff of General C. I. Walker, and major-general of the South Carolina division of the United Confederate Veterans and also historian of Camp Marion United Confederate Veterans.

McLUCAS, JOHN SHERWOOD.—Assistant professor of English in Clemson College. Was born in Marion, South Carolina, September 11, 1872. Attended the Marion Graded Schools, and graduated from the South Carolina College in 1893, and from Harvard University in 1899. Was instructor in mathematics at the South Carolina College one year.

McMAHAN, JOHN JOSEPH.—State superintendent of education. Son of J. J. McMahan and Susan N. Haynsworth McMahan. Born December 23, 1865, in Fairfield County, South Carolina. Graduate of South Carolina College with degrees of Bachelor of Arts and Master of Arts. He is unmarried. Practiced law at Columbia. Member of Constitutional Convention of 1895. Presidential elector in 1896.

McMASTER, FITZ HUGH.—General manager of the "Evening Post" Publishing Company. Son of George H. and Mary Flenniken McMaster. Born July 22, 1867, at Winnsboro, South Carolina. Of Scotch-Irish descent. One ancestor was a signer of the Mecklenburg Declaration of Independence. Attended Mount Zion Academy, and graduated from South Carolina College in 1888 with Bachelor. of Arts degree, and in 1889 with Bachelor of Law degree. Married Miss Elizabeth Waring, November 2, 1892. Practiced law in Columbia and edited the "Daily Record." Member of South Carolina Legislature. Captain on staff of Colonel E. H. Sparkman, First South Carolina Regiment of Cavalry.

McMASTER, GEORGE HUNTER.—Was born in Winnsboro, South Carolina, April 27, 1828. Son of John and Rachel (Buchanan) McMaster. Was educated at Mt. Zion Academy under I. W. Hudson, and at the South Carolina College under William C. Preston, president, and Dr. Thornwell, a professor. Taught school in Pineville and Liberty Hill three years, then traveled in Europe one year, and taught under I. W. Hudson one year. Married Miss Mary E. Flenniken, of Chester, November, 1855. Merchandised with R. S. Ketchin until the war, during which he assisted Rev. R. W. Barnwell and other members of the South Carolina Hospital Association in establishing and managing hospitals in Virginia. Superintendent of the South Carolina Soldiers' Home in Richmond from its establishment until the close of the war. Since the close of the war he has merchandised in Winnsboro. In 1873 he aided in establishing the Winnsboro National Bank, of which he was vice-president until 1885, then was made president and served as such until 1895. Member of the Legislature from 1880 to 1884 and of State Board of Equalization from its organization until 1892. In August, 1876, he was married a second time to Miss Lou P. Gregg, of Mars Bluff.

McMILLAN, JOHN CICERO.—Son of Sidney McMillan and Mary E. Palmer. Born in Marion, South Carolina, June 25, 1859. Of Scotch and English descent. Attended the com-

mon schools and Vanderbilt University, then graduated from
Bellevue Hospital Medical College in 1883, and took a post-
graduate course at same college. Married Mattie, daughter
of J. N. Robson, of Charleston, South Carolina April 11, 1888.
In early life was a printer, clerk in drug-store of his uncle
several years. Since graduation has practiced his profession at Marion, South Carolina. Appointed coroner of Marion County by the governor. President of the Marion Improvement Company and member of the South Carolina Medical Association.

McNEILL, DONALD TYNISH.—Son of William D. McNeill
and Jane Bryden (McRee) McNeill. Born November 29,
1853, at Clarkton, Bladen County, North Carolina, of
Scotch-Irish descent. Attended school in his native county,
then Fusculum High School, Melrose, North Carolina, and
Cape Fear Academy, Waynesville, North Carolina. Married
Mary E. Cromaike, daughter of Alex. A. Cromaike, April 23,
1878. Farmed in early life. In January, 1882, he moved to
Conway, South Carolina, and has since been engaged in mercantile and steamboat business, and for the past fifteen
years superintendent, secretary and treasurer of Waccama
Line of Steamers. In March, 1899, he was elected general
manager and treasurer of Conway and Seashore Railroad
Company.

McNEILL, JAMES PURDIE.—Born in Bladen County,
North Carolina. Attended the Clarkton, Cape Fear and Tus-
culum Academies, and the normal department of the university of North Carolina at Chapel Hill. Taught school three
years and entered the law school at Greensboro, North Carolina, presided over by judges B. P. Dick and J. H. Dillard
and graduated therefrom in 1881. Began the practice of his
profession with Honorable J. T. Walsh at Conway, South
Carolina. After practicing there for about two years, he removed to Florence, and has continued in his profession since
that time. For more than eleven years he was judge of probate for Florence County, declining re-election in 1900. For
a number of years he was one of the commissioners of the

Florence Graded School. One of the promoters of the Commercial and Savings Bank, and is a director and attorney for that institution. Also attorney for the Florence Loan and Investment Company, and local attorney for the Atlantic Coast Line Railroad. Married Miss Alma Chase, of Florence, South Carolina, December 18, 1888.

McRAE, ALEXANDER.—President of Red Bluff Cotton Mills at Clio, South Carolina. Was born at Queensdale, Roberson County, North Carolina, in August, 1827. Attended the public school in the neighborhood; married Miss Margaret McRae October 4, 1859. He is farming.

McSWEENEY, MILES BENJAMIN.—Governor of South Carolina. Born in Charleston, South Carolina, April 18, 1855. His father died of yellow fever in Charleston when the son was four years old. At ten he sold newspapers, and later clerked in a book-store, and attended night school. Served apprenticeship as a job printer, and worked on newspapers in Charleston and Columbia. Won the scholarship in Washington and Lee University offered to Charleston Typographical Union, but because of lack of means to meet outside expenses only attended a short time. In 1877, he moved to Ninety-Six, Abbeville County, South Carolina, and published the "Ninety-Six Guardian" until 1879; since then publisher of the "Hampton County Guardian." Was chairman of the county Democratic Executive Committee from 1884 to 1894. Member of the South Carolina Legislature 1894. Lieutenant-governor from 1896 to 1899. Succeeded to governor on the death of Governor W. H. Ellerbe. Elected governor in 1900. Several years member of the State Democratic Executive Committee, and for eight years president of the South Carolina Press Association.

MACE, JOHN CULPEPPER.—Son of John M. and Jane Watson Mace. Born in Marion County June 26, 1870. Ancestors were among the early settlers of the Pee Dee section of Marion County. Attended the Marion graded schools, and the College of Physicians and Surgeons, Baltimore, Maryland, graduating in 1891. Married Agnes Griffin, daughter of Mr. William K. Griffin, of Newberry, January 30, 1895. Since graduation has been practicing medicine at Marion, South Carolina. In connection with his practice he conducts a drugstore. County physician several years. Now serving second term as coroner of the county. Member of the State Medical Association. Editor and publisher of the "Marion Star."

MACKEY, JOHN FRANK.—Has practiced medicine at Lancaster since the war. Was born in that town on May 23, 1836. Is of Scotch descent. Attended the common schools of Lancaster and Kershaw, and was two years at Furman University, but did not graduate. Was assistant surgeon in the Confederate army, president of Lancaster County Medical Society, and member of South Carolina Medical Association. Has an interest in the leading drug firm of the town and takes an interest in all public enterprises. Married Miss Mary Berry, of Lancaster, South Carolina, February 4, 1869.

MAGILL, DAVID HADDON.—Born May 3, 1857, at Due West, Abbeville County, South Carolina. His early training was received in the primary schools of his native town, afterwards entering Erskine College, from which institution he was graduated in 1877. Married Miss Mary Ellis, of Hodges, South Carolina, January 19, 1882. Was elected a member of the House of Representatives from Abbeville County for six consecutive years, and held the same position from Greenwood County two years, which position he now holds. He at one time held the position as chairman of the committee on Incorporations in the House of Representatives for three years. Was also chairman of the committee on Privileges and Elections four years. Is a member of the bar at Greenwood.

MAGRUDER, JAMES MITCHELL.—Pastor of the Church of the Advent, Spartanburg, South Carolina. Was born in Richland, Holmes County, Mississippi, August 4, 1865. Son of W. H. Magruder, professor of English language and litera-

ture in the Agricultural and Mechanical College of Mississippi. He has been thoroughly identified with the educational interests of the South since the Civil War, in which
he fought as captain in the Confederate army. Was married in January, 1894, to Miss Margaret McKie Mosby, of
Canton, Mississippi. Graduated at the Agricultural and Mechanical College of Mississippi and taught school until studies for the ministry were begun. He pursued theological
studies at the Theological Seminary of Alexandria, Virginia,
and the Theological department of the University of the
South at Sewanee, Tennessee. He was admitted to the Dea-
conate (the first order of the ministry of the Protestant Episcopal Church) by the Right Rev. Hugh Miller Thompson, S.
T. D., Bishop of Mississippi, and later advanced to the priesthood by the same Bishop in St. Columbus Chapel, Aberdeen,
Mississippi, remaining there four years. At the request of
Bishop Capers he came to South Carolina and took charge
of the churches at Marion and Darlington. Remained there
three years, when he resigned to accept the rectorship of
the Church of the Advent, Spartanburg, South Carolina, October 1, 1899, which position he maintains ,at the present
time. Since moving to South Carolina he has declined several calls to supply churches in Mississippi, and St. Luke's
Church, Atlanta, Georgia. A delegate from South Carolina
to the International Sunday-school Convention held in Atlanta, Georgia, in 1899; also a delegate to the Domestic and
Foreign Missionary Society of the Protestant Episcopal
Church at the Ecumenical Missionary Conference held in
New York, April, 1900.

MAHON, GABRIEL HEYWARD.—Member of the firm of
Mahon & Arnold, large dry goods merchants of Greenville,
South Carolina. Was born at Cokesbury, Abbeville County,
South Carolina, January 21, 1863. His ancestors were of
Scotch-Irish descent. Was married to Miss Mary T. Brown,
daughter of Dr. W. F. Brown, of Williamston, South Carolina,
January 8, 1884. Began business at the age of nineteen, at
Williamston and later merchandised at Pelzer for five years.
A director in the Carolina Loan and Trust Company. In

connection with his mercantile business he was for eleven years traveling salesman for a large Baltimore house.

MAJOR, JOHN ROBERT TURNER.—Editor of the "Pee Dee Advocate." Son of Joseph M. and Mary E. Stacey Major. Was born in Grenada, Mississippi. Came to South Carolina in early childhood and located at Greenwood, South Carolina. Obtained education from the Greenwood Graded schools and graduated from Wofford College in 1898. Principal of the Lowndesville High School from 1898 to 1899; and the Marlboro graded school from 1899 to 1901. Was literary editor of the college journal, president of the senior class, president of the Preston Literary Society, and vice-president of the Young Men's Christian Association. Represented Wofford College in the Southern Students' Conference at Knoxville, Tennessee, in 1897. He is not married.

MAJOR, JOSEPH MARSHALL.—Son of Rev. S. B. and Matilda S. Major. Born in Abbeville, now Greenwood, County September 17, 1844, near the old Rock Church. He was prepared for college at Bethlehem Academy, but instead of going, entered the Civil War in the Army of Northern Virginia in 1867. Married Miss Mary E. Stacy December 25, 1867. He remained on the farm until 1892, when he was elected county commissioner of Abbeville, and served two years. At the formation of Greenwood he was elected county supervisor, which office he continues to hold.

MALLOY, WILLIAM HERBERT.—Merchant of Florence, South Carolina. Son of Dr. A. Malloy and Henrietta C. Malloy (nee Coit). Born at Cheraw, South Carolina, July 30, 1859. Of Scotch-Irish descent. Attended the common schools and Cheraw Academy. Twice married, first to Kate Wilson in 1885, and second to Hanna Pauline Waring, January 28, 1892. Was clerk and kept books in Cheraw several years. In 1891 went to Florence and kept books for E. F. Douglas & Company. Traveled in Texas one year. Is now serving his second term as mayor of Florence, to which position he was elected without opposition.

MARION, JOHN HARDIN.—Born near Richburg, Sumter
County, South Carolina, October 23,
1874. Was prepared for the South
Carolina College in the neighborhood
schools, entering the College in 1890,
and graduating in 1893 with the degree of Bachelor of Arts and Doctor of
Laws. He began the practice of law
at Chester in the summer of 1893, being admitted to the bar by special
act. Was county attorney for four
years; lieutenant of the First Regiment, South Carolina Volunteers, in
the Spanish-American War; was
elected at the head of the Chester delegation in the House
of Representatives, but did not stand for re-election. Was
elected major, Third Battalion, First Regiment, South Carolina Volunteers, Infantry (Militia), February, 1900, which position he still holds. Is general counsel for the Carolina &
Northwestern Railroad.

MARSHALL, JOHN.—Lineal descendant of Chief Justice
Marshall. Born at Markham, Virginia, January 10, 1866.
Graduated at the Cleveland High School, and was a student
at the University of Virginia. Married Miss Mildred R.
Thompson, a daughter of Colonel J. S. R. Thompson, of Spartanburg, in 1892. Was for four years professor of French
and German at Wofford College, and is now city editor of
the "News and Courier" at Charleston, South Carolina.

MARSHALL, JOHN QUITMAN.—Was born April 1, 1849,
at Columbia, South Carolina. Son of J. Foster Marshall, of
Abbeville. His earlier training was acquired from the village schools in Abbeville, and he graduated from the South
Carolina University in 1873, and also graduated in law in
1874, and was admitted to the bar. Married Miss Janie
Adams Brooks June 11, 1890. He was trial justice from 1876
to 1885. Bears the distinction of having sworn in Wade
Hampton as Governor in 1876. Secretary of the State from

20

1887 to 1890. Organized the Columbia Street Railway and Electric Power Company and was president thereof eight years. Is now practicing law in Columbia, and represents Richland County in the State Senate. Colonel of Palmetto Regiment from 1880 to 1887, when he resigned.

MARTIN, C. V.—Magistrate of the town of Donalds. Was born January 20, 1852, near Donalds, Abbeville County, South Carolina. Educational advantages were limited. Was appointed magistrate in 1883, which position he continues to hold. Is chairman of the local Democratic club, and was intendant of town of Donalds. His last wife was Miss Mamie Purkison, whom he married in 1895. He is also in the employ of the Southern Railway.

MARTIN, COLUMBUS BEN.—Instructor of Latin in Furman University. Was born at Youngs, South Carolina, November 14, 1876. Graduated from Furman University in class of 1899, and taught Latin and mathematics in high school at Hendersonville North Carolina. Not married.

MARTIN, SAMUEL MANER.—Son of Captain Benjamin and Catherine (Maner) Martin. Born in Allendale, Barnwell County, October 30, 1875. His father served through the entire Civil War as aide on General Hagood's staff, since which time he has been engaged in planting in Barnwell and Hampton counties. Graduated from the South Carolina Military Academy in the class of 1896. The first year after graduation he was assistant in the Johnston Institute, and served one year as superintendent of this institute, after which he was elected to a position at Clemson College and is now assistant professor of mathematics in that college and also major of First Battalion.

MARTIN, WILLIAMSON HENRY.—Prominent member of the Laurens bar. Was born in the northern portion of Laurens County August 21, 1852. Attended the common neighborhood schools and later pursued studies at home. Was admitted to the bar in 1881, formed a partnership with the late

General R. P. Todd at Laurens, and continued with him until the death of the latter, and since has been practicing alone. In November, 1876, he married Anna L. Sitgraves. Has been notary public since the beginning of his professional career. Was city attorney for two terms. Appointed on the staff of Governor McSweeney in 1901 with the rank of lieutenant-colonel.

MATHESON, ALEXANDER JAMES.—Born in Marlboro County, South Carolina, in 1848. His father, Donald Matheson, was a native of Attadale, Scotland, and came to this country when a young man and practiced law. The Civil War interfered with his education, and he had the advantages only of the country school. In 1869 he accepted a position as foreman on a farm in Marion County. The next year he operated a three-horse farm, receiving a portion of the crop as compensation for his labor, doing the hardest kind of manual work.

During the year 1870 he married Miss Ellen Garnigan. The next year he rented a small farm, and operated a limted mercantile business, which proved unsuccessful. He was disccuraged and went West, visiting many States beyond the Misssissippi, but finding no location that suited him, he returned home and started to work with renewed determination. He embarked in the mercantile business again, and from the first was successful and made money very rapidly. In 1873 purchased a twenty-five horse cotton plantation in the Pee Dee section, most of it on a credit. He continued his mercantile business, thereby amassing wealth rapidly, and year after year adding more land to his holding. Later he moved to Blenheim, seven miles south of Bennettsville, where he continued merchandising. He is the largest real estate owner in his section, and operates about two hundred plows. His numerous plantations are provided with telephones, artesian wells, retail stores, modern barns and improvements generally. His wealth is estimated at $100,000, and he employs more farm laborers than any other one man in the State. He has traveled extensively in Europe, is largely interested in real estate at Bennettsville, and is at the head of the Marlboro Wholesale Grocery. In August, 1900, he entered into co-partnership with C. E. Exum in the wholesale business and buying cotton; is also manager of the Matheson Real Estate Company of Bennettsville, which is engaged in buying and selling real estate, investing money and negotiating loans. He is a member of the Presbyterian Church and a great Sunday-school worker.

MATHEWS, EDWARD MILES.—Secretary of the Darlington Manufacturing Company. Son of William R. and Eliza Peronneau Mathews, of Charleston, South Carolina. Born October 8, 1869, in Habersham County, Georgia. Married Mary Randolph Hubard, of Nelson County, Virginia, October 28, 1896. Was bookkeeper for the Laurens Manufacturing Company four years.

MATTHEWS, BAILEY.—Elected supervisor of Saluda County in 1900. Born in Edgefield, now Saluda, County June 7, 1845, and was son of Cary Matthews. Received only that education which could be obtained from the common schools. Was also a farmer and merchant, and has been successful as a business man. November 11, 1866, he was married to Miss Martha Black.

MATTISON, JAMES OLIN.—Engaged in insurance busi ness in Charleston, South Carolina. Son of John W. and Sallie Mattison. Born June 29, 1870, at Donalds, Abbeville County, South Carolina, June 29, 1870. Attended the county schools of Donalds up to the age of fourteen, when he entered the Anderson Military Academy, taking a business course. Married Miss Cora H. Sykes, October 14, 1891. Clerked in stores at Donalds and Anderson up to twenty-one years of age, when he embarked in insurance business, having been located at Anderson, Vernon, Texas, Rock Hill; is now in Charleston. Member of Masonic Lodge, Mystic Shriners,

Knights of Pythias, and most all leading fraternities of the day. Chairman of stewards of St. Andrews Society of Charleston. District agent of the Mutual Benefit Life Insurance Company of Newark, New Jersey, having charge of the business in lower section of State.

MATTISON, JOHN WILLIAMS.—Bookkeeper and salesman for W. R. Dunn, Donalds, South Carolina. He was born near Donalds, Abbeville County, South Carolina, January 16, 1839. Education limited to the schools of that time. Married Miss Barmore on November 5, 1867. Volunteered in the Confederate army, July 19, 1861, Company G. Was severely wounded at Gaines' Mill in June, 1862, and at Petersburg, September 30, 1864. Was captured at Petersburg, Virginia, on April 2, 1865, and imprisoned at Hart's Island, New York, until June 18, 1865.

MAULDIN, IVY M.—Born December 17, 1875, at Pickens, South Carolina. Graduated at Clemson College in 1896, being a member of first class to graduate from that college. Was captain of Company K, Second Regiment, South Carolina Infantry Volunteers during the Spanish-American War. Served as such for one year. Was elected to the Legislature from Pickens County, and is now actively engaged in the practice of law, and serving his county as a member of the Legislature.

MAXWELL, JEFFERSON DAVIS.—Special agent for the Liverpool and London and Globe Insurance Company for South Carolina. Born in Oconee County June 5, 1881. His great-grandfather was Colonel Robert Maxwell of the Revolutionary War, and his grandfather Captain John Maxwell was a member of the Legislature and one of the signers of the secession ordinance. He received his education from Professor W. J. Ligon, the foremost educator of his time at Pendleton, South Carolina. When he first went to Anderson he secured a position as bookkeeper for B. F. Crayton and Sons. Afterwards went into the insurance business, both life and fire. Organized the Anderson Building and Loan

Association in 1883. Stockholder of the Hotel Chiquola, and was on the building committee of the new court-house and jail. Was an alderman of the city. Member of board of assessors for eighteen years. Secretary and treasurer of the first Democratic Club ever organized in Anderson. In 1886 was appointed on Governor Richardson's staff with rank of Colonel. Charter member of the Knights of Pythias and Woodmen of the World. Married Alice Von Borstelon October 19, 1875.

MAXWELL, JOHN H.—Son of Captain John Maxwell and Elizabeth Earle, natives of Greenville County. Their youngest son, Dr. John H., was born near old Pendleton, in Anderson County, on December 19, 1832. He spent his early boyhood in Pendleton, where he received his literary education. At the age of nineteen he entered the University of Virginia, and commenced an academic course preparatory to the study of medicine. His last session there was devoted entirely to the study of medical science, and in the fall of 1853 he entered the Jefferson Medical College of Philadelphia, Pennsylvania, and graduated there on March 11, 1854. After his return home he settled at Fair Play, Oconee County, South Carolina, and commenced the practice of medicine with his brother, Dr. Robert D. Maxwell. After two years' practice there, he returned to his native home. His health began to fail and for this reason he moved to Greenville, South Carolina, where he has confined his practice entirely to the city, with special reference to diseases peculiar to women. In 1860 he married Miss Mary E. Alexander, daughter of Colonel E. Alexander of Pickens, South Carolina. Member of the Baptist Church more than forty years, also Knight of Honor, and a Democrat.

MAYER, ORLANDO BENEDICT.—Son of Dr. Orlando Benedict and Carrie (DeWalt) Mayer. Was born August 23, 1853, at Newberry, South Carolina. On December 12, 1894, married Miss Hattie W. Jones, daughter of W. W. Jones, of Laurens, South Carolina. Graduated from the South Carolina Medical College March, 1874, and immediately began the practice of his profession in Newberry, South Carolina, where he continues to practice, not only in his native county, but in adjoining counties and other portions of the State. In 1885 he was elected president of the South Carolina Medical Association and has contributed at various times numerous papers on obstetrics and surgery. Member of the American Medical Association and has served several years as member of the State Board of Medical Examiners, which position he continues to hold. He is professor of physiology in Newberry College. In 1894 the degree of Master of Arts was conferred upon him by Newberry College. He is a trustee of Newberry College, a director of Newberry Cotton Mill, vice-president of Commercial Bank, and president of Newberry Land and Security Company. For two consecutive terms served as mayor. Newberry College is indebted to his generosity for a thousand-dollar scholarship. The Mayer Memorial Lutheran Church was erected by him in memory of his father, Dr. O. B. Mayer, Sr.

MAYES, GEORGE GREGG.—Born in Mayesville, Sumter County, South Carolina, September 18, 1866. Prepared for college at the Fort Mill Academy by Professor A. R. Banks. Entered Davidson College in the fall of 1884, and the sophomore class of the South Carolina College in 1885, and graduated with the degree of A. B. 1888. Entered Princeton Seminary the same year, and at the same time entered Princeton University as a post-graduate. Graduated from Princeton Seminary in 1891, and obtained from the University the degree of A. M. Was licensed to preach by the Harmony Presbytery at Sumter in 1890. Ordained and installed pastor of the Walhalla Church by the South Carolina Presbytery June, 1891. In connection with this work he also supplied Bethel and Ebenezer churches 1891 to 1894; Bethel and Richland 1894 to 1897. Was then called to Edgefield, and supplied Trenton, Johnston, and Roper churches, having remained there only a short time when he received a call to the Second Church, Greenville. Was stated clerk of the South Carolina Presbytery five years, and twice elected moderator of Presbytery.

MAYFIELD, WILLIAM DAVID.—Son of William and Lillian Blythe Mayfield. Born near Benton, Polk County, Tennessee, June 22, 1854. His parents returned to South Carolina soon after the Civil War.

He was prepared for college at Cane Creek Academy, and graduated with second honor from Hiawassee College, Monroe County, Tennessee, in 1875, and taught school a few years. Elected school commissioner of Greenville County, 1878, and to this office he was four times elected. He established the first teachers' institute in the State in 1879, and organized the splendid system of graded schools in the city of Greenville. Elected State superintendent of education in 1890, which office he held four terms of two years each. He was admitted to the bar in 1880, practiced at Greenville, South Carolina. Upon the retirement from office of State superintendent of education, he located at Columbia for the practice of law. He married Caroline Hartwell Bonds, of Newberry County, on November 8, 1882.

MEADOWS, WILLIAM PASCHAL.—Presiding elder of the Spartanburg District, South Carolina annual conference, Methodist Episcopal Church, South. Son of Paschal Mattey Meadows, a native of South Carolina. Was born in Laurens County, South Carolina, May 15, 1854. Was reared on a farm and attended the best schools of the time and neighborhood, but on account of the condition of the country just after the war he was deprived of a college education. He applied for license and was admitted into the Conference December, 1876. For four years he was presiding elder of the Charleston District, the largest field in the Conference. Has been twice married, first to Miss Kate Boyce English, of Union County; second to Miss Janie Belle Hutchison, of Abbeville County, whom he married on March 22, 1882 Has occupied important fields in the Conference.

MEANS, DAVID HARPER.—Born at Barnwell Court-house, South Carolina, March 31, 1856, and reared in Fairfield County, South Carolina. His father, Isaac H. Means, was a Confederate soldier, and secretary of the State of South Carolina four years. His mother was a sister of ex-Governor Johnson Hagood. He was educated at the King's Mountain Military School, leaving a few days before graduation to accept a position with a corps of Railroad surveyors, in which occupation he continued until 1878, when he was called to Columbia to take the position of general agent of public lands of South Carolina, which position he still holds. He was graduated Bachelor of Laws from the law department of the South Carolina College in 1893, winning the Clariosophic Society Medal. In 1892 he drew an act which became a law without amendment, and which for the first time enabled the State to make good tax titles for, and enforce the collection of taxes upon, about six thousand parcels of fortified land, the accumulation of about twenty years of previous defective legislation. By invitation he delivered an address to the State convention of United Confederate Veterans in May, 1901. He was admitted to the bar in 1893, but never practiced his profession.

MEDLOCK, JOHN TRAVIS.—Cashier of the Bank of Greenwood. Son of J. Travis and Cornelia Jones Medlock. Was born in Laurens County, South Carolina, August 18, 1856. He had the advantages of the common schools of Laurens and Abbeville counties. Graduated from the commercial department of Kentucky University, Lexington, Kentucky, in 1885. Taught school three years. Was engaged in the mercantile business in Laurens County with W. Z. McGhee of Hodges, South Carolina, from 1881 to 1885. Bookkeeper and salesman for T. J. Simmons of Greenwood in 1888, and in that year became bookkeeper for J. K. Durst and Company, and remained with them until 1891, when he was elected assistant cashier in the bank, and later to the position he now holds. He married Kate, daughter of R. M. Bullock, of Greenwood County, South Carolina, December 15, 1892.

MELCHERS, THEODORE A. W.—Member of the wholesale grocery firm of Melchers and Son of Charleston, South Carolina. Son of Casper A. and Marie Melman Melchers. Born November 5, 1833, in the city of Cloppenburg, Germany. Common school education received in Germany. Came to Charleston, South Carolina, in December, 1848, when only fifteen years of age, and entered the dry-goods business. Married Helen J. P. Muller, daughter of Rev. Dr. L. Muller, who was pastor of St. Matthews Lutheran Church for over fifty years. President of the German Friendschuftsbund, German Rifle Club, South Carolina Wholesale Grocers Association, director of Merchants' Exchange, alderman of the city of Charleston, member of Camp Sumter United Confederate Veterans, German artillery, Past Master of Walhalla Lodge 66 F. A. M., Past High Priest Germania Chapter 12, R. A. M., Past Eminent Commander South Carolina Commandery No. 1, and Knights Templar. Was presented by lodge with handsome jewels as token of their appreciation of his services. Entered active service in 1860 as sergeant-major of the First Regiment of Rifles South Carolina Militia, commanded by Colonel Branch. Served on Sullivan's Island during the bombardment of Fort Sumter in April, 1861, and was with the command at Rockville. Served on James and Wadmalaw Island until the State troops were disbanded, when he volunteered as a private in the German Hussars, Third Regiment, South Carolina Cavalry, and was identified with that company for eleven months following. Was then appointed by General Beauregard as signal officer and was on duty in that capacity at Fort Sumter, Fort Johnson, and several other points to intercept the enemies signal. At the evacuation of Charleston he was one of the escort of General Taliaferro as far as Cheraw, when he received orders to report to Colonel Tiger commanding First Brigade of Georgia Regulars at Chesterfield Court-house. Being sent out with two recruits to reconnoitre Sherman's advance, he succeeded in capturing and bringing in three Yankee stragglers Remained with Colonel Tiger until Fayetteville, North Carolina, was reached, when losing his horse, he attached himself to Sparkman's Battery, fighting at Averasboro, and Bentonville, and surrendering at Greensboro with Johnson's army. He was wounded during the war once on Johns Island. After the war closed he returned to Charleston to start in the world anew. Through friends in New York he succeeded in starting up a dry-goods business in 1866, which business he carried on until 1877, when he sold out to his partner and went with the house of H. Bischoff and Company of New York, wholesale grocers, to whose business he succeeded in 1887 as head of the firm of Melchers and Company.

MELTON, WILLIAM DAVIS.—Lawyer. Son of Dr. W. C. D. Melton and Mary Jane Poag. Born May 26, 1868, near Richburg, Chester County, South Carolina. Was of Scotch-Irish ancestry. Attended the University of Virginia from 1887 to 1890. Graduated in law at the South Carolina College in 1892. Married Caro Belser of Summerton, South Carolina, May 11, 1898. Clerked, kept books and merchandised from 1883 to 1887. Commenced to practice law in Columbia, South Carolina, in 1893. Alderman from ward in city of Columbia.

MILFORD, CHARLES ARLINGTON.—Druggist of Abbeville, South Carolina. Son of Charles S. Milford, of Anderson County. Was born near Townville, Oconee County, June 15, 1869. His father was a native-born South Carolinian of Irish descent, his ancestry having emigrated to South Carolina from Ireland in 1776. Educated in the common schools of Anderson County, and entered Patrick Military Institute in 1887. Graduated in 1889. Entered the Maryland College of Pharmacy of Baltimore, and graduated from same as valedictorian of his class in 1895. Was captain of the Abbeville Volunteers one year, and when volunteers were called for to take part in the Spanish-American War, his was the first company to respond. Served only six months, being mustered out at Columbia in November, 1898.

MILFORD, JESSE CUNNINGHAM.—Prominent merchant of Honea Path. Was born November 26, 1855. After having attended school under Professor Ligon, he entered Furman University. Just after leaving school he was married to Sallie, daughter of J. R. Latimer, on October 8, 1885. He remained on the farm until 1886, when he moved to Honea Path and engaged in the mercantile business. He is also vice-president of the Citizens Bank of that place.

MILLER, ANDREW HILL.—President of the Orangeburg Institute. Was born in Wellford, Spartanburg County, August 5, 1877. Son of J. J. Miller who is connected with the Arlington Cotton Mill. Education was acquired from the common and high schools of Wellford, South Carolina. Graduated with the degree of M. A. from Furman University with first honor in 1898. Read law and was admitted to the bar the following year, but never practiced. Was married to a Miss Vaughan, of Harris, Louisa County, Virginia, August 1, 1900. Assistant observer of the United States Weather Bureau, Columbia, Missouri, in 1898. Instructor of mathematics in Pantops Academy, Charlottesville, Virginia. Professor of chemistry in Furman University in 1900, and taught Latin the same year.

MILLER, HENRY FREDERICK.—Son of Daniel and Emily L. (Strohecker) Miller. Born November 15, 1852, at Charleston, South Carolina. Education was obtained from the Charleston public schools. Past Master Orange Lodge No. 14, A. F. and A. M. Lieutenant-colonel on staff of Governor John Gary Evans. Now general manager of the Miller Hardware Company.

MILLER, JONES FULLER.—Son of Jacob and Martha Miller. Was born in Abbeville County on November 15, 1855. Lived on the farm until 1871, since which time he has resided in the city of Abbeville. His early training was re-

ceived from the public schools of Abbeville. He married Miss
Ione D. Allen on May 7, 1881. Has been engaged in the
mercantile business for twenty years; served as city treasurer for ten years, and served two terms as mayor of Abbeville.

MILLER, WILLIAM CAPERS.—Son of Dr. William C. and
Elizabeth M. Miller. Born February 25, 1858, at George-
town, South Carolina. Educated at Furman University,
Greenville, and the University of Virginia, at Charlottesville.
Married Miss Georgia Gordon October 13, 1887. Attorney at
law and member of firm of Webster, Rhett, Miller & Whealey.

MILLER, WILLIAM JOSEPH.—Son of Joseph and Mary
Cathcart Miller. Born near Rock Hill, York County, South
Carolina, August 12, 1845. Attended the Ebenezer Academy
until the spring of 1861, when he entered the army, joining
the Twelfth Regiment South Carolina Volunteers at the age
of fifteen. Served through the war and surrendered at Appomattox. After the war closed he went to work on a small
farm, and now owns a thousand acres of land including the
old homestead that has been in the family over one hundred
and ten years, having original grant from State. He has often been solicited to enter the political field, but loved private life too well to enter that doubtful field. He is a Democrat. Married Miss Josephine Roddy, in November, 1866.

MILLIGAN, WILLIAM EMERY.—County superintendent
of education for Charleston County. Born July 21, 1844, at
Charleston, South Carolina. His great-grandfather, Captain
Jacob Milligan, was born in Charleston in 1730; and in the
bombardment of Fort Moultrie by the English fleet June 28,
1776, headed a party which boarded the British frigate Ac-
tean that had run aground. Captain Milligan succeeded in
getting the flags and ship's bell and had hardly left the
vessel when it blew up. His early life was passed in securing an education at the public schools, which was completed
at the high schools. On leaving school he entered his father's employ and in 1872 was actively engaged in the com-

mission and auction business. Appointed clerk of the board of county commissioners and held that office until 1878, when he was appointed deputy sheriff. Held this until 1880, when he accepted an offer from the custom service. He is Past Master of Solomon Lodge No. 1 A. F. M. and Past High Priest of the Carolina Zerubabel Chapter No. 1 R. A. M. Member of the Hibernian Society, and ex-president of St. Patrick's Benevolent Society, and member of the Knights of Honor. Served in Confederate army on the coast when hostilities began and afterwards in provost marshal's office on detached duty until close of war. Married Miss Martha Withington of Charleston, South Carolina, April 5, 1866.

MILLS, WILLIAM WILSON.—Pastor of the Presbyterian Church at Camden since 1884. Born December 21, 1837, near Mayesville, Sumter County, South Carolina. Of Scotch-Irish descent. His ancestors were prominent and active in the Revolutionary War. He spent 1856 and 1857 at Mt. Zion Institute, Winnsboro, and graduated with distinction from the South Carolina College in 1860. Entered the Columbia Theological Seminary in the fall of 1865 and graduated in the spring of 1868. Served in various capacities throughout the late Civil War. Twice seriously wounded. Served most of the time in Virginia under General Robert E. Lee. Was ordained a Presbyterian minister in the fall of 1868 and has supplied several churches. In 1900 the degree of Doctor of Divinity was conferred upon him by Davidson College, North Carolina. Member of the board of directors of Columbia Theological Seminary about ten years, and is at present its secretary. Married Miss Edith A. Smith, of Pendleton, South Carolina, December 23, 1868.

MIMNAUGH, JOHN LANTY.—Born in the north of Ireland in 1856. Attended the public schools of Ireland, and came to America in 1873. Served apprenticeship in drygoods business with James A. Gray and Company in Augusta, Georgia. Married Miss Missouri Williford December 28, 1879. Started in business in 1878 with $500 capital in Winnsboro; came to Columbia in 1883, and it was not long before he was recognized as a power in its business life. He may now be properly called Columbia's merchant-prince. By his own business sagacity he has become practically a semi-millionaire, having accumulated nearly $500,000 in twenty-two years by his own unaided efforts. Is the owner of two immense stores in Columbia, which he still personally manages; owns the new Wright's Hotel and is a director of the Central National Bank. Has always declined public position, and devotes himself entirely to his business.

MOBLEY, JOHN GLOVER.—Son of Dr. John G. and Fannie C. (Means) Mobley. Born in Fairfield County, South Carolina. His family on both sides were among the early settlers of the State. He received his education in Columbia, and at Kings Mountain Military School under Colonel Coward. Read law in the office of Wallace, Baxon & Moore at Columbia, South Carolina, and admitted to the bar in 1884. Entered into a partnership with Colonel William Wallace and practiced with him two years.

Then went into farming and stock-raising in Fairfield County, and has done much to develop that interest in this State. He is a director of the State Agricultural Society. Elected to the Legislature in 1898, and in 1901 was made a director of the State penitentiary, which office he now holds.

MOBLEY, SAMUEL GOODE.—Son of Dr. William S. Mobley and Harriet Goode. Born in Edgefield County, near Saluda. His father represented Edgefield County in the Legislature several terms, and was a popular and distinguished physician. Received a very good English education in the high schools of ante-bellum days. He has been thrice married. His last wife was Miss Mary E. Carwile, whom he married December 15, 1892. He has been actively engaged in the practice of medicine since May 1, 1856, and was assistant surgeon in the war between the States.

MOFFATT, JAMES STRONG.—Son of William S. Moffat. Born July 17, 1860, in Wheeling, Fulton County, Arkansas. Spent one year at a high school in Ohio and one year at St. Clairsville High School, Ohio, two years at Erskine College, South Carolina. Also two years at Muskingum College, Ohio; graduating there in 1883. Graduated from United Presbyterian Theological Seminary, Allegheny, Pennsylvania, in 1886. Married Miss Jennie Moffatt Grier, of Due West, South Carolina, November 23, 1886. Taught in the public schools of Ohio two years, and tutored one year at Muskingum College. Member of board of trustees of Erskine Theological Seminary, and treasurer of the same institution. and of the McMillan fund. Member of Board of Home Missions of the Associate Reform Presbyterian Church. Secretary and treasurer of the Board of Church Extension. Has been pastor of the Associate Reform Church of Chester for nearly fifteen years.

MOFFETT, GEORGE H.—Member of the Legislature from Charleston County. Son of George H. and Elizabeth (Simonton) Moffett of Charleston, South Carolina. His father was adjutant and inspector-general of Hagood's Brigade, Confederate States of America. Obtained education from public and high schools of Charleston and the Charleston College, graduating in class of 1889 from South Carolina University. Taught school two years and was admitted to the bar in December, 1891, practicing law as partner of W. Huger Fitzsimons. This firm was dissolved January 1, 1900, and Mr. Moffett has since practiced alone.

MOISE, EDWIN W.—Born in Charleston, South Carolina, May 21, 1832. Educated in the common schools of the county, and at the Academy of John S. Crisp and Sachtleben & Miles in Charleston, South Carolina. Married Esther Lyon at Petersburg, Virginia, September 20, 1854, at the residence of her uncle, Mr. Goodman Davis. Was appointed commander of the Tenth Georgia Regiment, Young's Brigade, Butler's Division, Hampton's Corps. The Regiment was made up from the Georgia companies of the Seventh Confederate Cav-

alry. He served in the last battles of the war at Bentonville and Averysboro, North Carolina. Assisted General
Wade Hampton in the struggle of 1876, and that same year
was elected adjutant and inspector, re-elected in 1878, and
declined candidacy in 1880. The second year he filled this office he donated his entire salary to the public schools. In
1880 he was elected presidential elector. Was chosen as one
of the judges of the World's Fair, at Chicago, in 1893. Burnt
the bridge at Smithville, North Carolina, thus preventing the
retreat of General Joe Johnston after the battle at Bentonville.

MOISE, MARION.—Lawyer. Former mayor of Sumter,
South Carolina. Was born on Sullivan's Island, South Carolina, June 14, 1855. His education was limited, having the
advantage of only a year at the Virginia Military Institute,
and in 1872 he entered the South Carolina College, but left
there with others when the negroes were admitted in 1873.
He was elected State Senator from Sumter County in 1886 and
again in 1889. He is a prominent member of the bar from
Sumter, South Carolina, and is engaged in the practice of
his profession with R. D. Lee. He is President of the school
board of Sumter Graded School. Married Miss Isabel De-
Leon Moise, November 7, 1877.

MONROE, WILLIAM M.—Son of David and F. A. Monroe.
Born December 3, 1857, in Marion County, South Carolina.
Of Scotch descent. Attended the common schools of his native town. Married Mary A. McMillan, May 16, 1882. Engaged in merchandising at Marion, South Carolina.

MONTAGUE, ANDREW PHILIP.—Was born September 27,
1854, in Essex County, Virginia. Educated in the University
of Virginia. Received A. M. and Ph. D. degrees from Columbian University, and LL.D. from Richmond College. Married Miss Christian Montague November 3, 1881. Held the
position of tutor in Columbian University, Washington, District of Columbia. Professor of Latin and principal of the
preparatory department; Dean of Columbian College. He is

21

now president of Furman University. Editor of "Letters of
Cicero," and "Letters of Pliny." Presiding officer of the
American Baptist Society in 1900, and appointed to say fare-
well to the National Education Association in Charleston, in
1900. Deacon in Pendleton Street Baptist Church, Greenville. Member of the American Philological Association, and
also of the Cosmos Club, Washington, District of Columbia.

MONTGOMERY, JOHN HENRY.—President of the Spartan
Mills and the Pacolet Manufacturing Company. Was born
on a farm in Spartanburg County, fourteen miles west of
Spartanburg, December 8, 1833. He is a son of Benjamin F.
Montgomery, also a native of Spartanburg County. Born in
1810. His ancestors emigrated to America from the north
of Ireland, and first settled in Pennsylvania. Captain John
H. Montgomery spent the first nineteen years of his life on
the farm where he was born. He obtained a very good common-school education, and at nineteen his father put him in
a store to clerk. He held this position one year, for which
he was paid five dollars a month and board. From there
he went to Columbia, and clerked four months. In the fall
of 1855 his parents, brothers and sisters removed to Texas,
leaving him the sole member of his family in South Carolina.
His brother-in-law with whom he was connected in business
at Hobbysville also went to Texas, leaving him to pay back
the capital with which they had started in business. He continued in business until 1858, when he moved his stock to a
store owned by his father-in-law two miles distant. There
he continued business until the opening of the Civil War. In
December, 1861, he volunteered his services to his country,
and was enrolled in Company E, Eighteenth South Carolina
Regiment as a private. Upon the reorganization of the regiment he was appointed regimental commissary with the rank
of captain. This office was soon after abolished and he was
made assistant commissary of the brigade. In 1864 this office was also abolished and he was then made assistant division commissary and continued as such until the close of
the war, surrendering with General Lee at Appomattox April
9, 1865. Returning from the war he had no means whatever,

his only property being a small stock of leather. In 1874 he removed to Spartanburg and gave his attention exclusively to fertilizers, becoming a partner of Colonel Joseph Walker and Dr. C. E. Fleming. He thus continued until 1884 when he retired from the firm. In the meantime, in 1881, the firm of Walker, Fleming & Company, to which he belonged, purchased a water-power on Pacolet River, thirteen miles east of Spartanburg, and, in 1882, began the erection of the Pacolet Manufacturing Company. This was completed in 1883. This company was incorporated in 1881 with Captain Montgomery as its president and treasurer, which position he has since held. The mill on its completion had twelve thousand spindles and three hundred and twenty-eight looms. These were increased in 1887 to twenty-six thousand two hundred and twenty-four spindles and eight hundred and forty looms. Captain Montgomery is a director in the Whitnet Manufacturing Company and a stockholder in the Clifton Manufacturing Company, both of Spartanburg County. He is also a stockholder in Beaumont, and a director in the National Bank, and a stockholder in the Iron District Fire Insurance Company. Captain Montgomery was married in 1857 to Miss Susan A. Holcombe, daughter of David Holcombe, a native of Union County. Mr. Montgomery is one of Spartanburg's most influential citizens, and has done and is doing much for the material and social prosperity of the city.

MONTGOMERY, WILLIAM JOSEPH.—Born May 20, 1857, at Marion, South Carolina. Graduated at Wofford College in 18875. Married Annie Stackhouse December 13, 1877. Member of the Legislature from 1882 to 1883. Member of the House from 1898 to 1899. Mayor of the town of Marion two terms. He is a lawyer and treasurer of the Farmer's Bank since its organization in 1889. Member Constitutional Convention of 1895.

MOODY, THOMAS CRAWFORD.—Son of B. Moody and Sarah Crawford Moody. Born in Marion County February 14, 1839. Of English descent, who were among the earlier settlers of the Pee Dee section of South Carolina. Attended common and academic schools of the county. Married Eliza E., daughter of Captain W. S. Ellerbe, December 20, 1883. Elected clerk of the court of Marion County in 1860, re-elected in 1864. In 1869 turned out of office and disfranchised by an act of Congress for refusing to subscribe an oath of allegiance. Between 1869 and 1878 was a member of the county and State conventions. In 1878 elected to the Legislature, and in 1884 was elected to the Senate from Marion County again in 1888, and declined re-election in 1892. Took an active part in the redemption of the State in 1876. Now engaged in farming.

MOONEY, JOHN ALLENDER.—Was a most successful member of the Greenville bar. Was born in the village of Gowensville in the Dark Corner of that county in 1863. Attended the Gowensville Seminary, which was under the control of Thomas J. Earle. Was at one time trial justice of his native county, and represented that county in the Legislature for several years. Also an alderman of the city of Greenville. He made his home in Greenville, but was associated in the practice of law with Messrs. Gentry & DePass of Spartanburg, South Carolina. Married Miss Margaret Montgomery.

MOORE, ANDREW CHARLES.—Professor of biology and geology in the South Carolina College. Son of Thomas J. Moore and Mary E. Anderson. Born at Moore Station, Spartanburg County, South Carolina, December 27, 1866. His ancestors were Irish and among the early settlers of the Tiger River section of Spartanburg County. Attended the Reidville Male Academy from 1881 to 1883. Graduated from the South Carolina College in 1887. Junior president of the Clariosophic Society, and valedictorian of graduating class of same society. Married Vivian May, of Hale County, Alabama, September

20, 1900. Superintendent of Spartanburg graded school in 1888. Organizer and superintendent of Camden graded schools from 1889 to 1890. Principal of the High School of Birmingham, Alabama, from 1890 to 1898. Resigned to take post-graduate course at Chicago University. Elected Fellow in Botany in Chicago University in 1900. Elected assistant in department of botany; resigned to accept the position he now has. In 1896 he studied in the University of New York City, and in 1901 in the Marine Biological Laboratory at Woods Hale, Masssacbusetts.

MOORE, GORDON BEVERLY.—Teaching in Furman University. Is a native of Virginia. Was born in Amherst County April 1, 1854. The foundation of his education was laid in White Gate Academy. Graduated from Richmond College, and also from the Southern Baptist Theological Seminary. Has a diploma from Chicago University. Married Miss Virginia Carpenter, October 28, 1882. Was pastor of the Darlington Baptist Church about nine years. Professor of political science and philosophy in Furman University. Associate editor of the "Baptist Courier" since 1891. One of the directors of the summer school.

MOORE, JOHN SWANN.—Son of George J. and Mary E. Moore. Born September 3, 1832, at Pittsboro, North Carolina, both lineal descendants of Governor James Moore. Prepared for college at the Caldwell Institute, Hillsboro, North Carolina. Graduated from the University of North Carolina in 1853. Read under W. H. Battle and Richmond Pearson, both judges of the Supreme Court of North Carolina. Married Laura A. E. Cook, daughter of Honorable William J. Cook. Was practicing law in Goldsboro, North Carolina, when the war came on. Volunteered and was appointed a lieutenant in the Goldsboro Rifles, the first company in the State ordered into service. Resigned this position and went into the Wilmington Light Infantry as sergeant and was with them at Appomattox. Taught school over twenty-five years. Then engaged in merchandising, and was twice burned out and was then appointed United States commissioner.

MOORE, MAURICE HERNDON.—Lawyer. Son of Dr. J. Nott Moore and Lucy Herndon. Born at Cedar Grove, Spartanburg County, South Carolina, October 18, 1866. Of English, Irish and Welsh descent. Graduated from Wofford College with degree of A. B. in 1884, and from law department of South Carolina College in 1887. Unmarried. Taught school two years. Began the practice of law in 1890 under the firm name of Robertson & Moore, of Columbia. Upon the withdrawal of Mr. Robertson to enter the banking business formed a partnership with Thompson. Elected city attorney for Columbia in 1900. Elected adjunct professor of law in South Carolina College in 1901.

MOORE, WALTER BEDFORD.—A prominent merchant of Yorkville, South Carolina. Was born October 7, 1863, in Yorkville, South Carolina. Educated at the Kings Mountain Military Academy. Member of the city council six or eight years, and served three years as mayor. While mayor built water-works at Yorkville. Was a prominent factor in organizing the Carolina Buggy Company and served as treasurer of that institution, and represented it on the road as salesman. Accepted the superintendency of agencies for Mutual Life Insurance Company of North Carolina in 1891 and 1892. He returned to Yorkville and went into his present business in 1893. Was appointed captain of the Jasper Light Infantry Military Company. He is largely interested in the telephone business and has built the lines connecting several towns with Blacksburg. Married Miss Annie Lee Adickes October 20, 1884.

MOORMAN, ROBERT.—Magistrate of the city of Columbia, and lawyer. Son of Thomas S. Moorman and Maria W. Wardlaw. Born November 14, 1873 at Newberry, South Carolina. Of English, Welsh and Scotch-Irish descent. Attended private schools of Newberry and graded schools of Columbia, graduating from South Carolina College in 1893 with degree of LL.B. Married Virginia C. Talley December 15, 1897.

MOORMAN, THOMAS SAMUEL.—Librarian of the Supreme Court. Son of Robert Moorman and Mary L. Kenner. Born March 25, 1842, near Goshen Hill, Union County, South Carolina. Of English descent. Graduated from Wofford College in 1860 when a little over eighteen years of age. Married first Marie W. Wardlaw in 1871 and Jane D. Wardlaw in 1900. Been practicing law since 1866. Magistrate a number of years. Served in Civil War in Company E of the Third South Carolina Regiment Infantry, Kershaw's Brigade, McLaw's Division, Longstreet's Corps, Army of Northern Virginia for about twelve months as private, then as third and second lieutenant. Promoted to first lieutenancy just at the close of the war. When General Johnston reorganized his army in North Carolina was wounded at the battle of the Wilderness.

MORGAN, BENJAMIN ARTHUR.—Son of Benjamin F. and Mary Hammett Morgan. Was born at Dacusville, Pickens County, June 14, 1864. Received his education from the Pickens Institute at Pickens, South Carolina. Read law under G. G. Wells, and James L. Orr, and upon admission to the bar in 1896 became a member of the firm. Was for several years special attorney for the Richmond & Danville Railroad, and also the Central Road and Banking Company of Georgia. Attorney for the city of Greenville four years. In 1900 was a candidate for the Legislature from Greenville County with fifteen others in the race, receiving almost three-fourths of the total vote, and being the only one nominated at the first primary election, leading the ticket over the next hightest man nine hundred and forty-six votes. His ancestors on paternal side were of Welsh descent. Three brothers settled first in Virginia, one went to Alabama and the other came to South Carolina. His father was a merchant, and held various public offices in Pickens County. He is now a prominent member of the Greenville bar. He was united in marriage with Miss Jennie Rose, of Fayetteville, North Carolina, February 14, 1893.

MORGAN, THOMAS REDMAN.—Lawyer. Son of Thomas O. and Annie R. Morgan. Born May 3, 1863, in Cook County, Illinois. Removed to Aiken, South Carolina, in 1869. Father a native of England and mother of Maryland. Attended the common schools of Aiken and took a special course at the South Carolina College. Admitted to the bar in 1889. Appointed United States Commissioner in 1885 while a law student; held same ten years when he resigned. Elected mayor of the City of Aiken in 1898; declined re-election.

MORGAN, WILLIAM DOYLE.—Son of John and Mary Morgan, natives of Ireland. He was born in New York City, February 5, 1853. A few months later his parents removed to Georgetown, South Carolina, where he has since resided. Attended the local school of Georgetown. His father died just after the close of the war, and he was compelled to go to work to support his mother and sisters. He is not married. Was mayor of Georgetown; president of the Bank of Georgetown and also several building and loan associations. He has been president of the Georgetown Bank since its organization in 1891; also president of the Eureka Building and Loan Association and a director in other local institutions. Mayor of the city of Georgetown since April, 1891, serving five terms without opposition for nomination or election.

MORRIS, THOMAS EDWARD.—Son of John J. and Sara Morris. Born December 30, 1855, in Williamsburg County, South Carolina. The common schools of the neighborhood, with one year at Palmetto Academy in Marlboro County, and two years at Cokesbury Conference school were the only opportunities of this kind open to him. Married Miss Isabel McColman, of Richmond County, North Carolina, November 10, 1880. Taught school two years, and then entered the South Carolina Conference, and has supplied churches in Columbia, Charleston, Bamberg, Laurens, Union, Marion and Chester. Member of the board of trustees of Columbia Female College.

MORRISON, JAMES B.—Son of Richard S. and Eliza A. (Venning) Morrison, of Charleston County. Born in Barbor County, Alabama, January 28, 1847. Of Huguenot and Scotch-Irish ancestry. Good common-school education. Married Miss Eliza H. Leland, of Abbeville County, South Carolina, December 22, 1870. He is engaged in farming. Member of the Legislature from 1888 to 1889. Elected sheriff of Berkeley County in 1891, which position he is still filling. Served in Civil War and surrendered with Johnston's army at High Point, North Carolina, 1865. His grandfather on maternal side fought in Revolutionary War.

MORRISON, WILLIAM SHANNON.—One of Clemson College faculty. Was born in Winnsboro, South Carolina, April 7, 1853. His parents, Wm. A. and Nancy (Carlisle) Morrison, moved to Blackstock, South Carolina, in 1869, where they still reside. His early education was received in private schools and at the Mt. Zion Institute in that town. He attended the preparatory department in 1867. In 1869, 1870 and 1871 he worked on the farm near Blackstock, studying at night and on rainy days, and in October, 1871, he entered the freshman class of Wofford College, from which college he was graduated with distinction in June, 1875. He at once began teaching. He established the high school at Wellford in Spartanburg County, February, 1876, and continued it until 1884, when he was called to organize and superintend the city schools of Spartanburg. After two years service there he was called to Greenville, where he organized the city schools in 1886, and which he superintended until 1892, when he was elected to the position he now holds. In addition to his duties as professor of history at Clemson College, he organized and had charge of the Fitting School there, which was abolished in 1899. He was a lay representative to the Annual Conferences held in various places since 1880. Professor Morrison was married on December 12, 1878, to Miss Maggie Jackson, of Wellford, Spartanburg County, South Carolina.

MOSELEY, HARTWELL ROBERT.—Son of Colonel George F. and Harriet Moseley (nee Lester). Born June 20, 1863, at Laurens, South Carolina. Of English descent. Attended the common schools, Greenville Military Institute, and graduated from Furman University with degree of A. B. and from the Southern Baptist Theological Seminary. Married Etna Oliphant December 5, 1888. President of Madero Institute, Satillo, Mexico; missionary in Mexico; pastor of the Rock Hill Baptist Church; pastor of Florence Baptist Church; general missionary in Eastern Cuba. Degree of D. D. conferred in 1898 by Furman University. Member of the board of trustees of Furman University and Greenville Female College. Now missionary to Cuba.

MOSS, ADAM HOLMAN.—Lawyer, and member of the House of Representatives from Orangeburg County. Son of James M. Moss, of Orangeburg County. Born September 16, near town of Cameron, in Orangeburg County. Graduated from Wofford College in 1892. Member of county board of education ten years. Taught school two years, one in county, and one in the Orangeburg graded schools. Second-lieutenant in the Spanish-American War. Promoted to captaincy and served with such rank both in the United States and Cuba. He is at present lieutenant-colonel on Governor McSweeney's staff. He is unmarried.

MOSS, BENJAMIN HART.—Born January 17, 1862, at Orangeburg, South Carolina. Educated at the Orangeburg High School and Wofford College, leaving college in 1881 to read law under Honorable Samuel Dibble, and was admitted to the bar in 1883. Married November 16, 1892, Frances Agnes Dibble. Was at one time a member of the Legislature, but declined re-election. Was also trial justice of Orangeburg, county attorney, and presidential elector. He now holds the position as president of the Orangeburg Knitting Mill, vice-president of the Orangeburg Manufacturing Company, and the Edisto Savings Bank. Mr. Moss is now actively engaged in the practice of law under the firm name of Moss & Lyde.

MOSS, JAMES MARTIN.—Son of ex-Sheriff W. W. Moss. Was born June 20, 1869, near Richland, in the central portion of Oconee County. His early schooling was acquired from the common and high schools. Graduated from Wofford College in 1892; a member of the county board of education, and principal for six years of Walhalla High School. His whole life has been devoted to teaching, having taught in Marion and Clarendon counties, and is now teaching in Walhalla. Married Kate S. Holleman, December 30, 1896.

MOSS, WARREN W.—Was born in Oconee County, South Carolina, April 3, 1836. Son of Martin Moss, whose parents were Scotch-Irish, and settled in Virginia before the Revolutionary War. His early schooling was had from the common schools of that day. He was three times elected county commissioner, and twice elected sheriff. Volunteered in Orr's Regiment Rifles in 1861; was twice wounded. Married Arretha S. Robinson, daughter of James Robinson, in 1865.

MOUNCE, JOHN HENRY.—An enterprising merchant of Pendleton, South Carolina. Son of William H. and Belle Verida Mounce. Born July 3, 1864, in Greenville County, South Carolina. Attended the public schools until the death of his father at the age of ten, when he secured a position as clerk. He has been very successful and is in business for himself. Married Miss Fannie A. Smith, December 27, 1888.

MOWER, GEORGE SEWALL.—Member of the Newberry bar. Was born April 20, 1853 at Greene, Maine. His preparatory training was received in the Newberry schools. Entered Bowdoin College in 1869 and graduated with the degree of Bachelor of Arts in 1873, and Master of Arts in 1876. He was editor of the "Bowdoin Orient," librarian of Pencinian Literary Society. Married Fannie D. Jones in 1876. An alderman of Newberry 1878 and 1879. Assistant counsel of South Carolina in Coosaw Phosphate case, and registration cases. A member of the House of Representatives from 1888 to 1890. Senator from 1893 to 1896 and 1896 to 1900. His time expires in 1904. Delegate to South Carolina Constitutional Convention in 1895. Treasurer and trustee of Erskine College. Vice-president and trustee of Newberry College. Member of school board of examiners of Newberry County. Trustee of Newberry graded schools from 1889 to 1893. Vice-president and director of Newberry Savings Bank; director of Commercial Savings Bank; director and secretary of Newberry Cotton Mills, Carolina Manufacturing Company, Piedmont Manufacturing Co.; director and vice-president Newberry Cottonseed Oil Mill and Fertilizer Company.

MULALLY, LANE.—Son of Rev. F. P. Mulally, D. D., and Elizabeth K. Adger. Born near Pendleton, Anderson County, South Carolina. He acquired his education from Adger College, South Carolina, and Washington and Lee University, Lexington, Virginia. He then graduated in medicine from the South Carolina Medical College at Charleston. Married Miss Caroline Hampton Lowndes. He was demonstrator of anatomy in the medical college of South Carolina, and lecturer on diseases of children. He is a member of the Medical Society and the Medical Association of South Carolina.

MULLER, JUSTUS A.—Was born at Sandy Run, Lexington County, South Carolina, September 16, 1858. From six to ten attended school at Sandy Run. His parents then removed to Buffalo, New York, where they lived two years, during which time Justus A. attended the grammar school of that city. Owing to severe climate, parents were compelled to leave Buffalo, going to Baltimore where they resided several years, during which time he attended a private school under Mr. Martin. Went to Newberry College several years, and from there to Washington and Lee University, of Lexington, Virginia where he graduated in 1880. Admitted to the bar of South Carolina in 1881, and the same year formed a partnership with Major H. A. Meetze of Lexington, South

Carolina, and practiced law with him until January, 1899, since which time he has practiced alone. Married Miss Mary B. Meetze, daughter of Major H. A. Meetze, in 1885. Has been connected with the council of his town for about ten years, served two years as intendant. Elected trial justice and held the office several years, previous to John Gary Evans' term as governor, and was holding such when he came into office, but not being able to support Evans, the position was given to an Evans man. He has also held the office of United States Commissioner.

MURFREE, EDWARD HUNTER.—President of Greenville Female College, was born at Murfree's depot Southhampton County, Virginia, September 18, 1845; his early training was obtained from the preparatory schools in Virginia, and received the degree of A. M. from the University of Alabama. He secured the position of professor of military science in University of Alabama. Superintendent of Mississippi Military Institute; professor of logic and mathematics «University of Arkansas, and President of Alabama Central College. He married Miss Adella Otis Manning on March 4, 1873. Received degree of Doctor of Laws simultaneously from two colleges.

MURRAY, WILLIAM JACOB.—Was born at St. George, South Carolina, March 9, 1856. Attended the common schools, and graduated from the medical department of Vanderbilt University. Married Miss Mary A. Connor November, 1885. He is one of the leading business men of Columbia. Is connected with a number of enterprises, and has made a signal success of the Murray Drug Company, the big Columbia wholesale concern, of which he is president and manager.

NARDIN, WALTER H., JR.—Practicing physician of Anderson, South Carolina. Was born in that county on January 1, 1876. Graduated from Patrick Military Institute in 1893, and the medical department of New York University in 1897. Was secretary and treasurer of the Anderson County Medical Society, professor of chemistry and physiology at the Patrick Military Institute, Anderson.

NASH, JAMES WRIGHT.—Was born in the northern portion of Laurens County, South Carolina, August 13, 1870. Received certificate from the Clinton Academy, under Mr. J. B. Parrott, in 1886. Took the A. B. degree from Wofford College in 1890, and the A. M. degree in 1899. Graduated from the South Carolina College with the degree of Doctor of Laws in 1893. Married Miss Fannie Boyd October 4, 1899. Taught the Hebron Academy in Marlboro one year. Principal of the Batesburg Graded School in 1891 and 1892. Is now associated in the practice of law with Congressman Joseph T. Johnson of Spartanburg.

NEEL, GEORGE PRESSLY.—Surgeon for the Pennsylvania Richmond and Western Central and Southern Railways. Practices his profession at Troy, South Carolina. Was born in that town February 12, 1866. Graduated at Erskine College in October, 1882. Then attended the Baltimore Medical College in 1886. In April, 1888, graduated from Jefferson Medical College, and was employed as house physician one year at St. Agnes Hospital, Philadelphia.

NEEL, JAMES D.—Born in Newberry County, December 5, 1837. After receiving a common-school education in Newberry County, entered freshman class of Erskine College in 1853, graduating in 1857. Graduated from Jefferson Medical College, Philadelphia, in 1859. Married Miss M. E. Pressley in 1860. The issue from this marriage was five children, upon the education of whom he spared neither efforts nor means. They are: Mrs. Emma, who is the widow of the late Dr. L. N. Kennedy, of Troy; Mrs. O. Y. Bonner, of Due West; Dr. George P. Neel, of Greenwood; Miss M. Lavinia Neel, who is a missionary at C. Del Maiz, Mexico; and Dr. Katie Neel Dale, who is a medical missionary at Ceritos, San Luis Potosi, Mexico. Dr. Neel was surgeon of the Fifteenth

South Carolina Regiment from 1863 to the surrender. Served two terms as representative in the State Legislature. Was a prominent factor in the promotion of the Atlanta & Knoxville Railroad. His attainments are many, and his scientific and practical research in his profession has proven of great value and usefulness both to himself and to his younger colleagues, to whom he has always shown unremitting generosity and kindness. He has enjoyed an extensive practice for thirty-six years. He is quick in judgment, prompt in action, an indefatigable worker and untiring at all times in the fulfillment of what he deems to be his duty.

NEELY, HYDEN A. D.—Appointed county treasurer of York County in 1881 and re-appointed every two years since. Was born on a plantation in the eastern part of York County, South Carolina, January 13, 1843. Ancestors were among the emigrants who came from Pennsylvania and setted in York, Chester and Lancaster counties, then called the Indian lands. Only the advantage of a common-school education, and experience in teaching began at eighteen years of age. Married Miss Martha M. Neely, of Chester County.

NELSON, PATRICK HENRY.—Lawyer. Son of Colonel P. H. Nelson who was killed in the battles around Petersburg, Virginia, June 24, 1864, and Emma S. Cantey, of Camden, South Carolina. Acquired education from the schools of Camden and the University of the South, at Sewanee, Tennessee. Married Henrietta Shannon, daughter of Colonel W. M. Shannon November 25, 1878. Member of the Legislature from 1885 to 1886. Appointed solicitor of the Fifth Judicial Circuit March, 1887; served as such until 1896. Admitted to the bar November 1877. Practiced at Camden until 1884 in co-partnership with General John D. Kennedy. Moved to Columbia in 1896 and has since practiced his profession there. Served on staff of Brigadier-General John D. Kennedy as major and on staff of Governor John P. Richardson with rank of colonel.

NESOM, GEORGE EDWARD.—Was born May 29, 1870, on a farm near Erata, Jones County, Mississippi. His early training was received in the country schools and the Montrose High School Jasper County, Mississippi. Graduated from the Mississippi Agricultural and Mechanical College. Took a three-year veterinary course at the Iowa State College, Ames, Iowa. Was assistant in the Ellisville Graded School and is veterinarian at Clemson College, South Carolina, and the South Carolina experiment station. Was married at Starksville, Mississippi, to Miss Bessie O'Brien, July 10, 1899.

NEVILLE, WILLIAM GORDON.—Was born in Walhalla, South Carolina, July 2, 1855. With the exception of one year spent at Princeton University his entire education has been obtained in his native State, having spent three years at Newberry College, one at Adger College, two at the Seminary at Columbia, and one at Princeton. With the exception of a year or two at Frankfort, Kentucky, his ministry has been passed in his native State and the greater portion of it in Bethel Presbytery. Before entering the ministry he taught school a few years. His first charge was composed of Cokesbury and Ninety-Six, churches in the South Carolina Presbytery. From these he was called to Concord Church in Bethel, from thence to Frankfort, Kentucky, and is once more in Bethel Presbytery as the pastor of Yorkville Church, in very many respects one of the finest churches in the Synod. He was appointed chairman of the committee on Synodical Home Missions in South Carolina three years. Member of the General Assembly's committee on the Twentieth Century Fund. Chairman of the Committee on Twentieth Century Fund in the Synod of South Carolina. Trustee of Davidson College, North Carolina, since 1893. Director in the Theological Seminary of Columbia, South Carolina, since 1897. Member of the Pan Presbyterian Council which met in Washington, District of Columbia, in 1899. Mr. Neville married Miss Virginia Aiken, daughter of the late Colonel D. Wyatt Aiken, November 7, 1883.

NEWBERRY, JAMES B.—Son of Rev. James Newberry. Was born in Sumter County, June 21, 1837. In 1840 he moved to Darlington County, and there grew to manhood with only such school advantages as could be had at that time. In 1860 he married Miss Tirzah, daughter of Rev. John Burdine, of Anderson County. July 1, 1861, he enlisted in Company K., Captain S. D. Goodlet, and went immediately to Summerville where the Sixth Regiment was organized, was hurried to Virginia, reaching Bull Run on the 21st of July. At the end of first term of enlistment he joined the Twenty-fifth Battalion as a private. Was soon elected lieutenant, which office he held until the close of the war. In 1873 he moved to Pickens, South Carolina, and has four times been elected intendant of the town. In 1887 he was appointed probate judge, which position he still holds.

NEWMAN, CHARLES CARTER.—Son of Col. J. S. Newman, professor of agriculture at Clemson College. Was born in Sparta, Georgia, September 6, 1875. Spent three years at the Agricultural and Mechanical College of Alabama and one year at the Georgia Military Academy, and took special course at Clemson College in 1897 and 1898. Elected assistant horticulturist at Clemson College in June, 1899. Elected professor of horticulture of South Carolina experiment station in June, 1900, which position he is still filling.

NEWMAN, JAMES STANLEY.—Was born in Orange County, Virginia, in 1836. Son of James and Mary Scott Newman. His father was a progressive, educated farmer. His early life was passed on a farm where he took an active part in all kinds of field and orchard work. Graduate of the University of Virginia in 1859. Married Alberta Lewis, August 3, 1863, in Georgia. Taught school ten years in Virginia and Georgia. Entered the Confederate army. After the war closed he farmed two years in Hancock County, Georgia. Was for five years State statistical agent of the United States Department of Agriculture, and editing clerk of the State Department of Agriculture for Georgia for eight years, during which time he prepared a manual for sheep husbandry, manual on

22

cattle, manual on poultry, manual on the hog, farmer's scientific manual, and other publications. For six years he was editor of the agricultural journal, "Southern Enterprise," and in 1883 was elected to the chair of agriculture and directorship of the State experiment station, at Auburn, Alabama. In 1884 was appointed State agent of the United States Department of Agriculture for Alabama, also elected president of the Alabama State Agricultural Society, and the Interstate Farmers Congress. Served three years as president of the State Agricultural Society, and declined re-election. Since 1872 he has been a life member of the American Pomlogical Society, and vice-president for Alabama eight years. Is now vice-president of the Alabama State Alliance, and has recently been elected to the chair of agriculture at the Clemson Agricultural College, South Carolina.

NEWTON, HOPE HULL.—Born February 16, 1845, at Marlboro, South Carolina. Graduated with degree of Bachelor of Arts at Wofford College, and received degree of Master of Arts from the same college. Has been three times married, his last wife being Katie Monroe McCall. Member of the House of Representatives from 1880 to 1881. Solicitor of the Fourth Circuit from 1883 to 1888. Member of the General Conference Methodist Episcopal Church, South, at Nashville, Tennessee, in 1882 and at Memphis, Tennessee, in 1894. He is now a lawyer and steward in the Methodist Church.

NICHOLLS, GEORGE WILLIAM.—Prominent member of the Spartanburg bar. Was born December 5, 1849, at Spartanburg, South Carolina. He obtained his education from Furman University. Held the position as probate judge for Spartanburg County ten years, also attorney for Merchant and Farmers Bank, Peoples Building & Loan Association, and the Morgan Iron Works, and attorney for the Western Carolina Railroad Company. Once Worshipful Master of Spartanburg Lodge A. F. M. Married Miss Mary L., daughter of Rev. Samuel Jones, Doctor of Divinity, May 29, 1884.

NICHOLSON, ALBERT RHETT.—Son of Dr. John O. Nicholson and Elizabeth Threewitts. Was born seven miles north of court-house in Edgefield County, March 12, 1843. Of Irish, German and English descent. His father was a member of the Legislature one term, but most of his life was given to the practice of medicine. Attended the country schools, and in 1860 entered the Military Academy of Columbia. In 1861 joined the First South Carolina Volunteers, Captain Adams, Edgefield Rifles, Gregg's Regiment. In Hampton's Legion, until the war closed, as a private, and for a year before the war closed was a member of the staff of General M. W. Gary. Surrendered at Appomattox. Married Miss Sallie Hughes, December 22, 1868. He has engaged in farming most of his life and at the same time conducted a mercantile business on his farm in this county. Elected county superintendent of education in 1896, which office he is still creditably filling.

NICHOLSON, BENJAMIN EDWARD.—Born near Ridge Spring, South Carolina, in Edgefield County, January 15, 1875. Son of General B. E. Nicholson, a distinguished Confederate soldier, who was given a vote of thanks by the General Assembly of South Carolina for his gallant conduct at the first battle of Manassas, where he captured a Federal flag. After war he married Lizzie Hughes, the mother of the subject of this sketch. Attended the South Carolina College for two years (1891, 1893). Left college after entering junior class, and taught school for three years, and was engaged in farming one year. Read law in office of Sheppard Brothers, and was admitted to the bar in 1898. Has been practicing law at Edgefield Court-house since admission to bar. Is county attorney for Edgefield County.

NICHOLSON, EMSLIE.—Born in Union, March 14, 1863, Son of William A. and Rebecca E. Nicholson. Educated at the Academy of Union, the Bingham School, and later graduated at Davidson College, North Carolina, in 1882. Organized and was treasurer of the Banking House of William A. Nicholson & Son, and is now its president. Is secretary and manager of the Union Oil Manufacturing Company, the first manufacturing enterprise ever established in Union. Mr. Nicholson organized and is president of the Excelsior Knitting Mills, the largest and most complete hosiery manufacturing plant in the South. Is a director in the Union Cotton Mills, Buffalo Cotton Mills, Monarch Mills, Aetna Cotton Mills, the Union Shoe Company, the Union Real Estate Agency, the Union Hardware Manufacturing Company, the Union Furniture Manufacturing Company, and is interested in many other public enterprises of the town and county.

NICHOLSON, ROBERT EDWIN.—Elected superintendent of education for Anderson County, South Carolina, in 1897. Re-elected without opposition in 1899. Mr. Nicholson was born March 2, 1866, near Walhalla, Oconee County, South Carolina. He graduated from Davidson College, North Carolina, in 1887. Married Miss Eudora M. Jones, January 1, 1896.

NORMENT, BENJAMIN C.—Practicing physician of Darlington, South Carolina. A native of Virginia. Born April 25, 1833. Attended the Richmond College and the University of Virginia. Graduated at Jefferson Medical College in 1853. Married Louisa H. Nettles May 7, 1857. President of the Pee Dee Medical Society two years.

NORRIS, D. KEATING.—Was born in lower St. Matthews, Orangeburg County, on November 1, 1846, and moved to Anderson County January, 1877, where he now resides on his estate, "Hickory Flat."  He joined the army in Company F, Second Regiment South Carolina Heavy Artillery. Was badly wounded at the battle of Bentonville, North Carolina. Married in 1877 Miss Bessie Caldwell of Abbeville, South Carolina. He is recognized as one of the leading farmers of the State, and a member of the Alliance both State and national. Delegate at large to National Farmers Congress in 1892. Delegate at large to Cotton Growers Convention, Jackson, Mississippi, in 1895. Delegate at large to Southern Intersate Industrial and Immigration Convention, Augusta, Georgia, in 1894. Delegate at large to Cotton Growers Protective Association, Augusta, Georgia, in 1897. Delegate at large to the Quarantine Convention, South Atlantic States, Mobile, Alabama, 1898. Delegate Third District Cotton Growers Convention, Galveston, Texas, in 1897. Delegate Third District National Farmers Alliance, St. Louis Missouri, 1889. Delegate Third District National Democratic Convention, Chicago, Illinois, in 1892; Honorary member Farmers National Congress, Parkersburg, West Virginia, in 1894. Member of the committee Pan Republic Congress in 1891. Master Grange in the seventies. President of the county Alliance six consecutive terms in the nineties. He took an active part in the inauguration of the Farmers movement in South Carolina, and was president of the State Farmers Association two years. Hon. Thomas G. Clemson, knowing and appreciating his interest in agriculture, appointed him trustee of Clemson Agricultural College. He is president of the Pendleton Farmers Society, the oldest in the State, and second oldest in the United States. Elected State Senator in 1894 and 1898; president prō tem of the Senate in 1897 and 1898. President and treasurer of the Norris Cotton Mills.

NORRIS, JOHN B.—Merchant. Son of John M. Norris and Mary Bøuknight. Born in Edgefield, now Saluda, County, South Carolina, November 9, 1849. Ancestors were English and came over with William Penn, settled in Pennsylvania, then Virginia and South Carolina. Attended the common schools, but the war prevented further educational advantages. When he became of age he went to Augusta and went into the mercantile business. In 1875 he removed to Trenton, South Carolina where he remained in the mercantile business until 1897. He took an active part in redeeming the State in 1876. Alderman and intendant of Trenton several times. President of Shaw's Club in 1876 at Trenton. Married Etta Rainsford, of Edgefield County, December 12, 1877. He is now in business with his nephew, the firm being Norris Cooner & King, Mr. Norris being president.

NORTHROP, HARRY PINCKNEY.—Son of Claudian and Hanna E. Northop. Born May 5, 1842, at Charleston, South Carolina. Attended Georgetown College, District of Columbia, from 1853 to 1856; St. Mary's College, Maryland, from 1857 to 1860, and in 1860 entered St. Mary's to study for priesthood, and to American College, Rome, in 1864. Ordained in 1865. Returned to Charleston and assisted at St. Joseph's Church until 1871. Served as missionary in eastern North Carolina, headquarters at Newbern. Assistant at Cathedral in Charleston until 1877. Appointed pastor of St. Patricks Church of that city in 1882. Vicar-apostolic of North Carolina, titular Bishop of Rosalia 1882. 1883, transferred to Charleston, made Bishop with the vicarick of North Carolina until 1888.

NORTON JAMES.—Was born October 8, 1843, in Marion County, South Carolina. Received an academic education. Left school in 1861 to enter the army. Served through the war in the Army of Northern Virginia. Was several times wounded, a ball at one time passing through his body and right lung. From this wound he had sufficiently recovered to be able to return to the army just at the time of the capture of Petersburg. After the war he re-entered school, but did not complete the course. Was elected county school commissioner in 1870 and re-elected in 1872, but did not serve. Was a member of the House of Representatives from 1886 to 1891. Was elected comptroller-general of the State in 1894, and re-elected in 1896, which office he resigned to accept a seat in the Fifty-fifth Congress, to fill the vacancy caused by the resignation of Hon. John L. McLaurin. He was re-elected to the Fifty-sixth Congress.

NORWOOD, GEORGE ALEXANDER.—Son cf Joseph and Sarah A. (McIntosh) Norwood. Born in Darlington County October 23, 1831. Ancestors were of English and Scotch descent and were the early settlers of Darlington County. Attended Wake Forest College of North Carolina two years and one session at Furman University. Finished college in July, 1852. Just after leaving college he taught school for a short while, and was connected with newspaper work at Darlington; then farmed a few years and engaged in merchandising six years, in connection with which business he ran a turpentine distillery. In January, 1873, he moved to Charleston and went into the commission business, handling cotton and naval stores for eleven years. In 1884 he moved to Marion and organized and became president of the Bank of Marion, remained there until 1890, when he moved to Greenville, where he is now engaged in the banking business. At present is president of the City National Bank. Married Miss Mary L., daughter of Rev. S. B. Wilkes, on March 28, 1858.

NOTT, THOMAS EDWIN.—Born near Grendel, Union County, South Carolina, September 24, 1830. His father was a distinguished physician, the eldest son of Judge Abraham Nott. His father moved to Limestone Springs, Spartanburg County, in 1837 for the purpose of educating his children. Thomas Edwin received his classical education at Limestone Spring, entered the South Carolina College in October, 1847, and graduated in 1849. Married Miss Julia Wallace, daughter of Hon. Daniel Wallace, in 1862. She having died, he married again, to Miss Mary Wallace, in 1882. He studied medicine and graduated at the Charleston Medical College in 1852, practiced in Union County until 1873, at which time he moved to Spartanburg and is still actively engaged in the practice of his profession. He served as private in Carpenter's Company, Fifth South Carolina Regiment the first year of the war between the States. At the close of the war was acting surgeon in the South Carolina Regiment, and was captured near Petersburg, when Grant succeeded in breaking Lee's lines, a few days before the surrender at Appomattox.

O'DONNELL, NEILL.—A native of Ireland. Born in Donegal, December 23, 1859. Came to the United States in 1874. For three years he attended the Wyoming Seminary in Pennsylvania, but his early education was obtained in the common schools of Ireland. Was, for two years, a member of the city council in Sumter, now serving eighth year as member of the board of education. Has been engaged in the mercantile business since January 1, 1883. Prior to that he was employed as traveling salesman for F. W. Wagner & Company, of Charleston. Married Miss Kate Bogin of Sumter County, February 2, 1887.

OLIVER, WILLIAM BENJAMIN.—Pastor of the Baptist Church at Florence, South Carolina. A son of James Francis and Lucy A. (Jones) Oliver. Born August 2, 1861, at New Fields, Bladen County, North Carolina. Of Welsh, French and English descent. Attended High School, Mt. Olive, North Carolina; Bingham School, and Wake Forest College, North Carolina; and the Southern Baptist Theological Seminary at Louisville, Kentucky. Married Sara Moseley, of Halifax County, Virginia, October 26, 1887. Taught school two years. Pastor of the Baptist Church at Mt. Washington, and Plum Creek, Kentucky; Marion, South Carolina; Durham, Fayetteville, Wilmington, North Carolina, and Florence, South Carolina. He was for two years editor of the "North Carolina Baptist."

ONSLOW, GEORGE.—Cashier of the Peoples Bank of Darlington. He is a son of George and Mary (Wells) Onslow. Born September 6, 1852, at St. Louis, Missouri. Attended the public and high schools of St. Louis. Married Desdemona B. Simpson, December, 1875. Held the position as telegraph operator and railroad agent. Elected teller of the Peoples Bank of Darlington, and has since been promoted to the position he now holds.

ORR, JAMES LAWRENCE.—Born August 29, 1852, at Abbeville, South Carolina. He received his early training in the primary schools of Anderson, South Carolina. On leaving there he attended the Kings Mountain Military Academy, at Yorkville, subsequently entering the University of Virginia. Married Bettie Bates Hammett on November 12, 1873. Was elected to the Legislature from Abbeville County in 1874, and re-elected in 1878. Mr. Orr was elected solicitor of the Eighth Circuit from 1881 to 1888. Has since been president of the Piedmont Manufacturing Company, Orr Cotton Mills; also vice-president of the American Spinning, and the Mills Manufacturing Companies. Is now a director of the National Bank, American and Peoples Bank of Greenville, South Carolina, also the Easeley and Cox Manufacturing Companies. He has for some time held the position as trustee of the South Carolina Medical College, and Converse College. Is also one of the largest cotton manufacturers of the State.

OSBORN, ABRAHAM COLES.—President of Benedict College, Columbia, South Carolina. Born at Scotch Plains, New Jersey, February 20, 1831. In August, 1851, he entered Madison University, in Hamilton, New York. Later he entered Gouveneur Seminary, without a dollar. Entered into an engagement to serve as janitor to pay for his books and tuition. He also sawed, split and corded wood for a villager, to pay his board, and thus worked his way through college. After graduation he was elected to a position as teacher of mathematics in the high school of Columbia, where he remained one year. In October, 1856, he entered Hamilton Theological Seminary, and there devoted two years to the study of theology, graduating in 1858. In September, 1858, he took charge of the Jefferson Street Baptist Church, in Louisville, Kentucky. In 1861, he went to Europe for the purpose of studying German. On the 29th of December, 1861, he was married to Sara E Matthews, member of the board of education of Louisville. In 1862, he accepted a call to the pastorate of the Fourth Baptist Church of St. Louis, Missouri. Degree of Doctor of Divinity conferred by Shurtleff College, at Alton, Illinois. In 1867, he was elected to the presidency of the New Hampton Literary and Theological Institute, at Fairfax, Vermont. He founded the Home Savings Bank of St. Louis and was a director in same. In 1869, he accepted the pastorate of the Tabernacle Baptist Church of Brooklyn, New York. In 1895, he accepted the presidency of Benedict College.

OSBORNE, OTIS A.—Merchant at Blacksburg, South Carolina, and member of the city council. He was born in Fitchburg, Massachusetts, August 18, 1845. Came South with his parents when about nine years of age. Educated in the common schools of that time. He was a bookkeeper and clerk for several years at Abbottsburg, North Carolina, and in St. Louis, Missouri. A director of the Blackburg Spinning and Knitting Mill. He was also engaged in the manufacture of brick in Lancaster, for several years. On December 31, he married Miss Jennie M. Brew.

OSTEEN, CHARLES PORTER.—Born in Sumter, South Carolina, December 10, 1866. Eldest child of N. G. and E. A. Osteen (nee Doar). After attending the public schools of Sumter, until about fifteen years of age, entered his father's printing-office, and while learning the trade continued his studies under a private teacher at night. Continued in the newspaper business until 1890, when he entered the Medical College of South Carolina, completing one session. In 1891, he entered the medical department of the University of Nashville, and graduated in the class of 1892. Since, has devoted his time to the practice of his profession in Sumter County, until January, 1901, when he removed to the town of Darlington to practice. Member of the State Medical Association and the Sumter County Medical Ascsociation. He was the winner of several medals while at college.

OSTEEN, HUBERT GRAHAM.—Born December 25, 1870, at Sumter, South Carolina. Educated in the common schools of Sumter. Won the Peabody scholarship in the Normal College, Nashville, Tennessee, in 1887; but was refused admission on account of being under the age. Succeeded, however, in winning the scholarship the following year, and graduated with the degree of L. I. in 1890. Married Elizabeth Duval, of Cheraw, South Carolina, July 28, 1898. He was for two years a teacher in Burke County, Georgia, from 1890 to 1891. Assistant for one year in the Graded School, Sumter, South Carolina. Is editor of the "Sumter Watchman & Southron;" also editor and proprietor of the "Sumter Daily Item," established October 15, 1894. He has been president of the Sumter Democratic Club since 1892, and for several years vice-president of the South Carolina State Press Association.

OSTENDORFF, J. HERMIE.—Son of J. H. Ostendorff and Carrie A. (Ansel) Ostendorff. Born at Walhalla, South Carolina, February 9, 1869. Of German descent. Attended the public schools, and Adger College, of Walhalla. Married Miss Louise Knobeloch in May, 1899. Engaged as salesman for John Hurkamp & Co. five years, and junior partner five years. In 1895, he became . proprietor of The John Hurkamp & Co., Charleston.

OUZTS, WILLIAM HOLLOWAY.—Son of Daniel Ouzts, of Edgefield County. He was of German descent. Born in the upper portion of Edgefield County, South Carolina, August 2, 1839. Only a common school education. Married Miss Isabel Adams, November 29, 1866. Engaged in farming until the year 1880, except four years service in the Confederate army. Was three times wounded, the last time in September, 1864, left leg was shattered by ball at battle of Petersburg, on Jones's farm. Is still suffering with wound, it never having healed. Elected sheriff of Edgefield County in 1880, and has served continuously ever since, having served in that capacity longer than any sheriff in the State, except Mr. Gilreath, of Greenville, who has been in office twenty-four years.

OWENS, CLARENCE JULIAN.—President of the Sumter Military Academy and Female Seminary. Son of Alfred Owens and Fannie R. Easterling. Born in Augusta, Georgia, July 4, 1877. Ancestors of Welsh and English descent. Obtained education from the Houghton and Williston High School, Cornell and Columbian Universities, receiving M. A. degree from the latter. Principal of the Greenland Public Schools, of Greenland, South Carolina. Professor of English, in Orangeburg College three years. President of Orangeburg College three years. Founder and president of

the Sumter Military Academy. Deputy Grand Chief Templar Independent Order Good Templars of South Carolina. Vice-president of the Baptist Young People's Union Convention of South Carolina.

OWENS, WARREN EDGAR.—Was born March 19, 1860, at Clinton, South Carolina. He is a son of Captain Robert S. Owens. His education was acquired principally at Clinton, and at the Reidville High School. He commenced clerking at the age of fifteen, and was made a member of the firm at the age of twenty-one. He has been engaged in the mercantile business at Clinton for nineteen years. Elected intendant of the town of Clinton at twenty-five years of age. Appointed county commissioner by the governor. Was member of the State Democratic Executive Committee, from Laurens, two years; declined re-election. A member of the board of visitors of the Thornwell Orphanage; a trustee of the Presbyterian College of South Carolina, at Clinton. Married Miss Mary Bailey, of Greenwood, South Carolina, October 27, 1885.

PARK, JAMES BRADDOCK.—Mayor of Greenwood, South Carolina. A native of Laurens County. Son of J. Fowler Park. Born at Parks Station, November 28, 1873. Was prepared for college at the Laurens Male Academy, and entered the Davis Military School at Winston, North Carolina. Graduated in law at the University of Virginia. Practiced at Laurens until 1897, when he moved to Greenwood, South Carolina, where he is still engaged in the practice of law, with J. F. J. Caldwell, under the firm of Caldwell & Park.

PARKER, LEWIS WARDLAW.—Was born at Abbeville, South Carolina, in 1865. He is a son of the late William Henry Parker, one of the most distinguished jurists in the State. His mother was Lusia G. Wardlaw, daughter of that eminent judge, D. L. Wardlaw. After attending the village schools and acquiring a good academic education, he graduated at the South Carolina College in 1885, with the degree of Bachelor of Arts, and in 1877 took the degree of Doctor of Laws. Married Margaret Smith, daughter of Austin Smith, of Richmond, Virginia, June 6, 1893. Immediately after graduation, he taught school for three years, and then removed to Greenville in 1889, and began the practice of law. He continued the practice of law for ten years. In 1897, however, owing to his wonderful capacity for business, he was elected president and treasurer of the Victor Manufacturing Corporation, engaged in cotton manufacture, located at Greers, South Carolina. He was manager of the loan department of the Piedmont Savings and Investment Company from its organization, from 1890 to 1900, when he resigned and was elected vice-president of this organization. Assisted by Thomas T. Parker, he organized the Monaghan Mills, at Greenville, of which he is still treasurer. He was mainly instrumental in the organization of the Bank of Greers, in 1900, of which he is still president. He is a director in numerous other corporations.

PARKER, THOMAS FLEMING.—President of the Monaghan Mills, Greenville, South Carolina. Was born in Charleston, South Carolina, December 28, 1860. His father, Thomas Parker, was killed in the battle of Secessionville, in 1861, in the twenty-ninth year of his age. At the time of the breaking out of the Confederate War, Mr. Parker was engaged in business in Charleston, having in this somewhat diverged from the custom of his family, who for several generations had occupied positions at the bar. The present Thomas Fleming Parker, after attending the school of Mr. A. Sachtleben, in Charleston, became a member of the class of 1882 of the College of Charleston. Owing to an injury to his eyes at the close of his sophomore year, he was obliged to forego further study, and to live an out-door life. During this time Mr. Parker became president of the Linville Land Improvement Company of North Carolina, in which both Northern and Southern capital was interested, and, in February, 1900, his eyes being very much improved, he withdrew from this enterprise, to return to his native State, and engaged in the rapidly developing industry of the new

South, the manufacture of cotton. The Monaghan Mills, of which Mr. Parker is president, are among the largest and best equipped mills in the State. Mr. Parker married, on April 6, 1887, Lisa deVaux Foulke, of Philadelphia.

PARKER, WILLIAM HENRY.—Was born in Abbeville County, January 1, 1828. His parents originally resided in Charleston, South Carolina, and moved to Abbeville about 1825. His great-grandfather was William Henry Drayton, chairman of the Council of Safety in Revolutionary days, and chief justice of South Carolina. His grandfather, Thomas Parker, was a prominent member of the Charleston bar. His father was also a lawyer, but gave up the profession and went to Abbeville, to engage in planting. His mother was a daughter of Rev. Thomas Frost, rector of St. Phillips Church, Charleston. Educated principally in Charleston at the schools of T. P. Allen, Samuel A. Burns, and C. C. Cotes, all eminent educators. Entered the sophmore class of the South Carolina College December, 1843 and graduated December, 1846, sixth in class. Married Lucia Gary Wardlaw, daughter of Judge David Lewis Wardlaw, January 1, 1856. Studied law with Messrs. Thomson & Wair, at Abbeville. Admitted to the bar December, 1849. In January, 1869, he formed a partnership with Honorable Sam McGowan, which was dissolved by his election to Supreme Bench, December, 1879. In January, 1890, he formed a partnership with W. C. McGowan, which terminated by the latter's death in 1898, and the present style of firm is Parker & Green. In December, 1861, he volunteered as a private in company commanded by Captain Cunningham, afterwards Company G, Nineteenth South Carolina Volunteers. Was appointed first sergeant, and on re-organization of regiment was appointed adjutant with rank of first lieutenant and served as such until honorable discharge in 1862. In 1880 elected to the House of Representatives, and successively in 1882, 1884 and 1886. Served as member of judiciary committee in 1882 and chairman of Incorporations, from 1880 to 1886. Served one year as chairman of Judiciary Committee. He assisted in compiling the

"General Statutes of South Carolina" in 1882. Withdrew from public life until general election in 1900, when he was returned to House of Representatives, and is now member thereof. Served two terms as mayor of the town of Abbeville; president of Farmers Bank, and director in Abbeville Cotton Mill.

PARKS, JAMES THOMAS.—Editor of the "Orangeburg Patriot." Son of William L. Parks and Sarah A. Cartledge. Born at Parksville, Edgefield County, South Carolina, May 12, 1865. Education very limited. At seventeen years of age he entered the common schools, entered Roanoke College, Salem, Virginia, in 1884. Taught and went to college alternately until 1888, when lack of funds compelled him to stop. Married Emma M. Yeldell, daughter of W. H. Yeldell, November 22, 1888. Taught seven years. Principal of Hodgson Institute, Burke County, Georgia, from 1889 to 1890. First assistant in the graded schools of Edgefield in 1892. Gave up teaching and went into the newspaper work, editing the "Edgefield Farmer," and later the "Marion County Farmer." For the past six years has been editor of the "Patriot." Appointed mail clerk of Senate by Lieutenant-Governor M. B. McSweeney in 1896. In 1897, was elected State printer to fill out the unexpired term of Mr. Calvo.

PARROTT, JAMES BARNEY.—Pastor of Clinton Baptist Church, since 1898. Born in Darlington, South Carolina, January 15, 1853. His early training was received from the Reidville Male Academy. Was two years at Worcester Academy, Worcester, Massachusetts, graduating in June, 1874; then spent one year at Brown University. Married Mary Elmore Freeman, of Nova Scotia on October 11, 1876. He was elected principal of the high school at West Springs, Union County, and Clinton Academy. Was pastor, at various times, of Baptist churches in Laurens County. Has been pastor of the Clinton church, since 1896.

PATE, JOHN THOMAS.—Member of the South Carolina Methodist Episcopal Church South. Was born in the city of Sumter, South Carolina, June 27, 1856. He attended the schools of his native city, and also Wofford College. He was licensed to preach, and entered the Conference in December, 1877. The next year he was given a circuit. He has steadily risen, and has supplied pastorates in Charleston, Greenville, Orangeburg and Camden. He was selected as one of the speakers of the Pan-American Congress of Religion and Education, held in 1895, at Toronto, and his address on "Christ, the Ideal Teacher," was an excellent production. He has traveled over various portions of the United States and Canada. He was married, in 1879, to Alice Godbold of Marion County, South Carolina.

PATRICK. JOHN MILLIGAN.—He is now merchandising in Anderson, South Carolina. Was born January 4, 1864, in Columbia, South Carolina. Graduated from Greenville Military Institute in 1881, and took the degree of M. A. from Furman University, Greenville, South Carolina, in 1883. Married Miss Carrie McCully February 20, 1889. He was commandant of cadets at Patrick Military Institute, and instructor in Latin and Greek.

PAYSEUR, L. C.—Started with a few hundred dollars and has made a success. He was born in Lincolnton, North Carolina, October 18, 1850. Only a comon school education. He was head clerk in J. A. Henneman's jewelry store at Spartanburg, South Carolina, four years. Married Miss Mary A. Hudson, a niece of Judge J. H. Hudson, October 18, 1864. Mayor of Lancaster for two years, and director in the Bank of Lancaster, since its organization; also director in Lancaster Cotton Mill six years.

PEARLSTINE, ISAAC M.—Merchandising in Charleston, South Carolina. He was born in Triestena, Russia, in 1843, and came to Charleston with his father in 1854. Ancestors were Russians. Attended the schools of his native country, but his education was principally self-acquired. Married in New York in 1866. Merchandised in Abbeville just after the Civil War. During the war his father made buckles for the

Confederate government. After the close of the war, he and his father went into dry goods business in Charleston. He also merchandised in Forsyth, Georgia. Then went to New York City, and was in the brokerage business until 1876, then went to Charleston and engaged in carriage and buggy business. In 1882, he opened up a store in Charleston, and has continued this business up to the present time. The firm is now known as J. M. Pearlstine & Sons. Alderman of Charleston four years from Ward II.

PEARMAN, SILAS NATHANIEL.—Was born August 29, 1845, near Mount Bethel Church in Anderson County, South Carolina. Attended the old field schools until fifteen. Entered the Confederate army as volunteer at the age of eighteen. Belonged to Company E, Twentieth Regiment under Captain Cowan. Married May 9, 1869, to Sarah O. Pruitt. Held commission as lieutenant in a company of Red Shirts during Hampton's administration. Member of the Legislature from 1892 to 1893. Magistrate of Broadway Township of Anderson County. He is a farmer.

PELHAM, WILLIAM ELLERBE.—Son of Professor Charles P. Pelham and Jane Dunlop Pelham. Born June 19, 1854, at Columbia, South Carolina. He had the advantage of the high schools of Columbia, under Hugh S. Thompson, James Wood Davidson, and other prominent educators; and graduated from the South Carolina College in 1871. He married Brantly Caroline, daughter of Colonel John R. Leavell, on April 5, 1876. Immediately after graduation, he took a course in pharmacy and was established in the drug business in Newberry, South Carolina, in 1875. He is chairman of the board of trustees of the Newberry Graded School; president of the South Carolina Sunday School Association, and is now chairman of the Executive Committee of the South Carolina Association. A commissioner to the General Assembly of the Presbyterian Church, New Orleans, Louisiana, in 1898. Member of Lodge 87, A. F. M., also Newberry Lodge Number 75 Knights of Pythias, Past Chancellor.

23

PELL, ROBERT PAINE.—President of the Presbyterian College for Women, at Columbia, South Carolina. Son of Rev. William E. Pell and Virginia Caroline Ramsay. Born June 12, 1860. Of English and Scotch-American descent. He is also a descendant of Rolfe. Graduated with degree of A. B. from University of North Carolina in 1881. Took postgraduate course at same university and studied at the Union Theological Seminary, now located at Richmond, Virginia. Married Anness Huske Shepherd, of Fayetteville, North Carolina. Instructor of English in North Carolina State Summer School. Evangelist of the Presbyterian Synod of North Carolina. Pastor of Presbyterian Church at Newberry, South Carolina.

PENNEY, WILLIAM THOMPSON.—Has been engaged in the drug business at Abbeville since 1865. Was born January 11, 1838, in Laurens County, South Carolina. Educated principally in the old field schools. Was reared on the farm, but went to Abbeville when nineteen years of age. Clerked in a dry goods store three years, then went into the drug business with Branch and Parker. Entered the Confederate army in 1862; served until April, 1865. Upon returning from the army he began business for himself. Served one term as city warden in 1872. Married Miss Mary A. Shillito of Abbeville, in 1859. Member of Clinton Lodge Number 9 F. A. M. and has held at various times nearly all the offices of the Masonic lodge.

PERRIN, JOHN LIVINGSTON.—Elected clerk of the court of Abbeville County, November 6, 1900. A native of that county. Was born November 5, 1860. His early training was received from the public schools; and he graduated from Erskine College in 1881. He clerked for several years, and then merchandised. Enlisted in Company H, Spanish-American War, and was appointed captain of the company. Served until mustered out of service at Augusta, Georgia, April 19, 1899. Married Mrs. Ella Penney on November 23, 1887.

PERRIN, LEWIS WARDLAW.—Was born May 21, 1839,
in the village of Abbeville, South Carolina. His parents
were Honorable T. C. Perrin and Jane E. (Wardlaw). Was
educated in the schools of the village, and entered the South
Carolina College in December, 1855. In 1859, after graduation, he entered the counting rooms of Messrs. Wardlaw, Walker & Company, in Charleston. Upon the secession of the
State, he joined the Rutledge Mounted Riflemen, Cleland K.
Huger, captain; and was called into active service on January 9, 1861, the day on which the Star of the West was
fired into. He joined Company B, Captain James M. Perrin,
of Orr's First South Carolina Rifle Regiment, September,
1861; and served with them on the coast of South Carolina
till December 24, 1861, when he received from Governor
Pickens a commission as second lieutenant in the First Regiment South Carolina Infantry (Regulars), Colonel William
Butler commanding. He served on the coast of South Carolina and the forts in Charleston Harbor until the evacuation of Charleston in 1865. During the retreat of the Confederate army, under General Joseph E. Johnston, through the
Carolinas, his regiment was a part of Rhett's Brigade, Talia-
fero's Division, Hardee's Corps. He had been promoted to
a captaincy in his regiment, and was placed in command of
Company C. He was captured by the Yankees, under General Sherman, two days after the battle of Bentonville, the
last pitched battle fought by General Johnston; and was imprisoned in Fort Delaware until about the twenty-third of
June, when he was discharged. Reached home on the 5th
of July, 1865. For some time after the surrender, he merchandised; and in 1875, entered the law office of Perrin &
Cothran, where he has continued during the various muta-
tions of that firm. In 1900, he was appointed master in
equity for Abbeville County. Since 1887, he has been the local attorney for the Seaboard Air Line Railway, and is the
attorney for the City Council of Abbeville. In 1879 he was
elected grand dictator of the Knights of Honor for South
Carolina. Appointed referee in bankruptcy in 1898. He was
married on the 21st of May, 1870, to Miss Mary M. McCaw,

daughter of Governor Robert G. and Belle (Bratton) Mc-
Caw, of Yorkville, South Carolina.

PITCHFORD, CHARLES W.—President and treasurer of
the C. W. Pitchford Company, dealers in general merchandise
and fertilizers. Son of Wesley Pitchford. Was born in Clayton, Georgia, May 8, 1863. His education was acquired from
the Newberry and Adger Colleges at Walhalla, South Carolina. He married Miss Carrie, daughter of J. S. Bauknight.
December 7, 1887. Was intendant of the town of Walhalla.
and secretary and director of Walhalla Cotton Mills.

PITTS, MILLEDGE THEODORE.—Son of James W. and
Elizabeth (Webb) Pitts. Born at Big Creek, Edgefield County,
South Carolina, January 8, 1870. Attended the Big Creek
Academy until about sixteen years of age, then entered the
South Carolina College and remained one session. Married
Miss Emma Belle Coleman. Elected clerk of court of Sa-
luda County, South Carolina, in 1900. Most of his life has
been devoted to farming.

PLAXCO, WILLIAM ALEXANDER McELWIN.—He is pas-
tor of the Associate Reformed Presbyterian Church in Clinton, South Carolina. Was born on November 15, 1856, at
Clarks Fork, York County, South Carolina. In early life his
educational advantages were meagre. In 1876, he entered
Kings Mountain Military Academy. Graduated from Erskine
College in 1881, with the degree of A. B. Same year he entered the Theological Seminary and graduated in 1883. In
April of that year was licensed to preach at Charlotte, North
Carolina. Married Mary Elizabeth Whitesides on November
6, 1883. His first charge was Shiloh Church in Lancaster
County, South Carolina. Remained there seven years, and re-
signed to do missionary work. After nine years service in
this capacity, gave it up to serve the church at Clinton,
South Carolina.

PLOWDEN, EDWIN RUTHVEN, JR.—Son of E. R. Plowden and Kate (Haynesworth) Plowden. Born June 7, 1854, at
Fork of Black River, in Clarendon County. Ancestors of

English and French descent. Attended the common schools
and took a two years course at Coits Military and Commercial School. Is engaged in farming. Member of the Legislature from Clarendon County from 1886 to 1890. Married
Miss Floride Oliver, December 20, 1884.

POE, NELSON CARTER.—Born in Montgomery, Alabama,
November 7, 1851. Son of William Poe and Ellen Cannon
(Taylor), daughter of Colonel Joseph Taylor and grand-
daughter of Colonel Samuel Taylor, a colonel in the Revolu-
tionary War. His great-grandfather, John Poe, came from
Londonderry, Ireland, to Baltimore in 1745. General David
Poe, the grandfather of Edgar Allan Poe, and his grandfather,
William Poe, were the oldest and youngest sons of John Poe.
In 1855, his mother and family came to South Carolina, a few
months after the death of his father. Owing to reduced cir-
cumstances caused by the Civil War, his education consisted
of a few years attendance at the Pendleton Male Academy.
In 1875, he commenced business in Greenville, South Carolina,
and has been identified with many of the most prominent
enterprises of this city. He is at present connected with a
number of cotton mills, several banks, is vice-president of
the F. W. Poe Manufacturing Company, and for the past
twenty years has been an active member of the firm of Wilkins, Poe & Co. In 1880, he married Miss Nannie Crawford,
of Pendleton, South Carolina, by which marriage he had
five children, three of whom are now living, Nelson, Ellen
and Wilkins.

POOL, STEPHEN M.—Supervisor of Oconee County. Son
of C. P. and Frances T. Pool. Was born in Greenville
County, March 31, 1842. His early training was acquired
in the common schools of that day. He served in the
Civil War four years, joining Orr's Regiment, McGowan's
Brigade. Was desperately wounded at the battle of Now-
ells Station, in Virginia, May 23, 1864. Was chairman of
the pension board for Oconee County two years. Married
Miss Alice M. Lay, May 5, 1878. Is now actively engaged in
farming.

POORE, JAMES EDWARD.—Practicing physician. Born February 24, 1876, at Belton, South Carolina. Academic education was obtained at Belton High School; collegiate, from Furman University, Greenville, South Carolina. Graduated from the medical department of Bellevue Hospital, New York, in 1897. First lieutenant and asistant surgeon, Second South Carolina Volunteer Infantry in Spanish-American War. Not married.

POOVEY, GEORGE W.—Practicing physician and surgeon of Lancaster, South Carolina. Born in Hickory, North Carolina, July 16, 1867; graduated from Rutherford college, North Carolina, and from the College of Physicians and Surgeons, Baltimore, Md. Married Miss Nannie Cauthen May 8, 1894. County physician, insurance examiner, and health officer of Lancaster.

POPE, JOSEPH DANIEL.—Professor of law in South Carolina College. Born April 6, 1820, at St. Helena Parish, South Carolina. Son of Joseph James Pope and Sarah Jenkins. Attended the private schools on St. Helena Island; Waterloo Academy. Graduated from the University of Georgia in 1841. Read law under James L. Pettigrew, of Charleston; and admitted to the bar in 1845. Formed a partnership with Richard DeTreville, of Beaufort, where he remained several years. In 1850 he was elected to the House of Representatives from St. Helena. In 1860 he was elected a member of the Secession Convention. Was a mover in organizing Confederate government and locating it at Montgomery. When Beaufort fell, in 1861, he moved to Columbia. In 1862 was elected to the Senate of South Carolina, which position he held until the close of the war. Appointed by President Davis head of Revenue Bureau, to raise supplies for the war. Also appointed to superintend insurance of the currency. After the close of the war, he resumed the practice of law. In 1842, he married Miss Catherine Scott, daughter of Dr. John A. P. Scott. His ancestors were English and Welsh.

POPE, YOUNG JOHN.—Born at Newberry, South Carolina, April 10, 1841. He was educated at the Newberry Male

Academy, under the management of Leonard W. Means and F. W. Pope, and at Furman University, from which institution he graduated in 1860. Married Sallie H. F. Rutherford, December, 1874. First a private in Company E, South Carolina Regiment, then from April 16, 1862 the adjutant of that regiment after which he acted as assistant adjutant-general of Kershaw's Cannon Brigade. He was elected district judge of Newberry from 1865 to 1868, and was for one year a member of the House of Representatives of South Carolina. He was elected by the Legislature associate counsel to the attorney-general in bond cases. In 1890 he was elected attorney-general of South Carolina, and in the following year he was promoted to the office of associate justice of the Supreme Court of South Carolina, which position he still holds. He has twice been elected county chairman of Newberry. He was also elected president of the State Democratic Convention in 1888 and the same year was elected State Senator from Newberry, South Carolina, and has filled at five different times the position as mayor of that town. He has also been, for twenty-four years, a member of the Board of Trustees of the Newberry College, and for eight years an ex-officio member of Board of Trustees of the South Carolina College. Has the distinction of having been placed on the honor roll of the Confederate army by the ladies at Richmond, Virginia.

PORCHER, WALTER PEYRE.—Born February 25, 1858, He is a son of Dr. F. Peyre Porcher. In 1876 Dr. Porcher went to Union College, Schenectady, New York, where he spent two years preparatory to entering the South Carolina Medical College. He graduated in 1881, taking first honor in his class. He had the good fortune to compete evenly with Dr. John Keith, of Richland County, and Dr. George G. Kinloch of Charleston, and the unusual distinction was made that year by the faculty of the College of conferring a first honor medal upon three men, an event which had not occurred before in the history of the institution. The striving was not even, but the results of the striving were. By virtue of his stand in the class, Dr. Porcher served for one year as house surgeon to the Roper Hospital, and was elected at the end of his term as service clerk of the city registrar, by the Charleston City Council. In 1883, subsequent to the reorganization of the city dispensary service, he was appointed to a position as city physician in charge of the Shirras Dispensary and he spent the following three years in laboring for the sick poor of the city. After devoting three years more to the pursuit of private practice he went North to perfect himself still further in medicine, and finding that his knowledge of each branch was so imperfect, he determined to devote himself to the acquirement of one alone. Having been especially interested in physical diagnosis the selection of laryngology and rhinology was a natural one. In 1882 Dr. Porcher received the compliment of a Fellowship in the American Laryngological Association; an organization consisting of the most distinguished men in that department in America, the membership of which is limited to seventy-five men. In 1900 he was elected president of the South Carolina Medical Association and had the honor of presiding at the semi-centennial celebration in his native city, the birthplace of the association. In 1897, Dr. Porcher was married to Miss Mary Long Porcher, daughter of Mr. S. Porcher, now of Minneapolis, Minnesota. Dr. Porcher has made many contributions to medical literature, most of which were read before the South Carolina Medical Association during his long membership in that body. His most elaborate articles, however, have been the chapter on "The Neuroses of the Larynx, Pharynx and Dysphagia," in Burnett's "System of Diseases of the Ear, Nose and Throat," published in Philadelphia in 1893; more recently, the chapter on "Atrophic Rhinitis" in "The American Text-Book of Diseases of the Eye, Ear, Nose, and Throat," by Deschweinitz & Randall, in 1899. Dr. Porcher has made two trips abroad in the interest of his specialty.

PORTER, WILLIAM STEPHEN LEANDER.—Clerk of the court of Lancaster County. Born in that county, November 13, 1860. Had very limited educational advantages in early life. Went to boarding school under the instruction of Professor L. Shurley, in his twenty-third and twenty-fourth years; continued to improve his education by teaching and studying very hard himself. Married Miss Julia Lane Warwick, of Lancaster County, on June 10, 1886. Began teaching after having obtained a first grade certificate, and has supplied several schools in Lancaster County. Elected to the office of clerk of court in 1896, and re-elected in 1900. Member of county board of education four years.

POWER, WILLIAM CARR.—Son of John Power and Jane Daniel Montague. Born March 2, 1831, in Abbeville County, South Carolina. Attended the common schools; and completed education at the Cokesbury Conference School in 1857. Married Martha Louisa, daughter of General William Evans, of Marion, South Carolina, March 20, 1867. College agent fifteen months. Army chaplain four years. Secretary of the South Carolina Conference fifteen years, the longest period the office has ever been held by one man. Presiding elder twenty years; he is now presiding elder of the Marion District.

PRENTISS, STEPHEN ELLIOTT.—Minister. Son of Rev. W. O. Prentiss and Mariah Jenkins. Born in Charleston, South Carolina, March 6, 1862. Of English and French-Huguenot ancestry. Attended the H. C. C. Institute of Charleston. Took theological course at the Western Theological Seminary, of Chicago. Married Miss Annie M. Waring of Charleston in 1888. Married a second time Martha D. Egleston of Winnsboro, South Carolina, April 25, 1894. Reporter and editor about six years. He is now pastor of the Holy Apostle Church, at Barnwell, South Carolina. He is also engaged in planting, stock-raising, and dairy farming at Barnwell.

PRESSLEY, WILLIAM LAWRENCE.—President of Erskine Theological Seminary, since 1891. He is a native of Due West, South Carolina. Was born May 9, 1837. Graduated from Erskine College, in 1857, and received his theological training from Erskine Theological Seminary, Due West,

South Carolina. He married Frances Elizabeth, daughter of Adam Wideman, of Abbeville County, on December 23, 1859. He supplied churches of Concord and Genevoster in Anderson County, South Carolina, from 1862-1871; and for nineteen years was pastor of A. R. P. Church at Due West. He is secretary and treasurer of Board of Foreign Missions of Associate Reformed Presbyterian Church.

PRESSLY, JOHN LOWRY.—Youngest son of Rev. James P. Pressly, D.D., who was for nearly forty years professor of Greek in Erskine College, and also in Erskine Theological Seminary. Was born December 31, 1857, at Due West, South Carolina. Graduated at Erskine College in the class of 1877. Two years later, he married Miss Josephine Le Gal. He merchandised at Due West from 1879 to 1889. From that time until 1892, he was principal of the Erskine College Fitting School. He was one year temporary professor of Latin and French in Erskine College. Since October, 1895, he has held the position of professor of Latin and French in the Due West Female College, and he is also professor of Greek in Erskine College. He has been a director of Due West Female College for several years.

PRINCE, GEORGE HOWARD.—Was born January 24, 1855, in Abbeville County, South Carolina. He was prepared for college at Wiliamston, South Carolina. Entered Wofford College in 1872, and graduated as valedictorian of his class in June, 1876. Was a professor in Williamston College three years. Was attorney for the city of Anderson four years; has been attorney for the Merchants and Farmers Bank since its organization. He is one of the attorneys for the Pelzer Mills, Orr Cotton Mills, Piedmont Mills and the Anderson Mills, and also the Cox. Is a director in Orr Cotton Mills. One of the promoters of the Anderson Graded Schools, having been chairman of the board since its organization seven years ago. Trustee of Wofford College. Member of the Constitutional Convention of 1895. Was a member of the House of Representatives for the year 1899 and 1900. Is a member of the present House. Was lay delegate to the General Con-

ference of the Methodist Episcopal Church South in 1898.
He married Miss Mattie Lander, daughter of Dr. Lander, of
Williamston, South Carolina, on the 24th of January, 1878.
He is a member of the law firm of Tribble and Prince, at
Anderson, South Carolina.

PROBST, GEORGE C.—Practicing dentistry at Walhalla,
South Carolina. Son of Rev. J. F. Probst, of Maryland. Was
born March 1, 1856, at Smithsburg, Maryland. Attended
Pennsylvania College, Gettysburg, Pennsylvania, and graduated from the University of Maryland in 1891. Married Lillian R. Steck on October 2, 1884.

PURDY, ROBERT O.—Lawyer. Son of James Purdy, of
Lawrenceville, Virginia. Born February 11, 1857, near Lawrenceville, Virginia. Attended the common schools, and was
two years at Virginia Argicultural and Mechanical College.
Then took degree of Bachelor of Laws, at Universtiy of Virginia. Moved to South Carolina in 1881. Married Hattie H.,
daughter of the late Dr. James I. Ingram of Manning. South
Carolina, December 18, 1883. Mayor of Sumter one term,
and now a member of the city council. Elected Circuit Judge
in 1902.

PYATT, MAHAM W.—Born at Georgetown, South Carolina,
November 10, 1867. Attended Winyah Indigo School, Dr.
Porter's School and the Citadel, at Charleston. Unmarried.
Member of House of Representatives from Georgetown Coun-
ty from 1894 to present time. Read law in office of R. Do-
zier, Esquire, and is practicing law at Georgetown, South
Carolina.

QUATTLEBAUM, EDWIN G.—Dentist. Son of Dr. Joseph
Quattlebaum and Lucy A. Merritt. Born March 15, 1864, in
Fairfield County, South Carolina. Of German and Scotch-
Irish descent. Graduated with degree of A. B. from South
Carolina College in 1886. Married May Tindal September 2,
1896. Graduated from the Philadelphia Dental College in
1891, and has since practiced dentistry at Columbia.

QUATTLEBAUM, JOSEPH M.—Dentist. Son of Dr. Joseph Quattlebaum and Lucy Merritt. Born November 13, 1856, in Orangeburg County, South Carolina. Of German and Scotch descent. Attended private schools of Blythewood and the Baltimore Dental College. Married J. Belle Merrit, at Ridge Spring, December 13, 1883. Reared on a farm.

QUATTLEBAUM, THEODORE ADOLPHUS.—Was born at Ridge Springs, Saluda County, South Carolina, February 4, 1876. Son of Dr. B. J. Quattlebaum, and grandson of Paul Q. Quattlebaum, of Lexington County. His mother was a daughter of William A. Merritt of Ridge Springs, South Carolina. Spent several years at Mount Zion College, Winnsboro, South Carolina, where his parents removed in 1883. Went to Furman University, where he studied for three sessions, ill health preventing his completing the course. In 1896 he took one course at South Carolina Medical College. Went from there to Vanderbilt Medical College; completed his second and third years' work, graduating in March, 1899, at the age of twenty-three. After graduating he retired to his home at Winnsboro, where he practiced his profession one year. Then removed to the prosperous town of Batesburg, South Carolina, where he is now following his chosen life work.

RAIFORD, LEMUEL CHARLES.—Instructor in drawing and textile chemistry in Clemson College. Born in Southampton County, Virginia, on August 2, 1872. Was educated in the public schools of Virginia, the Maryland College of Pharmacy and Brown University. Was appointed instructor in chemistry in Brown University.

RAMAGE, CARROLL JOHNSTONE.—Was born May, 1874, in eastern portion of what is now Saluda County, then Edgefield, near Wyse's Ferry. Graduated from Newberry College with honor, winning one of the medals for English essay and history. Dr. G. W. Holland, president of the college, took an unusual interest in him while a student. Took A. M. degree after graduation. Admitted to the bar in 1897, and has practiced successfully at Saluda since, giving his attention principally to civil court. Is specially interested in the early history of that section of South Carolina in which he resides.

RANDOLPH, HARRISON.—President and professor of mathematics in the Charleston College. Born December 8, 1871, at New Orleans, Louisiana, where his father was living temporarily, they being originally from Virginia. Education received in Virginia. Took M. A. Degree from University of Virginia in 1892; L. L. D. Washington and Lee University in 1899; instructor of mathematics in University of Virginia, 1890 and 1895; professor of mathematics University of Arkansas from 1895 to 1897. He has never married.

RAY, ARCHIBALD WADSWORTH.—Judge of probate of Richland County. Son of Dr. Duncan W. Ray and Sally F. Weston. Born July 23, 1860, at Adams Hill, in Richland County, South Carolina. Graduated at Union College, Schenectady, New York, and from the Albany Law school of Albany, New York, in 1884. Admitted to the bar in spring of 1884. Elected probate judge of Richland County to fill out an unexpired term. Re-elected in November, 1894, and again in 1898. He is unmarried.

RAYSOR, THOMAS MIDDLETON.—State Senator from Orangeburg County. Son of Captain P. A. and Ann M. Raysor. Born in Orangeburg County, South Carolina, May 26, 1859. Of English and Irish descent. Prepared for college in the public schools of Orangeburg and graduated from Wofford College in 1878 with degree of A. B. Read law under Hon. Samuel Dibble and admitted to the bar in December, 1880. Married Mattie M. Rogers. Member of the Legislature from 1884 to 1890. Chairman of graded school board for a number of years. Also chairman of commissioners of public works. Member of State board of education. He is actively engaged in the practice of law at Orangeburg.

RECKLING, WILLIAM AUGUSTUS.—Photographer. Son of Augustus Reckling of Vienna, Austria. Born September 4,

1849. Came to America when only four years of age. Attended St. Mary's College at Columbia. Married Ella Gertrude Radcliffe, daughter of Major Thomas W. Radcliffe, of Colorado, September 4, 1874. At seventeen years of age, began work with Wern & Hix, photographers of Colorado. Served in the Civil War. At the age of twenty-one went to Rome, Georgia and opened up a photograph gallery. He is now engaged in the same business at Columbia, South Carolina. He is a member of the National Photographers Association.

REDDING, JAMES F.—Son of John and Elizabeth Redding. Born December 9, 1848. Descended from one of the oldest families in Ireland. Parents came to this country from Tipperary, Ireland, in 1840. Obtained his education from public schools of Charleston. Left school at age of fourteen and tried to enter Confederate army but was refused. For twelve months made cartridges in the citadel, then entered service on steamship Fannie, a blockade runner. Clerked in United States quartermaster department. In 1870 opened a real estate office in Charleston. Commanded Montgomery Guards in 1876. Ex-president of Hibernian society. President of Winnsboro Granite Company, and Equitable Fire Insurance Company. Director in Peoples National Bank and Hibernia Trust and Savings Bank. In 1872 married Miss Nora M. Tierney, of Charleston. Served twelve years on city council.

REDFERN, ALEXANDER MAY.—Surgeon of Clemson College since the opening of the college in 1893. Was born in Anson County, North Carolina, March 21, 1862. Attended Furman University. Graduated from Wake Forest College in 1884, and from Long Island College Hospital, New York, in 1886 as valedictorian of the class. Married Miss Annie Streyhorn, June 4, 1891. Was county physician of Chesterfield County, and mayor of town in 1890. He is a Mason, Knight Templar and Shriner.

REED, CLIFTON AUGUSTUS.—Son of Judge J. P. Reed and Mrs. T. C. (Hammond) Reed. Born at Anderson, South

Carolina, June 5, 1845. Was prepared for college in the Anderson School and entered the South Carolina Military Academy at Columbia, South Carolina. October, 1864, he was married to Miss Fannie E. Kingsley, of Dalton, Georgia. On February 19, 1863, he joined the Confederate army under the command of Colonel William Trenholm. Early in the year 1864, this division was transferred to the army of Northern Virginia, and formed the Seventh South Carolina Cavalry, commanded by Colonel A. C. Haskell. He lost his right hand and was seriously wounded in the battle of Hawes Shop, Virginia, thus ending his military career. He has since been engaged in the mercantile business in Anderson, South Carolina.

REEVES, JOHN BOUNETHEAN.—President of State Savings Bank of Charleston, South Carolina, and treasurer of Carolina Rice Company. Was born November 5, 1847, in Charleston, South Carolina. His education was obtained from the public schools of that city and Dr. Henry M. Burns' School of Orangeburg, South Carolina. Master of Orange Lodge No. 14, A. F. M. Alderman of Charleston. President of South Carolina Fire Insurance Agents' Association and of the Building and Loan Association. He is still interested in the fire insurance business. He served in the Confederate war as lieutenant in a company which went from Orangeburg, South Carolina, in November, 1864, and remained until the war closed. Married Miss Mary Stone Bissell October 21, 1873.

REID, EBENEZER LEONIDAS.—Born November 3, 1867, in Mecklenburg, County, North Carolina. Of Scotch-Irish parentage. Entered Erskine College in 1884 and graduated from same institution in 188. Pursued post-graduate course in Johns Hopkins University, Baltimore, two years. Married Miss Gray Atkins, of Virginia, in 1897. Held a position in Macon High School, of Charlotte, North Carolina, for three years after graduation. Since 1894 he has been professor of chemistry and geology in Erskine College. Board of trustees of Erskine College conferred degree of A. M. one year after graduation.

REMBERT, EDWARD ENGLISH.—Merchant and planter. Was born April 25, 1864, at the old family homestead, "Sunny-Side Plantation," where he now resides. Was educated at Porters School, Charleston, South Carolina, the Carolina Military Institute, Charlotte, North Carolina, and the Citadel Military Academy of this State. Both the Rembert and Gaillard families came over from France with the first Huguenots, from which time these families have been identified with the religious, social and progressive growth of their adopted home. He married Miss Christine E. Sanders June 11, 1890.

REYNOLDS, JOHN SCHREINER.—Lawyer. Son of George N. and Susan Eliza Schreiner. Born September 28, 1848, at Charleston, South Carolina. Of English and German descent. Attended graded schools of Charleston until 1862. Then entered Mt. Zion Institute, Winnsboro, South Carolina. Spent one year at the University of the South at Sewanee, Tennessee. Married Sue Gadsden Edwards, December 9, 1880. Instructor of belles lettres, Kings Mountain Military School, Yorkville, from 1870 to 1875. Admitted to the bar in 1876. Removed to Columbia in 1887. Member of the Democratic conventions of Richland County. Delegate to the State convention of 1896, where he led the fight for a resolution instructing the State delegation in the national convention to abide by the action of that body. Elected to the Legislature from Richland County in 1896, and was the author of the measure known as the Reynolds Printing Bill. Author of the resolution urging the amendment of the Federal constitution so that United States Senators might be elected by a direct vote of the people. Entered the Confederate service in 1864, serving for a time in the State troops and then with the battalion of Arsenal Cadets till May, 1865, when discharged.

RHAME, JAMES A.—Was born October 1, 1850, on the farm of his father, the late Colonel John Coleman Rhame, in Sumter County. Received his education in the common schools of the town. Engaged almost entirely in farming, except for a few years when he was bookkeeping. In 1877 he was married to Miss M. Olivia Keels, of Sumter. In 1876 he was among the foremost in the redemption of the State, and from that time has been continuously a member of the county in State and Congressional conventions. In 1876, he was commissioned by Wade Hampton a lieutenant in the Jefferson Davis Light Infantry, a military company of which M. E. McDonald was captain. Was appointed in 1884 by the Governor and commissioner of agriculture as a member of the South Carolina Commission, to aid the Agricultural Department in having the resources of the State properly represented at the World's Industrial and Cotton Centennial Exposition, at New Orleans in 1884 and 1885. Correspondent for the United States Department of Agriculture. Member of the convention in 1890 that nominated Haskel for governor. Mason and Knight of Pythias.

RHETT, ROBERT GOODWIN.—Son of A. Moore and Martha Goodwyn Rhett. Born March 25, 1862, at Columbia, South Carolina. Of English descent. Attended Porter Academy, the Episcopal High School of Virginia, and graduated from University of Virginia with degree of M. A.; then in law department in 1884 with degree of Bachelor of Law. Married Miss Helen Smith, daughter of W. B. Whaley, November 15, 1888. Elected president of South Carolina Loan and Trust Company in 1896, and since November, 1899, president of Peoples National Bank. Also president of Land Pebble Phosphate Company and four building and loan associations. Member of firm of D. Middleton & Company, fire insurance agents. Treasurer and director of Chattanooga, Augusta and Charleston Railroad Company. Director of Bank of Barnwell, Enterprise Bank of Laurens, Charleston Importing and Export Company, Johnston & Crews Company, Charleston Dry Goods Company, Mutual Carpet Company, Smith McIver and Company, Granby Cotton Mills, Columbia, Courtenay Manufacturing Company, Newry, South Carolina, Alderman two terms, and mayor pro tem one term. Practicing law as member of firm Trenholm, Rhett, Miller & Whaley.

24

RICE, ENOCH BREAZEALE.—Director in the Anderson Cotton Mill. Native of Anderson County. Volunteered in 1861 to serve his country, joining the Palmetto Riflemen of Anderson, Colonel Jenkins, Longstreet's Corps. Went to Richmond and was in the battles around that place. Was at Appomattox at the time of General Lee's surrender. After the war he returned to Belton, South Carolina, and began merchandising. Later went into the oil mill business.

RICHEY, WILLIAM RASOR.—Born in Abbeville County, near Cokesbury, September 24, 1854. Very limited education, only being able to attend school at such times when his services were not needed on the farm. Clerked for W. Z. McGhee at Cokesbury from November, 1872, to February, 1873. Later clerked and kept books for McGhee & Cason at Hodges, South Carolina, until 1875, at which time he formed a partnership with John M. Miller and continued to do business until 1881, when Miller withdrew and he continued the business alone until 1886. In the meantime he had begun the study of law under J. T. Johnson at Laurens, South Carolina, and was admitted to the bar in the spring of 1885. The following year he moved to Laurens and formed a partnership with J. T. Johnson under the firm name of Johnson & Richey, and practiced law at Spartanburg and Laurens until said firm was mutually dissolved January 1, 1898. Since that time he has been practicing alone. In 1875 he married Miss Julia, daughter of Dr. B. C. Hart, of Cokesbury, South Carolina. Served two terms as intendant of the town of Hodges in 1883 and 1884. Was elected one of the commissioners of public works in the city of Laurens in 1896, which position he resigned in 1896 to accept that of mayor of Laurens. Re-elected in 1899 and declined to run in 1901. Director and attorney for the Bank of Laurens. President and secretary and treasurer and general manager of the Laurens Telephone Exchange Company. Also director of the Perpetual Building and Loan Association, of Laurens. Secretary of the Wares Shoal Land Company and is connected with several other financial institutions.

RIDGELL, JAMES ALEXANDER.—Elected sheriff of Saluda County in 1901. Is a son of Norris F. and Anna (Hunter) Ridgell. Born March 4, 1860, near Mt. Willing, in Edgefield County (now Saluda). Ancestors were of Irish and English descent. Very good education obtained from common schools of the county. Married Miss Mattie Matthews January 29, 1891. In early manhood clerked a short while at Leesville; then engaged in sawmill business and farming, which occupation he followed until elected to the present office.

RIGGS, WALTER MERRITT.—Born at Orangeburg, South Carolina, January 24, 1873. Educated at private schools of Orangeburg and at the Alabama Polytechnic Institute, and in the summer of 1894 did special work at Cornell University. Was post-graduate in department of English at the Alabama Polytechnic Institute 1893 and 1894. Instructor in charge of laboratory at the same institution 1894 and part of 1895. Appointed to take charge of electrical engineering at Clemson College in February, 1895. Took first honors in the junior and senior years on the course of electrical and mechanical engineering, and won the sophomore declamation medal. Is a great athlete, and the first coacher of the Clemson football team. Designed, built and equipped the laboratory at Clemson.

RIKARD, HENRY HUDSON.—Master of Newberry County. Born December 27, 1864, near Pomaria, in Newberry County. Education was acquired in the common schools, the Prosperity High School, one session at Erskine College, and graduated at the Newberry College in 1887. After graduation he spent several years teaching in the county, but his health failed and he returned to the farm. Has also clerked at Prosperity for several years. Being urged by his friends he entered the race for Master of his county in 1900, and was elected by a large majority, which office he now holds. Married Miss Mary C. Wheeler, daughter of J. M. Wheeler, of Prosperity, February 22, 1888.

RILEY, JOHN RUTLEDGE.—Pastor of the Presbyterian Church at Pickens. Born in Abbeville District, South Carolina, April 12, 1829. Was a student in the Presbyterian High School at Greenwood, South Carolina. In 1849 he was a student in the East Tennessee University, at Knoxville, and graduated from the South Carolina College in 1854. His theological studies were pursued in the seminary in Columbia. He supplied the Presbyterian Church at Laurens from 1860 to 1877. While in Laurens he was a professor in the Laurensville Female College and part of that time he was president. He was elected to a professorship in Adger College at Walhalla, and made chairman of the faculty. He remained there until called to his present charge. Degree of D. D was conferred by Newberry College in 1882. Married Miss Anna A. Donnelly September 19, 1860.

RILEY, THOMAS F.—Born in Abbeville, now Greenwood, County August 12, 1845. Had only the advantage of the common schools. Merchandised at Greenwood until 1870, at which time he went into the hotel business. Entered the army, joining McGowan's Brigade, Hill's Division, Stonewall Jackson Corps, Army of Northern Virginia. One of the prime movers in getting the county of Greenwood organized, and securing the railroads from Augusta and also Seaboard Air Line.

ROBERTSON, EDWIN WALES.—President of the Loan and Enchange Bank of Columbia, South Carolina. Son of Thomas J. Robertson and Mary O. Caldwell. Born September 3, 1863, at Columbia, South Carolina. Of Scotch-Irish descent. Attended Emerson Institute, Washington, District of Columbia, Hopkins Grammar School, New Haven, Connecticut. Graduated from Yale in 1885, and completed law course at South Carolina College in 1887. Married Evelyn P. Fitcomb, daughter of James A. Fitcomb, of Maine, September 29, 1886. From 1887 to 1894 practiced law at Columbia. President of the Canal Bank of Columbia from 1892 until its consolidation with the Loan and Exchange Bank January 1, 1898. Is also president of the Central National Bank, of Columbia. Director in First National Bank of Batesburg, South Carolina, State Bank and Trust Company of Columbia and the South Carolina and Georgia Railroad Company.

ROBERTSON, FRANCIS MARION.—Member of insurance firm of Ravenel, Johnson, Robertson & Company of Charleston, South Carolina. Born in Summerville, South Carolina, October 27, 1864. Entered the South Carolina Military Academy in 1882 upon the re-organization of the academy and completed the course in 1886. Married Miss Minnie Rogers Robertson, May 7, 1890. After leaving school was in the employ of the Clifton Manufacturing Company at Spartanburg a few months. In 1887 accepted a position as transmit man in United States hydrographic survey of Savannah River and harbor at Savannah, Georgia. In 1888 went into insurance business under the firm name of Pelzer & Robertson at Charleston, South Carolina, and in 1892 formed a partnership with the above company, and is still connected with them.

ROBERTSON, JOHN T.—Member of the principal mercantile firm of Clinton. Born December 10, 1858, near Waterloo, Laurens County, South Carolina. Had only the advantage of the country schools. After leaving school he spent several years as salesman in the J. W. Copeland & Company store, and is now secretary, treasurer and business manager of that firm. He married Miss Alma E. Griffin December 2, 1886.

ROBINSON, CHARLES EVANS.—Son of Dr. George E. and Sarah R. Robinson (nee Child). Born December 9, 1861, in Pickens County. He is of Scotch-Irish descent. His father was a surgeon in the Confederate army, and a member of Trenholm Squadron. On account of the war he was unable to obtain anything but a good common school education.

Read law under his uncle, R. A. Child, then a member of the bar, but now a Methodist preacher. Has practiced law since 1883 at Pickens. On May 30, 1888, he was married to Miss Nannie Cox of Pickens. He has at different times held the position of warden of the town and intendant of the town. Trial justice two years and edited the "Pickens Sentinel" in 1893. Elected to the Legislature in 1898, and re-elected in 1900.

ROGERS, ROBERT LEE.—Pastor of the Walhalla Presbyterian Church. Born in Laurens County, South Carolina, July 26, 1869. Graduated from the Presbyterian College of South Carolina at Clinton, in 1890, and from the Theological Seminary, at Columbia, South Carolina, in May, 1897. After leaving college he taught school two years, and in the meantime read law and was admitted to the bar in December, 1892. Married Miss Ella Blanche Steck, daughter of Rev. J. Steck, D. D., December 20, 1899.

ROGERS, WILLIAM ANSON.—Minister. Son of William Rogers and Ann Jane McCullum. Born at Bishopville, Sumter County, South Carolina, September 29, 1849. Attended school at Bishopville Academy and Washington College under the presidency of Robert E. Lee. Graduated from Wofford College in 1872. Married Annie M. Anderson March 22, 1876. Taught school a few months and in 1872 entered the ministry, joining the South Carolina Conference. Trustee of Wofford and is now on her board. Has supplied churches in Spartanburg, Charleston, Greenwood and other places.

ROLFS, PETER HENRY.—Professor of botany in Clemson College. Was born at LeClaire, Scott County, Iowa, on the April 17, 1865. His primary education was received in the graded and high school of his native city. In March, 1886, he entered Iowa State College at Ames, Iowa. Graduated in November, 1889, with the degree of B. S. In 1890 he took a post-graduate course at this institution in botany and entomology, receiving in 1891 a second diploma with the degree of M. S. He also studied at the botanical laboratory of Washington University, and the Missouri Botanical Garden at St. Louis. Before receiving his M. S. degree he was principal of the graded school at Garrison, Iowa, and of the Lawler graded school. In 1890 he accepted the position as assistant professor of botany in the Iowa State College, and State Agricultural Experiment Station. In 1891 he accepted the position of entomologist and botanist to the Florida agricultural experiment station at Lake City, Florida, and in June of the following year he was elected professor of natural science in the Florida State Agricultural College. He is the author of several books and pamphlets on agricultural subjects. Married Miss Effie Stone, daughter of H. G. Stone, August 25, 1892 at LeClaire, Iowa.

ROLLINS, RICHARD DAVID.—County treasurer of Williamsburg County since 1890. Son of Rev. J. L. and R. D. Rollins. Born near Timmonsville, in what is now Florence County, February 14, 1846. Ancestors were from France and Wales. Educated in the common schools and the High School of Timmonsville. Merchandised at Indian Town and Lake City several years, and at same time handles naval stores. He has also farmed. He took an active part in the redemption of the State in 1876 and escorted Hampton's campaign party from Manning to Georgetown. Entered the Confederate service in 1863, joining Company G, Twenty-Sixth South Carolina Volunteers. Served in the campaign around Petersburg. Twice wounded, once knocked down by a negro in a hand to hand fight at the Crater. Was a first lieutenant in Williamsburg Light Dragoons in 1876, and for more than ten years was first lieutenant in Lake City Light Dragoons. He represents several insurance companies, and a director in the Bank of Kingstree. Married Miss Ida I., daughter of Dr. Thomas B. Bars, January 27, 1872.

ROPER, LEWIS MURPHEE.—Pastor of First Baptist Church of Spartanburg, South Carolina. Born March 21, 1870, at Eden, Laurens County, South Carolina. Received Bachelor of Arts degree from Columbia University, A. M. Furman University, full graduate of Rochester Theological Seminary,

Rochester, New York. Married Miss Leonora A. Mauldin, of Hampton, South Carolina, September 5, 1893. He was pastor of First Baptist Church, Canton, Ohio, from 1896 to 1900. Trustee of Furman University. Took gold medal from Columbian University, and also first honor from Furman University.

ROSBOROUGH, WILLIAM LEONIDAS, JR.—Son of W. L. and Martha A. Rosborough. Born at Ridgeway, South Carolina, September 3, 1871; attended the common schools in Fairfield County, and graduated at Erskine College, Due West, South Carolina, in 1891. In 1900 he was elected county superintendent of education of Fairfield County, which position he is now filling.

ROWELL, ANDREW CLARK.—Son of Wilson and Mary Rowell. Ancestors were Dutch. Born in Lancaster County, South Carolina, April 26, 1874. Education was limited, but by pluck and perseverance he saved money from his own labors and thereby was enabled to take a business course. Married Miss Mary L. Plyler, October 11, 1900. Taught in common schools eight consecutive years, and clerked one year. Elected county superintendent of education in 1900, which position he is still holding.

ROWLAND, MARCUS OBADIAH.—Prominent physician of Spartanburg County. Was born near Boiling Springs, South Carolina, June 4, 1836. Obtained education from common schools of the county, and two years under Wiliam Irwin, of Spartanburg. Assistant surgeon in Confederate army. Member of Legislature from 1890 to 1896. Member of Constitutional Convention, director of State penitentiary, and engaged in farming.

RUCKER, ELBERT MARION, SR.—Born at Ruckersville, Elbert County, Georgia, June 15, 1888. Graduated from the University of Georgia, at Athens, and Harvard University, Cambridge, Massachusetts. Elected to the Georgia Legislature in 1853 from Elbert County. Member of the Southern

Rights Convention held at Milledgeville in 1851. Delegate to Democratic Convention of 1872. In that year he moved to Anderson, South Carolina. Elected to Legislature in 1880 and again in 1884. Married Sara Francis Whitner, November 3, 1853.

RUCKER, ELBERT MARION, JR.—A grandson of Judge J. W. Whitner, of Anderson, South Carolina. Born in that town March 15, 1866. Attended Adger College, at Walhalla, and later South Carolina College, where he graduated in the regular course and in law. Married Miss Bessie Kinard, of Columbia, December 15, 1886. Was appointed United States attorney by Secretary Hoke Smith in June, 1893, which position he retained until 1897. Returned to Anderson in 1898 and was elected to the Legislature in 1900. Formed partnership with J. E. Brazeale for the practice of law in 1901.

RUSSELL, DAVID HAMILTON.—Editor of the "Daily Mail," published at Anderson, South Carolina. Born January 4, 1841, in Anderson County, South Carolina. His early training was received under Rev. J. L. Kennedy, and later he attended the University of Virginia. Married Miss Frances E. Smith December 14, 1865. Was school commissioner six years and magistrate for four. Member of the Constitutional Convention of 1895 and also editor of the "Peoples Advocate." United States census supervisor in 1900 for Third South Carolina District. A private in Fourth South Carolina Volunteers and First South Carolina Cavalry under General R. E. Lee for four years. For eighteen months served in the signal corps of General J. E. B. Stewart.

RUTH, ABRAHAM MILES.—Born in Old Beaufort District, now Hampton County, South Carolina, January 31, 1841. His father, Hon. A. M. Ruth, was a wealthy planter of St. Peter's Parish. He was State Senator at the time of his death, which occurred while attending the sessions in Columbia in 1854. Captain Ruth, the subject of this sketch, was among the first to volunteer in the commencement of the war, and joined the cavalry of the Hampton Legion. He fought in the battles of Bull Run, Second Manassas, Sharpsburg and others, and in the great cavalry fight at Brandy Station in 1862. He was severely wounded in a hand-to-hand contest with Yankee officers, and for his bravery he was promoted to a captaincy. Married, in 1862, Miss Annie Goethe. Is sheriff of Hampton County, and has held the office twenty years. Is a Mason of high standing, and a strong supporter in the Baptist Church.

RUTLEDGE, BROOKS.—Son of Robert K. and Susan Rutledge (nee Richburg). Born May 18, 1857, at Summerton, South Carolina. Of Irish and French descent. Graduated at Furman University, Greenville, South Carolina, in 1885; then attended the dental department of the University of Maryland. Married Ella, daughter of J. K. Chase, of Nashville, Tennessee. In early life farmed and taught school in Greenville County, but since 1885 has practiced dentistry at Florence. Elected recording secretary of the State Dental Association in 1890, and in 1896 elected president. In 1900 he was elected a member of the State Board of Dental Examiners for five years. In 1899 appointed a trustee of Furman University and Greenville Female College for three years. Alderman of Florence since 1896.

RUTLEDGE, JAMES ROSE.—Manager of the real estate and insurance office of J. R. Rutledge & Company, Greenville, South Carolina. Born in that city April 19, 1870. His earlier schooling was received from the Patrick Military Academy and later attended Furman University, and the South Carolina College. He bought cotton nine years, and has been in his present business four years. Married Miss Edith S. Taylor January 4, 1899.

SALLY, GEORGE LAWRENCE.—Clerk of the court of Orangeburg County. Son of Nathaniel M. Sally. Born in Orangeburg County, South Carolina, February 28, 1847. Education obtained from the common schools. Married Mattie D. Stokes December 12, 1876. Supervisor of registration ten years.

SAMS, ROBERT OSWALD.—Born at Beaufort, South Carolina, September 4, 1841. Educated at the Beaufort College;
and at the South Carolina Military Academy, graduating in
the class of 1861. Was assistant professor at the Citadel before graduating. Professor of French in Military Academy,
Montgomery, Alabama; principal of High School, Spartanburg, South Carolina; co-principal Limestone Female College;
co-principal Gaffney Male and Female Seminary, and also
superintendent of the Gaffney Graded School. Member of
the battery that fired on the "Star of the West" that endeavored to re-enforce Fort Sumter. This was the first shot fired
during the Civil War. Lieutenant in battalion of State Cadets to the end of the war.

SANDERS, ARTHUR K.—Born in the Rafling Creek Section, of Sumter County, on July 3, 1860. Educated in the
common schools of the neighborhood, until February, 1874, at
which time he entered the Carolina Military Institute, at
Charlotte, North Carolina, graduating in 1879. Married Eva
J. McLeod, of Sumter County, on December 16, 1885. He was
elected to the House of Representatives, in 1888, allied with
the "Straightout" faction, and was re-elected in 1890, 1894,
and 1896. A member of the board of directors of the State
Penitentiary. After two years service, was re-elected to the
same position, and is now filling the position as chairman of
that board. In 1898, was appointed by the State Legislature
to examine the books, accounts, etc., of the State Dispensary.
1899, Governor Ellerbe appointed him as a delegate to the
National Prison Congress, which met at Hartford, Connecticut. He is a very successful farmer.

SARRATT, ROBERT C.—Born October 21, 1860. Was educated at Wofford College. Is principal of a flourishing school
at Boiling Springs, South Carolina. Served one term in the
House of Representatives, from Spartanburg County, in 1890
and 1891. Is now in the middle of his first term as Senator
from Cherokee County. Married Miss Fannie Amos Sarratt.
on July 6, 1887.

SASS, GEORGE HERBERT.—(Barton Grey.) Author. Was born in Charleston, South Carolina, December 24, 1845. A graduate of the College of Charleston, and valedictorian of his class. December 20, 1883, married Anna E. Ravenel. Many years literary editor of the "Sunday News and Courier." Has delivered literary addresses, and now holds the position as master in equity of Charleston County.

SAWYER, CLAUDE E.—Lawyer. Son of Colonel William Earl Sawyer and Louisa W. Fox. Born in Lexington, now Aiken County, South Carolina. Taught by parents at home; then went to Blythewood Institute, and Eastman Commercial College, Poughkeepsie, New York. Read law, in New York City, and completed the course at Aiken. Stenographer of the Second Judicial Circuit. Member of the Legislature from Aiken four years. Member of many State conventions. Presidential elector, in 1888. Director of the State Penitentiary in 1882 and 1884. Solicitor of the Second Judicial Circuit. Grand master of Masons of South Carolina, from 1894 to 1896; grand tribune of Knights of Pythias. On staff of Governors Hampton and Simpson; captain of Company L., First South Carolina Volunteers, during Spanish-American War; Captain of Thirty-eighth Infantry in the Philippines, and in command of the battalion at different times.

SAWYER, JEROME HAMILTON.—Cashier of the Central National Bank of Columbia. Born in Utica, New York, October 1, 1826. Attended the common schools in Alexandria, Virginia, from 1836 to 1838. Twice married. Connected with the Adams Express Company, from 1849 to 1857. Superintendent of the Baltimore office and lines south to Charleston, from 1853 to 1857. Chief clerk of the Ordnance Bureau, during the war. He invented a rule for finding bank discount, which is to be found in Sanford's Arithmetic.

SCARBOROUGH, ROBERT BETHEA.—Born October 29, 1861, at Chesterfield Court-house, South Carolina. Educated at Mullins Academy, Marion County, South Carolina. Married Mary J. Jones, December 15, 1882. In 1896 he was elected

State Senator from Horry County; appointed president pro tem of that body January, 1899. On the death of Governor Ellerbe he succeeded to the office of lieutenant-governor of the State, in June, 1899, lieutenant McSweeney, becoming governor. He was elected to Congress from the Sixth Congressional District, in 1900. Admitted to the bar, in 1884, and has since been actively engaged in the practice of law, at Conway, South Carolina.

SCARBOROUGH, WILSON DUPREE.—Was born in upper Salem, Sumter County, South Carolina, July 3, 1842. The subject of this sketch was raised on the farm, and partially at the plow handles, and had very limited educational advantages. He entered the freshman class, of the South Carolina College, to take a full course, five months before the beginning of the Confederate War, when he left school and entered the army on his nineteenth birthday. Served in Virginia seven or eight months; then joined Company E., Palmetto Battalion of Light Artillery. He entered this Company as private, but was soon appointed sergeant, and soon thereafter was elected senior second lieutenant. Was put in command of a heavy battery, with half his company, about seventy men. Commanded his company in its last fight at Bentonville, North Carolina. A captain's commission was issued him, which he did not receive however on account of immediate evacuation of Richmond and the termination of the war. He did a great deal towards breaking up lawlessness in this State just after the war. He has never refused to serve the people when prompted by duty. He has served as road overseer, sub-county commissioner, special constable, and deputy, school trustee. Chairman of local board of education. President of Democratic club. Was elected to Lower House of Legislature in 1878, and again in 1880. Was elected to the State Senate in 1892 but lost his seat by fraudulent means. He was commissioned as aide to Governor Johnson Hagood in 1882.

SCHAIDT, JOHN GEORGE.—Pastor of Evangelical Lutheran Church at Walhalla, South Carolina, since 1895. Was born of German parents at Lonaconing, Maryland, on July 31, 1846. Attended parochial school of German Lutheran Church, in Cumberland, Maryland, for about four years, and the Alleghany County Academy at the same place, one year. Graduated from Muhlenberg College, Allentown, Pennsylvania, June, 1872. In the fall of 1872, he entered the Theological Seminary of the Evangelical Lutheran Church at Philadelphia, Pennsylvania, and graduated in May, 1875. Has since supplied churches in Knoxville, Tennessee, and North Carolina. He also taught school several years before entering college. Married Miss Annie L., daughter of General S. Stansill, on June 23, 1881.

SCHERER, MELANCHTHON G. G.—Son of Rev. Simon and Sarah Annie Scherer. Born March 16, 1861, in Catawba County, North Carolina. His ancestors came from Germany about the middle of the eighteenth Century, settled in Pennsylvania, and then came South. He is a graduate of Roanoke College, Salem, Virginia. Studied theology at the Lutheran Theological Seminary of the same place. Was ordained Evangelical Lutheran minister, in 1883. Held pastorates at Grafton, West Virginia, Mt. Holly Springs, Pennsylvania, and Concord, North Carolina. In June, 1896, he was elected president of North Carolina College, at Mt. Pleasant, North Carolina, in which capacity he served until June 1899. Then he accepted a call to the Lutheran Church of the Redeemer, Newberry, South Carolina, of which he is now pastor. Elected secretary of the United Synod of the Evangelical Lutheran Church in the South in 1896, and still maintains that position.

SCOTT, DAVID CUNNINGHAM.—President of the Bank of Kingstree. Was born on November 23, 1849, at Kingstree, South Carolina. Son of John E. and Mary Gordon Scott. His ancestors on both sides were Scotch-Irish, and were among the pioneer settlers of Williamsburg County. Educated at private schools. Taught school two years, devoting his spare moments to the study of medicine. Graduated from the South Carolina Medical College, in 1876. Has since been engaged in the practice of medicine, in his native town.

Married Martha E. Brockinton, daughter of Dr. John F. Brockinton, in 1884.

SCOTT, THOMAS COWDREY.—A native of England. His ancestors came from Scotland and Ireland. First saw the light on August 12, 1847, in London, England. Attended only the common schools of those days. He was present at the laying of the foundation of the Thornwell Orphanage in 1876. Has since then been connected with that institution. Volunteered at the beginning of the war in Captain Blassingame's Company K., changed to Fifth Regiment Palmetto Sharpshooters, in Jackson's Brigade, Longstreet's Corps, Army of Northern Virginia. Served in many hard-fought and prominent battles until the close of the war.

SEASE, THOMAS SIDNEY.—Solicitor of the Seventh Circuit. Was born in Newberry County, on August 25, 1867. His early educa-

tion was acquired from the public schools, Newberry College. Graduated from the South Carolina College with the degree of A. B. Studied law at the South Carolina College, and was admitted to the bar in May, 1892. He was awarded two medals at the South Carolina College, one for declamation and the other for debating, both in a contest with several others. After graduation he returned to Newberry and was elected clerk and attorney for the County Board of Commissioners for that county. Chairman of the Newberry County Democratic Party. Master in equity for Newberry County. Elected solicitor of the Seventh Circuit, in 1896; and re-elected in 1900, without opposition. He married Miss Lula Caughman, of Edgefield County, on the eighteenth of July, 1893.

SEIBELS, JOHN T.—He is the oldest son of the late Edwin W. Seibels and Amanda Hyatt. Born in Columbia, South

Carolina, July 29, 1850. Prepared for college at the Columbia Male Academy, under Hugh S. Thompson and graduated from the South Carolina University, in 1870. In the fall of 1870, he entered the law department under Major C. D. Welhon, graduating in June following. Having been admitted to practice, he formed a partnership with Colonel James M. Baxter, of Newberry, which continued until the death of the senior member, in 1881. In October, 1876, Mr. Seibels married Carrie Thompson, daughter of Governor Hugh S. Thompson. He was appointed master for Richland County, in 1883. Retired from said office, in 1895; and his successor was appointed by Governor John Gary Evans. From 1876 to 1888, he was secretary of the County Democratic Executive Committee. He is a member of Trinity Church (Episcopal).

SHAFFER, ALEXANDER CASNER.—President of the Colleton Cotton Mills of Walterboro, South Carolina. He was born in Stillwater, New Jersey, June 2, 1838. His education was acquired from The Newton Collegiate Institute, Newton, New Jersey. He was captain of the New York Volunteer Cavalry at the close of the war, stationed at war department in Colleton County, and organized the labor on the rice plantations. Was clerk of the court six years, and county treasurer four. He is also a large merchant in Walterboro. He married Miss Amelia Jane Terry, daughter of John K. Terry, July 24, 1874.

SHAND, GADSDEN EDWARD.—Member of the firm of W. B. Smith Whaley & Company, engaged in cotton mill engineering, power plant work and architecture. Son of Robert W. Shand, of Columbia. Born in Columbia, South Carolina, March 21, 1868. Of English and Scotch descent. Graduated from South Carolina College in 1888, in course of civil engineering. Studied architecture in private office, and one year at Columbia College, New York. Married Patience Bonham, daughter of General M. L. Bonham, Superintendent of work of completing State House, 1888 to 1890. Private practice of profession, from 1891 to 1893.

SHAND, ROBERT WALLACE.—Lawyer. Son of Rev. Peter J. Shand and Mary Wright. Born in Columbia, South Carolina, February 27, 1840. Paternal ancestors came from Scotland, and his mother was a native of Charleston, South Carolina. Graduated from the South Carolina College, in 1859, with degree of Bachelor of Arts. Read law under Gen eral Maxcy Gregg. Admitted to the bar, in 1860. Married Louisa Coffin Edwards, April 15, 1863. Sergeant of Company C., Second South Carolina Volunteer Infantry, Kershaw's Regiment, until discharged on account of ill health, in 1863. He was in the battle of Manassas, Savage Station, Maryland Heights, Sharpsburg, and Fredericksburg. Member of the Legislature from Union County, from 1878, to 1879. State reporter from 1879 to 1895. Published thirty-four volumes of State reports. Compiled a book called "Shands Manual." Chancellor of the Episcopal Diocese of South Carolina. Practicing law at Columbia, since 1883.

SHANNON, WILLIAM McWILLIE.—Captain of Kershaw Guards three years, taking command in 1882. He was born in Camden, October 11, 1856. Early education was obtained from the Camden Academy, under Mr. McCandless. Then took junior and intermediate courses at University of the South, Sewanee, Tennessee. Married Miss Camilla A. Nelson, April 29, 1879. Democratic county chairman, in 1884 and 1885. For about ten years trustee of school district Number 1, and chairman of board when brick school building was erected in 1893. Studied law in his father's office. Was ad mitted to the bar in 1880. He is a director in most of the business corporations of Camden, and is attorney for Bank of Camden; Camden Building & Loan Association; Camden Cotton Mill; DeKalb Cotton Mill; Camden Pressed Brick Company; Atlantic Cotton Oil Co.; Seaboard Air Line Railway, and other corporations. His life has been devoted to professional work, and he has never aspired to political position.

SHEALY, FRANK W.—Elected at August primary, 1900, treasurer of Lexington County, and appointed by Governor McSweeney, February 7, 1901. Born October 19, 1870 near

Lewie Ferry, on the south side of Saluda River, in Lexington County. Son of James M. and Elizabeth L. Shealy. Of German descent. Attended the free schols of the county until thirteen years of age. Since that time, his education has been self-acquired. He was assistant postmaster and express agent, at Summit, South Carolina, about six years. Married Miss Nannie J. Shirey, March 8, 1896.

SHELOR, JOSEPH WARREN.—Son of Thomas Ryland and Susan Ann Shelor, Virginian by descent. Born March 29, 1853, at Tugalo, Oconee County, South Carolina. Attended the common schools of the county until 1872, when he entered the high school at Senoia, Georgia. Entered Newberry College, in 1874, and graduated at Adger College, in 1878. His first wife was Lou Neville. His second wife was Lizzie Hix. whom he married, in February, 1883. Studied law in the office of the late J. J. Norton, and was admitted to the bar, in January, 1880. Served four years as magistrate. Was attorney for the County Board of Commissioners twelve years; member of the State Democratic Convention three terms. Appointed United States commissioner, by Judge Simonton, in 1890. Trustee of Furman University, in 1899. Joint editor of the "Keowee Courier," a paper published at Walhalla.

SHEPARD, CHARLES UPHAM.—Tea-grower. Was born October 4, 1842, in New Haven, Connecticut. Graduate of Phillips Academy, Andover, Massachusetts, Yale College, University of Gottingen, Germany. Married Ellen Humphrey in 1872. He was professor of chemistry in the Medical College of the State of South Carolina, where he and his father signed diplomas, for over half a century. Chemist to the Board of Agriculture of South Carolina. Special agent for tea culture, United States Department of Agriculture. Specially interested in phosphates, both in field and laboratory.

SHEPPARD, JOHN C.—Near the old star fort, in Edgefield County, South Carolina, on the fifth of July 1850, John C. Sheppard, whose name stands at the head of this sketch, was born. His early education was received at Bethel Academy in Edgefield County. Later attended Furman University,

Greenville. In December, 1870, he left college to enter the office of Butler & Youmans for the purpose of reading law. The following year he was admitted to the bar, in Edgefield. Immediately afterwards the partnership of Butler & Youmans was dissolved, and Mr. Sheppard entered into partnership with Leroy F. Youmans for the practice of law. The firm continued for three years, when Mr. Youmans removed to Columbia, and Mr. Sheppard continued the practice alone until 1875, when he took his brother Orlando into partnership, and this firm continues to practice at Edgefield. In 1876 John C. Sheppard was elected a member of the House of Representatives. In 1877, Judge Wallace, then speaker of the House, was elected circuit judge, and Mr. Sheppard was elected to fill the vacancy thus caused. He was re-elected in 1878, and again chosen speaker. In 1882 he was elected lieutenant-governor of the State, and re-elected in 1884. During that term, Governor Thompson was appointed assistant secretary of the Treasury under President Cleveland, and Mr. Sheppard succeeded to the governorship, filling out the unexpired term of Governor Thompson. At the end of that term, he returned to his law practice in which he is still engaged. Is also president of the bank at Edgefield. On the 23d of May, 1879, Mr. Sheppard was married to Miss Helen Wallace, daughter of Judge W. H. Wallace.

SHEPPARD, ORLANDO.—Has been engaged in the practice of law twenty-five years. Before this time was a farmer. He is a son of James and Louisa Sheppard. Was born on the old family homestead, in Edgefield County, December 6, 1844. Graduated at South Carolina Military Academy, in the class before the surrender. Married Miss Ella, daughter of Colonel B. F. Griffin of Newberry, South Carolina, December 22, 1870. Has been for a number of years moderator of the Edgefield Baptist Association. In December, 1899, was elected grand master of Masons of South Carolina, and was re-elected in December, 1900.

SHERARD, JESSE LOUIS.—Principal of the Laurel Street School of Columbia. Son of D. J. Sherard and Margaret

Woodside. Born in Anderson County, March 28, 1876. Of Scotch-Irish descent. Graduated from the South Carolina College in 1898. Principal of the Winyah Indigo Academy of Georgetown, from 1898 to 1899. Principal of the Prosperity Graded School, from 1899 to 1900. Unmarried.

SHERIDAN, HUGO GROTIUS.—Head master of the Carlisle Fitting School, at Bamberg. Son of Hugo G. and Sarah A. Dantzler Sheridan. Born in Colleton County, South Carolina, April 7, 1862. Was prepared for college by his father. Entered Wofford College, and graduated in 1881. Married Effie E. Dantzler August 11, 1886. Taught in the Sheridan Classical Institute, founded by his father in Orangeburg, until 1890. Founded the Holly Hill Classical Institute in 1890. Remained in charge until 1901.

SHIRLEY, JOHN FLETCHER.—A practicing physician of Honea Path, South Carolina. Was born in that town on August 16, 1861. His education was acquired from the common schools. Graduated in medicine from the Baltimore Medical College in 1883. Married Emma Clinkscales April 30, 1889.

SHIRLEY, JOHN JASPER.—Was born, July 18, 1825, near Honea Path, South Carolina. Had only the advantage of the old field school. Is a farmer. Was railroad agent at Honea Path eighteen years. Organized Company E., Twentieth Regiment, South Carolina Volunteers, and was elected first lieutenant. Remained with this company two years. Then acted as scout around Charleston most of the time.

SHIRLEY, ROBERT M.—Son of John J. and Francis Shirley. Was born March 14, 1858, at Honea Path, South Carolina. He received a good English education from the high schools of his native town. Married Sallie Erwin, daughter of Malcolm and Maggie Erwin, November 13, 1890. He was assistant postmaster and express agent. Served on city council several terms. Past chancellor of Knights of Pythias Lodge. A director of Honea Path Oil Mill. He is now engaged in merchandising and farming.

SHIVER, FRANK SCOTT.—An officer in the association of official agricultural chemists of the United States. Was born in Columbia, South Carolina, March 28, 1871. He attended the Barnwell High School, preparatory to entering the South Carolina College. Took a post-graduate course at the South Carolina College in 1890 and 1891. Married Rebecca Calhoun, of Abbeville County, South Carolina. Assistant instructor in agricultural chemistry in Clemson College.

SHORE, GEORGE D.—Merchant. Son of H. W. Shore and Lavinia E. Boyer. Born January 14, 1862, at Salem, North Carolina. Ancestors were of Swiss descent, and early settlers of western North Carolina. Attended the common and high schools of Salem, and the Moravian Male Academy. Married Miss Charlotte C. Doar, of McClellanville, South Carolina, October 23, 1888. Kept books in Winston and Sumter. In 1890, went into the wholesale brokerage business. Member of the Board of Health of Sumter several years. Alderman one term. Member of the County Board of Control.

SHULER, FREDERICK HAWKINS.—Son of Frederick and Jane E. Jones. Born in Orangeburg, October 3, 1866. His ancestors were German and French, and were among the early settlers of South Carolina. Graduated from Wofford College in 1895. Married Mary Whitmore, of Greenville, South Carolina. Raised on a farm, but traveled in the West several years. Minister and member of the South Carolina Conference.

SIMKINS, LEWIS W.—Was born at Abbeville, South Carolina, January 9, 1854. Attended the Abbeville schools and Willington, Abbeville County. Later spent two years at the Washington and Lee University, Lexington, Virginia. On the 10th of June, 1881, he was married to Miss Mary A. Moorman. He clerked in the office of Moorman & Schumpert Moorman & Simkins. At one time associated with M. L. Bonham as editor of the "Newberry News." Represented Laurens County in the General Assembly for two years. Is now practicing law at Laurens under the firm name of Ball & Simkins. Was mayor of Laurens two years.

SIMKINS, SAMUEL McGOWAN.—Was born December 15, 1858, at Abbeville, South Carolina, under the roof of the late Samuel McGowan who was an uncle by marriage. His mother was Miss Wardlaw, daughter of the late Judge Wardlaw, of Abbeville. His father was Colonel John C. Simkins, of Abbeville, who was killed in a night battle at Battery, July 18, 1863. Attended the Porter Military Academy, Charleston, South Carolina; then went to the University of the South, Sewanee, Tennessee. After leaving school, farmed a few years. Then studied at Newberry, and was admitted to the bar from that county in 1882. Soon after this, he moved to Edgefield, the home of his father and ancestors who located and settled the town of Edgefield. He has been practicing law there since. Made a most creditable race for the Constitutional Convention in 1895, but was defeated, having as his opponents such men as Ex-Governor Sheppard, Congressman Tolbert, Senator Tillman, and Ex-State Treasurer Timmerman. Represented Edgefield County in the Lower House of the General Assembly, sessions of 1897 and 1898. Was the author of the present grand jury law. Married Miss Sara Raven Lewis, of Charleston, South Carolina, February 21, 1887.

SIMMONS, JOHN HARMON.—Clerk of the court of Manning, since 1896. He is a son of Thomas Simmons and Harriet J. (Ridgeway) Simmons. Born August 29, 1863, near Manning, in Clarendon County, South Carolina. Of Irish descent. Education limited, only that of a common school. He has been twice married. His first wife died in 1001. His second wife was Ellen Tobias, whom he married January 9, 1899. Taught school from 1886 to 1890. Was magistrate from 1890 to 1896, at Manning, South Carolina. He is also farming.

SIMMONS, JOSEPH T.—Was born in Laurens County, on the 5th of September, 1850. Educational advantages very limited, only that training which the common schools gave at that time. Married Mrs. Grace Finley, of Nova Scotia, on

November 12, 1877. Now merchandising at Greenwood. Interested in many banking and manufacturing corporations.

SIMMONS, OSCAR B.—Was born in Laurens County, May 4, 1856. At the age of fourteen he moved to Abbeville, South Carolina. Education limited, only that of the country schools. In 1878, he accepted a position as clerk in a store at Hodges, South Carolina. Formed a partnership, in 1883, with M. A. Cason. In 1884, he bought Cason out, and he and his brother formed a partnership. In 1888, moved to Laurens, and opened up a grocery business. In 1889, he built and assumed charge of an Oil Mill at Laurens, soon after he resigned and went into the dry goods business. He is president of the Bank of Laurens. He was married to Miss Clardy of Laurens County, on the 28th of February, 1884.

SIMONS, JAMES.—Son of James and Sarah (Wragg) Simons. Born at Charleston, South Carolina, November 30, 1839. Ancestors were French-Huguenots. Obtained education from private schools of Charleston, the South Carolina College, at Columbia, and then at the University of Leipzig, Germany. Married Miss Elizabeth Potter Schott October 16, 1890. After leaving college, entered Confederate service as first lieutenant of infantry, and at close of the war, was in command of a battery of light artillery. Member of Legislature many years, speaker of the House eight years. President of the State Society of the Cincinnati of the State of South Carolina.

SIMONS, MANNING. — Son of James and Sarah Lowndes Simons. Born May 6, 1846, at Charleston, South Carolina. Obtained education from public schools and Charleston College. Professor of clinical surgery in Medical College of South Carolina. Professor of general surgery, and demonstrator of anatomy in same. President of Southern Surgical and Gynaecological Association. Member of American Medical Association. Surgeon to city hospital, and St. Frances Xavier Infirmary. Local surgeon of Southern Railway, at Charleston. Vice-president of State Medical Association of Virginia and the Carolinas. Not married.

SIMONTON, CHARLES HENRY.—Judge. Born at Charleston, South Carolina, July 11, 1829. Graduated at the Charleston High School, and entered the South Carolina College in 1846. Graduated in 1849, with first honor. Taught school one year. Then studied law, entering the bar in 1857. Married Ella Glover, daughter of the late Judge T. W. Glover, of Orangeburg, in 1852. He was, for many years, speaker of the House of Representatives; chairman of the Judiciary Committee, and a leader in the Legislature. Has been United States district judge; United States circuit judge; chairman of the City Board of School Commissioners in Charleston County; trustee of Charleston College, and of the South Carolina Medical College. He entered the Confederate army, in 1861, as Captain of the Washington Light Infantry. In 1862, was elected colonel of the Twenty-fifth Regiment, which he commanded until the close of the war. He was appointed district judge by President Cleveland, September 6, 1886, and later appointed circuit judge, being a colleague of Judge Nathan Goff.

SIMPSON, RICHARD WRIGHT.—Second son of Richard F.

Simpson and M. Margaret Taliaferro. Born September 11, 1840, near the town of Pendleton, Anderson County, South Carolina. Graduated at Wofford College in 1861. Left college to join Company A, Third South Carolina Regiment, encamped at Columbia. He served in this regiment between one and two years when, on account of ill health, he was discharged. Returned to the army and was a second time discharged. From that time until the close of the war, he served in other departments of the Confederate government. He was educated for the bar, but on account of his ill health after the war, he was forced to remain on the farm. In 1875, however, he was admitted to the bar and has since been actively engaged in the practice of law at Anderson, South Carolina. In 1874, without his solicitation, he was elected a member of the Legislature from Anderson County, and served one term. He took a prominent part in advocating the Straight Out Movement, and was a member of the convention which nominated Governor Hampton. In the campaign of 1876, he was conspicuous in shaping the policy by which the State was redeemed, and was again elected to the Legislature. He was appointed chairman of the Ways and Means Committee. The Radical party had left the State in an almost bankrupt condition, and there were many opinions as to the best course to pursue to obtain relief therefrom. Colonel Simpson devised the plan, and secured its adoption, which reduced the debt of the State to its present small proportions. During his services in the Legislature, recognizing the necessity for an agricultural college to meet the changed condition resulting from the war, he became an earnest advocate of such an institution, and induced many to coincide with his views, which resulted in the founding of Clemson College. He is president of the board of trustees of this college. He has taken all the degrees in A. F. Masonry except the thirty-first, thirty-second and thirty-third. Married Miss Maria Louise Garlington.

SIMPSON, STOBO J.—Senior member of the law firm of Simpson & Bomar. Born at Laurens, South Carolina, March 14, 1853. Son of J. Wistar Simpson, Esquire, and Anne Patillo Farrow. Attended the village schools during boyhood, and prepared for Princeton College at the Laurens Male Academy, then conducted by Colonel John W. Ferguson. In the fall of 1871, he entered the sophomore class of Princeton College. Being unable to return to college, and complete his course, he began teaching at Laurens, South Carolina, in 1873. During the year 1874, he was principal of what was then known as the Clinton High School, and in 1875 he was again elected principal of the Laurens School, and taught there that year. During the spare hours of that year, and in the early part of 1876, he read law, and was admitted to practice at Greenville, South Carolina, at the spring term of 1876. In June, 1876, he settled in Spartanburg, entering into partnership with his uncle, Colonel W. D. Simpson. This partnership continued until 1879, when he entered the firm of Evins & Bomar, the firm then becoming Evins, Bomar & Simpson. This firm continued until the death of Colonel Evins, in 1884. The firm then continued as Bomar & Simpson until the death of Major John Earle Bomar, in 1899. Mr. H. L. Bomar, the youngest son of Major John Earle Bomar, had entered the firm about a year before his father's death, and on his death the firm became Simpson & Bomar. In 1886 Mr. Simpson was elected to the Legislature; served that term; but retired and did not offer for re-election. He was a member of the Judiciary Committee. In 1892 he made the race for the Senate as the representative of the anti-Tillman or Conservative party. In 1895, when delegates were being elected to the Constitutional Convention, factional feeling being still unabated in Spartanburg County, full tickets were put forward by both parties, and Mr. Simpson was again chosen as the representative of his party, and defeated by a strict party vote. May 18, 1886, he married Miss M. Eloise Simpson, daughter of Chief Justice W. D. Simpson. He is an elder in the First Presbyterian Church of Spartanburg; trustee of Converse College, and a director of several business enterprises of Spartanburg.

SIMS, JAMES LOYAL.—Born August 8, 1850, on Mount Ararat plantation on the Cooper River near Charleston, South Carolina. Educated in the graded schools of Charleston, South Carolina. Married Rosa Mouzon of Kingstree, South Carolina. Was married a second time in 1889 to Georgia Sheridan, of Orangeburg, South Carolina. He was connected with the "Charleston Courier" at the time of its consolidation with the "Charleston News." After working on some other journals, he bought an interest in the "Spartanburg Herald," which he sold in a few years. Went to Orange-

burg in 1888, and founded the "Orangeburg Democrat," later
on bought out the "Orangeburg Times," and consolidated
the two papers, making the present "Orangeburg Times and
Democrat," of which he is editor and proprietor. Mr. Sims
has several times represented his county in State Democratic Conventions, but has never held any public office
except commissioner of elections.

SIRRINE, GEORGE WILLIAM.—Son of Captain William
and Emma Sirrine. Was born December 20, 1847, in Monroe, Connecticut. His mother died when he was only five
years old. He came with his father in 1856 to Americus,
Georgia. He was placed under the instruction of Major J. E.
Rylander until his fourteenth year, when his teacher went
to the army and his school days ended. He entered the
Confederate army in the spring of 1864, serving as drummer
and then orderly to the regiment, and in the battles around
Atlanta as private. On the fall of Atlanta he joined Harvey's Scouts, which company was detailed for special duty
under General W. H. Jackson and during Hood's campaign
in Tennessee. Was under General N. B. Forrest, until the
end of the war. After the close of the war he returned to
Americus, Georgia, and went into the carriage business.
Moved to Charlotte, North Carolina, in 1875, and in 1876 accepted the position as superintendent of the Greenville Coach
Factory, which position he still has. He is president of the
Neblett Free Library Association and the Greenville Hospital Association. He married Miss Sarah E., daughter of
Captain Matthew E. Rylander, in October, 1867.

SIRRINE, WILLIAM GEORGE.—Born at Americus, Geor-
gia, December 30, 1870. Son of George W. and Sarah E.
(Rylander). Removed to Greenville in 1876. Attended the
Greenville Military Institute, Furman University, and Uni-
versity of South Carolina. Engaged in newspaper work with
"Greenville News," afterwards with "Philadelphia Times,"
and other papers there, and from 1891 to 1894, with "The
New York Evening Post." Entered the office of Cothran,
Wells, Ansel & Cothran and began to read law in May, 1894.
Admitted to the bar in May, 1895. Raised a company when
the war with Spain was declared, and served ten months

in the Second South Carolina Infantry, in the United States
and Cuba, as captain. Is now a practicing lawyer in Greenville.

SISKRON, JOHN.—President of the Peoples Bank of Darlington, South Carolina. Son of Edward and Caroline Ells
Siskron. Born in New Haven, Connecticut, September 15,
1838. Of English and French descent. High school education obtained at New Haven and other places. He was president of Holkon Bros. Manufacturing Company, of New Haven, Connecticut, several years. In 1873 he came to Darlington and engaged in the manufacture of carriages, wagons,
and furniture for about twenty years. Elected vice-president of the Peoples Bank at its organization, and has since
been elected president of same. Member of the city council
several years, treasurer of the city two years. Director in the
Darlington Manufacturing Company.

SITTON, JOSEPH J.—Was instrumental in organizing the
Pendleton Oil and Fertilizer Company, and was elected secretary and treasurer of same. Was born in Pendleton, South
Carolina, August 21, 1854. His ancestors came from England, and settled in South Carolina. Attended the public
schools, and Newberry College, while located at Walhalla,
taking only a partial course. Was for ten years engaged in
the carriage and hardware business. In 1889 was instrumental in organizing the bank at Pendleton, and accepted
the position as cashier, which position he still holds. Was
elected mayor three or four times, and declined re-election.
Married Miss Sue Hall Gaillard, July 26, 1876.

SLOAN, PAUL H. E.—Son of B. F. Sloan, of Anderson County. Was born in Franklin County, Georgia. His
literary education was obtained from the Citadel, Charleston,
South Carolina. He then took the medical course at the
Medical College of South Carolina. He was appointed assistant surgeon in the Confederate Army, and served as such
until the close of the war. From 1890 to 1901 he was secretary and treasurer of Clemson College. Was married in
April, 1863, to Miss E. V. Maxwell, daughter of Dr. Robert

Maxwell. Entered Fourth Regiment and served until close of Civil War.

SLOAN, PAUL HAMILTON EARLE.—Son of Dr. P. H. E. and Eloise Vernon Sloan. Was born February 9, 1866, at Pendleton, South Carolina. He was educated in the common schools of Pendleton, and at the Charleston High School. He married Miss Susie J., daughter of Colonel R. W. Simpson. He was made a master mason in 1887, served as junior warden in 1888 and 1889; elected secretary in 1890, and served in that capacity until 1898, then elected worshipful master and is now serving his third term. He has been reporter of Knights of Honor since 1892. Is engaged in the drug business with his father since 1883.

SMITH, AUGUSTUS WARDLAW.—Born at Abbeville, South Carolina, April 29, 1862. Educated in the common schools of the neighborhood, at the University of the South, at Sewanee, also at the South Carolina College. He assisted in the organization of the Woodruff Cotton Mill, and was elected president and treasurer of same. He also founded the Woodruff Bank, and is now president of that also. Married Miss Mary Bratton Noble, of Abbeville, South Carolina.

SMITH, CHARLES BETTS.—Pastor of the Methodist Church in Bennettsville, South Carolina. Son of William H. and Mary I. (McLeod) Smith. Born October 14, 1858, in Lynchburg, Sumter County, South Carolina. Educated in the common schools of the community, and completed the junior year at Wofford College. Married Mary E. Moore, of St. George, South Carolina, December 22, 1885. In December, 1882, he joined the Conference of the Methodist Church. Has been stationed at Columbia, Bamberg, Anderson, Orangeburg, and Darlington. In 1895, he was elected professor of psychology and economics in Wofford College; held this position four years.

SMITH, DRESDEN AARON.—Son of Whitaker Guyton Smith and Mariah E. Lewis. Elected without opposition probate judge of Oconee County in 1898. Was born in Anderson County, South Carolina, near Pendleton, on February 3,

1842. His education was acquired principally under the instruction of his father. A member of the South Carolina Methodist Conference several years. A trustee of the Grand Lodge Knights of Honor two terms; senior warden and treasurer of Blue Ridge Number 9 A. F. M., of Walhalla, South Carolina. He has been connected with the newspaper business since 1858, and is now connected with the "Keowee Courier," Walhalla, South Carolina. Married Miss Kathleen Small, of Abbeville, South Carolina, January 15, 1879.

SMITH, JEHPTHA P.—President and treasurer of Liberty Cotton Mills. Was born April 1, 1853, in Anderson County, South Carolina. His primary education was received in the common schools, and later he attended Thalian Academy, a high school under the management of Rev. J. L. Kennedy. Principal of an academy at Equality, Anderson County, four years. Secretary of State fertilizer department, from 1891 to 1901, at Clemson College. Resigned this position in 1901 to accept the position he now has. Married Carrie Glenn, daughter of F. M. Glenn, of Anderson County.

SMITH, JEREMIAH.—Son of Daniel and Celia Smith. Of English descent. Born August 11, 1840, in Horry County, South Carolina. His educational advantages were limited, he only being able to attend school two sessions of nine months each. Has been thrice married. His present wife was Miss Lizzie J. Caldwell, of Newberry County. Farmed until 1896, when he began the hotel business at Conway. Trial justice of Horry County from 1874 to 1880. Then elected to the House of Representatives, re-elected in 1882. Served in the Senate from 1884 to 1888. Member of the Constitutional Convention of 1895. In 1898 was again elected to the House of Representatives. Entered the Confederate service in 1867 as second-lieutenant. He was at home on a sick furlough when his battalion was re-organized, thereby losing his commission. He then joined Tucker's Cavalry, Wallace's Company, which was subsequently attached to the Seventh South Carolina Cavalry, Gary's Brigade, and was appointed second-sergeant. Wounded at Ridley's shop, near Richmond, Virginia. In 1863 he was again given a furlough.

Recovered and returned to active service in the retreat from Richmond, surrendered, and was paroled at Appomattox.

SMITH, JOHN ROBERT.—Son of Joel F. Smith, merchant and farmer, and Lelitice Hill Jones, daughter of General A. C. Jones. Born at Brewerton, Laurens County, South Carolina, July 20, 1843. He was educated at the neighborhood schools, and at Andrews Chapel Academy, in Abbeville County, where he was prepared for college. Entered the freshman class at Erskine College, 1859. In August of 1861, a boy of seventeen, he volunteered in Company C, Fourteenth Regiment South Carolina Volunteers. He was with his company in the several engagements in which they took part. Was wounded in both legs at Gettysburg, losing his right leg. Left upon the field, he fell into the hands of the enemy, and was sent a prisoner to Davids Island, and Fort Delaware, until 1864, when he was exchanged. Returning home, he commenced the study of medicine, graduating from the South Carolina Medical College in 1867. He was married to Miss Mary Cowan Smith, on December 15, 1870. Was president of the Laurens County Medical Society. Was a member of the Democratic Convention, 1876, that nominated Hampton for governor and W. D. Simpson for lieutenant-governor. Again represented his county in the Democratic Convention of 1878 and 1882. In 1895 he represented his county in the House of Representatives, the first Legislature held under the new constitution of 1895.

SMITH, ROBERT ATMAR.—A prominent dentist of Charleston, South Carolina. He is a son of William Bell Smith and Sarah Rogers Atmar. Born January 12, 1852, at Charleston, South Carolina. He is a descendant of Solomon Logan. He was prepared for college by Dr. Henry M. Bruns. Entered the sophomore class of the Charleston College; graduated March, 1843, with A. B. degree. He afterwards completed the course at the Philadelphia Dental College, with degree of D. D. S. Married Miss Mary E. Capers, December 19, 1882. After college work, began the practice of dentistry; January 15, 1902, will end twenty-five years in present office. He has attained all honors conferred by subordinate lodges or councils in the orders of Masonry, Knights of Pythias, and Junior Order United American Mechanics. Has been president in both the Charleston and South Carolina Dental Associations, and has held the position of recording secretary in the latter for many years. He is at present president of the R. Atmar Smith Dental Supply Co, King Street, Charleston, South Carolina.

SMITH, RUFUS FRANKLIN.—A practicing physician at Easley, South Carolina. Son of J. M. Smith. Was born August 17, 1858, at Slabtown, Anderson County, South Carolina. Attended Adger College at Walhalla, and graduated from the medical department of the University of Virginia, in 1881. Took post-graduate courses at Jefferson Medical College of Philadelphia, and the University of the City of New York. Married Miss Ida Hollingsworth, daughter of Colonel C. L. Hollingsworth, of Pickens, in 1888. He taught a public school for a few years after graduation. Moved to Gainesville, Georgia, where he practiced medicine, and was assistant surgeon of the Southern Railroad. He is now running a drug store in Easley in connection with his practice. Was a member of the Constitutional Convention of 1895.

SMITH, WATTIE GAILLARD.—President and treasurer of  the Enterprise Cotton Mill, of Orangeburg. Son of Henry J. Smith and Sallie E. Cobb. Born May 9, 1861, at Williamston, Anderson County, South Carolina. Of Scotch-Irish descent. Attended the common schools of Barnwell County, the Marietta Street Grammar School of Atlanta, and Wofford College. Married Mary A. Begg, in 1885. On October 19, 1898, married Lucia C. Weatherbee. After leaving college, he entered into the employ of the Clifton Manufacturing Company, and remained twelve years. After which was elected president and treasurer of the Bamberg Cotton Mills, where he remained eight years. He then bought the Enterprise Cotton Mill of Orangeburg, and organized a company of which he was elected president and treasurer. Director of the Edisto Savings Bank of Orangeburg. For a few years he was vice-president of the Orangeburg Knitting Mill, secretary and treasurer of the Young Men's Business League of Orangeburg. First-lieutenant in the Morgan Rifles of Spartanburg. Has been a member of several State conventions.

SMITH, WILLIAM CHESLEY.—Son of J. M. and Hester A. Smith (nee Watkins). His ancestors were of Scotch-Irish and Welsh descent, and settled in Anderson County about 1828. His father was a large farmer and merchant at Slabtown, Anderson County, South Carolina, for over fifty years. Was born January 8, 1862, at Slabtown, South Carolina. Was educated at Davidson College, North Carolina, In 1889, he bought out his father's interest in the mercantile business and continued under the firm name of W. C. Smith. Then closed out this business and accepted the position of cashier in the Easley Bank at its organization in 1891. Married Miss Mary Lee, daughter of Captain George A. Rankin, of Anderson County, November 20, 1883. He is a director of the Easley Bank, and the Easley Cotton Mill, president of the Easley Oil Mill Company and secretary and treasurer of the Easley Roller Mill Company.

SMYTH, JAMES ADGER.—Eldest son of Rev. Thomas Smyth, D. D., for over forty years pastor of Second Presbyterian Church of Charleston, South Carolina. Born in that city in 1838. Attended the high school of Charleston and graduated from Charleston College with first honor in March, 1858. Married Miss Annie R. Briggs, March 14, 1860. Alderman of Charleston sixteen years. Mayor of Charleston two, terms of four years each. President of Cotton Exchange five years. Enlisted in Confederate Army in April, 1862; and served until April, 1865. Grand master of Masons of South Carolina three years. Grand high priest of Royal Arch Masons three years. Master of Union Kilwing Lodge

26

high priest of Union Chapter. Has taken thirty-two degrees in Scottish Masonry and is a Knight Templar. Is elder in Presbyterian Church.

SMYTH, ROBERT ADGER.—Member of the firm of Adger & Smith, cotton merchants and brokers, of Charleston, South Carolina; also member of the New York and Charleston Cotton Exchanges. He was born July 25, 1871, at Charleston, South Carolina. He is a son of J. Adger Smyth, and grandson of Rev. Thomas Smyth, D. D. Attended the public schools of Charleston, and the South Carolina Military Academy. Elected commander of the United Sons of Confederate Veterans upon organization at Richmond, Virginia, 1896. Elected commander of the Northern Virginia department, second to command in chief. Unanimously elected commander-in-chief in 1897 at Nashville, Tennessee, and re-elected in Atlanta, Georgia, reunion, in 1898. Re-elected at Charleston, South Carolina, in 1899 for third term, but declined to serve, believing that some one else should take a turn at the work. Elected grand treasurer of Phi Kappa Alpha Fraternity, a purely Southern college order, in 1899. Has been filling the place since. Is also editor-in-chief of the "Shield and Diamond," the official magazine of that order. Deacon in the Second Presbyterian Church, and member of the standing committee.

SMYTHE, AUGUSTINE THOMAS.—Lawyer. Was born in Charleston, South Carolina, October 5, 1842. Son of Thomas and Margaret M. (Adger) Smythe. His father, a native of Ireland, was for forty years pastor of the Second Presbyterian Church of Charleston. His mother was a daughter of James Adger, a prominent merchant of the same city. He was educated at the schools of Charleston, and at the South Carolina College, Columbia, South Carolina, where he remained until the outbreak of the Civil War. On April 10, 1861, he entered the service of his State as a private of the South Carolina College cadets, and about one year later was mustered into the Confederate army as a member of Company A. of the Twenty-fifth South Carolina Volunteers. He continued in the service until the close of the war, at which time he was a member of Logan's Brigade, Butler's Division, Confederate cavalry. On the return of peace, he began the study of law in the office of Simonton & Barker, of Charleston. After his admission to the bar, in 1866, entered upon a successful and constantly increasing practice. During his professional career, he has been connected with the firms of Smythe, Bruns & Lee, Smythe & Lee, and Smythe, Lee & Frost, and at the present time is a member of the latter firm. He has always been interested in politics, but never consented to accept nomination for public office until 1880, when he was elected to the State Senate. After continuous service of over fourteen years, he resigned, and returned to private life. Mr. Smythe has been prominent as a Mason, and has held such high offices as master of the Lodge, high priest of the Chapter, eminent commander of the Commandery, grand master of the Grand Lodge, and grand high priest of the Grand Chapter of South Carolina. In the Scottish Rite he has taken all the degrees up to and including the Thirty-second. He is a member of several other organizations, civil and military, and has been active in every enterprise for the benefit of his city. In 1865, he was married to Louisa R., daughter of Colonel D. J. McCord, of Columbia, South Carolina.

SMYTHE, ELLISON ADGER.—Son of Rev. Thomas Smythe, D. D., and grandson of James Adger. Born in Charleston, South Carolina, October 26, 1847. Educated in the private schools of Charleston. Joined the Confederate States army in 1864. Appointed a cadet to the South Carolina Military Academy, and was with them at the close of the war. Married Miss Julia Gambrill, of Baltimore. A member of the Charleston Board of Health, during Mayor Courtney's administration. Appointed by president McKinley, a member of the United States Industrial Commission. Captain of the Washington

Artillery Rifle Club, in Charleston, in 1876, and for a year before and four years later. Captain of the Greenville Guards of Greenville, South Carolina, in 1892 and 1895. President of the Pelzer and Belton Manufacturing Companies, Moneyrick Oil Mill, Dexter Broom and Mattress Company, and the Chicora Savings Bank. Director and vice-president of about ten cotton mills, eight banks, three insurance companies, and also vice-president of the National Manufacturers' Association.

SPAHR, HERMAN L.—Born December 18, 1875, at Macon, Georgia. Moved to Orangeburg, South Carolina, in 1880. Received his early education at the Mellichamp High School, and the Sheridan Classical School. Entered the South Carolina College in 1891 and graduated in 1895. He immediately thereafter went to Germany, where he studied at the University of Heidelberg. On his return he was elected instructor in modern languages, and later in mathematics, at the Orangeburg Institute. He resigned at the breaking out of the Spanish War to enter the army with his company, the Edisto Rifles, Company C, Second South Carolina Volunteer Infantry. He was elected first-sergeant, but soon promoted to second-lieutenant. After serving in Savannah, Cuba, and Havana, he was mustered out in Savannah. He is now professor of modern languages in the South Carolina College. Took a special course at Amherst, Massachusetts, in summer of 1900; and at the University of Chicago, in 1901.

SPARKMAN, EDWARD HERIOT.—Was born on Birnfield plantation, in Georgetown County, South Carolina, March 5, 1846. Eldest son of James R. Sparkman, M. D., who practiced his profession for over sixty years, and died in the eighty-third year of his age. His educational advantages were very limited, owing to the fact that before he was sixteen, in January, 1862, he entered the Confederate service. Enlisted for the war as a private in Pickens Cavalry which in 1864, formed Company A. of the Seventh South Carolina Cavalry, under Colonel A. C. Haskell, Gary's Brigade. Captured at Willis Church, Virginia, August 14, 1864. Was sent as a prisoner of war to Point Lookout, and there confined until April, 1865, when he was exchanged and liberated on parole. In November 1866, he left his native town, and went to Charleston seeking employment there. Was the guest of his father's life-long friend, Colonel D. L. McKay, president of the Peoples National Bank, who allowed him to make himself useful about the bank without pay until he could do better. There being no banks in Charleston at the time, the business increased very rapidly, requiring a large force to handle it, and it was not long before the lowest position in the bank was open to him at a salary of twenty-five dollars per month. He being attentive to duty was soon rewarded by being given the position as bookkeeper, which he held until 1880. Was then given the position as cashier, which he still holds. He is also cashier of the Savings Bank and a director in both institutions. Married December 19, 1878, Eliza Augusta Kirk.

SPARKMAN, JAMES R.—Engaged in general insurance business at Georgetown, South Carolina. He is a son of James R. Sparkman, M. D., and Mary Elizabeth Herriot. Born at Georgetown, South Carolina, September 2, 1847. Of Scotch and German descent. Attended private schools of Charleston, and Military Academy at Hillsboro, North Carolina. He left college to enter the Confederate army at age of seventeen. Served with the Marion Artillery of Charleston, and surrendered with them at Greensboro, North Carolina, May 7, 1865. He is a large rice planter. Attended all the County and State conventions held in recent years, and is prominently identified with the political movements of the State. Commander of State Cavalry at Georgetown, South Carolina, being a full colonel.

SPARKMAN, WILLIAM ERVIN.—Born at Plantersville, Georgetown County, South Carolina, June 11, 1857. Graduated from Holy Communion Institute, Charleston, in 1875, and completed the course in medicine at University of Maryland, Baltimore. Married Hattie McGilvery, daughter of

Honorable W. L. Buck, of Horry, in 1881. Member of South Carolina Medical Association. Chairman of Board of Health, Georgetown, South Carolina. Commander of Camp Arthur Manigault Sons of Confederate Veterans. Practicing physician at Georgetown, South Carolina.

SPEARS, JAMES MONROE.—Son of Jacob Spears. Born at Lamar, South Carolina, February 15, 1874. Had only the advantage of the country schools. Married Miss Agnes Moore December 2, 1892. Elected intendant of the town of Lamar at the age of nineteen, receiving more than twice as many votes as his three competitors combined. Magistrate at Darlington two years. Member of the Legislature. Admitted to the bar in May, 1898. At present senior member of the law firm of Spears & Dennis, Darlington, South Carolina.

SPEEGLE, JAMES ELLIS.—County supervisor of Greenville County. Was born in Burke County, North Carolina, February 16, 1859. Educational advantages were not of the best, but having good common sense, has made good use of what he had. He was married to Miss Susan Cooksey on April 4, 1890.

SPENCER, ALMON EDWIN.—President and professor of Greek of the Presbyterian College of South Carolina. Born in Tuskegee, Alabama, December 14, 1867. Graduated with the A. B. degree, from Central University, Richmond, Kentucky in 1888; and took Master of Arts degree the summer of 1897. Took a business course, and graduated in bookkeeping and stenography from the commercial department of the University of Kentucky, Lexington. Married Mattie Estell Calvert on December 30, 1891. Has made teaching his life work.

SPRATT, JOHN McKEE.—Director of the Fort Mill Manufacturing Company and vice-president of the Savings Bank. Is a son of the late Thomas D. Spratt, and a great-grandson

of Thomas Spratt, "Old Kanawha," the first settler of the
Fort Mill section. He was born in Fort Mill Township, near
the Old Spratt homestead, April 28, 1849. Spent his boyhood and early manhood on his father's farm. Though not
yet sixteen years of age, he was just preparing to enter
the Confederate service, when he received the news of Lee's
surrender. The next few years he devoted to farming. In
1871, on account of the indiscriminate manner in which the
United States government was arresting certain citizens of
the Fort Mill neighborhood, left the State and went to Florida. Remaining there only a short time, however, he went
to west Tennessee, and engaged in teaching school. Returned to Fort Mill in 1873, and again engaged in farming.
Shortly afterward he became interested in a general merchandising business; and, in 1879, took charge of the railroad
and telegraph offices at Fort Mill. In connection with his
duties in this position, he built up a profitable business in
lumber, cotton-seed and fertilizers. When the question of
building a cotton mill at Fort Mill, in 1887, was agitated,
Mr. Spratt took an active interest in the project, and it was
largely through his efforts that the enterprise was carried
to a successful completion. He was married in 1876 to Miss
Sue E. Massey, a daughter of the Honorable B. H. Massey.

SPRINGS, LEROY.—Born on November 12, 1861, at Springfield, near Fort Mill, South Carolina. Was prepared for college at Charlotte, North Carolina, and attended the University of North Carolina, entering the sophomore class at the
age of seventeen. Left at the end of the junior year, to
engage in the mercantile business. He married Miss Grace
Allison White, of Fort Mill, South Carolina, on December
28, 1892. He is president of the following corporations: Bank
of Lancaster; Lancaster Cotton Mill; Eureka Cotton Mill.
Chester, South Carolina; of the Lancaster and Chester Railroad Company, Heath Springs Company, Camden, South
Carolina; Columbia Compress Company, Columbia, South
South Carolina. Is general manager of the Fort Mill Manufacturing Company. Fort Mill, South Carolina. Was one of

the organizers of the Heath Springs Company, and the head
of that company until it was dissolved, being succeeded by
the Lancaster Mercantile Company, of which he is vice-president. Is also senior member of the firm of Springs & Shannon, Camden, South Carolina. Was colonel on Governor
Richardson's staff for four years; was chosen as delegate
from his district to the National Convention in 1898, and was
placed on committee to notify Mr. Cleveland of his nomination. Was a director for five years of the Charlotte, Columbia and Augusta Railroad until its   reorganization into the
Southern System.

SQUIER, WILLIAM HENRY.—Auditor of Richland County.
Son of A. C. Squier and Emeline Britton. Born in Columbia,
South Carolina, June 15, 1848. His early education was very
good, though the Civil War interfered with the completion
of it. Married Margaret Grace Kennedy January 15, 1874.
Clerked until July, 1863. Entered the army with the Eighteenth Texas Regiment at the age of fifteen. Was wounded
February 19, 1865. Clerked until 1897 when he was elected
to the position he now holds.

STACKHOUSE, JAMES.—Son of Colonel E. F. and Anne

Fore Stackhouse. Born the 17th of
January, 1849, near Marion, South Carolina. Ancestors were of Scotch and
French descent and among the earlier
settlers of Marion County. Attended
the common schols and took a partial
course at the South Carolina Military
Academy, leaving to enter the army.
Married Florence E. McAllester, June
8, 1871. He was mayor of Marion several years. Represents Marion County in the State Senate by more than
three-fourths of vote of entire county.
He is also a dealer in agricultural supplies.

STACKHOUSE, ROBERT EDGAR.—Son of H. M. Stackhouse, for many years State Senator from Marlboro County.

R. E. Stackhouse was born in Marion, South Carolina, October 21, 1866. His early training was had in the country schools of the neighborhood. Graduated from the State Normal College of the University of Nashville. He married Miss Annie P. Green, of Greenwood, South Carolina, December 6, 1891. After graduation taught in the Montgomery Bell High School, of Nashville, Tennessee, until admitted into the ministry of the South Carolina Conference, in December, 1888. Has supplied numerous churches since. Filled the chair of natural science in the Columbia Female College two sessions. He is now on the Pendleton Circuit and preaching at Clemson College.

STACKHOUSE, THOMAS BASCOM.—Born November 23, 1857, near Little Rock, Marion County, South Carolina. Family, on both father and mother's side, were early settlers of the county of Marion. Was prepared for college at the Little Rock Academy; entered Wofford College, October, 1877; graduated June, 1880. Taught for two years, in Marlboro County, and at Little Rock, South Carolina. Merchandised at Little Rock, South Carolina, from 1881 to 1886. In 1892, was appointed deputy collector of internal revenue for the district of South Carolina. He is cashier of the bank at Dillon, South Carolina, and president of the Dillon Cotton Mills. Married Lizzie M. Hamer October, 1885.

STEADMAN, JOHN MARCELLUS. — Pastor of Methodist Church in Lancaster, South Carolina. Member of conference board of missions. Born in Lexington County, South Carolina, May 15, 1866. Educated at Leesville College, under the presidency of Rev. J. E. Watson. He has supplied churches in Newberry, Parksvile, Greenwood, Lancaster, Charleston, and Yorkville. Married Miss Lizzie K., daughter of Dr. J. C. W. Kinnerly, November 27, 1887. Served on Conference committee of examination, and four years on Conference board of education.

STECK, J. A.—Son of Rev. J. Steck. Born in Tiffin, Ohio, November 3, 1875. His parents removed to South Carolina when he was only six years old. He entered as an apprentice in the office of the "Keowee Courier," Walhalla, South Carolina, at the age of thirteen; served four years. Worked as journeyman on the "News and Courier," Charleston, South Carolina, two years; with C. A. Calvo, Columbia, South Carolina, one year; and as job printer and stationer at Walhalla, South Carolina, two years. Entered as junior member of firm of Jaynes, Shelor Smith & Steck, Walhalla, on April 1, 1898. Is still a member of this firm, the editors and publishers of the "Keowee Courier."

STEPHENSON, WILLIAM GRIFFITH.—Superintendent of King's Mt. Military Academy. Son of Rev. James Edwin Stephenson and Mary Annie (Griffith) Stephenson. Born December 9, 1871, in Southampton County, Virginia. His early childhood was spent on a farm owned by his grandfather. Attended the common schools of Virginia, and four years at William and Mary College. Principal of Orange Graded School, Orange, Virginia, 1891 and 1894. Took post-graduate course from William and Mary College in 1894, and a post-graduate course at University of Chicago in 1899. Married Miss Caroline Bennett, of Craigsville, Virginia, on July 7, 1899. Professor of pedagogy in William and Mary College; professor of English and history in Missouri Military Academy; and also principal of New London Academy, Bedford Springs, Virginia.

STEPPE, JOHN BROADUS.—Physician and farmer. Born July 7, 1862, at Flat Rock, Greenville County, South Carolina. Entered the Greenville Military Institute in 1879, finishing in 1882. Graduated from the Atlanta Medical College in 1887, taking the prize offered to the class in surgery. Began practicing in Atlanta, but on account of ill health, he gave up this work in 1889. Married Rosa Lee Switzer December 18, 1889. Located at Switzer, South Carolina, and began farming on an extensive scale.

STEVENS, PIERCE CANSAS.—Engaged in the mercantile business at Johnstons for the past three years, with Alvin Ethridge, wholesale and retail. He is a son of Elisha and Sarah (Saddler) Stevens. Born September 28, 1860, at Eulala, South Carolina. Of English and Irish descent. Has a common English education. Married Miss Lucy, daughter of Charles Carson, January 30, 1889. In early manhood was engaged in farming and milling in this section. Appointed by the Constitutional Convention of 1895 one of the commissioners to lay off the county of Saluda.

STEVENSON, WILLIAM FRANCIS.—Was born in Iredell

County, North Carolina, November 23, 1861. Attended the public schools in winter, and worked on the farm in summer. Was prepared for college in the academy at Taylorsville, North Carolina, and graduated from Davidson in June, 1885. On November 13, 1888, he married Miss Mary E., daughter of General W. L. T. Prince. He was mayor of Chesterfield while living there, mayor of Cheraw; member of House of Representatives; chairman of committee to investigate penitentiary; speaker of House of Representatives; president of Merchants & Farmers Bank; also of Chesterfield and Lancaster Railroad and the Chesterfield County Oil Company. He has twice been a member of the Presbyterian General Assembly; moderator of Synod of South Carolina, the only layman to occupy that position up to the present time. He was a director of the Seaboard Air Line; was president of the Democratic State Convention, in 1900.

STEWART, EUGENE MARCELLUS.—He is supplying a group of Presbyterian churches in Edgefield County.

making his home at Edgefield Court-house. He was born August 22, 1871, in Hinds County, Mississippi, near Edwards. Afterwards moved to Crystal Springs, in Capiah County. Took the full course at the French Camp Academy, Mississippi, and after some providential hindrances was able to spend three years in Southwestern Presbyterian University, Clarksville, Tennessee. In 1897, entered the Home Mission Work, Daphne, Baldwin County, Alabama. After one year there went to Mobile, Alabama, and supplied the Broad Street Presbyterian Church one year. Then went to Columbia, South Carolina, to take a course in the Theological Seminary.

STEWART, JAMES M.—Was born in Pickens County, South Carolina, May 16, 1839. Educated in the common and high schools of Pickens, South Carolina. He was twice married, his second wife being Miss Bessie Hamilton, whom he married on February 23, 1898. Served in the Confederate War as captain and major. Ordained to the Baptist ministry in 1880. Served as a missionary under the State Board of Baptist State Convention, in Pickens and Oconee Counties, and Transylvania and Judson Counties, North Carolina. Served twelve years as clerk of the court of Pickens County.

STOKES, J. WILLIAM.—Was brought up on a farm. Attended the ordinary schools of his county and town until nineteen years of age. Graduated from Washington and Lee University in 1876. Taught school for twelve years, in the meantime studied medicine, and graduated from Vanderbilt University, Nashville, Tennessee. In 1889, he returned to the farm, assisted in the organization of the Farmers Alliance, and was president of the State Farmers Alliance two terms. Elected to the State Senate in 1890. Was a delegate to the National Democratic Convention in Chicago, and was presidential elector on the same ticket the same year. Was a member of Congress for three consecutive terms.

STOPPELBEIN, JOSEPH LEE.—Editor of "The Truth," a weekly paper published at Spartanburg, South Carolina. Born at Summerville, South Carolina, July 29, 1864. Educated in the city schools of Charleston. At the age of twelve years, entered business at the bottom round of the ladder as an office boy. From his earliest boyhood his ambition was to become a lawyer. He steadily rose in commercial life, filling every position in the counting house. Was admitted to the bar, and entered upon the practice. He was made master in equity for Berkeley County. Was largely instrumental in the formation of Dorchester County, framed the bill and went before the assembly in its interest. Upon the formation of the county, he was elected probate judge, which office he resigned to move to Spartanburg. Entered the military service of his State as a private in 1888; elected sergeant, then elected lieutenant, and afterwards appointed brigade adjutant with the rank of major. Subsequently he was unanimously elected by the Third Regiment as its colonel, and in the reorganization of the State troops in 1895, being the ranking colonel, he was promoted by the Governor to brigadier-general, in command of the largest brigade of cavalry in the United States. He is the ranking military officer in South Carolina. In 1899, he came to Spartanburg and entered journalism. He is now editor of "The Truth" and president of The Truth Publishing Company. Is serving his second term as first vice-president of the South Carolina State Press Association. He is a member of the Knights of Pythias, D. O. K. K., Knights of Honor, W. O. W., a Craftsman, a Red Man, and is a Mason of the first degree.

STRAIT, T. J.—Was born in Chester, South Carolina, December 25, 1846. Being only fifteen years of age at the time the Civil War commenced, he enlisted in Company A, Sixth South Carolina Regiment, among the first. He was transferred to Company H, Twenty-fourth South Carolina Regiment in 1863. Appointed third sergeant, and was mustered out at the close of the war with that rank. He married Miss Kate A. Lathrop of Abbeville County, South Caarolina, in 1869. In 1871, went to Mississippi and entered the Cooper Institute in Lauderdale County. After completing a three years' course he returned to Chester County, began teaching school, and continued until 1876. Afterward, he went to Ebenezer, York County, and remained in charge of that school until 1879, when he removed to Lancaster, and taught until 1881. In 1883, he entered the South Carolina Medical College and was graduated in 1885. In the fall of 1890 he was elected to the State Senate; in the fall of 1890 to Congress, succeeding John J. Hemphill. He served in Congress ten years, and was succeeded by D. E. Finley.

STRIBLING, JAMES PAUL.—Son of W. W. and Emily R. (Dendy) Stribling. Was born in Oconee County, South Carolina, July 9, 1862. He spent three terms at Adger College and then entered the North Georgia Agricultural College, where he graduated at the head of his class in 1886. He married Miss Bessie May Conger, of Athens, Georgia, on December 10, 1901. After graduation, he taught for a time in country schools, and went into farming and stock raising. Success crowned his efforts and soon he ranked as one of the leading farmers of the up-country. He is intimately associated with several of the leading enterprises of his County.

STRIBLING, JESSE WALES.—Cashier of the Bank of Seneca. Was born in Seneca, Oconee County, April 28, 1838. Spent several years in the common and high schools, taught by Rev. J. L. Kennedy, at Equality, South Carolina. Married first Miss Sarah E. Shelor. His second wife was Mrs. Sarah C. Cherry, nee Creswell, whom he married September 18, 1889. He served four years in the Confederate War. When Pickens District was divided into Oconee County, he was elected first clerk of the court for Oconee County, and continued in office sixteen years consecutively. He organized Seneca Bank in 1885, and was elected cashier of same.

He has filled the position of intendant of the towns of Walhalla and Seneca several terms. Was president board of trustees of Walhalla Female College. Trustee of Adger College, Walhalla, South Carolina, and also of Furman University, Greenville, South Carolina.

STROTHER, WILLIAM A.—Was born in Edgefield County, South Carolina, February 14, 1845. His father was George J. Strother. Born in Edgefield County, in 1815. Was a direct descendant of William Strother, who emigrated from England to Virginia before the Revolution. Closely related to General William Strother of the War of 1812, and founder of the once noted Mount Zion Institute, of Winnsboro. On account of the war between the States which he entered from school, only received such educational advantages as could be obtained from the common schools. Served during the Civil War in South Carolina Heavy Artillery, which defended Charleston during the entire war. Married Hassie M. Mickler, daughter of Captain J. P. Mickler, in 1871. After the war, moved to West Union, in Oconee County. Engaged in merchandising. Interested in manufactures. Captain of a company of Red Shirts during the Hampton campaign.

STUCKEY, ALBERT BROOKS.—Lawyer. Son of Captain J. W. and Elizabeth Reames. Born at Bishopville, South Carolina, November 8, 1858. Of Scotch-Irish descent. Attended the academies of Reidville and Bishopville, and graduated from Wofford College, with degree of B. S. Married Leila C., daughter of William K. Dickson, of Bishopville, South Carolina, December 24, 1879. Taught school at Bishopville and Darlington. Farmed from 1875 to 1885. Read law in the office of R. W. Boyd, at Darlington. Admitted to the bar in December, 1885. Practiced at Bennettsville until 1886. In 1887, moved to Sumter, and has since been practicing law there. Appointed trial justice in 1888, and served several years, afterwards auditor of the county. Elected mayor of Sumter in May, 1900, which position he still holds. Director of the Peoples Building and Loan Association.

STURKIE, TYRONE C.—Son of C. R. Sturkie, of Lexington. Was born in that town on February 7, 1878. Earlier training was received from common schools, and later entered the Orangeburg College. Read law under Ex-Judge James F. Izler, of Orangeburg, South Carolina. Admitted to the bar in the spring of 1899, and has practiced law at Lexington since.

SULLIVAN, JAMES MATTISON.—Was born in Anderson County, September 8, 1855. His early training was received under the instruction of Professor W. J. Ligon. Graduated from Davidson College, North Carolina. He has been an alderman of Anderson, city assessor, was a delegate to the Constitutional Convention of 1895, member of the House of Representatives in 1897 and 1898, and since then has been senator from Anderson County. He is a school trustee; president of Anderson Board of Trade; director of the Bank of Anderson, Anderson Light Water & Power Company and the Anderson Fertilizer Company. He is interested in various other local enterprises; was influential in establishing the present system of public schools. He married Miss Mary A. Wannamaker, of Orangeburg, on the 16th of May, 1877.

SULLIVAN, PAUL WARREN.—Son of Dr. James M. and Elizabeth Sullivan. Was born November 5, 1861, in Greenville County, South Carolina. His early training was acquired in Williamston. Later attended the Patrick Military Institute, at Greenville. Married Ena Agnew on December 11, 1882. He was engaged in farming and merchandising, but is now cashier of the Citizens Bank at Honea Path, South Carolina.

SUMNER, CHARLES EDWARD.—Son of George W. and Martha D. Sumner. Was born November 18, 1858, near Little Mountain, South Carolina. By close attention, obtained a thorough education from the common schools of Lexington County. He was married to Leonora C. Sease, January 2, 1879, who died August 20, 1884. Again married a younger sister, Mary Jane Sease, January 3, 1886. In 1888, he moved to Newberry. Has been elected on city council; served two terms. Is now commissioner of public works for town of Newberry; vice-president, secretary and treasurer of the Newberry Warehouse Company, vice-president and director of the Handle & Shuttle Company; director of Newberry Knitting Mill, also of Land & Security Company, and a member of the business firm of Summer Bros., Newberry, South Carolina.

SUMNER, GEORGE WALTER.—Son of George W. and Martha D. Sumner. Born July 15, 1861, near Little Mountain, Lexington County, South Carolina. He had only the advantage of the common schools of the neighborhood. Married Polly Lavinia Long, of Newberry County, October 13, 1881. He moved to Newberry in November, 1884. He is identified with several enterprises in Newberry. President of the Newberry Warehouse Company; director in Newberry Cotton-seed Oil Mill, the Commercial Bank of Newberry; and is a member of the large business firm of Sumner Bros., Newberry, South Carolina.

SWANDALE, GEORGE TUPPER.—Has been engaged in practicing medicine in Greenville twenty-three years, with the exception of one year spent in a hospital in New York. Was born July 17, 1855, at Greenville, South Carolina. His ancestors were of English and German descent. His literary schooling was acquired from the Kings Mountain School. Graduated from Bellevue Medical College, New York, March 1, 1878. On the 2d of October of that year he was married to Miss Fannie E. Keels. He is a member of the State and County medical societies, and ex-president of the County Medical Society.

TAYLOR, BENJAMIN WALTER.—Physician. Son of B. F. Taylor and Sallie W. Coles, of Virginia. Born February 28, 1834, at Columbia, South Carolina. Of English and Irish descent. Graduated from South Carolina College in 1855. Graduated from South Carolina Medical College in 1858. Married Anna Heyward Taylor December 14, 1865. Surgeon

27

at Fort Moultrie when Fort Sumter fell. Medical director of Carolina Camp C. V. A. and president of the South Carolina Medical Association. Chairman of the State Board of Health. President of the board of regents of the South Carolina Hospital for Insane. Member of the American Medical Association and the Gynaecological Association. Delegate, in 1875, to the World's Fair medical congress at Philadelphia.

TAYLOR, JOHN THOMAS.—Son of Alfred Taylor. Born at Chick Springs, Greenville, South Carolina, December 26, 1859. Reared on a farm. Received a common school education. Married Fannie C. Brandon, of Suwanee, Gwinnett County, Georgia, October 24, 1884. At the age of twenty-one, he went into the mercantile business, at Taylor's Station, Greenville County. After remaining there about eighteeen months, sold out and took a position as flagman on the Air Line Railroad. Served in the position as flagman and baggage master twelve months. Was promoted to conductor of passenger train. After leaving the service of the Southern Railway, in 1897, accepted the position he now holds as general manager of the Pickens Railroad.

TERRELL, CHARLES JEFFERSON.—Son of Dr. Thomas J. Terrell. Was born August 17, 1862, at Warren Plains, Warren County, North Carolina. His ancestors were Irish. Education was obtained from the Warrenton High School. For twenty years he was connected with the railway service. January 1, 1899, he bought the Johnston paper, then a four-page paper. Now it has eight pages, its advertising patronage has more than doubled, and subscription list nearly doubled. Not married.

THOMAS, ALBERT SIDNEY.—Pastor of the churches in Marion, Florence and Darlington. He is a son of Colonel John P. and Mary (Gibbes) Thomas. Born in Columbia, South Carolina, February 6, 1873. He is a descendant of Rev. Samuel Thomas, first missionary to South Carolina, sent out by the Society for Propagation of the Gospel in foreign parts. Graduated at the South Carolina Military Acad-

emy in 1892, with first honor. Captain of Company B.
Graduated from the General Theological Seminary in New
York in 1900. Ordained deacon in the Protestant Episcopal
Church by Bishop Elison Capers, in Trinity Church, Colum-
bia, in 1900, and to the priesthood the following March.
Taught in the Columbia city school from 1892 to 1895.
Principal of the Laurel Street School from 1895 to 1897.

THOMAS, ANDREW JACKSON SPAARS.—Editor of
the "Baptist Courier." Was born December 14, 1852, near the
town of Bennettsville, South Carolina. He is a son of Rev. J.
A. W. Thomas, a Baptist minister, for nearly fifty years in
Marlboro County. His early training was received from the
Bennettsville Academy. He then entered Furman University. Having decided to enter the ministry he took a course
at the Southern Baptist Theological Seminary. Supplied a
church at Batesburg three years, also the First Baptist
Church of Charleston, South Carolina, four years, and later
at Orangeburg. Then became joint proprietor and editor
of the "Baptist Courier," at Greenville, South Carolina. He
received degree of D. D. from Columbian University, Washington, District of Columbia. A trustee of Furman University, and of Greenville Female College. Has been a trustee
of the Southern Baptist Theological Seminary for seven
years. He traveled extensively in Europe during the summer of 1890, and went as a delegate from Southern Baptist
to meeting of Evangelical Baptists. He was supervisor of
Fourth District United States Census, 1900. He was married
to Miss Isabelle, daughter of A. F. Roempke, of Charleston,
South Carolina, August 21, 1877.

THOMAS, ROBERT GIBBES.—Was born on July 22, 1859,
in Columbia, South Carolina. He is a son of John Peyre and
Mary (Gibbes) Thomas. Received academic education at
Columbia Male Academy, under Hugh S. Thompson, and
graduated from the Carolina Military Institute, Charlotte,
North Carolina, in 1877. Assistant professor, at Carolina
Military Institute, of mathematics and physics from 1878
to 1880, and from 1881 to 1882. Assistant engineer West-

ern Northern & Central Railroad 1880; and held the same position with other railroads. Was United States assistant engineer of river and harbor work from 1883 to 1889 in South Carolina, Georgia, and Florida. Since November, 1889, he has been professor of mathematics and engineering in the South Carolina Military Academy, Charleston, South Carolina. In 1894, became a member of the society for the promotion of engineering education, and in 1898, was elected a member of its council. Member of St. Andrews Society of Charleston.

THOMPSON, HENRY TAZEWELL.—Agent and director of the New York Life Insurance Company, at Columbia. Born in Columbia, South Carolina, July 6, 1859. He is a son of ex-Governor Hugh S. Thompson. Married February 1, 1883, Miss Fannie C. McIver, of Society Hill, South Carolina. Took Bachelor of Arts degree at Union College, Schenectady, New York, in 1889. Assistant professor in the South Carolina Military Academy from 1883 to 1884. Private secretary to the governor from 1885 to 1886. Admitted to the bar in 1884. Practiced in Darlington until the outbreak of the Spanish War, when he volunteered as captain of the Darlington Guards, promoted to major of Independent Battalion, and afterwards lieutenant-colonel Second South Carolina Volunteers. When latter regiment was mustered out, he was appointed by President McKinley a captain of the Twenty-ninth Infantry. He has for years been prominently connected with the military life of South Carolina.

THOMPSON, HUGH S.—Was born in Charleston, South Carolina. Spent his youth in Greenville, the home of his father, until he entered the South Carolina Military Academy, from which he was graduated in 1856. In 1858, he was appointed assistant professor of mathematics and French at the Arsenal Academy, with the rank of second-lieutenant. In 1859 he was made professor of French in the same institution with the rank of first-lieutenant. In October, 1861, he was promoted captain, and transferred to

the Citadel Academy, at Charleston, as professor of belles
lettres. The officers and cadets of the Military Academy
having, by act of Legislature, been organized as a battalion,
he served with that command in the operations in the defense of Charleston Harbor. In 1865 he was elected professor of the Male Academy, which soon became one of the
leading schools of the State. In 1876, though not a candidate for the position, he was nominated for superintendent
of education and was elected on the ticket with Governor
Hampton. In 1878-1880, he was re-elected to that office.
In 1882, he was elected governor and was re-elected in
1884. In 1886, he was appointed by President Cleveland
assistant secretary of the Treasury, which position he held
until the close of the first Cleveland administration. Shortly
before the expiration of that administration, President Cleveland appointed him the Democratic member of the Civil Service Commission, to which position he was re-appointed by
President Harrison, in May, 1889. He served in this capacity until April, 1892, when he resigned to accept the position of comptroller of the New York Life Insurance Company, to which he had been elected. Still holds this office.

THOMPSON, JAMES LAWRENCE ORR.—Was born at
Walhalla, South Carolina, November 21, 1869. Removed to
Pickens Court-house in October, 1874. Entered school at the
age of seven; remained until fourteen, standing high in
class in the Piedmont Institute, Prof. W. M. McCaslin, of
Clinton, being principal. In 1883, he entered the office of
the "Pickens Sentinel." In 1891, at the age of twenty, embarked in the newspaper business, as editor and owner, at
Brevard, North Carolina, going into a republican stronghold,
buying a republican sheet, and infusing South Carolina democracy into it. A portion of that teaching is still felt in
that section. On account of the ill health of his wife he
returned to Pickens, and worked on the "Sentinel." In 1893,
ran a paper at Westminister, South Carolina. In 1894, accepted the position as foreman on the Democrat, at Easley,
South Carolina. He was offered the editorship of the "Dem-

ocrat," an afternoon paper published in Greenville, but refused. In 1895, held the position as foreman on the "Peoples Journal," at Pickens. Then took a position on the "Sentinel," remaining until 1897, when he and his brother-in-law bought it out. He is now editor and business manager of the "Sentinel." Married Miss Dora Richey, second daughter of Sheriff H. A. Richey, on December 25, 1889.

THORNWELL, JAMES H.—Pastor of Fort Mill and Ebenezer Churches. Is a son of the distinguished philosopher and theologian of the same name. Has his residence at Fort Hill, and has been the spiritual leader of that community, since 1882. Born at Columbia, in 1846. Was appointed drill master with the rank of lieutenant, and while acting as adjudant of the Fourth Regiment of Reserves, was appointed to the Arsenal. Remaining there only one session, however, he again. entered the army connecting himself with Bolton's Cavalry Company, and continuing in active service until Johnston's surrender. During the next year he was engaged in farming, but in 1867 entered the South Carolina College. In 1869 studied law in Yorkville, under Wilson and Witherspoon. Admitted to the bar, he practiced law in Anderson about twelve months. In 1871, became student in the Theological Seminary at Columbia. Graduated from this institution in 1874, and was licensed to preach by the South Carolina Presbytery in September of the same year. After serving Concord Presbytery for several years as an evangelist, and officiating for some time as pastor of the Presbyterian Church at Poplar Tent, Dr. Thornwell accepted his present charge. He was married to Miss Florence Earle of Anderson, in 1869. Degree of Doctor of Divinity was conferred by Presbyterian College, at Clinton, South Carolina, and also by Davidson College. He is at present Supreme Keeper of Records and Seals of Grand Lodge of Knights of Pythias. He represented his church at Glasgow, Scotland, as delegate to Pan Presbyterian Council; delivered a speech at the reunion in May, 1901—subject: "The Birthright of our Children."

THURMOND, J. WILLIAM.—Son of George W. and Mary
(nee Felder) Thurmond. George W.
is the hero of two wars and is over
eighty years old. The subject of this
sketch was born in "Skippers, Georgia," Meriwether Township, Edgefield,
South Carolina, on May 1, 1862. Early
education entirely under his mother,
who was anxious to have him educated. Entered Corryton High School
in 1876, which he attended for several
sessions, under the management of
Professor A. S. Townes and Rev. Hugh
T. Oliver, respectively. He then
taught school, and later attended the South Carolina College
one session, entering the sophomore class. In 1887, taught
school, farmed and read law, entering law office of Sheppard
Bros. in October of said year. Admitted to the bar in
January, 1888. The Supreme Court in admitting his class
said, "Fourteen of the eighteen applicants have been admitted, ten passed creditable examinations and the manuscripts
of four are so excellent as to deserve special mention by this
court; they are those of J. William Thurmond, of Edgefield,
South Carolina, Folk, of Edgefield, Youmans, of Columbia,
and E. H. Herndon of Walhalla. In December, 1888, there
was a hot contest among a number of lawyers for the attor-
neyship of Edgefield County resulting in a big victory for
the subject of this sketch, he having secured all three
votes of the commissioners. This was his debut in politics, and he held this position as long as he desired it. In
1894, he was elected to the Legislature by an overwhelming majority. In 1896, he ran for solicitor of the Fifth Judicial Circuit, and defeated the encumbent by 874 votes;
was elected to this office in 1900, defeating his opponent by a
majority of between three and four thousand. When in the
House as one of a committee of three, made a minority report against the funding of bonds claimed by Samuel Lord
as receiver of the State Bank, and defeated said claim by a
vote of 72 to 29. Nominated Honorable B. R. Tillman for

the United States Senate, against General M. C. Butler. Nominated Honorable Ira B. Jones for associate justice of the Supreme Court. The result of the war left his parents with very little property, and not over fifty dollars was ever paid out for his education except what he made himself. Has been solicitor over five years, and has never had a single indictment quashed, or demurrer to one sustained. Was never defeated before the people.

TIGHE, TERENCE R.—Born in Charleston, South Carolina, December 12, 1852. Son of Owen H. and B. F. Tighe, natives of Ireland who emigrated to South Carolina in the early fifties. He obtained his early education at the school of Professor John Gadsden, of Summerville, South Carolina. Graduated from the Charleston College in 1870, the degree of Master of Arts being conferred the following year. Read law under Pressley, Lord, and Inglesby; and admitted to the bar in 1872. Taught school in Summerville about two years. Chosen warden of the town twice. Elected corporation counsel of same town twice, without opposition. Judge of probate for Dorchester County, which position he still holds. Solicitor of the Summerville Board of Improvement. Member of the auxiliary board of South Carolina, Interstate and West Indian Exposition. Resident correspondent of the "News and Courier" several years. He is still engaged in the practice of law.

TILLMAN, BENJAMIN RYAN.—Was born in Edgefield County, South Carolina, August 11, 1847. Received an academic education under the instruction of George Galphin, at Bethany, in the same county. Left school in July, 1864, to join the Confederate army, but was stricken with a severe illness, which caused the loss of his left eye, and kept him an invalid for two years. Followed farming as a pursuit, and took no active part in politics, till he began the agitation, in 1886, for industrial and technical education, which culminated in the establishment of the Clemson Agricultural and Mechanical College, at Calhoun's old home, Fort Hill. The demand for educational reform broadened into a demand for other changes in State affairs, and he was put forward by the farmers as candidate for governor in 1890. After an exciting and heated canvass, he received the nomination, in the Democratic Convention by a vote of 270 to 50 for his opponent, and was elected in November following. This was his first political office, and he was re-elected, in 1892, by a large vote. His term as governor was signalized by the passage of the Dispensary Law for the control of the liquor traffic of the State, and by the establishment of another college, the Winthrop Normal and Industrial College for Women, at Rock Hill. Entered the race for Senator against General Butler, and the two canvassed the State, county by county, with the result of Tillman's election, by the General Assembly, by a vote of 131 to 21 for Butler. His term of service will expire March 3, 1905.

TIMMERMAN, WASHINGTON HODGES.—Ex-lieutenant-governor of the State of South Carolina. Was born May 29, 1832, in Edgefield County, South Carolina. Attended the old field schools, and finished his literary course at Hodges Institute, Greenwood, South Carolina. Graduated in medicine from the Charleston Medical College in 1854. Was twice married, first to Miss Pauline Asbill, November 4, 1856; and second to Miss Henrietta M. Bell, May 6, 1879. He was vice-president and director of the Farmers Bank of Edgefield, also of the Farmers and Mechanics Bank of Columbia, South Carolina. President of the First National Bank of Batesburg, South Carolina. Was a member of the House of Representatives from South Carolina and also of the Senate. State treasurer of South Carolina, and is now president of First National Bank of Batesburg, South Carolina. Practiced medicine for about thirty years in the county, and has always lived there until elected State treasurer. Farmed in connection with his practice.

TIMMONS, MANLY.—Practicing dentistry at Edgefield, South Carolina. Was born February 7, 1857, in Edgefield County, South Carolina, now known as Pickens Township. Attended the schools in the neighborhood until the age of twenty. He then began the study of dentistry with Dr. H. Parker, at Edgefield, South Carolina. After remaining with him several years, entered Vanderbilt University, graduating in 1886. Married Mary E. Youngblood, daughter of Captain E. H. Youngblood, January 25, 1895. Has held various positions in fraternal organizations such as Knights of Pythias and Woodmen of the World.

TODD, FLORENCE MORGAN.—A native of Laurens County. Born on the 30th of May, 1872. His early training was received from the Reidville Male Academy. Spent two years at the Simpsonville Academy, and one at Furman University. He merchandised at Simpsonville for four years. Was manager of Simpsonville Oil Mill one year, and in July, 1899, was elected president of the Clinton Oil Mill, which position he still holds.

TODD, JAMES EBENEZER.—Born in Laurens County, at what is now Landford Station, January 17, 1853. He had the advantage of the common schools of the neighborhood, and the high school at Woodruff. Then entered Erskine College, and went through junior class. He first married Miss Janie Grier, daughter of Rev. R. C. Grier; his second wife was Hattie, youngest daughter of Rev. J. N. Young, both of Due West. Trustee of Erskine College and the Due West Graded School, vice-president of the Farmers Bank of Abbeville, South Carolina. Represented his county in the Legislature two terms. He is now actively engaged in farming and milling.

TOLBERT, WILLIAM JASPER.—Born in Edgefield County, South Carolina, in 1846. Educated in the schools of his native county and the academy of Due West, Abbeville, South Carolina. Served in the Confederate army throughout the war. After the war he engaged in farming, giving it his personal attention and labor. In 1880, was elected to the Legislature, and re-elected in 1882. In 1884 was elected to the State Senate. President of the State Democratic Convention, which nominated Tillman for governor, was chosen superintendent of the State Penitentiary, which position he held when elected to Congress. Has filled various positions in

the Farmers Alliance, and helped formulate the "Ocala Demands." Has been a member of Congress for four consecutive years.

TOLLEY, TAZEWELL THOMPSON.—City treasurer of
Columbia. Son of William H. and Agnes S. Tolley. Born
in Columbia, South Carolina. Of Scotch-Irish ancestry. Education was obtained under the instruction of Colonel Hugh
S. Thompson. Married Miss Coles February 17, 1891.
Clerk and auditor of Railroad; chief clerk to civil engineer;
city auditor of Columbia.

TOWNSEND, CHARLES PINCKNEY.—Son of Mekin and
Rachel I. Pearson Townsend. Born in Marlboro County,
South Carolina, July 1, 1835. Of English and Welsh descent.
Attended the Bennettsville Male Academy, and graduated at
the South Carolina College. Married Amanda McConnell in
1859. His second wife was Nannie Henley, whom he married October 3, 1889. Member of the Legislature three
terms; circuit judge, and assistant attorney-general of the
State. Senator McLaurin's private secretary for the past
three years. Captain of Company G., Fifth South Carolina
Volunteers, during the Confederate war.

TOWNSEND, JOHN BENNETT.—A practicing physician
of Anderson, South Carolina. Was born in Charleston, South
Carolina, July 18, 1870. Graduated from Davidson College,
North Carolina. Completed his medical course at the University of Virginia, and took a post-graduate course at the
New York Hospital. Married Miss Eliza Duckett, of Clinton, South Carolina, on October 14, 1896. Secretary of Board
of Health of Anderson, South Carolina.

TOWNSEND, JOHN HENRY.—Son of D. D. and Henrietta
M. Townsend. Was born on Edisto Island, June, 1840. Educated in Charleston until 1854, when, on account of ill
health, he went to Stephen Lee, at Asheville, North Carolina.
Was one year at Mt. Zion, Winnsboro. From there went to
the South Carolina College. Just at this time the war broke
out and he joined the army. After the close of the war, he

returned to his plantation on Johns Island, to eke out an existence of ten years fighting chills and fever, during the reconstruction period. In 1877, he accepted a position in Anderson County. Built the Anderson Oil & Fertilizer Mill, ten-ton capacity, which has been increased, from time to time, to forty tons.

TOWNSEND, WILLIAM HAY.—Appointed solicitor of the Second Circuit, in 1899, to fill a vacancy; and in 1901 elected Code commissioner. Son of William Hutson Townsend and Harriet Hay. Ancestors were English and Scotch-Irish. Attended the local schools and read law under Honorable James Aldrich of Aiken, South Carolina. Commenced the practice of law under Colonel William Elliott, of Beaufort, in 1889. In 1894, removed to Barnwell, and entered into partnership with Attorney-General Bellinger, which partnernership still exists. He is unmarried.

TRACY, THOMAS WALSH.—Pastor of the Church of the Redeemer, at Orangeburg, South Carolina. Born September 28, 1866, at Conway, South Carolina. He is a son of Honorable Joseph T. Walsh, a lawyer of Conway. He attended the McLean High School, of Marion, South Carolina. After teaching one year in the public schools, became postmaster at Sumter, South Carolina. In 1888, he went North to attend the Phillips Academy at Andover, Massachusetts. During the four years following, he was engaged in the retail book business in Philadelphia and Boston. He then went to the University of the South at Sewanee. While there, gave instruction in elocution; was elected president of several societies, and won the Louisiana medal for oratory. Graduated in August, 1896, with degree of D. D. Served Grace Church, Charleston, and then St. John's church, Walterboro. While at Walterboro he was advanced to the priesthood by Bishop Capers, in 1897. Married Mamie P. Fishburne, of Walterboro, April 19, 1899.

TRANTHAM, WILLIAM DUNLAP.—Was born at Flat Rock, Kershaw County, South Carolina, November 11, 1847. He attended the common schools, and Kings Mountain Military Academy. Graduated from Wake Forest College, North Carolina, June 1871. He served in the Legislature of South Carolina, from 1879 to 1880, and from 1888 to 1890. During the last term, he was a member of the Ways and Means Committee. He studied law under Captain James M Davis, of Camden, and was admitted to the bar in October, 1872, where he has since practiced his profession. From October, 1873, until the fall of 1878, he was connected with the "Camden Journal," and advocated, editorially and on the stump, the straight out movement of 1876. Has served several terms as Democratic County chairman. While in the Legislature, he advocated Clemson College. When the call was made for troops, in April, 1861, he, a mere boy, responded, joined Company G., Kershaw's Second South Carolina Regiment. In November, 1864, he applied to return to the same command, but being then seventeen years of age, he was assigned to the Seventh South Carolina Battalion of Reserves, and served in that command to the close of the war. Was a member of the South Carolina Press Association, and present when it was organized at Hibernian Hall, in Charleston, May 5, 1875. Married Miss Nannie E. Simmons, daughter of professor W. G. Simmons, of Wake Forest College, February 1, 1877.

TRAXLER, DAVID HENRY.—Born March 14, 1849, at

Charleston, South Carolina. In early life his educational advantages were limited. He attended the country schools for a few years before he was twelve years of age. Between the ages of fourteen and eighteen he attended a high school for one year. When South Carolina seceded from the Union, and the tocsin of war sounded, he ran away from home as a beardless youth, joined the Confederate army, and became marker for Company G., Eleventh South Carolina Regiment. Was in the coast service for four years. At the close of the war, he apprenticed himself as a machinist in Charleston, but, tiring of this, he entered the mercantile business at Scranton, South Carolina, in 1869. Later, he located at Timmonsville, and engaged in merchandising. He became an expert telegraph operator, and was railroad agent for nineteen years, when he re-entered mercantile life, in 1893. In the meantime, from 1882 to 1889, he served as treasurer for Darlington County. Was for many years an alderman of the city. When the Dispensary Law was enacted, he was chosen, by Governor Tillman, to organize that institution, and in this line he showed marked ability. He held this position during Governor Tilman's term, resigning when he became Senator. He is a business man of unusual ability; and, as a citizen, his course has been marked by enterprise and patriotism. He is a member of the State Democratic Executive Committee, one of the county commissioners of Florence County. Was a member of both the Cleveland and Bryan National Conventions. Quartermaster of the Second Regiment, and although comparatively a young man, has been successful in a marked degree. He began business, in 1869, without money and with limited education, but is now comfortably settled financially; and has educated his children at the best institutions in the land.

TRESCOT, EDWARD AMORY.—Youngest son of William Henry Trescot. Was born at Pendleton, Anderson County, South Carolina, September 15, 1869. Was educated in the private schools of Washington, District of Columbia University, and graduated from its law department in 1891. Admitted to practice before the Supreme Court of the District of Columbia. While pursuing his law studies, he was made secretary of the American delegation to the International American Conference, which was composed of representatives from the United States and the Central and South American Republics, the object of which was to bring about closer commercial relations between the countries. He located in Blacksburg, South Carolina for the practice of his profession. In 1894, he was appointed United States commissioner, by Charles H. Simonton, and re-appointed, in 1896, by Judge W. H. Brawley.

TRIBBLE, MILTON PYLES.—Born in Laurens County, South Carolina, August 27, 1840. Joined the State Guards, a company organized at Laurens Court-house, which became Company A., Third Regiment South Carolina Volunteers. With this company, entered the service, in April, 1861. He remained with this regiment until the reorganization, when he joined Company C., Seventh South Carolina Cavalry, Gary's Brigade. He served with this regiment until he surrendered at Appomattox. For the last three years of the war, he was detailed as a scout. In 1881, he was elected treasurer of Anderson County, serving two terms. In 1885, was elected clerk of the court of Anderson County, serving two terms of four years each. He secured his title of colonel during the campaign of 1876. In 1894, he was appointed postmaster at Anderson, by President Cleveland, serving three years. Now practicing law.

TRIMMIER, THOMAS RANDOLPH.—Clerk of the court of Spartanburg County. Was born in Spartanburg, South Carolina, March 28, 1855. The only son of Theodore G. Trimmier, and Mary L. Thompson. He attended Wofford College, from 1871 to 1873, and afterwards at Milan, Tennessee. In young manhood, he lived in Mississippi, holding the important position of bookkeeper with large cotton firms. He came to Spartanburg, in 1884, at the solicitation of Captain F. M. Trimmier, then clerk of the court of Spartanburg County, and entered his office as confidential clerk. In 1885, was appointed deputy clerk by Captain Trimmier, which appointment was confirmed by Judge W. H. Wallace. After the death of Captain Trimmier, in 1888, Governor Richardson appointed T. R. Trimmier to fill out the unexpired term of Captain F. M. Trimmier. This appointment was not made until after Mr. T. was nominated by the Democratic Primary, held September 11, 1888, at which election he was nominated by a majority

of 479 votes over four competitors, in the first race. In 1892, he was elected without opposition, he being the only candidate in the county who had no opponent. In 1896, and 1900, he was again elected by flattering majorities in both cases with first race, to the office of clerk of the court. On the 23d of September, 1890, he was married to Miss Mary Fleming, of Columbia, South Carolina.

TUPPER, GEORGE.—Son of Tristram and Eliza (Yoer) Tupper. Born February 3, 1839, in Charleston, South Carolina. Educa-

tion obtained from high schools of Charleston. Read law under his brother, James Tupper. Married Sarah C. Doar, daughter of Elias M. Doar, of Santee, South Carolina, July 30, 1860. He was president of the Phoenix Fire Insurance Company, of Charleston; was auditor of Colleton County; trial justice of Summerville; intendant of town of Summerville two terms; treasurer of town of Summerville six terms; president of Dorchester Democratic Club twelve years. Entered Confederate service, as private, in 1861, joining the Charleston Light Dragoons. In May, 1861, he was promoted to second lieutenant of South Carolina Rangers. Promoted to first lieutenant, June, 1862, and in February, 1863, was promoted to captain of Company D., Fifth South Carolina Cavalry. He was present at the capture of Fort Sumter, Yemassee and other places; in Virginia, at Winchester, Cedar Creek, Rappahannock, and many other battles. In North Carolina he participated in the battle of Averysboro, Bentonville, and many skirmishes. He was badly wounded twice. Was taken prisoner but escaped the night of his capture, and joined his command the next day. He was detailed June 30, to blow up the Ironsides of Charleston Harbor, by General Beauregard, because of her deadly fire on our works. He served until the surrender of Johnson's army, April 27, 1865. When South Carolina passed the Ordinance of Secession, December 20, 1860, at St. Andrews Hall, in Charleston, South Carolina, he conveyed the information to the "Charleston Courier," on East Bay; and a salute of seven guns was immediately fired. He was one of the twelve members of the Charleston Light Dragoons, who volunteered to relieve the exhausted gunners on the "Floating Battery," in the second day's siege of Fort Sumter. He was commissioned colonel of the First Regiment of Mounted Rifles, Volunteer State Troops, by Governor Wade Hampton, on the 16th of June, 1877. He organized the General James Connor Camp United Carolina Volunteers, in April, 1893; and was its first commander, serving until 1897. Appointed presidential elector, in 1900, but declined. He is treasurer of the town of Summerville, county chairman of Dorchester County, editor of the "Pineywoods Cracker," and conducts a real estate and brokerage business in Summerville, South Carolina.

TURNER, T. C.—Clerk of the court of Greenwood County. Was born in Abbeville County, South Carolina, July 9, 1853. Very limited education, only the advantage of the old field schools. Married Ella Calhoun, on the 13th of December, 1876. For some time he was engaged as salesman in a dry good store, and is now engaged in farming, as well as in filling the office of clerk.

TWICHELL, A. H.—Born at New York Mills, Oneida County, New York, February 13, 1841. Son of Winslow and Annie Carroll Twichell, the former a native of New Hampshire, and the latter of Ireland. When only four years of age, his father removed to Cohoes, New York, a manufacturing town where his son spent his youth. He received an academic education, at the Stillwater Academy, New York. In 1859, at the age of eighteen, he came to Spartanburg County, and took a position as bookkeeper in the cotton mill at Glendale, under the management of J. Bomar & Co. He continued in that capacity, until August, 1861, when he enlisted in Company C., Thirteenth South Carolina Regiment McGowan's Brigade; and served until the close of the war. He was transferred to the quarter master department in the early part of 1863, and there served about six months. He then returned to the line, remaining there about two months, when he was detailed to the paymaster's department. There he remained until a short time before the close of the war, when he was transferred to the commissary department. He was at Appomattox when Lee surrendered, after which he walked to his home in Spartanburg County. He resumed his position with J. Bomar & Co. About the year 1868, Mr. Bomar died; but the works were operated under his name for some time after his death. In 1870, Mr. Twichell took an interest in the mill, yet still performing the duties of bookkeeper, and, shortly after, the name was changed to the D. E. Converse Co. At this time was made treasurer of this company, and also of the Clifton Manufacturing Company, which was formed about this time. He held this position until the death of Mr. D. E. Converse, in October, 1899 when he was made president. He is a stockholder and director of the National Bank, and the Fidelity Loan & Trust Co., of Spartanburg, also of the Spartanburg Savings Bank. He was married December 21, 1865, to Miss Mary A., daughter of Washington Bomar, formerly of Charleston, South Carolina.

VANCE, SAMUEL FARROW.—Son of Robert Shaw Vance, of Clinton, South Carolina. Born December 13, 1829, at Clinton, South Carolina. Education was limited, having only the advantage of the common schools of that period. He has been merchandising at Clinton since 1849. In 1897 he took his son in as a partner, and since then the firm name has been S. F. Vance & Son. He volunteered in Company A., South Carolina Volunteers, Kershaw's Brigade, Early's Division and Gen. Longstreet's Corps. Was commissary sergeant for nearly three years. Was at first battle of Manassas, and present at Greensboro, North Carolina, when General Longstreet surrendered. Married Mrs. M. J. Metts, April 30, 1872.

VANCE, SAMUEL WATSON.—Born November 6, 1847, at Cokesbury, Abbeville County, South Carolina. Attended the High School of Cokesbury, the South Carolina College and the University of Edinburgh, Scotland. Married Mary Caroline Young, November 21, 1871. Assistant clerk of the House of Representatives; secretary of the Constitutional Convention of 1895. State liquor commissioner, and at the time of his death which occurred August 9, 1901, he held the position of State Phosphate Inspector, to which office he was elected April, 1899, upon the expiration of his term as dispensary commissioner. Farmed in Laurens County previous to his removal to Columbia, South Carolina, and also engaged in the insurance business. He was a Mason, Woodman of the World, and a member of the Ancient Order of United Workmen.

VERDERY, EUGENE FRANCIS.—Born near Augusta, Georgia, June 28, 1845. Attended the Summerville Academy and Richmond Academy until his seventeenth year, when he enlisted in 1863 as a private in the Oglethorpe Artillery from Augusta. Mr. Verdery saw much active service in the campaign from Chattanooga to Atlanta and, at the latter place, on July 20, 1864, in the battle of Peachtree Creek, received a severe fracture of the skull, necessitating his retirement from active service. Shortly after the termination of the war, he commenced the study of law, in 1863, was admitted to the bar and has since given the larger part of his time to his profession. He was married April, 1871, to Annie M. Winter, of Augusta, Georgia. In 1879, Mr. Verdery was elected president of the Augusta & Knoxville and Greenwood, Laurens & Spartanburg railways, being one of the principal promoters and organizers of these roads, and for seven or eight years afterwards continued as president and general manager of these corporations. He was for three years receiver of the Georgetown and Lanes Railroad of South Carolina. In 1897 he was elected president and treasurer of the Warren Manufacturing Company, a large cotton mill at Warrenville. Aiken County, South Carolina, which enterprise under his management is now being operated with marked success. For ten consecutive terms he was elected mayor of his native town, Summerville, Georgia, and has for many years been a member of the board of public education of his county and one of the trustees of Summerville Academy.

VERNER, JOHN D.—A private banker of Walhalla, South Carolina. Born at Retreat, in Oconee County, July 12, 1844. His ancestors are of Scotch-Irish descent. Educated at Retreat Academy, in Oconee County. Volunteered as a private in Company G., Seventh South Carolina Cavalry in Confederate army. Merchandised at Walhalla, and intendant of town for several years. Was president and treasurer of Walhalla Cotton Mill from 1895 to 1899. He has considerable farming interest in Oconee County and Franklin County, Georgia. Married Miss Mary J. Lovinggood, January 2, 1872.

VERNER, WILLIAM LEMUEL.—Born July 25, 1856, at Retreat, South Carolina. Educated at Newberry College, Newberry, South Carolina. Married Miss Fannie S. Haltiwanger, February 5, 1886. Clerked in a dry-goods store for a few years, cashier in J. D. Verner's bank. Member and treasurer of the town council.

VISANSKA, GEORGE A.—Son of Aaron Visanska, of Jerusalem, Palestine. Born in Suwalki, Russia-Poland, February 14, 1837. Attended mainly the Jewish religious schools and academic schools of Suwalki. Married Annie R. Winstock, of Due West, South Carolina, December, 1860. Was employed as salesman for W. E. Winstock for a few years. Entered the Civil War in 1860, joining Twentieth Regiment of South Carolina Volunteers, but soon took sick and was transferred to Richmond, where he did office work under Lieutenant Poindexter. Remained there until the war closed, and then returned to South Carolina to engage in the mercantile business. He was trustee of the graded schools of Abbeville, director in Farmers' Bank; vice-president of cotton mill, and a member of the water board of Abbeville.

WALKER, C. IRVINE.—Member of firm of Walker, Evans and Cogswell Co., bookbinders, printers and stationers, of Charleston, South Carolina. Born in Charleston, South Carolina. Son of Joseph and Cornelia M. Walker, great grandson of Richard Teasdale, who exported the first bale of cotton from America. On father's side Scotch and on mother's

English and French Huguenots. Obtained education from private schools of Charleston, and Kings Mountain Military School, Yorkville. Graduated from South Carolina Military Academy in April, 1861. Agent for B. F. Johnson Publishing Company school books. Entered Confederate service day after graduation as drill master; then adjutant of Tenth South Carolina Regiment, lieutenant-colonel of Company Tenth, South Carolina Regiment. President of Carolina Rifle Club, first rifle club organized in South Carolina, and on which all others were modeled. Was brigade-general Fourth Brigade South Carolina Volunteer Infantry. Member of Board of Visitors of South Carolina Military Academy. Has taken great interest in Confederate veterans organization, and was an original member and officer of first association organized in South Carolina. Since 1895 major-general commanding South Carolina Division United Confederate Veterans. Member of South Carolina Chickamauga Memorial Association, and to him was largely due the erection of the monument. Married Miss Ada Oriana Sinclair, June 20, 1866.

WALKER, JOHN FROST.—Clerk of the court of Richland County. Son of George E. Walker of Columbia and a native of Richland County. Acquired his education from the Columbia Male Academy, Kings Mountain Military School and the University of Virginia. Farmed and merchandised a while. Member of the Legislature two sessions; City treasurer of Columbia five years. Married Nannie V. Flannagan, December 17, 1873.

WALKER, JOSEPH.—Was born in a log cabin on Fair Forest Creek, Spartanburg County, April 18, 1835. His father was a son of Colonel John Walker, of Virginia, and his mother was the daughter of John Cannon, also of Virginia. Colonel Walker was reared upon the homestead farm, receiving a common school education. In 1853 he accepted a position as clerk for John B. Cleveland, and remained with him three years. From 1856 to 1860 he did business on his own account. In 1860 he married Miss Susan E. Wingo, daughter of Alexander Wingo, who was once sheriff of Spartanburg County. He volunteered at the breaking out of the war and was chosen captain of Company K, Fifth South Carolina Cavalry Regiment, April, 1861. He was in command of that company one year. In April, 1852, upon the reorganization of the South Carolina troops he was elected lieutenant-colonel of the Palmetto sharpshooters, a regiment composed of twelve companies, soon after this he was made colonel of the regiment and served as such until the close of the war. At the close of the war Colonel Walker engaged in the cotton trade, and that has since been his vocation. In 1871 he helped to organize the National Bank of Spartanburg, and is a stockholder and director therein. In 1888 he was one of the organizers of the Merchants and Farmers Bank, and has since been its president. He is a director in the Pacolet Manufacturing Company, Whitney, Beaumont and the Produco Mills, all of Spartanburg County. A director in the Columbia & Greenville, and the Spartanburg, Union and Columbia Railroad, director and vice-president of the Spartanburg and Asheville Railroad. Director in Converse College Company and Fidelity Loan and Trust Company. President and director of the Peoples' Building and Loan and the Columbia Phosphate Company. Has six times been mayor of Spartanburg, and served one term in the State Legislature.

WALKER, JULIUS HENRY.—Insurance business. Son of Rev. Charles B. Walker and Caroline Simkins Jeter. Born in Edgefield, South Carolina, March 31, 1853. Obtained education under Hugh S. Thompson. Graduated from South Carolina College with degree of Bachelor of Arts. Married Margaret Lowndes, daughter of Colonel T. Pinckney Lowndes, of Charleston, South Carolina, November 3, 1892. Cashier of Loan and Exchange Bank from 1896 to 1897. Vice-president of Central National Bank of Columbia from 1897 to 1901. Member of the Governor's Guards of Columbia from 1874 to 1877.

WALKER, LEGRAND G.—Member of the State Senate from Georgetown. Son of Hasford and Mary E. Walker (nee

Allen). Born January 28, 1850, at Georgetown, South Carolina. Of English descent. He was prepared for college at the
high schools of Marion, South Carolina, and graduated from
the College of New Jersey, now Princeton University, in class
of 1872. Married Miss Kate T., daughter of Rev. J. W. Kelley,
of Marion, South Carolina, December, 1873. He again married Mrs. Julia T. Hayes of Morganton, North Carolina, May
8, 1901. He read law under Judge A. J. Shaw, at Marion,
South Carolina, and was admitted to the bar June 18, 1873.
Taught school a few years, and is at present practicing law
at Georgetown. In 1894 he was elected State Senator from
Georgetown county to succeed Walter Hazard who resigned
and has since filled the position.

WALKER, NEWTON FARMER.—Eldest son of Rev. N. P.

Walker. Is the present superintendent of the South Carolina Institution
for the education of the deaf and blind.
Born in Spartanburg County, January
12, 1845. Was prepared for sophomore
class at South Carolina College at
Cedar Springs Academy, and St. Johns
Classical and Military School of Spartanburg. He has filled in succession
every office in above institution, from
clerk in the office to that of superintendent. Is a member of board of directors of Converse College and chair-
man of the board of trustees of the public schools of his
district. Is a member of the farmers' organization of his
State and county. Entered the Confederate army when sixteen years of age as a member of Spartan Rifles, Fifth Regiment South Carolina Volunteers. After the war he read
law in the office of Farrow & Duncan, at Spartanburg. Married early in life Miss Virginia Eppes, of Laurens, South
Carolina, January 22, 1867.

WALLACE, EDWARD BARTON.—Son of Colonel William
Wallace and Victoria McLemore, of Richland County. Born

October 9, 1860, in Columbia, South Carolina. Of Scotch-Irish descent. Attended the Columbia Male Academy under Hugh S. Thompson, and the South Carolina College. Married Mattie P. Black, of Richland County, August 18, 1885. Taught in the public schools of the county four years. Member of county board of education ten years. Elected county superintendent of education for Richland County in 1900, which position he still holds. President of the Richland County Teachers Association.

WALLACE, WILLIAM HENRY.—Son of John and Martha Wallace. Born in Laurens County November 4, 1848. Attended the common schools of the neighborhood, and graduated from Wofford College in 1871. Married Miss Alice A. Lomax, December 26, 1872. Taught five years in Columbia Female College, and was for five years superintendent of the graded schools of Newberry. Edited the "Greenville News" for a short time, but gave it up on account of ill health. Is now a part owner and editor of the "Newberry Observer."

WALLER, COLEMAN B.—Assistant professor of mathematics in Clemson College. Born at Greenwood, South Carolina, March 8, 1872. The foundation of his education was laid in the public schools of Greenwood, South Carolina. Entered Wofford College in 1889, and graduated in 1892. Afterwards took a post-graduate course at Vanderbilt University, remaining there two years. He was for three years superintendent of the public schools of Union, South Carolina, and later was assistant professor of mathematics in Vanderbilt University.

WALSH, JOHN TRAVIS.—Lawyer. Son of Michael P. and Mary Vardelle Walsh, born January 26, 1835, in Charleston, South Carolina. Attended the Charleston High School and entered the South Carolina College in 1850, at the age of fifteen. Left college during the "bread riot," in 1852. Went to Princeton and graduated with degree Bachelor of Arts, in 1854. Taught school and read law under Judge Munro and Charles H. Simonton. Married

Frances Congdon in 1857. Admitted to the bar in 1856 and settled in Horry County. Being a cripple, could not enlist in the Civil War. Elected to the Legislature after the war. Elected district judge and held office until put out by military rule. County chairman until 1878. First school commissioner of the county under the public school system. Moved to Marion, in 1881, and entered into partnership with Colonel James B. Blue. Subsequently formed a partnership, in Conway, with Robt. B. Scarborough. On account of sunstroke, in 1888, he moved to the cooler climate of Boston, where he remained twelve years as recorder for the hospital. In 1901, he returned to his old home in Horry and resumed the practice of his profession.

WALSH, THOMAS BARDELL.—Probate judge of Sumter County. Son of M. P. Walsh and Mary Bardell. Born April 12, 1833, at Charleston, South Carolina. Of Scotch-Irish and French descent. Attended Mount Zion School at Winnsboro and the High School of Charleston. Married Ellen Jane David, June 24, 1852. In early life kept books and was engaged in the railroad business. Entered the Confederate army in 1861, Captain of Company A, Cavalry, Holcombe Legion. Promoted to lieutenant-colonel of said regiment. On account of ill health was assigned to conscript service, in which he was actively engaged when the war closed. After the close of the war, he engaged in the mercantile business at Sumter, continued until 1876 when he was appointed trial justice. Held this position during the trying days of 1876 and 1877. Clerk of the county board of commissioners, which office he has held from that date to the present time.

WANNAMAKER, JACOB GEORGE.—President of the Wannamaker Manufacturing Company of Orangeburg. Son of J. G. Wannamaker and Matilda Colclasure. Born in Orangeburg County, April 4, 1852. Of German descent. Attended the common schools; and a short course at the South Carolina College. Graduated from the South Carolina Medical College in 1874. Married Carrie E., daughter of Lewis E. Connor, of Charleston, South Carolina, October 7, 1875.

Engaged in the drug business at Orangeburg, then associated in the drug business in Columbia. Firm name of Wannamaker & Murray Drug Company. Vice-president of the State Pharmaceutical Association and one of the commissioners of public works of Orangeburg.

WANNAMAKER, JOHN EDWARD.—Farmer. Born at Poplar Spring, Orangeburg County, South Carolina, September 12, 1851. Educated under private tutors, and the St. Matthews School, and graduated from Wofford College in 1872. On January 31, 1878, married Miss M. N. Duncan, daughter of Major D. R. Duncan, of Spartanburg, South Carolina. Headed the farmers movement in Orangeburg County, which resulted in the establishment of Clemson Agricultural and Mechanical College at Fort Hill, South Carolina. Without his knowledge or consent Mr. Wannamaker was elected a life trustee of the college.

WARDLAW, ALBERT GOODALL.—Pastor of Westminister Presbyterian Church of Charleston, South Carolina. Born in Fort Valley, Georgia, January 20, 1856. Was reared to the age of fifteen in Cuthbert, Georgia. At that age he was sent North for academic instruction, and at seventeen was sent abroad to study the modern European languages. On returning home he pursued his collegiate course at Randolph-Macon College, and subsequently completed his literary course at Emory College, Oxford, Georgia, graduating in 1879 with the degrees of A. B. and A. M. Having decided to enter the ministry, attended the Theological Seminary at Princeton, New Jersey. Graduated in May, 1882. Since then he has supplied churches in North and South Carolina and Georgia. Married April 27, 1887, to Miss Hattie Lee Field, of Christian County, Kentucky.

WARDLAW, COLUMBUS.—Pastor of the Baptist Church of Seneca, South Carolina. Was born in Anderson County, South Carolina, May 23, 1855. Was educated in the common and high schools of his native county, and at the University of Virginia where he studied law, completing his course in 1880. On December 14, 1881, he married Miss Ida

St. Clair, daughter of the late Daniel Brown, of Anderson, South Carolina. Practiced law at Anderson until 1894; was school commissioner of Anderson County from 1891 to 1892, and president of the State School Commissioners Association in 1892. In 1894 he moved to Lockesburg, Sevier County, Arkansas, having been elected to a position in the Hesperian High School at that place. In 1896 he purchased the Sevier County "Democrat," published at Lockesburg, Arkansas, which he edited and published until January, 1900, when he sold it and returned to Seneca, South Carolina. In 1896 he was ordained to the ministry in the Baptist Church at Lockesburg, Arkansas, since which time he has abandoned the practice of law and devoted his time to his work as a minister of the gospel. In 1897 and 1898 he was county examiner of the public schools of Sevier County, Arkansas.

WARDLAW, JOSEPH GEORGE.—Born at Abbeville, South Carolina, April 4, 1859. Son of Dr. Joseph James Wardlaw of Abbeville, South Carolina, and Mary A. Witherspoon, of Lancaster, South Carolina. Was educated in the village schools of Abbeville, and completed education at the Kings Mountain Military Academy, Yorkville, South Carolina, in 1879. For many years head accountant of Clifton Manufacturing Company; vice-president of the Cowpens Manufacturing Company. Vice-president of the National Bank of Gaffney. Vice-president of the Citizens Building and Loan Association. Director of the Gaffney Carpet Manufacturing Company. For twenty years connected with State Militia. For several years colonel of Third Regiment. Chancellor Commander Knights of Pythias. Secretary of the Gaffney Manufacturing Company, and also of Alpha Mills. Was twice married first, to Miss Sarah Fishburne Carroll, of Aiken, South Carolina, May 23, 1893; second, on December 20, 1900, to Miss Emmie Dozier Sams, daughter of Professor R. O. Sams. He was also in command of his regiment during the Darlington riot.

WARING, THOMAS RICHARD.—Editor of the "Evening Post," Charleston, South Carolina. Son of E. P. Waring and

Anna (Waties) Waring. Born December 7, 1871, at Charleston, South Carolina. Earlier training was obtained from Porter Academy, Charleston, and graduated with degree of B.L. from Hobart College, Geneva, New York, in 1890. Married Miss Laura Witte, November 23, 1898. He was employed four years in the traffic department of the South Carolina and Georgia Railroad. News reporter on the "Evening Post," and assistant editor, assuming the position as editor in February, 1897.

WARREN, JOHN LEE BERG.—Editor of the "Press and Standard" of Walterboro. Was born April 25, 1870, in Warren Township, Colleton County. His educational advantages were limited to the common schools. At the age of eighteen years he gained great local notoriety by attacking, through his county papers, then "The Colleton Press," the management of the common schools, taking the position that the prevalent custom of employing students of the higher institutions to teach the free public schools in the summer months was waste of the public money. A warm controversy ensued, in the conduct of which on his part surprising ability was shown. The result was that he was offered a position on the paper, which he accepted and on May 22, 1899, entered the newspaper field, in which he has labored ever since. Married April 14, 1897, Adelaide Geneva Weeks, daughter of Captain R. S. Weeks, of St. George, South Carolina.

WATERS, PHILEMON BERRY.—Lawyer and magistrate at Johnston, South Carolina. Born September 21, 1840, in Wilcox County, Alabama. Of South Carolina parentage. His family returned to South Carolina and he was reared in Edgefield County. His education was obtained from Mt. Zion Institute, Winnsboro, South Carolina, and the University of Virginia. Married Miss Mary Huiet, December 21, 1865. Appointed captain of Company K, Second Regiment Artillery, South Carolina Volunteers. First intendant of town of Johnston, South Carolina. He represented Edgefield County in the Legislature.

WATKINS, HENRY HITT.—Member of the firm of Bonham & Watkins. A native of Laurens County. Graduated from Furman University and took a summer course in law at the University of Virginia in 1890. Married Maud Wakefield December 27, 1892. Taught school a few years after graduation. Principal of preparatory department of Furman University 1887 to 1891, and for several years a trustee. Also a trustee of Connie Maxwell Orphanage and the Anderson Graded School. Captain of Company C, First South Carolina Volunteer Infantry in Spanish-American War.

WATKINS, JOHN BARNES.—Superintendent of Honea Path graded schools. Born September 18, 1855, in Laurens County, South Carolina. He was prepared for college by Rev. A. W. Moore and James A. Madden. Graduated with the degree of A. M. from Furman University in 1881. Has been engaged in teaching ever since. Married Miss Lela A. Burts, December 26, 1889. Member of Anderson County board of education two years and of Laurens County five. Was president of Laurens Teachers Association several terms. Superintendent Lawson Graded Schools seven years when he was elected principal of the Honea Path High School.

WATKINS, JOHN C.—Clerk of the court of Anderson County. Born in that county on March 20, 1851. Entered Newberry College in 1873 and graduated from there in 1876 with second honor. After graduation he taught school for several years, and then engaged in farming. In 1889 he was appointed county treasurer for Anderson to succeed W. H. Frierson who had resigned. In 1892 he was first elected to the position which he now holds.

WATKINS, JOHN S.—Pastor of the First Presbyterian Church of Spartanburg, South Carolina. Born in Halifax County, Virginia, January 4, 1844. Was educated in Brooklyn Academy, Hampden-Sidney College, and graduated from the University of Virginia, after which he entered the Theological Seminary of that State. The degree of D. D.

was conferred by the University of North Carolina. He was professor of Greek and Latin in the Fredericksburg High School, and also professor of moral philosophy Peace Institute, Raleigh, North Carolina. Pastor of the Roanoke Church, Virginia. Pastor of the First Presbyterian Church, of Spartanburg, South Carolina. Married Mary L. Coleman, August 4, 1871.

WATKINS, WILLIAM W.—Son of Colonel Thomas Camp Watkins. Born a few miles east of Pendleton, in Anderson County, October 13, 1852. Dr. Watkins received his early education in the country schools, and in Newberry College, and then entered the University of Virginia, in which institution he took a fine stand, laying the foundation for that success which has come to him in the years following. He received his medical diploma from the Maryland University, and then took a post-graduate course in the University of New York. In 1893 he married Miss Margaret Garlington, eldest daughter of Colonel R. W. Simpson.

WATSON, EBBIE JULIAN.—City editor of the Columbia "State." Son of Colonel T. Watson and Helen Mauldin. Born near Ridge Spring, Edgefield County, South Carolina, June 29, 1869. Attended the country schools until seven years of age, then the primary department of Columbia Female College, Thompson Military Academy, Columbia city schools, special course under Professor Von Fingerlin. Graduated with degree of Bachelor of Arts from South Carolina College in 1889. Married Margaret Smith, daughter of William  W. Miller, of Beech Island, December 20, 1896. Entered journalism soon after graduation as city editor of the "Columbia Record," which position he held until the establishment of the "State" in 1891, when he became city editor, and during the Spanish-American War acted as news editor. In

1899 commissioned lieutenant-colonel on staff of Governor M. B. McSweeney. Recommissioned in 1901. Member of county Democratic Executive Committee and city board of health.

WATSON, SAMUEL JAMES.—Son of James H. and Mary (Holland) Watson. Born in Edgefield County, December 25, 1866. Took a one year's course at Patrick Military Institute, Greenville, South Carolina, and later two years at Furman University. Left the latter institution in 1889 to accept a position in the Loan and Exchange Bank of Johnston. Elected cashier of same in 1890, holding the position until 1894. In that year the Loan and Exchange Bank consolidated with the Bank of Johnston and he was elected assistant cashier of the Bank of Johnston, which position he still holds. He was district deputy grand master of the Fifth Masonic District for three years. Grand representative of the Grand Lodge of F. & A. Masons of Wisconsin. Moderator of the Ridge Baptist Association two years, and superintendent of the Baptist Sunday-school. Married Miss Grace Lee Corley, October 8, 1890.

WATSON, WILLIAM FRANKLIN.—Professor Watson was born in New Brunswick, Canada, in 1861. Was educated at Colby, Maine, taking the A. B. degree in 1887, and the A. M. degree in 1890. He has studied also at the University of Pennsylvania and Chicago University, pursuing special courses. Came to Furman in 1887, having previously taught in grammar and high schools in the State of Maine. In addition to his work in the class-room, he has prepared several lectures which have been delivered with fine effect at a number of places in this and other States and Canada. In 1889 he married Miss Clara Norwood, daughter of Mr. G. A. Norwood, of Greenville, at that time living in Marion, South Carolina. He has written a text-book on "Experimental Chemistry," now being published by A. S. Barnes & Company, New York. He also writes for several journals.

WATTS, JAMES WASHINGTON.—Born in 1819 near the line of Newberry and Laurens Counties in South Carolina.

Son of James Watts, Jr., and Nancy Clark Williams, and the great grandson of Colonel James Williams of Revolutionary fame, who was killed at the battle of King's Mountain. He received his early education in the country schools, and his classical course in the academy at Laurens; but on account of ill health left school at the age of sixteen and went into business. He entered the army as first lieutenant of cavalry company. Then elected colonel of the regiment, which position he resigned, and later he was elected captain. May 16, 1844, married Sallie Jones. In 1852 he moved to North Georgia, and after a residence of three years, was urged to make the race for ordinary of Cass County, now Bartow, which he did and was elected, holding it four years, and declined re-election in 1859. Left home May 2, 1864, with General P. M. B. Young en route to Virginia to serve on his staff. General Young was wounded. Being left without a position he was ordered to Richmond, Virginia, to the treasury department, but was soon transferred to Columbia, South Carolina, where he remained until the burning of Columbia by Sherman. He again entered the commissary department, under Major J. K. Vance. After the war he began farming, and on August 8, 1865, married Mrs. Kittie G. Martin, and settled on the farm near Martin's Depot, now Goldville. Was a member of the Wallace House, re-elected two years later and made chairman of the committee on agriculture. Was president of several county organizations. Held the position of statistical agent for South Carolina. President of the Laurens County Tax Union. Chairman of the county board of equalization. February 22, 1894, he married Susan Constance Williams, of Laurens County.

WATTS, RICHARD CANNON.—Son of John Watts and Elizabeth Cannon. Born at Laurens, South Carolina, March 15, 1853. Obtained education from Laurens Male Academy and took a partial course at the University of Virginia. Has been twice married; first wife, Allune Cash, daughter of Colonel E. B. Cash; his last wife, Charlotte, daughter of Chief Justice McIver, whom he married April 16, 1896. He was appointed lieutenant-colonel on the staff of Governors Hampton and Simpson. Member of the Legislature from Laurens County from 1881 to 1882 and from 1893 to 1894. Elected judge of the Fourth Judicial Circuit December 1, 1893, which position he is still holding. Read law under Colonel B. W. Ball and was admitted to the bar at the age of twenty by a special act of the Legislature. Formed a partnership with Hon. Y. J. Pope which continued six years. Then formed a partnership with Colonel B. W. Ball, which lasted until 1890, which was then dissolved and he practiced alone.

WATTS, WILLIAM AUGUSTINE.—President of the Peoples Loan and Exchange Bank of Laurens, South Carolina. Was born in that county on December 16, 1846. Graduate of the Laurens Male Academy. Entered the Confederate service in January, 1864, joining Company B, Hampton's Legion, and surrendered at Appomattox, Virginia.

WAUCHOPE, GEORGE ARMSTRONG.—Associate professor of English, South Carolina College, since 1898. Born at Natural Bridge, Virginia, May 26, 1862. Son of Rev. Joseph W. Wauchope, chaplain of the Ninth Virginia. Graduate of Washington and Lee University, A. B., M. A., Ph. D., in 1889. Graduate student in Harvard University in 1898. German student in Berlin in 1889. Assistant professor of English and modern languages Washington and Lee University from 1879 to 1889. Assistant professor of English in University of Missouri 1891 to 1895. Professor of English in University Idaho 1895 to 1897. Married in Chicago, Illinois, August 8, 1899, Elizabeth Bostedo. Member of the Modern Language Association of America. Has written several articles for magazines.

WEATHERBY, COLIN W.—Director of the Bank of Marlboro and the Bennettsvile Manufacturing Co. Born at Clio, Marlboro County, South Carolina, September 12, 1842. Attended the common schools, and West Point Military Academy from June 1, 1859, to December, 1860. Married Mary G. McLeod, November 22, 1866. Is a planter and merchant. Entered the Confederate service at the beginning of the war

29

as second-lieutenant, Company G, Eighth South Carolina Regiment, Kershaw's Brigade, Longstreet's Corps. Wounded at the battle of Chickamauga. Was adjutant of regiment four years.

WEBB, BENJAMIN FRANKLIN.—Born in upper portion of Saluda County, South Carolina, May 26, 1870. Son of William M. and Elizabeth Webb. Attended college in Augusta, Georgia, in 1892, and later accepted a position as bookkeeper, which he filled five years. Married Miss Bennie, daughter of J. A. Griffin, March 6, 1898. Merchandised at Payne, South Carolina, until elected county auditor of Saluda County, South Carolina, in 1900, which position he is still filling.

WEBB, ROBINSON CORNELIUS.—Son of Elijah Webb, who was clerk of the court for twenty-eight years. His mother was Rosa H. Waller, whose parents came from England and resided in Charleston, South Carolina. He was born January 16, 1858, at Anderson, South Carolina. His education was acquired under the instruction of Professor W. J. Ligon, of Anderson. In 1882 he entered into partnership with C. F. Jones and continued in the mercantile business under the firm name of C. F. Jones & Co. until March, 1901. Now doing a jobbing and commission business under the firm name of Webb & Cater. Also travels a few months in the year for a large clothing house. Married Lillian M. Slough, formerly of Concord, North Carolina, on February 26, 1891.

WEBER, SAMUEL ADAM.—Son of John Weber and Ann Lander, of North Carolina. Born January 19, 1838, in Iredell County, North Carolina. Father of Dutch ancestry, and mother came from Ireland. Attended the home schools of Cleveland and Iredell Counties, and graduated from Wofford College in 1859. He was twice married, the second time to Mrs. Camila Jefferys, of Yorkville, South Carolina, in 1899. He has devoted his life to the profession of teaching. Was a professor in Cokesbury Conference School from 1859 to 1861; in Davenport Female College, North Carolina, 1866 to 1867; Williamston Female College, South Carolina, 1873 to

1876. Editor of "Southern Christian Advocate" 1878 to 1884; assistant editor of "Southern Christian Advocate," Charleston, South Carolina, 1898 to 1900. Degree of D. D. conferred by Emory College, Georgia, in 1892. He is a frequent contributor of newspapers and magazines. A pastor for twenty-five years, and trustee of Wofford College same number of years.

WELLS, WALTER HERBERT.—Son of Jacob H. Wells and Fannie McConnell. Born September 10, 1872, at Columbia, South Carolina. Of Scotch-Irish descent. Ancestors were among the early settlers of Newberry County. Graduated from the South Carolina College in 1894. Admitted to the bar in May, 1896, and moved from Marion, South Carolina, to Florence in 1895, where he is now practicing law. Is United States Commissioner. City attorney of Florence. Member of the House of Representatives from Florence County from 1901 to 1902. He has never married.

WEST, FRANCIS CORNELIUS.—Member of the Legislature from Spartanburg County. Was born in Glenn Springs Township, Spartanburg County, South Carolina, February 6, 1850. Upon the death of his father, Isaac West, a member of Company A, Eighteenth South Carolina Volunteers, who died in 1864, it devolved upon him and his two brothers the care and support of his widowed mother and family, thus depriving him of a collegiate education. In 1873, he with his two brothers formed a partnership and conducted a successful mercantile business for several years. In 1888 he was elected trial justice for his township, which office he held for seven years, and until Governor Evans appointed him Supervisor of Registration for Spartanburg County in 1895. Re-appointed in 1896 and served until 1897, when he was elected to fill an unexpired term in the Legislature. Was re-elected in 1898 and 1900, and he now fills a position on two of the most important committees of the House. He is actively engaged in the milling business and agriculture. Married Miss M. A. McArthur in 1869.

WEST, WILLIAM BENJAMIN.—A prominent merchant of Honea Path. Born at Fork Shoals, Greenville County, January 10, 1870. His primary training was obtained at Honea Path and later attended Furman University. Was superintendent of the Piedmont Graded Schools one year, and principal of the Belton High School from 1894 to 1900. President of the Philosophian Literary Society while in college. Married Mittie E. McKinney, December 26, 1895.

WESTERVELT, J. IRVING.—Son of Harmen Westervelt, who was a prominent dentist of Charleston, South Carolina. Was born November 11, 1862, at Pinopolis, South Carolina. Attended the country schools of Charleston County and three years at the Porter Academy. He was deputy registrar of Mesne Conveyance of Charleston, South Carolina. In 1880 he accepted a position as junior clerk for Arthur Barnwell & Company, Charleston, and remained with them several years. Secretary and treasurer of the Charleston Cotton Mill three years, then treasurer of the Pelham Mill eight years. He organized and is president and treasurer of the Brandon Mills of Greenville. He was married August 27, 1891, to Miss Melville Cain, daughter of W. H. Cain of Pinopolis, South Carolina.

WESTON, FRANCIS HOPKINS.—Born October 10, 1866, in the lower part of Richland County.

Was educated at the South Carolina College, and is the third generation of his family to graduate from that institution, his grandfather having graduated there in 1814, and his father in 1849. Has been a member of the Legislature since 1892, and is also a trustee of the South Carolina College. Is commander of the Sons of Veterans; secretary of the executive committee "Forty Movement;" member of the Ways and Means Committee of the House, and chairman of the committee for the State Hospital for the Insane. Has been elected president of the Farmers and Mechanics Bank. Made the address of welcome to the Sons of Veterans at the General Reunion, Charleston, South Carolina, and also delivered an oration at the unveiling of the monument to the unknown Confederate dead in the cemetery at Columbia.

WHARTON, JOHN HENRY.—Railroad commissioner. Born in Laurens County, South Carolina, October 8, 1847. Had only the advantage of the country schools of that period. Entered the Confederate army at the age of sixteen. Married Laura J. Harris, March 17, 1870. County commissioner four years, and member of the Legislature ten years. Clerk of the court of Laurens County six years. Member of the Constitutional Convention of 1895. Director of the State Penitentiary two years. He is at present engaged in farming and merchandising, also railroad commissioner. Director of the National Bank of Laurens.

WHEAT, HIRAM DANA.—Born August 6, 1859, at Saluda, Lexington County, South Carolina. Son of D. A. Wheat and Sara Bevel, both of Camden, South Carolina. Attended the common schools of the neighborhood. Has been in the mill business since boyhood, holding various positions until made superintendent at Glendale, South Carolina, in 1883. Held the same position with the Clifton Manufacturing Company from 1888 to 1898. In 1892 he built the Gaffney Manufacturing Company Mill and was made treasurer of same company. In 1896 built Tucapau Mill and filled the position as treasurer and general manager for some years. President and treasurer of the Alpha Mills at Charlotte, North Carolina. Director of the National Bank, at Gaffney. Alderman of the town of Gaffney, South Carolina. A Knight of Pythias for twenty-one years. Was largely influential in having carpet mill established at Gaffney, and was for a time a director of same. On June 22, 1888, married Miss Anna S. Cannon, of Spartanburg County, South Carolina.

WHISONANT, JEROME FULTON.—President of the Blacksburg Spinning and Knitting Mill. Born October 13, 1849, in York County, South Carolina. Education was obtained from the country schools of the neighborhood. Married Miss Mary L. Hamrick, August 16, 1870. In addition to the above position he is engaged in farming and merchandising.

WHITE, ALEXANDER LAWRENCE.—Was born in Charleston, South Carolina. Son of John Thomas Hamlin White, who was a grandson of John White, one of the original settlers of South Carolina, and Mary E. Parker. Married Lavalette, daughter of Captain Homer L. McGowan, of Laurens County. In 1880 he became auditor and treasurer of the Spartanburg and Asheville Railroad and secretary and treasurer of the Spartanburg, Union and Columbia Railroad. These positions he filled until the roads were consolidated. When the Merchants and Farmers Bank was organized in 1889 he was elected assistant cashier and in a few years he was appointed cashier, the position which he now holds.

WHITE, CHRISTOPHER GADSDEN.—Son of C. G. White, M. D., and Mary L. Gailard of St. Johns, Berkeley County. Born November 28, 1865. Attended the public schools of Charleston, won scholarship at South Carolina Military Academy and graduated in 1886. Attended University of Maryland 1887 and 1888. Then graduated in dentistry from Southern Dental College in 1893. In 1888 built some miles of the Newberry, Blackville, and Alston Railroad, and later in same year built part of Charleston, Sumter and Northern Railroad. In fifteen months had risen from lowest position to that of bookkeeper in a bank of $300,000 capital. After graduating in his profession, he was immediately taken as partner by one of the leading dentists of Oakland, California. Remained there until his health failed and he returned to his native State, settling in Charleston in 1895, where he has since resided.

WHITE, LEONARD WALTER.—Was born in Abbeville, July 7, 1843. Was prepared for college by his brother, William Henry White, who graduated at the South Carolina College in 1857. Entered the South Carolina College in 1860, but on account of the war never completed the course. On May 9, 1871, he married Miss Mary Helen, daughter of L. J. Jones of the Newberry bar. He entered the Confederate army before eighteen years of age. Was severely wounded in the battle of Gaines' Mill, June 27, 1862. Served through the entire war, and was at Appomattox Court-house when Lee surrendered, April 9, 1865.

WHITE, SAMUEL E.—President of the Fort Mill Manufacturing Company and one of the largest landowners in the county. Is a native of Fort Mill Township, and was born on the lands where he now resides, the same having been owned by his father, grandfather, and great-grandfather. After receiving a thorough military training in the Kings Mountain Military School at Yorkville, the Arsenal at Columbia, and the Citadel at Charleston, he spent a part of three years, 1858, 1859 and 1860, in Texas and Mexico. Returning home in the latter part of 1860 he volunteered for the war in 1861. Entered the service as lieutenant, promoted to captaincy and afterward received a severe and almost fatal wound in the head. After the war Captain White returned to his farm near Fort Mill. He invested largely in merchandising, and during the financial crisis of 1878 and 1879, in which all of Fort Mills merchants were completely bankrupted, he lost something over $15,000. After this misfortune he went to farming in earnest. President of the bank and the board of trustees of the high school. Married Miss Esther P. Allison, of Concord, North Carolina. He erected two monuments in the park at Fort Mill, one in honor of the trials of the Southern women during the Civil War, and the other to the faithfulness of the Southern negro to the women and children of the South during the war. The last-named is probably the only one of its kind in the South. He, in connection with John M. Spratt, erected a very creditable monument to the memory of the Catawba Indians during the French and Indian War, the Revolution and the Civil

WHITE, THOMAS HENRY.—Son of Matthew White, who was the great grandson of John White, who came from Ireland and settled in Chester County in 1767. T. H. White was born March 29, 1863, near Bullock Creek, York County, South. Carolina. Graduated at Erskine College in 1884. Married Loula, daughter of Captain J. W. Carlisle, Spartanburg, South Carolina, June 25, 1889. Kept books for Joseph Wylie & Company, Chester, from September, 1884 to October, 1890. Then began banking. Cashier of the Exchange Bank, of Chester, South Carolina, and secretary and treasurer of the Wylie Cotton Mills.

WHITE, WESLEY OLDRIDGE.—Master in equity of Oconee County. Son of Wm. N. White of that county. Born March 4, 1869, near Walhalla, South Carolina. Is of English and Irish ancestry. His early education was acquired from the country schools, and took a collegiate course at Adger College, Walhalla, South Carolina. He is assistant postmaster at Walhalla, South Carolina, and engaged in farming. Married Miss Carrie E. Crisp on December 21, 1893. He was also magistrate at Walhalla two years.

WHITESIDES, ROBERT WASHINGTON.—Engaged in farming and milling. Was born July 29, 1836, on a farm in York County near the waters of Clark's Fork. Had the advantage of a common school, limited to the English branches. Farmed until 1861 when he joined the Confederate army, Company B, Twelfth Regiment South Carolina Volunteers. Promoted to orderly sergeant in 1862, and served as such until promoted to captaincy. After the war he still farmed and served as county commissioner. Deacon in Associate Reformed Presbyterian Church for thirty-five years. Married Miss Mary M. Schumpert, February 21, 1860.

WHITESIDES, THOMAS B.—Physician of York County. Was born at Hickory Grove, South Carolina, November 19. 1839. Education was obtained at home and in Chesterville, South Carolina. He attended lectures in Charleston, and graduated from the Charleston Medical College in 1861. Married Miss H. M. Leech December 24, 1867, and has practiced medicine twenty-four years in York County. He is proprietor of the Whitesides Lithia and Mineral Spring at Blacksburg. Has given up the practice of his profession and is now engaged in farming.

WHITNER, WILLIAM CHURCH.—Born at Anderson, South Carolina, September 22, 1864. After attending school at Greenville under W. C. Benet, and at Anderson under W. J. Ligon, entered the South Carolina College, and graduated in civil engineering in 1885. Married Miss Katherine Roddey, daughter of Captain W. L. Roddey, of Rock Hill, South Carolina, in June, 1890. Was given the position as tutor in the South Carolina College for one year. Was chief engineer of railroad laid out from Newberry to Blacksburg in 1887, but never completed. Built the water and electric light plant in Anderson, South Carolina, in 1890; first long distance electric transmission plant in the South. Chief engineer of a similar plant on Chattahoochee River at Columbus, Georgia. Is now engaged in constructing an electric power plant at Indian Hook Shoals on the Catawba River, near Rock Hill, South Carolina.

WIDEMAN, JAMES WARREN.—Prominent physician of Due West, South Carolina. Born on Long Cane, in Abbeville County, September 16, 1846. Had the advantage of the country schools and two sessions in Erskine College. Would have graduated but lack of finances prevented. Married Emma L. Jordan on January 23, 1868. Entered the Confederate army, joining Company A, First South Carolina Cavalry, at the age of seventeen, but was honorably discharged at Hillsboro, North Carolina. Was twice president of the Abbeville County Medical Society, and a member of the State Medical Association.

WILHITE, JOSEPH OLIVER.—Was born at Anderson, South Carolina, September 18, 1859. Attended the University of Georgia at Athens three years. Graduated at the Jefferson Medical College of Philadelphia in 1881. Took postgraduate courses at the New York Post-graduate and the New York Polyclinic Medical Schools. He married Miss Meta Sloan, November 15, 1883. Was president of the Anderson County Medical Society. Member for some time of the board of health of Anderson, South Carolina. Is a general practitioner, and is at present conducting the business of Wilhite & Wilhite, wholesale and retail druggists. Chairman of board of health of Anderson.

WILKINS, WILLIAM.—Native of Greenville, South Carolina. Educated at the Bingham Military Institute and Poughkeepsie Business College, New York. His wife was Miss May Avery, of Atlanta, whom he married in October, 1893. He is a member of the firm of Wilkins & Poe, hardware merchants of Greenville, South Carolina.

WILLCOX, EDWARD TYSON.—Engaged in the milling business at Marion, South Carolina. Son of John and Sarah Clark Willcox. Born October 10, 1865, at Marion, South Carolina. Of Scotch-Irish and English ancestors, who were among the first settlers of Philadelphia, Pennsylvania. Educated at the Marion Academy. Married Miss Alice, daughter of the late William L. Buck, of Buckville, South Carolina, October 27, 1899. President of the board of health from 1894 to 1895. Alderman from 1896 to 1897. Elected mayor of Marion in 1899, and has been in office since. Engaged in the furniture business from 1887 to 1900. Sold out and built the Roller Flour Mill in 1900, and is now engaged in milling.

WILLCOX, JOHN.—Son of John and Caroline A. Wagener Willcox, a granddaughter of Wiliam Wayne, a soldier of the Revolution and cousin of General Anthony Wayne. His father was a prominent merchant and for twenty years judge of probate of Marion County. John Willcox was born February 21, 1847, at Marion, South Carolina. Common school education. Married Leila I. Smith, February 21, 1883. Sheriff of Marion County from 1879 to 1880. Clerk of the court from 1882 to 1892. Is now a bookkeeper in the office of C. A. Woods, a prominent attorney of Marion. At the age of seventeen he was sergeant-major of the Seventh Battalion South Carolina Reserves, and was in active service until the close of the war.

WILLCOX, PHILIP ALSTON.—Son of John and Sarah Clark Willcox. Born December 4, 1866, at Marion, South Carolina. Of English and Irish ancestry. Graduated from the South Carolina College in 1887. Read law in the office of C. A. Woods, of Marion, South Carolina, and admitted to the bar in 1889; since which time he has been practicing law at Florence. Vice-president of the Bank of Florence, and director in said bank and also the bank of Timmonsville. He is unmarried.

WALLACE, WILLIAM HENRY.—Born March 24, 1827. Attended the Union Academy for several years, and for one year the high school at Cokesbury, Abbeville County, South Carolina. In the fall of 1846 he entered the South Carolina College, in the first class that entered that institution under the presidency of William C. Preston, and graduated in 1849. After leaving college joined his father in Washington, where in the spring of 1850 he was married to Miss Lena Dunlap, who was a native of Newberry, South Carolina. After his marriage, returned to Union and settled on a plantation, where he remained until 1857, when he purchased a home in Union. Upon coming to Union purchased the "Union Journal" newspaper, which he changed to the "Union Times." He had associated with him Mr. Charles W. Boyd, a brilliant young man, who had taken first honors in the South Carolina College. At the time of engaging in this business they both began studying law, and in 1859 admitted to the bar. In the fall of 1860 was elected to the Legislature of South Carolina; and there voted for the bill that passed the ordinance of secession. Enlisted as a private in Company A, of the Eighteenth South Carolina Volunteers, and just a few days afterward was appointed adjutant of the regiment by Colonel James M. Gadberry. Was elected lieutenant-colonel

in May, 1861. Two weeks later the regiment was ordered
to Virginia. Upon the retirement of General Evans in 1864,
was made brigadier-general. Three days after the surrender at Appomattox, returned home and engaged in the
practice of law, carrying on planting at the same time. In
the fall of 1865 was, without his knowledge or solicitation,
elected to the Legislature. He was elected circuit judge on
December 7, 1877, immediately after the restoration of the
government of the State to the people, a position which he
held for fifteen years. Died 1891.

WILLIAMS, DAVID R., JR.—Son of David R. and Kate
Boykin Williams. Born October 11, 1858, at Society Hill,
Darlington County, South Carolina. Graduated at Washington and Lee University in 1876. He is a civil engineer, investment insurance and real estate agent. Married Miss Ellen Manning Williams, July 14, 1886.

WILLIAMS, GEORGE WALTON.—Born in Burke County,
North Carolina, December 19, 1820. Was twice married,
first to Louisa A. Wightman, in 1843, sister of Bishop William M. Wightman. His second wife was Martha F. Porter,
a daughter of John W. B. Porter, of Madison, Georgia, whom
he married in 1856. Having previously been favorably im-
pressed with Charleston, he visited that city in 1852 and established the wholesale grocery house of Geo. W. Williams
& Company. He was elected a director in the State Bank
of Georgia in Augusta, at the age of twenty-three. Just in
the prime of manhood, and at the breaking out of the war
between the States, Mr. Williams was at the head of two
of the largest commercial houses in the South, an alderman
of the city of Charleston and chairman of the Committee of
Ways and Means, which position he held during the entire
war. He was appointed by the State Legislature during the
war to procure food for the soldiers' families, and the poor
of Charleston. He at once adopted measures to enable him
to get the necessary supplies, which were issued under his
personal supervision, without charging for his services, or
rent for the buildings occupied. It was not Mr. Williams' in-

tention at the close of the war to again engage in the mercantile business, but to establish a bank. Before accomplishing this however, he was urged by friends and customers to return to his old business, and was the first house to resume business in Charleston after the war. He also opened a banking house, and in a short time was fully immersed in business.

WILLIAMS, JAMES THOMAS.—Engaged in the hardware business at Greenville, South Carolina, since 1875. Son of Dr. James T. and Anna Williams. Was born at Greenville, South Carolina, June 28, 1845. Only a common school education. Has been twice married, first to Miss Eliza Cleveland, of Greenville, who died in 1877, and three years later to Miss Sallie McBee, daughter of V. A. McBee, of Lincolnton, North Carolina. Served four terms as mayor of Greenville. At the age of sixteen he volunteered in the Confederate service and served throughout the war.

WILLIAMS, LEROY RUSSELL.—Merchant of Yorkville, South Carolina. Son of John S. and Jannett Williams. Born January 19, 1842, in York County, South Carolina. Owing to the Civil War his education was limited to that of a common English education. His ancestors were Scotch on mother's side, who crossed the Atlantic in 1818. After the Civil War he turned his attention to farming, and though penniless succeeded in his undertaking. Married Miss Clementine V. Williams, September 22, 1868. He has given up farming and moved to Yorkville for the purpose of giving his children better educational advantages than were permitted him.

WILLIAMS, THOMAS WEST.—Clerk of the court of Berkeley County. Born January 3, 1857, near Holly Hill, Berkeley County, South Carolina. Received his education principally at the St. George High School, under Professor M. C. Connor. Previous to this he attended the schools of his county. Married Miss Carrie M. Wiggins, March 13, 1881. Was elected magistrate in 1892, but being in that year appointed deputy treasurer for Berkeley County, never served as magistrate, but filled the former position for two years until 1894, when he was elected clerk of the court of common pleas, and was commissioned December 20, 1894, and served until 1898. Was re-elected without opposition in 1898, and still holds the position.

WILLIAMS, THOMAS YANCEY.—Practicing law at Lancaster, South Carolina. Son of David A. and Sarah A. Williams. Born August 20, 1866, at Lancaster, South Carolina. His primary training was received at Franklin Academy, Lancaster. Spent one year at Furman University, Greenville. Entered law department of South Carolina in 1884 and graduated June, 1886, with degree of LL.B. Married Miss Lela A. Poore, of Belton, South Carolina, April 25, 1888. After leaving Furman taught school one year in Lancaster County. Admitted to bar December, 1887. Formed a partnership with Mr. Ira B. Jones, which continued until 1895, at which time Mr. Jones was elected associate justice of South Carolina. Elected to Legislature in 1896, re-elected in 1898 and again in 1900. Member of judiciary committee, chairman of Committee on Incorporation. Delegate to Democratic National Convention, Chicago, 1896, and at Kansas City in 1900. Member of State Democratic executive committee.

WILLIAMS, WILLIAM BEATTY.—Auditor of York County. Born September 2, 1841, at Yorkville, South Carolina. Son of Hon. Geo. W. Williams, who died in 1868. His education was acquired from the Kings Mountain Military Academy, Yorkville, Ebenezer Academy, York County, and Mount Zion Academy, at Winnsboro. Married Miss Mary E. Thomas, Union County, South Carolina, February 25, 1867. Reading clerk in the Wallace House, magistrate in 1866 to reconstruction time. Entered the Confederate army June 3, 1861, Jasper Light Infantry, Company I, Fifth Regiment South Carolina Volunteers and in 1862 joined Company G, Palmetto Sharpshooters, Jenkin's Brigade. Participated in first Manassas and several battles around Richmond. Lost his right arm near shoulder on the morning of August 30, 1862, in second battle of Manassas.

WILLIAMSON, BRIGHT.—Born March 3, 1861, six miles east of Darlington Court-house. Son of B. F. and Martha McIver Williamson. Attended Sandy Ridge Academy and Kings Mountain School, under Colonel Asbury Coward, the University of Virginia, and Eastman Business College. Cashier of the Bank of Darlington in 1889. President of the Bank of Darlington in 1890. President of the Darlington Phosphate Company and the Darlington Oil Mill. Bought out the Darlington Brick Company and now owns same.

WILLIS, WILLIAM E.—Born at Cottageville, Colleton County, South Carolina, August 11, 1866. Was prepared for college at the Sheridan Classical School of Orangeburg, South Carolina. Graduated at Wofford in June, 1892, taking both the A. B. and the A. M. degrees, but owing to the college rules at that time the latter was not conferred until since 1893. Married Mary Octavia Riley of Orangeburg, August 13, 1896. He at one time held the position as principal of the Dothan High School, Marion County; and also assistant teacher in the Carlisle Fitting School, and at present head master of this school.

WILSON, BENJAMIN F.—President of Converse College, Spartanburg, South Carolina. Born March 20, 1862, in Sumter County, South Carolina. Up to the age of seventeen he had only the advantage of a common school. In the fall of 1880 when eighteen years of age he entered Davidson College of North Carolina, from which he graduated in 1884 with the degree of B. A. He won several medals both in his junior and senior years. He was elected valedictorian of his class by the literary society of which he was a member. In the fall of 1884 he entered the Theological Seminary at Columbia, and in the fall of the following year he entered Princeton Theological Seminary, at Princeton, New Jersey. from which he graduated in the summer of 1887. During his first year there he took the second scholarship prize in Greek

and the last year took the first scholarship prize in He-
brew. In the summer of 1889 he became pastor of the Presbyterian Church in Spartanburg. He spent the summer of
1888 in the University of Berlin. Was chosen alumnus orator by his Alma Mater for the 1889 commencement. In the
spring of 1889 was elected pastor of the First Presbyterian
Church, Richmond, Kentucky, and also at the same time to
the chair of Christian apologetics of Central University, Richmond, Kentucky, both of which he declined. In the winter
of that year he was elected president of Converse College,
a non-sectarian institution for young ladies, which position
he now holds. He married July 30, 1890, Mrs. Sallie Foster,
daughter of J. C. Farrar, a prominent merchant of Charleston.

WILSON, CHARLES COKER.—Architect. Son of Dr. Furman E. Wilson and Miss Coker, of
Society Hill, South Carolina. Born
November 29, 1864, at Hartsville
South Carolina. Graduated at South
Carolina College in 1886, studied civil
engineering in 1888 and took degree
of Civil Engineering. Took post-graduate course, taking degree of Master
of Arts. Studied architecture in
Paris, France. Married Codie M. Sel-
by, December 23, 1889. First assistant engineer on C. N. & L. Railroad.
Engineer in charge of surveys for the
Carolina Southern Railroad, a branch of the S. A. E. City
engineer of Columbia two terms. Has designed and built
many fine public and private buildings in Virginia, North
Carolina, Georgia, Florida and Alabama.

WILSON, HENRY FRANKLIN.—Master in equity of Sumter County. Born June 23, 1854, at Mayesville, Sumter
County, South Carolina. Educated at Davidson College,
North Carolina. Studied law and was admitted to practice
by the Supreme Court June, 1881. Was elected to the State
Legislature in 1886, and again in 1890. Served for fifteen
years as a member of the county school board. Was elected

mayor of Sumter in 1898. Married Miss Georgia Walton Law of Savannah.

WILSON, HUGH.—Born November 1, 1838, in Laurens County. His parents moved to Abbeville when he was an infant. His educational advantages have not been of the best, having only attended the common schools of Abbeville, South Carolina. He has never married; neither has he ever held a public office of any kind, except that of president of the State Press Association for one term. When quite young he became a member of the Clinton Lodge, A. F. M. Was one of the directors of the Abbeville Cotton Mill, and a large stockholder, and has always taken an active interest in all public enterprises. Is the editor of the "Abbeville Press and Banner." Served in the war between the States, and was wounded at the battle of Chickamauga, September 20, 1863.

WILSON, JOHN OWENS.—Member of the South Carolina Conference of the Methodist Episcopal Church, South, and editor of the conference organ, "The Southern Christian Advocate." Was born at Cedar Grove Plantation, Berkeley County, South Carolina, January 27, 1845. Son of Hon. John Wilson, M. D., for many years Senator and representative St. James (Goose Creek), and Mrs. Sarah E. Wilson, whose maiden name was Owens. Entered the Kings Mountain Military Academy, then conducted by Major Micah Jenkins, and Captain Asbury Coward, when lacking twenty-seven days of being thirteen years old, yet stood among the first in his class. In January, 1860, he entered the South Carolina Military Academy and held creditable stand until June, 1862, when with over forty cadets he left the institution to enter the Confederate army, and served as a private until the close of the war. After the war he studied law and was admitted to the bar in November, 1866, practicing at Kingstree and Marion. Entered the South Carolina Conference of the Methodist Episcopal Church, South, December 15, 1873, and served at Darlington, Camden, Greenville, Trinity (Charleston) and on the Florence and Greenville Districts. Has been a delegate to the General

Conferences, of his church held in 1890, 1894 and 1898. Member of the general Sunday-school board of same church since 1895. Wofford College conferred the degree of D.D. in 1896. Was a delegate to the Ecumenical Methodist Conference which met September 4, 1901, at London, England. He has been twice married; first, to Miss May O. Richardson, of Marion, South Carolina, April 27, 1871, and second to Miss Kathleen McPherson Lander, of Williamston, South Carolina, August 27, 1896.

WILSON, JOHN SIMONTON.—Elected probate judge of Chester County in 1890, and is still filling that office with credit. Born July 4, 1820, on a plantation on Rocky Creek, in Chester County, South Carolina. In early boyhood attended the various country schools in Chester and Fairfield counties, and in 1838 went to Mount Zion College, Winnsboro, and prepared for college under J. W. Hudson and graduated from the South Carolina College in 1842. Married Miss Jane Patton Rosborough January 12, 1847. Member of the Legislature from 1856 to 1861. United States commissioner for about fifteen years. Captain of Company D, First Cavalry. Served throughout the war and surrendered at Greensboro, North Carolina, under General Johnston.

WILSON, STANYARNE.—Born January 10, 1859, at York-

ville, South Carolina. He attended Kings Mountain Military School, and graduated from Washington and Lee University, Lexington, Virginia. Elected to the Legislature in 1884. Also served as State Senator. Member of Constitutional Convention of 1895. Is a prominent member of the Spartanburg bar. While in the General Assembly he was the leader in the contest which resulted in the repeal of the law exempting factory investments from taxation. Was author and champion of the law restricting to eleven hours a

day, sixty-six hours a week, the labor of women and children in cotton factories. Also acted as chief constructor of the present general railroad law of the State. In the Constitutional Convention he was chairman of the judiciary committee and of the Steering Committee. In Congress he led the Democratic side of the House in three contests: First, placing restrictions upon undesirable immigration. The bill passed but was vetoed. Second, opposing the bankruptcy bill in the shape introduced. It was very materially modified because of the debate, and passed much improved. Third, resisting the apportionment bill which proposed to reduce the representation of the South in Congress and in the electoral college. It was defeated. Mr. Wilson married Hattie W. Hazard, December 15, 1896.

WINGARD, JACOB BROOKS.—Born in the Dutch Fork Section of Lexington County, South Carolina, August 24, 1856. Is of German ancestors who have lived in Lexington County for perhaps two hundred years. His father was Job F. Wingard. Attended the common schools of the community in early life, and graduated at Newberry College in June, 1878, being the valedictorian of his class. In November, 1883, he married Miss Lucy Rice Hutcheson, of Virginia. Read law with George Johnston, of Newberry. Stood the examination before the Supreme Court in 1881, and was admitted to practice. He formed a partnership with his preceptor which still exists. They practice in both State and Federal courts. Mr. Wingard is the attorney for his (Lexington) county, and also the corporation's attorney for the town of Lexington, South Carolina, which position he has filled for several years. He has been sent as a delegate to both State and general synods of the Lutheran Church, of which he is a member. The honorary degree of Master of Arts was conferred on him by his Alma Mater in 1882, and he was commissioned an aide on the staff of Governor Hugh S. Thompson with the rank of lieutenant-colonel. For several years Mr. Wingard has served as a trustee of Newberry College.

WITTOWSKY, LEGRIEL ADOLPH.—Born in Camden South Carolina, May, 25, 1868. His early education was received in the public schools of Camden, South Carolina. Entered the South Carolina College in the fall of 1884, graduating therefrom in June, 1889, with the degrees, Bachelor of Arts and Bachelor of Laws. Immediately after graduation he commenced the practice of law at Camden, South Carolina. In January, 1894, he was appointed Master of Kershaw County, and has held the office ever since, recently appointed for another term of four years. Married Miss Estelle Heyman, of Chester, South Carolina, April 17, 1901.

WOLFE, CHARLES W.—Son of Charles W. and Eugenia P. Scott Wolfe. Born at Benson, Williamsburg County, April 4, 1870. Grandparents on father's side came from Switzerland, and on mother's side Scotch-English. Obtained education from Wofford College and South Carolina Military Academy. He is unmarried. Principal of the Blenheim High School one year, 1895 to 1896, and Bennettsville graded school two years, 1896 to 1898. Member of Legislature from 1899 to 1900 from Williamsburg County. Member of committee of education. Chairman of committee on public printing. Editor and proprietor of the "Williamsburg County Record" and founder of the "Georgetown Outlook."

WOLFE, WILLIAM CHEVALETTE.—Born in Orangeburg County, South Carolina. Son of Dr. W. C. Wolfe and Julia C. Rumff. He is a great-grandson of General Jacob Rumff, the Revolutionary patriot. Attended the Sheridan high school of Orangeburg, then entered Wofford College. Farmed after leaving college and then concluded to read medicine, but later decided to study law, and was admitted to the bar in 1893. Married Alma K. Sawyer, in 1893. Does special work for the daily papers of the State. Bought an interest in the "Cotton Plant" and with the late Dr. J. Wm. Stokes edited the "Cotton Plant" several years. Prominently connected with the Farmers Alliance. Elected to the Legislature in 1892, voluntarily retired from the Legislature after serving one term, and since then has devoted his entire time to the practice of law.

WOLLING, JOHN GEORGE.—Member of Legislature from Fairfield County. Born July 6, 1852, near Ocala, in Marion County, Florida.  Moved with his parents to Orangeburg, South Carolina, in 1857. Attended private schools in Orangeburg to close of the war, then the public schools of Charleston, South Carolina, until he went to work at E. Perrin's, in Charleston. He afterwards learned the trade of a machinist at Helena, South Carolina. Married Miss Lula G. Feaster, of Fairfield County, South Carolina, November 27, 1872. Took an active part in the campaign of 1876, and has been repeatedly elected to State and county conventions. Delegate to National Democratic Convention in Chicago, in 1896. Is now farming and merchandising and has been very successful. Chairman of county board of trustees fifteen years, and has built up one of the best school districts in the State.

WOOD, ADOLPHUS NOTT.—Son of James and Harriet Wood. Born December 17, 1846, on Pacolet River, about three miles from Pacolet Station, in Spartanburg  County. Attended the common schools in the country before and during the war. After the war he entered Captain J. Bailes' school at Limestone Springs, in 1866. Taught school for two or three years, and then went to Alabama, where he engaged in the mercantile business until 1875, when he went to Gaffney, South Carolina, and went into the mercantile business with N. Lipscomb. Firm dissolved in 1876, and he continued the business alone until 1887, at which time he went into the private banking business. Continued this business until February, 1901, when the Merchants and Planters

Bank was organized, of which he was elected president. Was with the Reserves in the Confederate army at Greenville, South Carolina, and Hamburg, South Carolina, for about four months. Left the Reserves and joined Company F, Fifteenth South Carolina Volunteers. Remained with said regiment till surrender near Greensboro, North Carolina. This company was commanded by Moses Wood, his brother. Was one of the originators of the Gaffney Manufacturing Company and held the office of president from the beginning until January, 1898, when he resigned. Is vice-president of the Cowpens Manufacturing Company, Cowpens, South Carolina, and was for several terms mayor of Gaffney. Was twice married; first to Mellie C. Draper, of Alabama, June 24, 1874, and second to Mrs. Annie E. Band, of Cheraw, South Caroina, on September 7, 1899.

WOOD, JULIUS ANDREW.—Physician of Sumter, South Carolina. Born in Lincolnton, North Carolina, April 22, 1854. His father, Rev. Henry M. Wood, was born in Charleston in 1819. Is of German descent. Prepared for college under Judge W. C. Benet at Cokesbury, and graduated from Wofford College in 1875. Graduated from the Medical College of South Carolina in 1879. Took post-graduate course at Medical College of New York. Married in 1876 Miss Alma Archer, of Spartanburg, and on February 13, 1882, married Janie Brogdon, of Sumter, South Carolina. Moved to Sumter in 1881. Member of the medical association of South Carolina. Appointed by Governor Ellerbe a surgeon of the First Regiment, South Carolina Volunteers, during the Spanish-American war. Served until discharged with the regiment. He has charge of a private hospital established in 1895.

WOODROW, JAMES.—In the old historic city of Carlisle, England, within six miles of the Scottish border, James Woodrow was born May 30, 1828. He is a son of Rev. Thomas Woodrow, a native of Paisley, Scotland. When James Woodrow was eight years old his parents removed to America, in 1836, settling at first in Canada, but subsequently coming to the United States in May, 1837, his father became pastor of the First Presbyterian Church at Chillicothe, Ohio, and this was his home for some time. He was taught at home by his father, but attended school in Canada and Chillicothe, Ohio. He entered Jefferson College at Canensburg, Pennsylvania, in 1846, graduating with first honor. He then taught school two years and in 1853 attended the Lawrence Scientific School at Harvard University. In January, 1853, he was elected professor of natural science in Oglethorpe University, Georgia, a position which he retained until January 1, 1861. In 1855 and 1856 he was studying in Germany, and took the degree of Ph.D. at Heidelberg. He was married in 1857 to Miss F. S. Baker, daughter of Rev. J. W. Baker, of Marietta, Georgia. In November, 1860, he was elected to the Perkins professorship of natural science in connection with Revelation in the Presbyterian Theological Seminary at Columbia. From 1861 to 1872 he was treasurer of foreign and domestic missions. From 1869 to 1872 he taught chemistry and geology in the South Carolina College. In 1865 he became editor of the "Southern Presbyterian." In 1872 he went to Europe with his family and remained there until 1874. In 1891 he was elected president of the South Carolina College. Degree of M.D. conferred by Medical College of Augusta, Georgia. D. D. by Hampden-Sidney College, Virginia, and LL.D. by Davidson College, North Carolina. His views on evolution caused a great stir in the Presbyterian churches several years ago.

WOODS, CHARLES ALBERT.—Born July 31, 1852, at Darlington, South Carolina. Son of Samuel A. Woods and Martha J. Woods (nee DuBose). His ancestors were Scotch-Irish and Huguenots. Graduated at Wofford College in 1892. Married Sallie J. Wannamaker, December 16, 1884. Has been practicing law in Marion, South Carolina, since 1873.

WOODS, EDWARD ORR.—Son of Samuel A. and Martha DuBose Woods. Born on November 14, 1862, at Darlington, South Carolina. Was prepared for college in the common schools of Darlington. Entered Wofford College and graduated in June, 1883. Took a course in law at the Albany Law School (Union University) and finished in 1885. A few years after graduation he was married to Miss Theodora Warley Wagner, February 19, 1889. Has never taken very much interest in politics. Held the position as assistant United States Attorney for the district of South Carolina during the second administration of President Cleveland.

WOODWARD, FRANKLIN COWLES.—Born May 27, 1849, at Fort Conway, King George County, Virginia. Graduated with the degree of A. M. from the Randolph-Macon College, Virginia, in 1874. Having completed the course to the satisfaction of the faculty and himself he was elected assistant instructor of Greek and English, which position he held for three years. Married Mary P. Leary, February 24, 1879. Member of the Virginia Conference, and for six years actively engaged in the ministry at the end of which time he was elected professor in Wofford College, holding this position for six years, from 1881 to 1887, being at that time elected one of the professors of the South Carolina College. In 1897 Dr. Woodrow resigned the presidency of the South Carolina College, and Dr. Woodward was unanimously chosen president of that institution, which position he now holds.

WOODWARD, HENRY HOLMES.—Member of Legislature from Horry County since 1898. Son of William P. and Elizabeth P. Rhuark Woodward. Born at Toddville, South Carolina, June 3, 1874. Attended common schools of Horry County. Taught in the public schools and read law, graduating in law from South Carolina College in 1898. Married Miss Grace Dusenberry, June 25, 1901. He is now practicing law at Conway, South Carolina. Owns controlling interest in Conway Publishing Company and is now editor of the "Horry Herald."

WOODWARD, THOMAS W.—Son of Colonel William T. Woodward and grandson of Thomas Woodward, the "Regulator," who was killed by British and Tories May 12, 1774. Educated under the instruction of J. W. Hudson at

Mount Zion College. Went to Wake Forest College, North Carolina, then entered the South Carolina College and went through the junior year. Married Cornelia M. Dantzler, and married a second time to Rebecca V. Lyles, of Fairfield. Member of the Legislature in 1860 and member of the Secession Convention. Senator in 1884 and again in 1888. Entered the Confederate army in 1860 as a private and was elected major of the Sixth South Carolina Regiment. Served on the coast and in Virginia. Was made quartermaster of Keith's Twentieth South Carolina Regiment. Served at Sullivan and Morris Island. Returned to Virginia and surrendered with Johnston at Greensboro. Returned home and took an active part in reconstruction. Member of several conventions and succeeded General Hagood as president of the State Agricultural and Mechanical Society.

WORKMAN, THOMAS MADISON.—Inventor. Born in Laurens County, near Clinton, South Carolina, November 4, 1847. Son of John C. and Caroline Blakeley Workman. Educated in the common schools and at the Laurens Male Academy. Father was a hat manufacturer and early life was spent at that trade and on the farm. Taught school and engaged in the sawmill business. Is the inventor of the first telephone of which there is a record. He called it "an electric speaking trumpet." Also invented automatic car-brake, press for making round cotton bales, and discovered in 1871 that mosquitoes conveyed malaria, advancing that theory in numerous newspaper articles which the medical fraternity at that time ridiculed. At work on other inventions and engaged in the lumber business. Married Hattie Senn in 1888. She died in 1900.

WRIGHT, CALVIN SHELOR.—Son of Calvin and Virginia C. Wright, of Gordon County, Georgia. Mr. Wright was born July 31, 1878, in Gordon County, Georgia. Graduate of the Georgia School of Technology, Atlanta, Georgia. Held the position as draughtsman for the National Tube Works, McKeesport, Pennsylvania, and instructor in machine shop, Clemson College, South Carolina.

WRIGHT, GORDON FLOWERS SALTONSTALL.—Son
of Charles T. and Rebecca Wright, nee Saltonstall. Born
in Marion, South Carolina, April 17, 1832. Attended the
Winyah Indigo Society, the oldest chartered school in South
Carolina. Graduated from the Baltimore Dental College in
1876. Married Miss Sarah M. B. Boinest, of Charleston,
South Carolina in 1852. Clerked in Charleston and Georgetown a few years. Then learned the trade of a machinist,
which work he followed a few years as engineer of river
boats. He was also in the sawmill business. Began the
study of dentistry under his uncle at Mobile, Alabama, in
1855. Entered the Confederate army as member of Company
A., Tenth Regiment South Carolina Volunteers of Georgetown, South Carolina and remained until close of war. In
1868 he moved to Pomaria, South Carolina, where he did his
first professional work. In 1869 he was elected secretary
and treasurer of The State Dental Association, which was
organized that year. He was associated with Dr. Boozer,
of Columbia, until 1882, when he removed to Georgetown.
In 1875 he was chairman of the committee on Legislation
and succeeded in getting a law enacted to regulate the practice of dentistry in South Carolina, and he obtained a charter
for the State Dental Association and was elected its president
in 1876. Member of Southern Dental Association since 1871.
President of Southern Dental Association in 1891. Member
of State board of examiners for past twenty-five years. Dr.
Wright now wears a Cross of Honor bestowed upon him
some years ago by the Daughters of the Confederacy.

WRIGHT, ROBERT ZACHEUS.—Born in Laurens County,
South Carolina, April 6, 1849. Education limited, only the
advantage of the common schools of the country. He entered the Confederate service under Colonel J. P. Thomas,
who had charge of the cadets at Columbia, remaining until
the close of the war. Married Miss Mamie C. Lee, March
30, 1879.

WRIGHT, THOMAS WISTER.—Born in Jackson, Mississippi, July 22, 1867. Attended the country schools near Jack-

son until ten years of age, when his parents removed to South Carolina, in 1877, and attended the private school of Rev. J. L. Holmes, at Laurens, South Carolina. He was assistant machinist at Pelzer four years, and four years an instructor in the machine-shops at Clemson College, and chief engineer of the Laurens mill three years. Not married.

WYLIE, HUGH SMITH.—Son of John and Caroline (Smith) Wylie. Born near Winnsboro, Fairfield County, South Carolina, August 18, 1866. His education was obtained from Mount Zion Institute, Winnsboro, South Carolina. Secretary and treasurer of the Fairfield Agricultural Society from 1888 to 1895. Secretary of the Fairfield County Alliance three years. Elected county treasurer in 1898 against strong opposition. Re-elected in 1900 without any opposition. Married Miss Mamie A. Rawls, December 17, 1895.

WYLIE, RICHARD EVANS.—Born February 8, 1860, at Lancaster, South Carolina. His father was Colonel John D. Wylie of the Fifth Regiment of South Carolina Volunteers. Graduate of the Carolina Military Institute, Charlotte, North Carolina. Entered the University of Virginia in 1879 and graduated with the degree of B. L. in 1881. Upon his return home he formed a partnership for the practice of law with his father, Colonel John D. Wylie, and continued uninterruptedly until the death of his father in 1894; since which time he has been engaged in the practice of his profession alone. He is now president of the Lancaster County Building and Loan Association. Married Miss Louise Gildersleeve Pratt, daughter of Rev. H. B. Pratt.

WYLIE, WILLIAM BROWN.—Clerk of court of York County, South Carolina, since first of January, 1889. Born at Hickory Grove, York County, South Carolina, September, 1854. Graduated from Erskine College in class of 1879. Married Miss Ida M. Kennedy, January 18, 1893. Taught school from the date of graduation up to the time of his appointment to clerk of court. He is registrar of Mesne Conveyances for York County, South Carolina.

This book may be kept